# THE MARKET MAKER'S EDGE

## Day Trading Tactics from a Wall Street Insider

Josh Lukeman

**McGraw-Hill**

New York   San Francisco   Washington, D.C.   Auckland   Bogotá
Caracas   Lisbon   London   Madrid   Mexico City   Milan
Montreal   New Delhi   San Juan   Singapore
Sydney   Tokyo   Toronto

**Library of Congress Cataloging-in-Publication Data**
Lukeman, Joshua.
    The market maker's edge : day trading tactics from a Wall Street insider
    / by Joshua Lukeman.
      p.    cm.
    ISBN 0-07-135975-3
    1. Day trading (Securities).   2. Electronic trading of securities.   I. Title
  HG4515.95 .L85   2000
  332.64'2'0285–dc21                                  00-021162

# *McGraw-Hill*

*A Division of The McGraw·Hill Companies*

This book is created for educational reasons only. In no way is this book intended to provide all of the answers for successful day trading. Day trading entails significant risks and should be undertaken only with money that you are comfortable never seeing again. Day trading can result in the loss of all of the capital that you are using to trade. Successful day trading takes a long time to develop and requires experiencing loss on a regular basis. If you use margin to trade, it is possible that you will lose more capital than you have, resulting in large and uncontrollable debt.

In no way whatsoever does the author, the author's employer at the time of publication, or the publisher assume any liability or responsibility for losses experienced from applying the lessons taught in this book. They cannot and do not assure you of any success in day trading as a result of reading the contents of this book. Any day trading that you do before or after reading this book is at your own risk.

2 3 4 5 6 7 8 9 0 FGR / FGR 0 9 8 7 6 5 4 3 2 1 0

ISBN 0-07-135975-3

*This book was set in Palatino by Inkwell Publishing Services.*
*Printed and bound by Quebecor/Fairfield.*

 This book is printed on recycled, acid-free paper
containing a minimum of 50% recycled de-inked fiber.

# CONTENTS

iii

# PREFACE

The on-line trading revolution is transforming the investment world at a dizzying speed. In a single year, between April 1998 and April 1999, the number of trading accounts opened on-line in the United States increased 25 percent, rising to over six million. At the beginning of the year 2000, over 8 million on-line accounts exist. The potential growth rate for on-line accounts is startling, given that they comprise fewer than 10 percent of all brokerage accounts.

CNBC reported that a majority of day traders go broke within their first six months of trading. Active day traders are responsible for 30 percent of the million-plus on-line trades executed daily. The combination of the huge number of Americans who are trading on-line and the high expected failure rate for beginners results in a potential powder keg: In the first years of the new millennium, more Americans will lose money day trading than ever before. There is a national need for an all-encompassing, simple, and effective day trading guide; thus, *The Market Maker's Edge*.

Day traders have been around since the inception of the stock market in 1792. Human beings have speculated on prices since the dawn of currency, and this trend will continue regardless of the state of the market.

Public interest, demand, and participation in day trading increased dramatically during the roaring bull market of the 1990s. Higher rates of return, advances in technology, ease of entry provided by on-line brokers that charge lower commissions, and a public that cannot afford to retire have all contributed to the explosion in ownership and interest in the stock market. Almost 50 percent of the American public had some sort of equity ownership in 1999. The majority of these investors and traders have unrealistically high expectations of the amount of money they can expect to receive from their investments, creating a need for education.

Many of the principles behind profitable day trading are simple. Yet time and again, people tend to complicate the decision-making process due to a number of factors, both internal and external.

Day trading magnifies the emotional pitfalls people face in everyday life, including greed, fear, attachment, shame, regret, and the search for security. These emotional and psychological traps that I call the internal factors are the most common causes of financial loss in the trading world.

To be successful, every trader needs an effective trading plan. The best plans are simple and comprehensive, addressing external factors such as risk control, entry and exit, technical and fundamental analysis, trend spotting, and trading tactics.

This book stands out from most books on trading in that it places special emphasis on both the internal and external factors. It is also unique because it is written from the perspective of the sell side of the trading world, shedding light on tactics and methods used by professional Wall Street traders.

The information that has not been readily available to the public is what market makers actually do, and what makes many of them effective day traders. Day traders have all sorts of misconceptions about market makers' roles and objectives. Market makers are incorrectly stigmatized as the enemy of day traders, when in fact the main enemies of day traders are day traders themselves.

Market makers come in all shapes and sizes. They range from small retail order flow shops that do not put up any risk capital, to the largest institutional global banks that consistently take large risk to facilitate order flow. Institutional market makers' strengths lie in their experience and technical expertise. One advantage they enjoy is that they understand the way that order flow works. Large buyers or sellers always leave traces through their activity. Their activity is visible to all who know how and where to look for it. *The Market Maker's Edge* helps to clarify this activity, providing traders who lack market making experience with information about how order flow works. This book sheds light on a simple way to take advantage of identifying short-term trends emanating from volume.

Another advantage market makers have over day traders is their large financial backing, which permits them to expand their risk profiles in order to withstand larger losses. The large global banks that have market making operations have the deepest pockets. A $10,000 loss may be large to a day trader, but to an institutional market maker it is simply the cost of doing business. Day traders can make up for their lack of large financial backing with proper risk control and realistic expectations, both of which they will learn about in this book.

Day traders who are in the early stages of development have to overcome their lack of experience, which is often only acquired either by learning what not to do or by making mistakes. This process can be very expensive, more so than many can afford. *The Market Maker's Edge* provides guidance in the form of a step-by-step process for developing and maintaining a diligent risk profile, which will help beginning day traders to weather the initial storm.

Information used to be a commodity that the top market makers enjoyed as a result of having well-endowed research departments. The Internet has broken down the information barrier between global banks and individual investors. The best research is now easily accessible on the Internet for all to see. Sometimes market makers are the last ones to catch wind of important information that is released on the Internet.

The best market makers and traders know that trading is like playing a game of chess or poker. A key to success is reading the market while disguising your own objectives. Ed Lasker, one of the greatest chess players who ever lived, said that for him chess was a psychological battle. During the game he would ask himself, "What is my opponent's present state of mind, and how can I worry him the most?" Lasker explained that he didn't simply look objectively at the board, but rather he made the moves he knew his opponent feared. "He sometimes achieved victory by boring his opponents to death, or by luring them into attacks when attacks weren't in their nature."* These are psychological issues that every trader must face, and that this book addresses.

---

*Investor's Business Daily,* "Leaders and Success."

*The Market Maker's Edge* will teach you how to trade with the best market makers, not against them. You will become adept at overcoming short-term gyrations by sticking to the methods and tactics provided in this book. *The Market Maker's Edge* will help you overcome fears or weaknesses by developing successful trading habits and focusing on your strengths. Your conviction and staying power will increase and you will become a better trader, less susceptible to the influences that are outside of your control.

JOSH LUKEMAN

# ACKNOWLEDGMENTS

I would like to thank my talented agent, Noah Lukeman of Lukeman Literary Management, whose guidance and foresight helped make this book a reality.

I would like to thank my fiancee, Yana Polischuk, for her understanding and support throughout the project.

I would like to thank Joseph Ferrarese for his instruction and influence in my development as a market maker.

Matthew Desalvo and Keith Brickman have also been instrumental in my career.

I would also like to thank my family for their continued assistance and encouragement development as a market maker in trading and I would like to thank them for their support.

I would like to thank John Mulheren for his guidance and tutelage during my earliest stages of development as a trader. David Schulman and Lenny Destefano were also supportive during this period and I would like to acknowledge them for their help.

I would like to thank Stephen Isaacs, Jeffrey Krames, and Philip Ruppel of McGraw-Hill for their help and their belief in the book from its earliest stages. Their professionalism and talent are of the highest caliber in the publishing industry.

Many thanks to Paul Bracco, Tommy Crocamo, John Procopion, Josephine Siciliano, Steve Suslow, Ronny Commerchero, and Daniel Uslander for their help and support in the trading world.

Thank you to CTS Charts and QMS Systems of Brass Utilities for allowing me to display their charts and NASDAQ Level III screens throughout the book.

I would like to acknowledge R. Aaron Mehlman, Sensei Toyotaro Miyazaki, Darrin Giglio, John Procopion, Anthony Tricario, and Carl Ashmowey for their expert advice and guidance along the way.

I would also like to thank my parents Gerry and Shoshanna, and the rest of my family, Melissa, Abram, Adam, Danny, Zoe, Remy, Leah, John, Fred, Regina, and Avi for their continued assistance and encouragement, without which this book would not be possible.

P A R T

# RISK CONTROL

1

# MANAGING MONEY TO SUCCEED AS A DAY TRADER

*After graduating from college, Avi Levichuk was eager to make big cash by day trading. He heard many stories about SOES bandits making thousands of dollars a day flipping in and out of stocks. Avi believed that all he needed to do was catch a couple of waves a day trading Internet stocks. If he did this, he would make anywhere from five to ten points, or five to ten thousand dollars, per day using 1,000-share lots.*

*Avi went to a SOES shop on Broad Street and plunked down his bar mitzvah money, $25,000, plus another $25,000 he borrowed from his grandfather. With the $50,000 he would qualify for 4 to 1 intraday leverage, providing him with $200,000 of buying power. He estimated this would be enough to allow him to trade high-priced Internet stocks such as Yahoo, Ebay, or Amazon.*

*On his first day of trading, Avi was briefly up $4,000 on a 1,000-share position in Ebay. Then the stock turned against him and he was quickly down $3,000—a $7,000 reversal. Instead of cutting his losses,*

*Avi bought another 1,000 shares, in order to "average down." Ebay sold off another 6 points and suddenly Avi was down $15,000, or 30 percent of his $50,000, in less than two hours. Unable to take the pain anymore, Avi sold his 2,000 shares—at the bottom of the move. Within three weeks Avi had lost all of his $50,000 dollars, and on top of that he owed the firm $3,000. If he had understood the principles of risk control, his chances for success would have increased dramatically.*

Risk control is the foundation of survival for all traders. It is one of the few aspects of the marketplace that a trader has control over. The most common error made by beginning traders is a disregard for risk control by taking overly large positions. Unreasonable expectations can cause beginners to gamble 50 to 100 percent of their portfolios on a single trade. Taking wild shots with huge positions is not trading—it's gambling. Successful trading is developed over time, by winning consistently and conserving capital.

Trading positions that are too large often results in huge losses; it is the most common reason beginning traders go broke quickly. Large positions go hand in hand with large emotions: The bigger the position, the more intense the feeling of either greed or fear. The large P&L swings associated with big positions usually cause traders who are just beginning to abandon discipline and to trade subjectively and emotionally. On one hand, it is harder for them to take the loss because of its size; on the other hand, it is harder to let the profits run on a position that's too big. Traders end up cutting their profits short and letting their losses run—the opposite of what they should be doing in order to be successful.

## TRADE ONLY WITH MONEY YOU CAN AFFORD TO LOSE

Sun Tzu said that "Every battle is decided before it is ever fought." He meant that through meticulous planning and preparation before a conflict, a person should be able to get into a position such that victory is assured. When the battle occurs, it will take place against an opponent that is already defeated—a result of the prior planning.* The same methodology should be applied to trading. Before trading, traders should put themselves into a position such that the victory can be assured by substantially reducing the meaning of their losses.

The emotional pitfalls of trading are magnified exponentially when you have to trade successfully in order to survive. The most successful traders have an almost complete disregard for money. The need to make money forces a person to be attached to the outcome. This attachment normally influences the decision-making process for the worse, because fear is magnified, distorting reality.

Traders must be comfortable with the worst-case scenario before they even consider the best. The most successful traders have become comfortable with the idea that they can lose it all; paradoxically, that idea provides them with a sense of security.

Only you can determine how much money you can afford to lose. The money you trade with should be money that you are comfortable with never seeing again. If you decide to invest in a career as a day trader, ponder this question carefully.

## SMALLER IS LARGER

The importance of financial management when applied to position size cannot be overemphasized. Wall Street is filled with stories about experienced traders who went broke after long and successful careers because they ignored the oldest and most important rule of money management: Don't take positions that are too big for your financial comfort level.

The urge to make money quickly will always tug at you when you're trading. Fight this urge so you don't have to learn a painful lesson the hard way. Successful trading is first and foremost about survival through financial preservation and consistency, not about

---

*Sun Tzu, *The Art of War*. James Clavell, ed. Delacorte Press, 1983.

hitting home-run trades with huge positions. It takes strict discipline and careful preparation to match your positions to your risk profile. The smaller your positions, the easier it will be to maneuver in and out of trades, whether you are adding to a winner, cutting a loss, or taking a profit.

There is a direct correlation between correct position size and higher profitability. Losses are inevitable; but smaller positions produce smaller losses, allowing quicker recovery and less emotional attachment. The key here is emotional attachment. Traders tend to develop a comfort zone for position size, given their financial capacity to take risk. If you trade a position that is too big, then your sense of detachment can be thrown out of whack, adversely effecting your ability to maintain objective discipline.

What causes a trader whose comfort zone is 2,500 shares to buy 10,000 shares? Traders take positions that are too large for a variety of reasons: greed, lack of understanding of money management techniques, faulty trading tactics, the ever-present ego, and unrealistic expectations.

Larger losses are the product of bigger positions. A big loss requires a higher gain in the future to offset it, because of slippage, time, and commissions.

It is much harder for a trader to trade out of a large hole than out of a smaller one. If a trader is down around 6 percent on the month, chances are that the trader's confidence and buying power will remain intact. Successful traders are not afraid of reasonable losses, because they have confidence that they will persevere to make back what they lost and more.

However, if a trader is down 50 percent on the month, it will be a lot harder to regain confidence and stability. Large losses sting, and can cause a trader to be gun-shy in the future.

It becomes increasingly difficult to recapture an unusually large loss when you trade position sizes that are not evenly distributed. In addition to making back the equivalent percentage lost on the bigger position, you'll have to make back the spread and commissions. Many traders who experience a skewed loss resulting from a position that was too big believe that the only way they can make it back is to take a large position again. When this occurs, a trader is operating at a psychological disadvantage arising out of desperation. The result is that the risk profile is endangered, and the trader loses the best source of protection.

## TRADE WITH BALANCED POSITION SIZE

Position size in trading should be adjusted for broadly uneven stock price levels. Uneven stock price levels result in uneven probabilities that a large percentage move will occur. If you hold both a $10 stock and a $100 stock, a one-point price change in each one will have an equal impact on the profit or loss of your portfolio if the position sizes are equal. However, a one-point move in each stock would represent very different percentage changes. A one-point move in the $10 stock represents a 10 percent price move; a one-point move in the $100 stock represents a 1 percent price move. The 1 percent price move in a stock is statistically less significant, and thus more likely to occur, than a 10 percent move. Therefore, it does not make sense for traders to take equal position sizes in stocks that have broad price discrepancies, although they do it all the time.

A $100 stock would have to move 10 points in order to yield an equivalent percentage change to a 1-point move in a $10 stock. The 10-point move would have 10 times the dollar impact on a portfolio if the position sizes were the same, an unbalanced risk allocation. Position sizes should be adjusted according to the price and number of stocks you are trading, such that an equal percentage price change will have an equal profit or loss impact on the portfolio.*

## THE 2 PERCENT RULE

One of the principles of risk management is the 2 percent rule. The rule states that no more than 2 percent of a total portfolio should be lost on any individual trade. Ideally this figure should include the costs of commissions and slippage. This means that the largest loss you should tolerate on any single trade is 2 percent of your portfolio. Some people misinterpret this rule to mean that only 2 percent

*Schwager, Jack, *Technical Analysis of Stocks and Commodities*. Technical Analysis, Inc., June 1999, p. 26.

of your trading equity should be allocated to each trade, but that's not the case. The 2 percent rule is designed to limit a trader's losses while preserving capital. It is powerful insurance because it provides a trader with a number; you know before you enter a trade how much you can afford to lose. Applying this principle, a trader can afford to be wrong numerous times and still live to see the next trading day.

Keeping your losses to 2 percent per trade often means that you will have to trade smaller positions. Many traders who are just starting scoff at the idea, thinking that bigger positions will allow them to strike it big and make a large monthly income through big profits. Nothing could be further from the truth. When beginning traders take on bigger positions, it often causes them to lose money faster because they have not built up the tolerance for accepting larger losses or bigger profits. They tend to take profits off the table faster when they are winning, because of the immediate gratification associated with being right. They also tend to let their losers run longer, because they are not willing to accept the pain associated with being wrong.

It is not uncommon for traders to enter into positions not knowing beforehand how much they are willing to lose, because they think they are going to win. When expectations for a trade are not met and no exit strategy exists, a trader is often forced to cut a position based on either emotion or financial pain. The goal of a trader should be to accept losses without letting them affect his confidence. This is accomplished through preparation *before* the trade, budgeting for losses just as you budget for an insurance bill.

The 2 percent rule is pivotal because the success of an individual is not necessarily correlated to the number of winning trades: Some of the most successful traders on Wall Street earn up to 80 percent of their profits from just 20 percent of their trades. This means that the majority of their trades may not earn them the big money. The reason they are profitable as a trader is that they have learned to quickly accept and manage loss, not disregard or try to eliminate it. Successful traders aim to keep loss controlled. When losses are controlled a trader is free to focus on and add to winning trades.

By limiting individual losses to 2 percent or less of your portfolio, you increase the odds that you will experience more break-even and winning trades. Over time, these trades tip the scales toward profitability, as long as losses are managed. The 2 percent rule is particularly beneficial for beginning traders. Your probabilities of success increase with the number of times you play. A 2 percent maximum loss guideline increases the life span of beginning traders, providing them with the opportunity to learn from their mistakes.

A loss of 6 percent to 8 percent is the maximum a trader should accept for the entire month. A trader who has four consecutive 2 percent losses should stop trading for the month and evaluate what's going wrong. You can always begin anew the following month. Taking time off after a string of losses is beneficial, because it provides you with an opportunity to regain your confidence. A trading time-out is similar to a basketball time-out after the opposing team has scored a number of unanswered points. The time-out slows the winning team's momentum and helps the losing team regain confidence with a pep talk and a breather. If you enter a trading day lacking confidence, close the shop and begin again tomorrow. Confidence in yourself and what you are doing is your strongest ally.

## MARGIN MADNESS

Using margin to increase buying power is an accepted and common practice among most day traders today. It is important for day traders to be aware of the risks of margin, and to learn how to handle the augmented buying power effectively if they choose to use it. Using excessive leverage through margin is a dangerous game. The sell-off in Internet stocks in the spring and summer of 1999 resulted in a huge number of margin calls for day traders and investors. The risks associated with margin require careful planning and tighter stop-loss criteria. Many investors are not aware of the risk inherent in using leverage, and should stay away from it. When the market turns against a highly leveraged position, a trader is often forced to liquidate it at the worst possible moment.

Even the brightest and most highly regarded traders on Wall Street are not immune to the danger of trading with excessive margin. During the predicament in the global financial markets in September 1997, the Long Term Capital Management (LTCM) hedge fund reported that it had lost $2.3 billion in high-risk trades and was on the verge of bankruptcy. Fund founder John Meriwether and his partners, Nobel laureates Myron Scholes and Robert Merton, traded with ridiculously high levels of margin. At times they took huge positions, putting only 5 percent down. Although they attempted to diversify the risk with long and short spreads in their bond funds, the bloated margin ultimately proved fatal. The amount of margin power that LTCM used is the equivalent of a stock trader buying $100,000 worth of stock with only $5,000 cash down. A small hiccup in price could easily wipe a trader out with such high degrees of leverage.

In a report issued on August 9, 1999, the North American Securities Administrators Association stated that it is not uncommon for some day trading firms to encourage day traders to borrow money from other traders in order to meet margin calls. This practice flies in the face of the most basic risk management practices and should be avoided at all costs. It is a clear sign that the trader is acting out of financial desperation and that the end is near.

When you choose to trade on margin, enforce strict risk-control standards geared to the amount of underlying cash you have to trade with. If you have $50,000 to trade with and you are using leverage through margin, your risk standards should be focused around the $50,000 in underlying cash, not the amount of buying power you are using. Applying the 2 percent rule, your maximum permissible loss will be $1,000 per position.

Success in day trading is first defined as survival. Your ability to survive as a day trader depends on your money management techniques. When you manage your money properly, you provide yourself with valuable risk insurance, which any business should have. The best way to control risk when trading is to manage your losses. Determine the most that you are willing to lose on any one position, which should not exceed 2 percent of your underlying equity.

Keeping your individual losses to 2 percent or less often requires that you trade smaller positions to start. Smaller positions can be empowering because they allow you to trade with less attachment, permitting you to cut your losses sooner and easier. The key to success in trading is to have the least possible emotional attachment to your positions. If you are trading because you have to win, chances are that your attachment to the outcome will be high, adversely affecting your decision-making process. When you trade only with money that you can afford to lose, your attachment will be minimal and your results will be better.

Risk control is a crucial component to successful trading. Improper risk standards result in trades that can easily wipe out even the most experienced traders. Traders last in the business because they have learned to manage their expectations and control their exposure. When addressing the risk factor, remember the importance of position size. Never allow yourself to trade a bigger position than you can afford. The temptation will always be there, but managing this urge through discipline is the mark of a successful trader. It is always better to start out small and add to your position, rather than starting out large and regretting it afterward. Remember the old saying:

*Discipline weighs ounces while regret weighs tons.*

# FIVE STEPS TO DETERMINE THE PROPER POSITION SIZE

Endurance in trading is the first step toward success. Especially when a trader is beginning, surviving means you can learn and become better. Living to see the next day in trading is the most basic and important goal of any trader. This sounds simple, but its importance cannot be overemphasized. The outcome of any trade is not within a trader's control; how much money you lose is. Controlling loss is the only security a trader has; without that security, catastrophe can strike.

The way to maintain a 2 percent maximum loss risk profile is to determine beforehand the proper position size. Determining the proper position size involves five simple steps. These steps should be taken methodically, every day, before trading.

## STEP 1. ALLOCATE CAPITAL PER POSITION

The first step is to determine the maximum capital per position, or the most money that should be invested in a single trade. This figure is calculated by dividing the total capital in your account by the number of positions you wish to take. If you have $100,000 of risk capital to trade with and you want to take four positions, allocate an equal dollar amount to each position:

$$\text{Capital per Position} = \frac{\text{Risk Capital}}{\text{Number of Positions}}$$

Risk Capital = $100,000

Number of Positions = 4

Capital per Position = $100,000 / 4 = $25,000

The maximum capital per position you should being willing to invest is $25,000.

## STEP 2. CALCULATE MAXIMUM SHARES PER POSITION

Once your capital per position is allocated, the next step is to calculate how many shares of each position to trade. Divide the risk capital per position, or $25,000 in this example, by the share price. Assuming there are four stocks you want to trade with prices of $100, $50, $25, and $10, the calculation is:

$$\text{Maximum Shares per Position} = \frac{\text{Capital per Position}}{\text{Stock Price}}$$

Capital per Position = $25,000

Stock Price = $100, $50, $25, and $10

Maximum Shares per Position =

$25,000 / $100 = 250 shares

$25,000 / $50 = 500 shares

$25,000 / $25 = 1,000 shares

$25,000 / $10 = 2,500 shares

These figures are maximums that take into account your buying power per position.

## STEP 3. DETERMINE 2 PERCENT DOLLAR RISK PER TRADE

To determine the maximum amount of money you can withstand to lose per trade, multiply 2 percent times your capital per position. In the example, using $25,000 per position:

Maximum Dollar Risk = .02 × Capital per Position
Capital per Position = $25,000
Maximum Dollar Risk = .02 × $25,000 = $500

In this example, $500 is the most you are willing to lose on a trade, given your capital allocation per position. Taking another example, if you have $100,000 to trade with and decide that you want to take two positions, then your dollar risk per trade is $1,000:

$$\text{Capital per Position} = \frac{\text{Risk Capital}}{\text{Number of Positions}}$$

Risk Capital = $100,000
Number of Positions = 2
Capital per Position = $100,000 / 2 = $50,000
Maximum Dollar Risk = .02 × Capital per Position
Capital per Position = $50,000
Maximum Dollar Risk = .02 × $50,000 = $1,000

## STEP 4. DETERMINE THE STOP-LOSS POINT

Various stop-loss strategies are covered in detail in Chapter 3. For now we'll determine our stop-loss point from initial entry. Stop-loss exit points vary greatly given the different price of stocks. In our example, a one-point move in the $100 stock (1%) would represent a small percentage change compared to a one-point move in the $10 stock (10%). It is prudent to use wider stops for higher-priced stocks and tighter stops for lower-priced stocks. Assume that, based on your calculations, you have identified a lower-priced stock with one point of risk. Using the $25 stock as an example, if the current market is quoted $25—$25⅛, then $24 is the stop-loss exit point if you are trading from the long side with one point of risk.

Adjusting for slippage on entry and exit can be difficult because many different elements determine what sort of executions you may receive, including liquidity, volatility, technology, the market environment, and the execution medium (see Chapter 13). Always provide enough room for a poor execution on exit. When adjusting for slippage, it is always better to prepare for the worst and be glad if you receive the best. For this example, we'll factor in an extra 1/4 of a point on each side of the trade for slippage.

Stop-Loss Risk = Current Bid − Exit Point + Slippage
Current Bid = $25

Exit Point = $24

Slippage = 1/4

Stop-Loss Point = $25 — $24 + 1/4 = 1¼ points

## STEP 5. CALCULATE MAXIMUM POSITION SIZE

After determining the 2 percent maximum dollar risk and the stop-loss point, you can calculate the maximum position size:

$$\text{Maximum Position Size} = \frac{2\% \text{ Maximum Dollar Risk per Trade}}{\text{Stop-Loss Point per Trade}}$$

2% Maximum Dollar Risk per Trade = $500
Stop-Loss Point = 1¹/₄ points
Maximum Position Size = $500 / 1¼ points = 400 shares

If you have $25,000 allocated for a trade and you have picked a stock that you believe has 1¼ points of risk, then the maximum position size is 400 shares. If the price of the stock is $25, you will use only $10,000 of buying power ($25 × 400 shares = $10,000), which is appropriate given your 1¼ stop-loss point and your $500 maximum tolerance for loss. In our example, because you're using only $10,000 of buying power for the $25 stock, you free up $15,000 in capital to allocate toward another position.

Step 2 provides guidance for the maximum position given your capital allocation:

Maximum Shares per Position =
$25,000 / $100 = 250 shares
$25,000 / $50 = 500 shares

$25,000 / $25 = 1,000 shares

$25,000 / $10 = 2,500 shares

Even though the maximum position size for a $25 stock is 1,000 shares given your capital allocation, you would not trade with that size because the loss you might sustain with a 1¼ point stop-loss would be larger than your $500 maximum loss risk tolerance. On the other hand, if you selected a $100 stock with the same 1¼ point stop-loss risk profile, then your maximum position size should be limited to 250 shares, because that would be the maximum you could buy given your $25,000 capital allocation.

Higher-priced stocks also normally require wider stops. Chances are that the $100 stock would have a wider stop-loss point because of higher slippage and volatility. With the 250-share position in the $100 stock, the maximum stop-loss point would be 2.

When you carefully prepare to manage risk before trading, the outcome will always be manageable. Trading with appropriate position sizes is extremely important for beginning and professional traders alike. Appropriate position size is determined by knowing beforehand how much you can afford to lose on any one position. When you know that figure, you can determine how large your position should be given your initial stop-loss point and the price of the stock.

# PROFIT BY MANAGING LOSS

Being wrong about a trade is okay. In fact, the only way for a trader to become comfortable with the notion of loss in trading is to experience it regularly, while developing the discipline to cut it out quickly without even thinking about it. Some of the most profitable traders are right marginally more than they are wrong. The most successful traders have developed the ability to accept loss as part of the game, and to cut it out before it cuts them out. This allows them to spend their time focusing on the winners rather than the losers.

*Substance is the inner quiet of mind, free of individual failings.*

ZEN SAYING

## HOW TO WIN WITH THE STOP-LOSS

Enter into trades only when you have established a sensible game plan, with a stop-loss exit strategy mapped out in case the trade is a loser. A stop-loss is your only insurance if the stock does not perform the way you hoped. If and when that initial stop-loss point is reached, it is crucial to get out of the position *without thinking about it*. A protective stop can be entered on the actual books of the New York Stock Exchange. However, most NASDAQ market makers do not accept stop-loss orders, so you have to keep track of stop-loss points mentally or on paper. There will be times when a stock will turn around moments after you were stopped out, but keep in mind that in the long run, this makes absolutely no difference.

Managing loss is what risk control is all about. Losing correctly requires inner strength, discipline, and resolution. It takes strict control to set a stop before you enter a trade. Setting a stop before trading means that you are considering the risk before going after the reward. The only way to last in trading is by preserving capital; adhering to predetermined stops will allow you to do this.

After you enter a stop, do not adjust it to give yourself more leeway if the trade is not working out. Why a trade is not working doesn't matter; you can always find rationalizations and excuses for loss. Price action, however, does not warp reality. The sooner your stop announces to you that your position is faulty, the better off you will be. By way of an analogy, on a multiple-choice exam, usually the first answer you pick is the best one. Statistics show that if you second-guess yourself by going back and changing your answer, you will probably be incorrect. Moving stops or ignoring them is similar to second-guessing yourself on a test—your first choice for a stop-loss is probably the best, and you should adhere to it.

There are different strategies for placing stops. With practice, most traders develop their own stop-loss strategies based on individual preferences.

## INITIAL STOP-LOSS

Initial stop-losses can be placed in many different areas. Depending on why you entered a position, the initial stop-loss will ensure that your original thought process remains intact. When a trade is initiated, a stop-loss should be placed immediately. There are various technical levels to place a stop, but a general guideline for long positions is that the initial stop-loss should be placed 1/8 point beneath the previous day's low. For short positions, the initial stop-loss should be placed 1/8 point above the previous day's high. Only after you choose an initial stop-loss can you take the steps, described in Chapter 2, to determine your proper position size.

The previous day's low and high prices represent the first technical price levels of daily support and resistance. Yesterday's low or high point was the furthest that the bears or bulls could push the stock before it changed direction. Stops tend to accumulate just below or above these price ranges. A move through the lows or highs of the previous day may trigger stops and tend to clear the path for further momentum. If, for example, Dell Computer is 40 bid and yesterday's low was 38½, your protective stop-loss order should be placed at 38³⁄₈.

## BREAK-EVEN STOP-LOSS

After the initial stop-loss is set, the next stop-loss order to use is a break-even stop-loss. After you have entered into a position and have your initial stop-loss protection in place, your objective would naturally turn toward implementing a superior exit strategy to use when the trade is earning you money. The first step toward exiting a winning trade is to protect your profits by moving the stop-loss order to your entry point.

With a break-even stop, you are in a sense catching a free ride on the tail of the market, and the worst-case scenario is nothing lost, except for commissions. A tightened stop-loss does increase the possibility of being prematurely stopped out while the trade still has a shot to meet your original objectives, but you can always get back into the position. The break-even stop-loss provides peace of mind along with a sense of detachment. When the trade is working and the break-even stop-loss is in place, you have successfully created an opportunity with little or no cost to you.

The best time to raise your stop-loss to the break-even level is subject to individual trading styles. A guideline that seems to work well when adjusting stops to the break-even point is the 1½ percent move. The 1½ percent move suggests that you should adjust your stop-loss to break-even after your position has moved at least 1½ percent above your entry point. For example, assume you bought DELL at 50 and your original stop-loss was 49. When DELL moves 1½ percent above 50, or 3/4 points to 50³⁄₄, you should slide your stop-loss up to your entry point of 50. The 1½ percent adjustment yardstick is useful because it can be applied across the board to broadly ranging prices. It is recommended that for lower-priced stocks, the minimum move before raising your stop-loss to break-even should be at least 1/2 point. For example, a 1½ percent move in a $25 stock is approximately 3/8 of a point. In this case you would wait for 1/2-point move first before using a break-even stop-loss.

The 1½ percent break-even parameter is meant to be flexible according to each trader's individual style and comfort level. Some traders raise their break-even stops immediately after the stock has moved 3/8 of a point in their favor. Others wait for a move of at least $1 or more. Experiment with this parameter and utilize its psychological advantage.

## TRAILING STOP-LOSS

If stocks have lingered in no-man's-land for the day—that is, they have not moved above the 1½ percent break-even stop-loss barrier or have fallen beneath the initial stop-loss point—they require a trailing stop. A trailing stop is an adjustment of the initial stop taking into account the price action of the current day when the market has closed. If the initial stop-loss was placed 1/8 below the previous day's close, then the trailing stop would be moved 1/8 beneath the current day's close. Assume that after you go long DELL at 50, it trades in a 49¼—50½ price range. During the day it fails either to pierce the initial stop-loss at 48¾ or to move above the 1½ percent mark of 51¾. In this case, the new stop-loss would be moved up to 49⅛, or 1/8 below the current day's low. Remember that you can always reenter a position after getting stopped out if you believe the trade still has potential. It's always better to reexamine the position with a clear mind and nothing at stake. If you still like the position after being stopped out, then your strategy was probably sound, based on objective reasons.

## PROFIT-TAKING STOP

Another type of stop-loss is one used to protect your profits. This is used when your position is working well and has moved at least 1/2 point above the 1½ percent break-even stop-loss zone. At this point your break-even stop-loss is in place and it's time to preserve some of your gains. Your objective is to move your break-even stop to 1/2 point below the 1½ percent profit-taking barrier. In our example, if after you go long DELL at 50, it moves to 51¼, your break-even stop would be moved upward from 50 to 50³⁄₄. The 51¹⁄₄ price represents a 1/2-point move above the 1¹⁄₂ percent break-even stop-loss entry zone.

Locking in some profits using a stop-loss strategy is an effective way to trade without worrying about losing your gains. It helps a trader to let profits run longer while not missing out on a solid gain. Depending on the trader's style and the type of stock traded, the stop-loss level used to lock in some gains could be adjusted. More aggressive traders may use wider stops to protect profits, while less aggressive traders would use narrower ones.

Developing a comfort level when using stops takes practice and discipline. Each stock has its own personality and reacts differently throughout the day. Some stocks advance and pull back quickly, while others may creep along steadily. After becoming familiar with the stock you're trading, you will be able to place stops more effectively.

Stop-loss orders are protective measures and are not perfect. Market forces can swing prices through stop points, resulting in larger-than-anticipated losses. Stops are still the most effective form of insurance a trader has. Successful traders have learned to exit their positions quickly when their stops are hit, without thinking about it. They understand that tomorrow is another day and they will have another chance. Stops give traders breathing room, discouraging them from being "psyched" out of a position due to choppiness or indecision. Stops provide peace of mind because they represent a decision that was made before the trade. Placing a stop-loss order means there is one less decision traders have to make while they have a position. When you take action and exit a position because of a prearranged stop, you are reinforcing discipline and confidence in your game plan. Remember to always stick to pre-arranged stops.

## TRADE LIQUID NAMES

Properly evaluating the liquidity and the volatility of a stock may mean the difference between a successful or a hapless outcome for market makers and day traders alike. One of the toughest jobs a market maker has is to properly size a market. This means correctly assessing the proper risk, given the current liquidity and volatility of a stock. Market makers are constantly putting up risk for accounts to capture larger order flow. This involves either buying or selling a block of stock at or very close to the inside market. For example, if AAPL's current inside market is 53—53$^1$/$_8$, with 2,600,000 shares traded on the day, what is the proper amount of stock the trader should be willing to buy or sell on the inside bid or offer? What is the most the trader should be willing to sell up or down 1/8 from the inside market? What kind of slippage, or movement, if any, would be involved before buying back or selling the size bought or sold?

A market that is oversized can easily lead to a large loss. If a market maker were putting up risk for a large order, the object of the next part of the trade would be to trade the order for a small profit, for a small loss, or flat. This would eliminate the up-front risk, allowing the market maker to trade the rest of the order for a profit, generally without risk. Day traders who are about to enter a trade should also be careful to judge how much slippage may be involved before they will be able to exit or enter the position.

Part of a market maker's job is to broadcast buy and sell interest messages in stocks through an electronic system called Autex (owned by Thompson Financial Services). These messages are sent out before market opening and throughout the day, with the goal of letting the street know what you want to do in a stock in order to attract an order. Brokers or traders can view these messages at will and respond accordingly with a phone call, depending on their particular interest.

Here's an example of a super message followed by an order: Apple Computer is trading actively, with 2,600,000 shares traded so far on the day. The market maker wants to get involved and notices that the stock is acting strong, with blocks of 25,000 and 50,000 going up on the offing side. He decides to offer the stock for sale, with the objective of accepting risk up front in order to get an order in the door. With AAPL's market quoted 113—113$^1$/$_8$, the market maker "supers" 100,000 shares at 113$^1$/$_8$, on the offer. An institutional trader who wants to buy sees this message and calls the firm.

*Jack, you just "supered" 100 AAPL at 113$^1$/$_8$ and I'm a buyer. I'd like to own the 100 here, and take 100 more to buy behind that.*

The salesperson relays to the trader:

*Apple, you just supered 100 at 113$^1$/$_8$. I bought those. Work 100 behind it at the market.*

The market maker is now short 100,000 shares of Apple on the offering at $113^1/_8$. The success of this trade will depend on the market maker's judgment as to the liquidity and volatility of AAPL, given the super message. His objective now is to buy back the stock that he shorted with the least market impact. He will adjust his market discretely in order to reduce his risk by buying as much AAPL as possible in order to service the account quickly.

## DIVERSIFY YOUR POSITIONS

Traders can spread out their positions in order to minimize market risk while optimizing their chances for success. Many professional Wall Street traders look for ways to increase their probabilities for success in a trade by diversifying the number of positions they take within a given sector. Diversification tends to increase the odds that if the sector does move in the anticipated direction, other stocks that the traders have selected will move that way too.

Diversification among individual stocks within one sector spreads out the alpha, or individual, risk inherent in each stock. Every stock in the marketplace is subject to both market risk (beta) and stock-specific risk (alpha). The market risk (beta) of a stock refers to how it moves in conjunction with the motions of the broader market. The beta risk of a position is the risk that the broader market will turn against you, pulling the stock you are long with it. Some stocks have higher betas than others, which means more exposure to the fluctuations of the market. Stocks that have a beta of 1 should move in step with the market. If the market is up 2 percent, a stock with a beta of 1 on average should also be up 2 percent. If a stock has a beta of 2, then it moves at twice the rate of the broader market. If the market were up 2 percent, a stock with a beta of 2 would be up 4 percent.

The alpha risk of a stock is the individual risk inherent in every issue. This includes risks that cannot be foreseen, such as fundamental news specific only to that stock. By selecting several issues within a given sector, traders protect their portfolios from the chance of having individual positions turn against them or alpha risk.

Suppose a sector trader is bullish on the hardware sector, for example. Instead of putting all your money into one stock, you can go long in several stocks by allocating less money to each one. Instead of buying $50,000 worth of International Business Machines

(IBM), you would buy $10,000 worth of five different stocks, such as
IBM, Dell Computer (DELL), Hewlett-Packard (HWP), Compaq
Computer (CPQ), and Gateway (GTW). The number of shares you
purchased of each would depend on their prices. All five of the
issues are correlated. This is called basket trading, and it reduces the
alpha risk of a portfolio but not the beta risk. Basket trading
involves added expense in terms of commissions and spreads, but it
provides insurance against individual stock risk.

Some traders look to reduce the beta risk as well. There are various ways to reduce the broader market risk, including hedging
with futures and options, pair trading, diversifying among sectors,
and using different long to short ratios.

One way to reduce broader market exposure is to hold both long
and short positions of correlated stocks. The ratio of your long to
short exposure should be in accordance with the current underlying
trend of the market, combined with individual stock selection. If the
trend as you perceive it is up, and you want to reduce broader market risk, then your long to short exposure ratio should be long by 2
to 1, but a minimum of 2 to 2. This means that for every two long
positions you hold, you hold at least one short position.

The long to short exposure ratio could be spread out among sectors so it would not adversely impact the conviction you have on a
specific industry. Reducing the beta risk by taking concurrent long
and short positions only works when the different sectors you have
selected have similar betas. For example, if you like the hardware
sector but don't especially like the software stocks, and you think
the broader market will rally as a whole, your strategy might be to
go long two hardware stocks and short one software stock. If you
are more neutral on the market, then you might hold two longs in
the hardware sector and two shorts in the software stocks. Because
the hardware and software sectors have similar betas, this strategy
should reduce your beta risk.

## STICK TO YOUR GAME PLAN

Sticking to your game plan is the hardest thing to do as a trader. The
reason it's so hard is that it takes strict discipline and an emotional
detachment from the outcome. Knowing what to do and doing it are

two separate issues. Trading involves so many unforeseen elements and market forces that mishaps and fuzzy thinking materialize even at the most advanced levels. The only way to trade successfully through this sea of uncontrollable elements is to have the discipline to stick to your game plan. Your plan is the shield that no market force can penetrate, unless you let it.

The main reason experienced traders lose is that they fail to follow their own rules. There are hundreds of reasons and excuses for deviating from a trading plan—for breaking your rules. In the long run, the reasons make zero difference. In the end, people are judged by their results, not the quality of their excuses. In an unstructured environment with multiple sources of reason pulling you in different directions, rules become the cornerstone for success.

A trading plan is predictable. It provides sources of reason given any number of existing circumstances. It filters out noise and encourages discipline. Remember that having a trading plan and sticking to it is invaluable. The simple recognition of this fact can provide the stimulus to adhere to your own plan.

The association a person attaches to losing can be deep-seated. Feelings of unworthiness or shame usually have their roots in childhood and can cause people to act in unpredictable ways. Loss in trading is unavoidable. The best traders do not get upset when they lose; they maintain equilibrium. Seasoned traders do not perceive loss as a personal or professional setback. Instead they acknowledge loss as a necessary and important step on the path toward success. Do not be afraid to lose. Act quickly to cut your losses without thinking about it.

C  H  A  P  T  E  R

# MIND GAMES THAT PROPAGATE FINANCIAL HAVOC

It is easy for traders to get hooked into subjective interpretations of what the market is doing, because their minds are playing tricks on them. Different people react in different ways to stress. Day trading takes an enormous amount of mental exertion, which requires physical energy. Successful trading is the by-product of a ruthless mentality that allows you to make quick decisions when there is a lot at stake. The best traders can make decisions objectively under stressful circumstances, without looking back.

Many traders fall into a middle ground wavering between subjective and objective interpretations. This happens because they are more attached to the outcome and what it represents than they should be. A trader who falls into a losing rut, for example, is more likely to perform poorly because of a negative state of mind. You tend to attract what you focus on. If you are in a losing streak, chances are that you are focusing on loss, thus attracting more loss.

Detrimental mind games start to kick in when you refuse to accept the fact that you were not able to achieve your desired outcome. When you accept loss gracefully and refrain from beating yourself up, your mind-set will improve and you will be able to focus on where you want to go. This will improve your chances for success.

## WHAT NOT TO DO

> *When you learn what not to do in order not to lose, only then can you begin to learn what to do in order to win.*
>
> EDWIN LEFEVRE, *REMINISCENCES OF A STOCK OPERATOR*

Successful trading involves two spheres of choice: action and inaction. The proactive course of offensive action is a step taken in order to win. It means that you have made a decision and are acting on it by putting yourself on the line. It should stem from a plan that provides contingencies for entering and exiting positions. It's an approach that requires doing something in order to benefit from it. It requires taking action now.

Playing offense by taking action, however, is only half of the equation. The other half of the equation that leads to successful trading involves inaction, or negative selection. Inaction involves refraining from trading in order not to lose; it is a preventive posture used for insurance. Not taking action under certain circumstances can be harder than taking action. It is very hard to be patient when you are bored, looking for excitement, and eager to make some money.

Many traders wrongly believe that they need to have a position in the market at all times. They ask themselves, "Should I be long or short here?" They rationalize that if they don't want to be long a stock anymore, then they have to be short it, or vice versa. Choosing not to trade, however, is also a decision. It's hard for some traders to admit that they may have no conviction on the current stock or market trend. There are times that having no position will statistically improve your chances of winning in the long run. If you consider being flat, along with being long or short, then you will begin to look at opportunities with more patience and less effort.

An example of defensive inaction in day trading is refraining from chasing a stock too far past your ideal entry point. Not chasing a stock is, in many cases, a way to avoid unnecessary loss. In day trading, entry is a crucial part of the equation and should not be done impatiently. If an entry point is missed, so be it. Take non-action. Choose not to chase. Wait for the next opportunity.

Traders should consider themselves to be on sentry duty throughout the trading day. Sentry duty is one of the hardest military assignments because most of the time nothing happens: It gets very boring. Even so, it requires careful attention to detail and concentration at all times, even though you may be bored. One little slip-up during a cigarette or coffee break could mean the difference between life and death, for the individual as well as the whole squad.

The human mind will go to great lengths to avoid boredom. Yet in trading the natural human tendency to avoid boredom is a negative quality that must be recognized and controlled.

Avoiding certain actions preserves a trader's life and provides a shield from unforeseen difficulties. Defensive trading means not taking a course of action that might cause you harm or lost money. Inaction in trading is like defensive driving: It's a technique that involves knowing what not to do in order not to get into an accident, such as not changing lanes before you look, or not gunning the gas when a light is about to turn.

In order to win, a successful trader must first learn how not to lose. Knowing what action not to take is just as important as knowing what action to take.

## BOTTOM FISHING

No stock is ever cheap or expensive; it just is. A common rationalization is that because a stock was trading at 80 last week and now it's at 40, it's cheap! Stock prices reflect the current supply and demand for an issue, regardless of past or future. A day trader's goal is to make money today, not to analyze long-term value. Each trading day must be approached with complete disregard for the past and future. Here and now is all there is. Today is when the money will be made, not yesterday and not tomorrow.

As a day trader, do not believe for a minute that the way to make money trading is to buy low and sell high. This is false in day trading. Attempting to buy low or to short high is the way to lose money, not to make it. Buying low and selling high is a description of bottom and top fishing, which are the enemy of all traders. Bottom fishing is the by-product of a faulty ego-based approach to trading. It involves a guessing game in which you are pitting yourself against the broader consensus. Let go of your desire to bottom fish.

> *In a bull market one should trade only from the long side. In a bear market one should trade only from the short side.*
>
> WALL STREET PROVERB

Although the above proverb sounds deceptively simple, experienced traders who attempt to pick bottoms and tops of trends lose fortunes. Bottom and top fishing seem like the comfortable, rational thing to do. However, in the less than zero-sum game of trading, comfort and rationalization are costly goals that should be avoided whenever possible.

The most successful traders make their profits from buying high and selling higher or from selling low and buying lower. The market does not take your opinion into consideration when it decides where it wants to go. When you buy high and sell higher, you eliminate a large part of the guessing game that so many traders get entangled in. Always allow the market to show you where it plans to go. Do not try to guess when it is going to stop. Allow yourself to do the uncomfortable thing, which is to buy strength and sell weakness.

## THE MYTH OF AVERAGING DOWN

A trader should never average down under any circumstances. Averaging down is buying more stock below the price that you paid for it, or shorting more stock above the price where you originally shorted it. Averaging down means adding to a loser and hoping it will turn around. Whenever you hear the phase "average down," run for the hills. "I'll average down" is really a coined excuse that means "I'll refuse to admit that I'm wrong."

Remember that you want to buy stocks that are moving in your direction, not against you. Your objective is to trade with the momentum. If you throw money into a losing position, you are fighting the momentum. Losses can easily become compounded in a snowball effect when you average down. Adding to a loser is similar to rolling the dice out of frustration or desperation. If you maintain discipline in the first place, you will not be caught in the painful position of watching the size of your loss grow exponentially because you have thrown more money into a losing pit.

When you add to a loss, you are throwing good money after bad. That money could much better serve you if it were put to work in a winning position. When you average down, a small manageable loss can easily be transformed into a large unmanageable one. As a simple rule, never, ever add to a losing position, under any circumstances.

## ROLLING THE DICE

Great traders have proven time and again that they can consistently win by speculating when the odds are in their favor. They have the ability to correctly assess and integrate a risk–reward ratio that statistically favors a profitable outcome. The outcome is based on a statistical distribution, whereby the probabilities are measurable when the same strategy is employed consistently. Both novices and professional traders often confuse speculation with gambling.

Speculation is derived from probabilities; pure gambling, on the other hand, is based on hope. Gambling is a less than zero-sum game in which the outcome is not based on any measurable probability. Traders sometimes gamble with positions, and gamblers sometimes count cards and play when the odds are stacked in their favor. When you become aware of the difference between speculation and gambling in trading, you'll be able to repeat profitable trading scenarios while cutting out blind gambling shots.

In gambling, the house is the one that stands to collect, because the odds are in its favor. A gambler who wins will never really be able to explain why, except to say that "luck" was favorable. If you are trading for excitement, you are probably gambling. Gambling will force a trader's hand when no plan or discipline exists.

Gambling is a sickness and an addiction in many people. Gambling is believed to increase dramatically during times of stress and pressure; many gamblers are unaware of or just don't care about their real probabilities of success. They rely on some untouchable or unexplainable gut feeling. There are between 4 million and 16 million compulsive gamblers in the United States, and a number of day traders may fall into this category. Gamblers in trading fall into the low end of the performance spectrum, if they last. They are usually influenced by some hyped-up sector that is receiving all the attention in the media. The impulsive gambling instinct causes them to trade from the hip, sometimes with an all-or-nothing destructive urge. It is hard for some gamblers not to trade if they fear they will miss the current craze.

Successful traders are diametrically opposed to the gambling types. They do not look for excitement in the marketplace; they come thoroughly prepared with a clear plan and a search routine that is methodical. Rational traders maintain superior discipline, which shields them from the human emotional biases, such as hope and boredom, that are prevalent in gamblers.

## SWINGING FOR THE FENCES

The desire to hit a home run in trading is the earmark of a beginner. The key to earning profits in day trading is consistency. Steadily hitting singles and doubles is how the pros fill the coffers with profits and produce dynamic results over the long run. Statistically speaking, a large swing occurring in a given stock at the precise time an order is entered is an anomaly. The stocks that make large and fast moves regularly are the ones that require a more diligent risk profile, translating into a smaller position with a wider stop-loss point.

Focusing on hitting singles and doubles does not mean that you cannot maximize your gains. It simply means that you are focusing on technique. When a batter hits a home run in baseball, it happens naturally, usually without any effort. The same holds true with a home run trade. The home-run trade should not be the focal point. Successful traders pile on the profits by focusing on technique and risk control, letting the profits take care of themselves. Successful traders tend to view trading as a business, like any other, in which wishful thinking is kept to a minimum.

A baseball batter who is attached to the idea of hitting a home run is distracted by the thought and usually performs worse for it. Successful batters first visualize correct technique before getting up to the plate. They stay focused on the motions and technique that lead to consistency and greatness, such as stance, eye contact, grip, swinging motion, and other details. Proper technique leads to home runs; home runs do not lead to proper technique. Correct routine in trading revolves around visualizing and implementing proper methods, not around the big swing.

Swinging for the fences in trading is destructive on several counts. The first reason it's destructive is that it's the product of unrealistic expectations. Having unrealistic expectations may set you up for a let-down in the future, because the odds can be slim that the hoped-for event will occur. When high expectations are not met, traders generally experience a sense of disappointment and frustration; emotions that interfere with optimal trading performance and could result in a downward confidence spiral.

Another reason swinging for the fences is destructive is that it often fosters an-all-or nothing mentality, and traders risk far more than they should on a single position. The extra-large position makes it harder for the trader to cut losses if the position turns the wrong way. A trader who is not willing to cut losses quickly will not last long. When traders focus on hitting home runs, their attention is diverted from other, profitable possibilities.

## POSITION SIZE ENVY

Traders often take larger positions than they should because they are experiencing size envy. Position size envy occurs when your ego whispers to you, "The sky's the limit." You may be in an environment in which other traders are taking positions larger than yours. You decide that if they can do it, so can you: You jump in without sticking your toe in the water first. If the water is ice cold, you could be in for the shock of your life. A trader's risk tolerance develops over time, given experience, confidence, and the emotional and financial ability to withstand losses.

Someone who can trade large positions has arrived at that point through a long and painful learning process. Most people cannot walk into a gym and bench-press 300 pounds if they are used to putting up only 150. The only way to get to the 300-pound mark is to slowly build up your strength and tolerance over time through a gradual increase in the weight lifted. The same holds true for increasing your position size. It should be a slow process based on your financial capacity and psychological and emotional development, discipline, and strength. *Traders should judge themselves by their own goals and nothing else.*

One reason traders take positions that are too big is the almighty greed instinct. Greedy traders have an insatiable attachment to money. Remember, the most successful traders on Wall Street have a disregard for money. When you are glued to your P&L as a trader, your ability to act objectively is limited. Everyone experiences greed to some extent, but traders have to keep this human trait under control. Attachment in trading is detrimental because it represents emotionally charged subjectivity. The fewer associations and attachments a trader has, the better.

Emotional attachment to money and what it represents is the main reason traders freeze and have a difficult time taking losses, especially large ones. They find themselves in situations they're unprepared for financially or mentally. One of the hardest things for a trader to do is to stick to a game plan when emotions blow things out of proportion. A trader who freezes is unable to act or think quickly. This hesitation usually makes the difference between a profit, a loss, or a huge loss.

Another reason why a trader might have a position that is too large is because he adds to a loser, or averages down. Adding to a loser is probably the most deadly sin in trading, but the vast majority of traders do it at one time or another. Many do it out of sheer hope or desperation, refusing to acknowledge that they were wrong. Adding to a loser is the worst excuse for a trader to have a position that is too big. Wishful thinking and hoping to make back what was lost often result in huge losses. A snowball effect is created, gaining size and momentum in the wrong direction.

One way to avoid adding to a loser is to realize that you can always cut your losses now and get back in later. Successful day traders are constantly selling stocks for small losses and reentering the position when they think the momentum has begun to move in their favor. Successful traders add to winning positions, not losing ones.

If losses set in that are above your risk tolerance, it becomes much harder to act quickly and to face the truth that you are wrong. As your account accumulates money, your position sizes should increase gradually. This will allow you to slowly build up your risk tolerance based on financial soundness. Position size in trading should be dictated by risk control, not high hopes. The anguish of being wrong in a trade grows exponentially when your positions get out of control. If the mind and wallet are not accustomed to taking large hits, it becomes very difficult to act swiftly and to cut your losses.

## VENGEANCE TRADING

Vengeance trading occurs after a trader takes a hit on a trade and wants to get even with the stock. The reason the trade went sour doesn't usually matter; the trader is angry, but not wanting to accept blame, will quickly place it elsewhere. This misdirected emotional firestorm usually translates into pure revenge. The only solution in this cloudy state of mind is for the trader to avenge honor and money lost by getting them back from the stock that took it. The stubbornness festers, and pretty soon it's an all-out battle.

> "The Internet stocks seemed likely to sell off hard this morning," thought Scott O'Riley, a market maker for a large firm. "They had a nice run yesterday, and with negative news out in AOL and AMZN, they should be down further." The Internet index was weak when Scott decided to short 2,000 shares of EBAY, which at the time was down 2 points. For some reason, AOL started to bounce off its lows and AMZN and EBAY followed along with it. "I can't believe this stock! This thing should be down ten points and for some stupid reason it's now up two dollars! I'll prove that I'm right and that the market is wrong and I'll get my money back by shorting another two thousand shares here." Scott added to his losing position and shorted 2,000 more shares. Soon after, EBAY ran another three points. By this time, Scott was red in the face and could not think of anything else but getting back at EBAY. He was cursing at EBAY, at the market in general, and at the computer screen.
>
> Throughout the day, EBAY continued to rally along with all the other Internet stocks. Scott refused to cut his losses. As the day progressed, he became completely irrational and frozen with fear. His eyes were glued to the computer screen and he even punched the computer and the desk. He kept blaming EBAY and continued to short more stock so he could get even, until he was short 7,000 shares with EBAY up ten points. By the end of the day, EBAY was up 15 points and Scott was down $100,000, and almost out of a job.

The problem with vengeance trading is that the initial loss probably occurred because the original direction of the trade was incorrect. Vengeance trades rarely take place in the opposite direction of the original losing trade. It takes a seasoned pro to change directions on a position after initially being wrong. The vengeance trade goes in the same direction because vengeance traders need to prove that they were right in the first place, that it wasn't their fault they lost money. They need to get even so their egos can be restored to their original perches.

The common misperception is that when you are trading, you are fighting the market, which is the enemy that must be defeated. Ameritrade recently ran an advertisement pitching on-line day traders and asking them if they were ready to take on the market with the following quote: "I don't want to just beat the market. I want to wrestle its scrawny little body to the ground and make it beg for mercy." This is faulty, ego-based, unrealistic thinking that will lead toward losses, not profits. The market is never wrong and it cannot be defeated. It is selfless. It does not experience feelings of victory or defeat. The market is a cold battlefield and its participants are engaged in a life-or-death battle against themselves.

> *Every battle that takes place, whether within the body and mind or outside of it, is always a battle against oneself.*
>
> ZEN SAYING

Vengeance trading can quickly turn into disaster, because revenge is one of the strongest and most stubborn of emotions. Vengeance trading is a futile exertion of time, energy, and money. Its grip only tightens, clogging clear thinking and profit; it drains the resources of a trader, sucking time away from other profitable opportunities by encouraging the trader to focus on where the losing trade did not go, rather than where another trade could go.

Instead of fretting over lost money and trying to get even with a market that does not care, use your time and energy to focus on other situations that will be more profitable.

You will immediately begin to improve as a trader when you stop wanting to control the outcome. The desire to control that which cannot be controlled creates a distorted reality, leading to stress and mind games that will thwart your success. It will be easier for you to acknowledge objective circumstances when you treat yourself kindly, and when you realize that each trade is just one step in the sphere of things to come. Acknowledging that you are not your results will help you to step outside of yourself and to trade with increased detachment and objectivity.

P A R T

# UNDERLYING CONDITIONS

5

# TREND SPOTTING IS THE KEY TO PROFITS

One of the most powerful methods in day trading is identifying and trading with the underlying trend. The underlying trend represents the gravitational pull of the market. The trend is the true force behind price action and sector momentum. It carries everything in its path with it.

Technology has made identifying trends easier than ever. The tools necessary for spotting trends are readily available in software packages today. The most effective way to spot a trend is to have a simple check and balance system.

Many who are interested in trading have heard the saying, "The trend is your friend." Why then do many novices and professional traders alike disregard the concept of trading with the trend? This is because many are not sure how to define a trend for their own trading objectives. Even when traders have developed a clear-cut definition of a trend, they often disregard their own rules because of their desire to catch the bottom or top of a move.

The middle part of the trend, or the "meat of the move" as many call it, is the part of the move that you should focus on catching and trading. The beginning or end of a move is inconsequential. You have not missed much when you miss the bottom or the top of a trend.

As a trend gets close to completion, it is the most ferocious, and it battles for every last breath. This occurs because as trends mature, they usually attract more attention and more volume. When a hot stock or sector's popularity is the greatest, many buyers already own the stock. When optimistic bulls or pessimistic bears push a trend to its very limits, heavy volume is often associated with the last desperate assault. This is called volume capitulation, which is a surrendering of the force moving it because they used up all of their buying or selling power. The reason the trend capitulated is that the supply–demand equilibrium shifted. If you are fighting for your life, you get a burst of adrenaline that allows you to push your strength to its limit. When the adrenaline wears off, you are weaker than ever. Volume capitulation is the market equivalent of adrenaline capitulation.

In effect, the top or bottom of a move is only a small part of the entire move. There is still a great deal of profit to be made when you climb on board to catch the middle of the trend. Traders who disregard the middle of the trend and instead attempt to buy the lows and sell the highs of a move are caught in never-never land. They have a strong desire to be completely right and to gain acknowledgment for calling the top or the bottom.

Trends come in many shapes and sizes. Short-term day traders should have different trend definitions from long-term investors. A long-term investor can use a 50-day moving average to define a trend; a short-term day trader would be better off using an 8-day moving average to define one. As a short-term day trader, your holding period will be from 2 minutes to 3 or more days. Three days is usually sufficient time for a short-term trend to play itself out. Most day traders prefer to go home flat overnight, so the daily trend is the most important. Regardless of whether you hold a stock for 2 minutes or 3 days, your short-term definition of a trend can be the same.

Many traders get caught up in the belief that identifying a legitimate trend is a complicated endeavor. This is far from the truth. A few of the basic techniques that will allow you to spot a trend are the 8-period moving average, the opening price signal, and the net price rule. When you know how to spot a trend, your profitability and entry effectiveness will immediately increase.

If you become comfortable with the idea that it is okay to miss the bottom or the top of a move, you will immediately become more profitable. Traders who look to catch the meat of a trend will be rewarded twofold. First, they will lose less money and time because they have stopped trying to guess when the stock or the market is going to stop. Second, they will earn more consistently, because they have developed the habit of trading after price confirmation, not before it. The odds of your making a successful trade increase dramatically after the price of a stock, its sector, and the broader market confirms your idea. By trading with the trend, you are listening to the market and letting it lead you, rather than trying to impose your own opinion upon it.

Some of the greatest traders have the simplest rules for defining trends, allowing them to trade with less effort. People tend to complicate trading because they believe that effort and strain will increase their effectiveness. Great traders win with simple plans and quiet minds. They have developed the ability to block out the noise and stay focused on what the market is telling them.

## NEWTON'S LAW OF MOTION

Isaac Newton developed scientific theories that explained the laws of momentum. Although it couldn't be seen at the time, Newton's famous laws of motion provided the first clue for successful day trading, some 350 years ago.

Newton's most significant discovery was the science of how objects move, or in day trader's terms, how prices move. Represented mathematically by the equation $F = ma$, Newton put forth that the acceleration of an object (the rate at which its velocity changes) is equal to the net force on the object divided by the object's mass.* For the trader, this law of physics applies to trends: It can be interpreted to mean that the acceleration of a stock's price, or momentum, is equal to the volume (net force) on the stock divided by the float (object's mass). Stocks that have a large net force and a small mass will move forcefully.

---

*Michael Hart, *The 100: A Ranking of the Most Influential Persons in History.* Citadel Press/Carol Publishing, 1989.

Newton's law of motion states that objects in motion tend to stay in motion until an outside force stops them. When applied to trading, the law of motion could be translated to mean that buying strength and selling weakness, or trading with the trend, is the right thing to do. This is because buying or selling stocks that are moving in your direction is compatible with the laws of probability. Probabilities show that prices, like objects, will continue to move along the path of least resistance until some outside force stops them. It takes more effort for an outside event or seller to halt the momentum than for the momentum to continue. If a train is moving at full speed, it takes time and effort to slow it down and to ultimately reverse its course.

## THE MOMENTUM OF A TREND

Momentum is the juice behind the development of overbought and oversold oscillators. According to Newton, momentum is the combination of mass and velocity. Newton said that momentum represents the ability of an object to move in one direction at an even speed until an outside force slows it down or stops it.

The risk involved with trading along trend-following techniques is the prospect of missing the initial reward when the trend is changing direction. The risk–reward ratio of picking the top or bottom of a trend does not work in favor of traders or investors in the long run. Attempting to go long at the bottom or short at the top of a trend has destroyed more traders than any other trading technique. The risk–reward ratio improves dramatically for traders who focus on catching the meat of the move by going long or short once a trend is in place.

One reason traders feel such a need to pick the bottom or top of a move is that many have a deep-seated desire to be proven right. Rather than selling part of a long position if they think the trend is at the top, or waiting for confirmation that a top has indeed formed, their egos coax them on, encouraging them to take a shot and go short. If the initial guess was wrong and the trend was not at the top, their egos tighten the grip. The traders, not wanting to feel half-witted, either add to their losers or let them run.

It seems reasonable to short a stock that has risen high, or to buy a stock that has swooped low; but what is high and what is low? Most traders have their own definitions of high and low. Successful traders do not make money by buying low and selling high; they make money by buying high and selling higher, or shorting low and buying lower.

Methods such as oscillators and basic chart patterns will help you isolate when a trend is in the process of changing, and allow you to wet your beak on some of the volatility that takes place when markets turn. The first step, however, is to use perceived inflection points of tops and bottoms of trends as areas to trade around existing positions. Rid yourself of the belief that for every successful trade there is one entry point and one exit point. The most profitable traders trade around a core position, constantly scaling in and out. If your signal is telling you that the market is forming a top, use that signal to sell part or all of your long position. Refrain from trying to short a perceived market top.

## SECTOR POWER

The first step toward trading with a trend is knowing what trend to look at. For every stock that you are trading, there are a handful of highly correlated issues that trade along with that stock and compose its underlying sector. The sector's movements as a whole have a strong impact on the direction the individual stock will take in the short term.

Along the road, many traders acquire the habit of focusing solely on the stocks they are trading, without regard for the price action of the underlying sector that the stock is part of. Traders have a tendency to become attached to an idea. When this happens, they have difficulty relinquishing the idea if the stock's sector or the broader market is not cooperating.

In order to trade with the trend, you should monitor three underlying instruments before determining whether to take a position. When all three are pointing toward the same conclusion, the chances are greater that your trade will be successful. The first instrument is the individual stock; the second is the individual stock's underlying sector; and the third is the broader market. Having the patience to wait for confirmation will increase your conviction, effectiveness, and profitability.

For example, if you are considering going long Dell Computer, the first thing that you should look at is the individual stock, DELL. The second is DELL's underlying sector, which is the Computer Hardware Index (HWI), traded on the American Stock Exchange

(AMEX). The third item to monitor is the broader market, which in this case is the NDX 100. The NDX 100 is one broader market to monitor when you are trading tech stocks.

DELL's price movements are correlated with other hardware stocks, such as Compaq Computer (CPQ), Gateway (GTW), International Business Machines (IBM), and Hewlett-Packard (HWP). These stocks are all part of the HWI. The HWI can be charted and tracked intraday just like any individual stock. The sector's trend throughout the day has more influence than any other factor on how an individual stock within that sector will perform.

The NDX 100 and the S&P 500 are two measurements of the broader market that should be monitored carefully before determining what side of the fence to be on. Your odds for success will increase dramatically when you go long a stock in the midst of an uptrend in the broader market, or if you short a stock when the market is selling off.

Taking the other side of the trend is a losing game. Although you may be intellectually right and the trade may eventually go your way, you could still be wiped out because of the short-term force of a trend reaching the end of its move. Remember that your objective is to earn profits today, not to sit with losing positions and hope they will turn around in order to bail you out.

Before taking a position, it is important to know which stocks are the leaders in the underlying sector that you are trading. Bigcharts.com has an extensive listing of stocks and their related sectors. Stocks that are leaders within groups should be monitored if the stock that you are trading has a high degree of correlation to it. For example, Applied Materials (AMAT) is a leading semiconductor capital equipment stock. Before you take a position in KLA-Tenor (KLAC), another semiconductor capital equipment stock, you should see what AMAT is doing. Stocks that have the heaviest weighting in their sectors often lead the rest of the group. It is a good idea to monitor the individual leaders along with the sectors that you are trading.

If there is strong price divergence within a sector between two leading stocks, then it may be better to look for a trade in a sector where there is no price divergence. A stock that is under pressure in a sector can act as a drag on its correlated stocks, even if the damaging news is company-specific. Sometimes it takes a while for analysts to sort out whether negative news in a company is really company-specific, or whether it suggests deeper problems within the industry.

For example, when Compaq Computer (CPQ) blew up in the spring of 1999, the bad news was attributed to the internal problems associated with assimilating Digital Equipment (DEC) in their recent merger. On the opening, all the P.C. stocks fell under the gun even though the news was company-specific. Later in the day, the other P.C. stocks did rally, but the news caused correlated stocks to come under pressure early on.

## TIME PERIODS FOR TRACKING THE TREND

Monitor multiple time frames when tracking a daily trend. The multiple-time approach will provide you with various degrees of confirmation, ranging from a weekly time period to 2 minutes. This approach requires that you track trends with a weekly chart, a daily chart, and two to three intraday charts.

The weekly chart is useful to help you initially identify an idea or appraise a current one. Weekly charts allow you to examine the broader picture, determining which direction the wider trend points to. Weekly charts do not have to be monitored intraday, but you should look at them before looking at the daily chart. When you receive weekly confirmation for an idea, you can flip over to daily and intraday charts.

Weekly trends do not always produce confirmation for daily ideas. There are times when a weekly trend will point in one direction while the daily trend points in another. Your odds for success increase when the weekly chart confirms the daily one.

There are daily ideas and trends that can be taken advantage of without weekly confirmation. At times day traders may lack the patience to wait for weekly confirmation before acting. Under these circumstances, it is still possible to trade the daily trend successfully; however, consider trading smaller positions than you normally would, with tighter stop-losses and increased flexibility.

When you have received weekly confirmation, the next time period to look at is the daily. The daily chart is the main medium for finding trading ideas. The daily chart should be monitored intraday, along with other intraday charts. Most software charting packages allow you to plot at least four charts on a single page. The daily chart should be one of the main charts on your page.

After the daily chart, you should monitor intraday time periods, preferably two or more, with each focusing on different time periods.

**Figure 5-1** Daily and Intraday Charts Showing Sell-Off in the NDX

Figure 5-1 *(Continued)*

Depending on your preference, the 60-minute and 15-minute periods work well as the first two time periods. The 60-minute and 15-minute are susceptible to less noise than the 5-minute or 2-minute periods. The 5-minute and the 2-minute are useful, but can be susceptible to faulty signals and insignificant price moves. They should be used in conjunction with the 60-minute and the 15-minute time frames.

The charts in Figure 5-1 (see pages 46 and 47) show the NDX selling off on November 30, 1999. The charts track different time periods: daily, 15-minute, 5-minute, and 60-minute. The NDX formed a daily shooting star on November 26, which is a short-term reversal pattern. It then confirmed this short-term reversal pattern on November 30, after it broke beneath the daily 8-period moving average. You can see that on the 29th, the NDX fell beneath the 8-period moving average on the intraday charts as well, which confirmed that the short-term trend had changed.

The advantage of tracking multiple intraday time periods is that your objectivity is enhanced. Intraday charts provide day traders with a good method for timing entry and exit and for staying with the current trend. When you are tracking intraday time periods, first look at the largest time period for confirmation, and end with the smallest time period. For example, if you are watching the 60-minute, 15-minute, and 5-minute intraday charts, you should receive confirmation first from the 60-minute chart, then look at the 15-minute chart then the 5-minute chart.

If you receive weekly, daily, and intraday confirmation of a trend for your individual stock, the underlying sector, and the broader market, then your conviction should be at its highest; your chances for being on the right side of the trend are very strong. When you stack the underlying conditions in your favor with multiple time frames and multiple underlying confirmations, you are choosing to win the game before you enter it.

The best way to catch a trend is to be prepared to catch one. First, it is important to be at peace with yourself when you miss the bottoms and tops of moves. Refrain from feeling regret because you didn't sell at the highs or buy at the lows. Remember that your objective is not to initiate trades at these levels; it is to exercise the discipline to trade the meat of the move. When you trade with the objective of catching the middle of the move, you can stop playing the guessing game and start trading when the probabilities are most in your favor.

# 6

# FOUR TRADING SIGNALS FOR SPOTTING A TREND

There are four signals that every trader can use to isolate and catch a trend. These signals are simple in nature. Their power resides in their objectivity and in their ease of use. As a market maker, it is crucial to be able to make a split-second decision as to whether the short-term trend is in your favor. These four trading signals will relay to you the market's opinion as to what the trend is, and they will clue you in to a change in the underlying sentiment.

## THE PREVIOUS SESSION'S HIGH AND LOW

The previous day's high and low serve as the shortest-term measures of support and resistance. These prices mark the extreme ranges of the strength of the bulls and the bears from the previous day. Stops tend to accumulate just above or below these prices, because once the price is broken the momentum usually carries the price further. Buyers or sellers are usually there to defend these prices. Buyers who missed the opportunity to get on board at the low prices the previous day will be back; they remember having missed that price and they regret it. Sellers who missed the previous day's high will often be back to sell; they regret having missed the opportunity to get out at the highs on the previous day.

A window of opportunity for entry presents itself when a stock crosses above its previous day's high or below its previous day's low. When a stock breaks above resistance or beneath support, the path is cleared toward further gains or declines. The stops that are triggered and accumulate just above or below these levels act like a spring, jolting prices further because of the sudden increase in demand or supply.

Stocks that are breaking down tend to fall harder with less volume than stocks that are breaking out. This is because more people are long the market than short the market, so fear tends to be greater on the downside. Day traders tend to be biased to the long side because of the great bull market of the 1990s, and because it is harder for them to go short due to the uptick requirements.

Market makers are often keyed in to important support and resistance levels. Their alarms go off when these levels are approaching or are reached. If they see that offers are starting to lift when the stock is at resistance, or that bids are starting to fade when it is at support, they may gun the stock, sweeping the street with as many as 25,000 shares going out to each market maker. This push may be all the stock needs to burst into new territory, like opening the walls of a dam.

An increase in demand or supply kicks in on a grander scale when prices break out to all-time highs, or collapse to all-time lows. When this happens, traders may scramble all at once to buy or sell the stock. The stops that are triggered are either physical with listed stocks and futures, or mental with NASDAQ stocks. Stops that are triggered in the S&P futures market cause a concurrent reaction in the stock market.

Locals in the S&P futures pit attempt at times to bid up the market just enough to trigger stops that are set above the previous day's high, in order to flip them out in short order when the market pops higher. These momentum plays carry prices quickly, so traders should be aware of the support and resistance levels in the S&P 500 and the NDX 100 futures markets.

The first levels of support and resistance that should be recognized are the previous day's high and low prices. When these prices are broken, the short-term daily trend will be clearly defined. Trade stocks that are trading above the previous day's high from the long side; and trade stocks that are trading below the previous day's low from the short side.

## THE 8-PERIOD MOVING AVERAGE

A short-term moving average is a simple and effective trend-following tool. It provides a powerful way to smooth out price action in order to determine the short-term trend, areas of support and resistance, and when a trend is reversing. For a short-term trader looking to capture the meat of the move, short-term moving averages offer an ideal way to decide what side of the price action you want to be on.

Many chartists believe that the only proper way to define a trend is by drawing trendlines. While trendlines are useful, they can leave too much open to subjective interpretation, deliberation, and fudging. Day traders need a quick and consistent method to determine if an idea has immediate short-term trend confirmation. Trendlines leave too much room for a trader to rationalize away a losing position. For example, a trendline drawn for a three-month daily chart might look completely different from a trendline drawn for a one-year daily chart. This sort of uncertainty is exactly what you want to avoid.

It is not uncommon for traders to use charts to rationalize a bad position or to distort reality. Without clear-cut trading rules and the discipline to stick to them, traders can look at charts and see only what they want to see. They might have a position that's causing some pain and, rather than cut the loss, use charts to provide them with a glimmer of hope. Sticking to the correct side of the short-term moving average will provide factual evidence of the short-term trend. This will discourage agitated day traders from cherry picking chart patterns to rationalize a loss.

A moving average smooths price action for a select number of periods. Moving averages usually default to the last closing price, but the closing bid price or ask price can also be used. Simple, exponential, and weighted moving averages are three types that can be employed. Exponential is the most widely used today, because it allocates greater weight to the last trading day, responds to changes faster, and factors in older data rather than dropping it.

If the price of a stock or sector has been consistently trading above its 8-period moving average on a daily chart, the short-term uptrend will been broken once the price opens and closes beneath the 8-period moving average. You can use that as a signal to take some profits if you are long, to be flat, or to trade from the short side. If a trader wants to catch a longer-term move and has wider tolerance for loss, you can use a longer-term moving average, such as the 15-day, the 21-day, or the 50-day.

Short-term moving averages can be used as discipline measures for keeping a trader out of trouble. As a simple trading rule, you should only have a position in a stock that is on the same side of the moving average. If a stock is trading above its 8-period moving average, you can trade from the long side but you should not trade it from the short side. If a stock is trading beneath its 8-period moving average, you can trade from the short side but not from the long side. If you stick to this rule, you will prevent yourself from bottom or top fishing because you will be trading on the same side of the short-term trend as defined by the moving average.

A simple and effective trading tactic is to initiate positions only on the side of the 8-period moving average. If the last price is above the 8-period moving average, then the trend is up. If the last price is below the 8-period moving average, then the trend is down.

The 8-period moving average should be used for individual stocks, sectors, and the broader market. For example, if you are considering going long Dell Computer, the ideal scenario would be for DELL, the hardware index (HWI), and the NDX 100 all to be trading above their 8-period moving averages.

The exponential 8-period moving average can be applied across multiple time frames, including the weekly, the daily, and the intraday. It can be used in conjunction with the opening price signal and the net price to key you in to the broader trend as well as the intraday movements of the market.

Which short-term time period you are using is not as important as remaining consistent with the time frame. For example, if a 5-day moving average works well for you, then stick to it. Don't switch to an 8-period from a 5-period in the middle of a trade because you want to nurse a losing position. The reason you are using the moving average in the first place is to remain disciplined in spotting and trading with the trend. From a short-term perspective, the 8-period time frame works well. Experiment with various periods. When you find one that you are comfortable with, give yourself time to get used to it.

The weekly 8-period moving average should be the first trend to look at, as it provides the longer-term trend picture and the broader measure of force. If the last price on the weekly time frame is above the 8-period moving average, then the weekly trend is positive. If the last price is below the 8-period moving average, then the weekly trend is negative (see Figure 6-1).

The chart in Figure 6-1 on page 54 shows Adobe Systems breaking above its weekly 8-period moving average on March 5, 1999. After it opens and closes above its 8-period moving average, it trends above it for the next 10 months in a stellar move. Any trader who used the 8-period moving average trend rule would not have traded ADBE from the short side during this entire period.

After looking at the weekly time frame, the next time frame to look at is the daily one. The daily charts provide a tighter measure of a trend than the weekly charts do. If the last price on the daily chart is above the 8-period moving average, then the daily trend is positive. If the last price is below the 8-period moving average, then the daily trend is negative (see Figure 6-2).

The chart in Figure 6-2 on page 55 shows Veritas Software (VRTS) breaking out above resistance and its daily 8-period moving average on September 2. From September 2 on, VRTS closed above its daily 8-period moving average in all but two instances. A trader following the 8-period moving average rule would not have shorted into this uptrend, and quite possibly would have profited nicely by simply trading on the right side of the trend.

The strongest measurement of a trend occurs when both the weekly and the daily trends confirm one another. Weekly trends often dictate daily trends. However, the daily trend is more important to the day trader, because you are concerned with the immediate market action today. If the situation you are interested in trading

adbc.q.1.1   105Weeks   1997/11/21-1999/1/19
Last=76 1   PC=210.71%   AVn=10205769
High= 79 0 (99/1/19)   Low=11 7 (98/09/04)

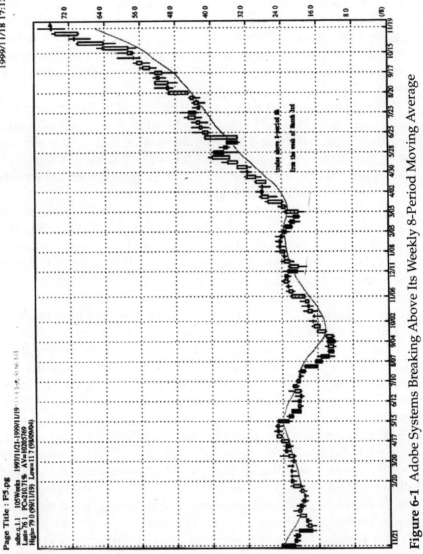

index above 8-period m.a.
from the week of March 3rd

**Figure 6-1** Adobe Systems Breaking Above Its Weekly 8-Period Moving Average

54

Page Title : vrts.pg

vrts.q.1.1  129Days  1999/05/17-1999/11/16
Last= 120.13  PC=206.53%  AV=2071294
High= 121.44 (99/11/15) Low=37.72 (9905/17)

trades above 8-period MA for 95% percent of up move

breakout above resistance

**Figure 6-2** Veritas Software Breaking Out Above Its Daily 8-Period Moving Average does not have mutual confirmation of the weekly and the daily trends, then go with the daily trend.

When you have received daily trend confirmation, the next step is to narrow down what the trend action looks like intraday. The intraday trend is positive when the last price is trading above the 8-period moving average, and it is negative when the last price is trading beneath the 8-period moving average. When examining the intraday trend, always begin by looking at the longer time periods. First determine if the last price is trading above the 60-minute, 8-period moving average. If it is, then determine if it is trading above the 15-minute, 8-period moving average. The 5-minute and the 2-minute 8-period moving averages are less reliable as trend indicators because they are subject to interference from false moves. These shorter-term time periods can be useful for taking profits on reversals, because they will lead the longer time periods first.

The most effective way to integrate intraday moving averages with entry is to make sure that the broader measures of the trend are intact. For example, if the last price is above the 8-period moving average on the daily chart, but beneath the 8-period moving average on the 60-minute chart, don't initiate any new longs or initiate any shorts. Use the move beneath the 60-minute, 8-period moving average to take profits if you are long. If the last price is above the 8-period moving average on the daily chart and on the 60-minute chart, but beneath the 8-period moving average on the 15-minute chart, don't initiate any new longs or any shorts. Use the move beneath the 15-minute chart to take profits if you are long.

Staying on the right side of the 8-period moving average is an excellent risk management practice. Depending on your holding tolerance, you can use the daily, the 60-minute, or the 15-minute time frame. This simple method will prevent a lot of traders from fighting the trend or from bottom fishing. It is a protective intraday entry and exit tactic that, when followed, prevents doubling down and allows you to spot short-term price direction.

Part of the advantage of watching the intraday 8-period moving averages is that you can spot when a trend has almost run its course and is in the process of reversing. When prices first break above or beneath the average after an extended move, take profits and adjust yourself for a possible price reversal.

Day traders should use the 8-period exponential daily moving average as the first category for determining if price action confirms their opinions. If the price is above the 8-period moving average, trade from the long side, but not the short side. If the price is below the 8-period moving average, trade from the short side, but not the long side. This simple rule does not dictate that you must have a position simply because the price is above or below the moving average. It does, however, give you an objective measurement for weighing ideas.

## THE OPENING PRICE SIGNAL

The opening price signal is a simple and effective gauge for determining the daily trend of a stock. The opening price signal is the last price minus the opening price. If the net difference between the last price and the opening price is positive by 1/4 point or more, it is a positive opening price signal. If the net difference is negative by 1/4 point or more, it is a negative opening price signal. Trade only in the direction of the opening price signal. The opening price signal formula is:

Opening Price Signal = Last Price – Opening Price

When the opening price signal turns from negative to positive, it is the first indication that the stock's underlying sentiment has changed to the upside. When the opening price signal changes from positive to negative, it is the first indication that the underlying sentiment has switched to the downside.

Trade only on the side of the opening price signal. From a short-term risk perspective, the opening price signal allows you to be on the correct side of the daily trend. If you adhere to this principle and respect what it is telling you, it will prevent you from fighting a trend and bottom or top fishing.

While the net price of a stock shows the market sentiment from yesterday's close to today's opening, the opening price signal displays the immediate market sentiment from today's opening price to the last price. With the opening price signal, you can determine whether the opening price was set by real demand or was due to an artificial markup. The opening price signal will let you know what kind of force is behind the market opening, which creates the opening price.

Market makers watch opening prices carefully. After the market opens, if the last price falls beneath a marked-up opening price, it is a signal to refrain from initiating longs or to possibly go short. If there is an excessive down opening and the last price rises above the opening price, it is a signal to refrain from initiating shorts or to go long. When stocks gap up or down, the opening price is the one gauge that market makers can use to determine whether stocks are going to go higher or lower.

Here is an example of a market maker using the opening price signal to take advantage of an artificial markup:

> At 9:28 AM the S&P futures were up 15 points, pointing toward a big opening for the Dow Jones Industrial Average and the rest of the market. The retail buy orders were lining up on a market makers' desks with smaller investors eager to buy stocks. The latest positive PPI report was noninflationary, signaling that the Fed would probably not raise rates any time soon. Retail order flow derives mainly from the nonprofessional trading community and is usually driven by emotional extremes. The majority of the larger sophisticated players do not chase excessive markups in the morning, but instead use them as opportunities to take profits or to sell the markup along with the market makers.
>
> With the positive market sentiment, WCOM was marked up in Instinet to 83, up 2 points from the previous night's close. The market makers with the retail buy orders in WCOM were jockeying for position on the inside 83¹/₄ bids. With the market locked, many market makers were using Select Net to preference other market makers who were at 83¹/₄ and let them know that they had to either sell stock or move off the offering.
>
> After the market unlocked, WCOM soon opened up at 83³/₈, up 2³/₈. The market and WCOM soon pulled back from the excessive markup on the opening retail orders. After WCOM opened at 83³/₈, within 15 minutes it sold off to 82¹/₂. Some market makers used the initial markup as an opportunity to short their retail buy orders at prices ranging from 83 to 83¹/₂, and earned a quick profit. The immediate clue of an excessive markup in WCOM was a negative opening price signal. Although on the surface the market and WCOM looked like they were in a strong uptrend, the opening price signal betrayed a different picture.

In the above example, the short-term trend for WCOM and the market looked as though it was positive, but it was actually in an overbought condition. The negative opening price signal provided the first clue that the short-term trend was negative, not positive.

The strongest trend indication occurs when both the opening price signal and the net price both point in your direction. When both the net price and the opening price signal are positive, trade from the long side. When both the net price and opening price signal are negative, trade from the short side.

A gap-up on the opening above the previous session's close produces a positive net price. If the stock sells off beneath the opening price but remains above the previous session's close, the result is a positive net price with a negative opening price signal. For example, if a stock opens up 2 from the previous session's close, and then pulls back 1/2 point, the opening price signal is –1/2, and the net price is +1$^1$/2. In this situation, market makers will use the opening price signal as their first measurement to determine what side of the market they want to be on for the short term.

It pays to wait patiently for both the opening price signal and the net price to point in your direction. When these two signals act in harmony, you have optimal conditions for trading from the correct side of the daily trend. Many times, however, market makers have to make a decision when the circumstances are not perfect, and the net price and opening price signal conflict with one another. When this occurs, the opening price signal serves as the more useful short-term trend indicator, because it evaluates how the stock is trading from today's opening, not just from yesterday's close. It also tends to act as a leading indicator for a change in net price. The opening price signal compares the last price to the current market sentiment, by taking into consideration all the news events that have materialized overnight or early in the morning.

The opening price signal can easily be monitored throughout the day with most software packages. Simply enter in the formula for each stock you are following, which is the last price minus the opening price. Tracking the opening price signal as it turns from positive to negative, or vice versa, provides a profitable entry tactic for timing a change in the underlying trend. The point in time when the opening price signal changes from one side to the other is called the inflection point. Always wait for the opening price signal to point in your direction by at least 1/4 of a point. The point when the opening price signal changes within 1/4 to 1/2 of a point is the best spot to enter.

Figure 6-3 is a snapshot of a monitor page with symbols and is an example of how a market maker tracks stocks. The monitor page includes the net price, the opening price signal, the bid price, a

| Symbol | Net | Signal | Bid | MA | Bounce | Retrace |
|--------|-----|--------|-----|-----|--------|---------|
| aapl | 0.5625 | -1.19 | 59.0625 | 69.3750 | 1.06 | 2.19 |
| qwst | .65625 | -1.56 | 28.375 | 29.1625 | 0.19 | 2.12 |
|  |  | 1.94 | 38.9375 | 142.0125 | 4.00 | 5.50 |
| inkt | -1.875 | -1.81 | 23.1875 | 132.0500 | 0.19 | 4.81 |
| mspg | -0.75 | -0.94 | 27.8125 | 28.8375 | 0.12 | 0.94 |
| elnk | -1.5 | -1.31 | 43.75 | 42.3500 | 0.19 | 1.62 |
| adbe | -0.5 | -0.50 | 110.125 | 108.0938 | 0.38 | 3.88 |
| erts | -0.5 | -0.50 | 73.9375 | 72.4375 | 2.38 | 1.62 |
| vrts | .65625 | -4.09 | 76.5 | 77.3000 | 0.09 | 4.91 |

**Figure 6-3** Monitor Page Showing Opening Price Signals and Other Indicators

short-term moving average, and the amount by which the stock has bounced off its lows or retraced off its highs.

Here is another example of a trader using the opening price signal to position a trade.

*EBAY was trading up 4 points at 134 with a positive opening price signal of +2. It had gapped up 2 points on the open from the previous day's close of 130, to open at 132, and had rallied 2 points from there. As the Internet index began to sell off, EBAY's opening price signal went from +2 to –1, with the last price moving from 134 to 131. EBAY was still up 1 point on the day, but was now trading beneath its opening price by 1 point. This change in the opening price signal forecasted a change in momentum. A Wall Street trader named Bin shorted 15,000 shares EBAY, which was half of his intended position. He only shorted half of his intended position because EBAY was still net positive on the day.*

*Soon after the opening price signal turned negative, EBAY broke beneath its previous night's close of 130. At this point, Bin shorted another 15,000 shares, bringing his total short position to 30,000 shares. EBAY continued to sell off and ended up closing at 123, down 7 points on the day. Bin rode EBAY for the meat of the move and ended up making a tidy profit on the trade.*

The change in the direction of the opening price signal was the first clue to sell longs and to be prepared to trade from the short side.

The inflection point is a valuable entry area for an intraday change in net price. When a stock's net price changes from positive to negative or vice versa, the underlying daily sentiment has changed. Use this change as an entry point or as a stop-loss point. A change in the opening price signal will always lead a change in the net price, so it can be used as a leading indicator for a change in the underlying psychology and market tone.

## THE NET PRICE RULE

The net price rule states that you should trade only on the side of the net price. If you want to go long a stock, the net price should be positive. If you want to go short a stock, the net price should be negative. If the net price is positive, you should not be short; if it is negative, you should not be long.

The net price rule should be used for a stock, the stock's underlying sector, and the broader market. If you are contemplating trading an Internet stock, the first thing to look at is the net price of the stock itself. If it is net price positive, trade from the long side but not the short side. If the net price is negative, trade from the short side but not the long side.

After looking at the net price of the individual stock, look at the stock's underlying sector. If you are trading an Internet stock, you might look at the Internet Index (DOT). If the DOT is net positive on the day, trade from the long side but not the short side. If the DOT is net negative on the day, trade from the short side but not the long side.

After looking at the net price of the DOT, look at what the broader market as a whole is doing. If the NDX 100 is net positive on the day, trade from the long side but not the short side. If it is net negative on the day, trade from the short side but not the long side.

You will not always receive mutual net price confirmation between a stock, its sector, and the broader market. The odds of being on the right side of the trend increase when all three are in your favor. If all three are not in your favor, use the net price of the stock and its sector as the two guidelines to follow.

The net price of a stock or sector indicates which side the market consensus is on. A positive net price votes in favor of the bulls, while a negative net price votes in favor of the bears. The net price reflects the market's judgment as to whether this stock should be higher or lower today than yesterday's closing price.

The reason a stock is trading higher or lower than the previous day's close is irrelevant. Traders can get caught fighting a trend or bottom fishing when they analyze and think too much. Once a rigid opinion is formed, it is hard to admit defeat because your ego is involved. This is even more evident when you announce your opinion to others. Traders make up all sorts of rationalizations to avoid looking "stupid" or wrong in front of other people.

The net price is the quickest measurement of the market's opinion of how a stock should trade today compared to yesterday. When you listen to the market's opinion, your trading will take place along the path of least resistance. The direction of net price is a crucial piece of information that does the thinking for you.

One of the benefits of trading on the side of the net price is that it will prevent you from fighting the trend. If you isolate a trade for the long side and you're itching to trade it, a negative net price will prevent you from buying it. The negative net price tells you that the gravitational force is not pulling in your direction.

Nonprofessional traders often go long in stocks that are net down on the day because they think the price is low. People love to get a bargain, especially when they are eyeing a piece of merchandise that was more expensive a few days before, or even a few hours before. When traders buy stocks that are down on the day because the stock looks "cheap," they get what they pay for—something that is not worth very much.

Remember, it takes more energy and power for an object in motion to stop and reverse course than it does for it to continue along its path of motion. Always remember that, as a day trader, you should buy or sell stocks that are moving in your direction, not against you. Prices do reverse course intraday; there is no question about that. Big price reversals are more the exception than the rule, however. When prices do reverse course, you will still have ample opportunity to profit after the net price has turned in your direction. Price reversals normally provide excellent opportunities to climb on board after the net price turns in your favor, because large price reversals have momentum on their side, and that normally continues.

Here is a summary of the time periods to examine along with the most favorable conditions for catching a trend. You will not always be afforded the luxury of locating an idea when all the trend factors point in your direction. When you do find ideas that have the maximum trend signals pointing in your favor, then your conviction should be at the maximum. When all the factors are not in your favor but you still like an idea, the more of the signals that are in your favor, the better.

## Weekly

The first chart to look at is the weekly chart. The strongest measure of a weekly uptrend includes price action with these characteristics:

a. Price above the previous week's high.
b. Price above the weekly opening price.
c. Price above the 8-period moving average.
d. Price above the previous week's closing price.

## Daily

After determining the strength of the weekly trend, the next trend to look at is the daily one. The strongest measures of a daily uptrend are similar to those for a weekly trend:

a. Price above the previous session's high.
b. Price above the previous session's close.
c. Price above the 8-period moving average.
d. Price above the opening price.

## Intraday

Intraday trends are the most immediate signals for short-term price action. These trends provide the first clues for entry or exit. The distinction between an intraday trend and the daily trend is the intraday price action. The intraday moving average provides a quick way to assess which way the wind is blowing. If a sector is trading above its 8-period moving average on 60-minute and 15-minute intraday charts, the short-term trading trend is positive. The last price should also be above the opening price and the previous session's close:

a. Price above the intraday 8-period moving average.

Remember that your objective as a day trader is not to catch the entire move. Attempting to catch an entire move is unrealistic and the by-product of faulty guesswork and wishful thinking. As a day trader, you are best served when you resist the urge to being completely right, and instead stay focused on trading with the middle of the trend. The probabilities for catching a trend increase with the number of signals that are in your favor.

One reason it is important to stay focused on catching the middle of the trend is that it is the easiest part to catch. It is the easiest part to catch because prices in motion tend to stay in motion. The objective tools you can utilize to identify a trend in motion include the daily and the intraday short-term moving averages, the opening price signal, the net price, and the previous sessions high and low price. When all three factors point in your direction, then you can act decisively.

P A R T

III

# FUNDAMENTALS

7

# FUNDAMENTAL CATALYSTS

Market makers act with increased conviction when the fundamentals and technicals work together in harmony. Both fundamental and technical analysis are of great value. There is no reason why you should not combine the two so you can act with increased conviction. From a strategic standpoint, a day trader should know what fundamental news has the strongest tendency to trigger a forceful streetwide reaction.

When you are trading with fundamentals, always wait for the price action to confirm your opinion. Remember that your objective as a day trader is to make money, period. Do not get caught up with excessive thought or analysis. It is better to make money than to be right. Allow the market to interpret the fundamental information for you through price action. Remember that the market's opinion is what really matters, not yours.

Knowing why an institutional trader takes action can help you think and act with the pros. There are fundamental catalysts that cause large holders to act with ruthless speed. Although mutual funds classify themselves under broad categories such as value, growth, momentum and so forth, many act on fundamental information, especially when the news is negative. Portfolio managers have a low tolerance for certain chinks in the armor of the companies that they hold near and dear to their hearts.

Market-moving fundamental catalysts change from year to year, depending on the state of the market and on what approach has garnered the most attention through recent performance. During aggressive cyclical bull markets, an aggressive-oriented momentum approach is favored because investors are looking for capital appreciation instead of conservative income. During correctional phases or cyclical bear markets, investors are more nervous; the defensive-oriented approach that targets stocks with stronger book ratios and higher yields is the favorite.

A *Barron's* article pointed out a survey of institutional investors, asking them the main reasons they buy or sell stocks. Among the responses, earnings surprises, return on equity, and analyst revisions to earnings ranked as the top three in late 1999.*

## EARNINGS SURPRISES

Institutions act quickly when a company surprises to the downside. A quick reaction on the part of an institution means that some of the biggest holders could be out in force, slamming the stock. An earnings surprise is viewed as a fundamental trend that is likely to continue.

Portfolio managers do not want to be held accountable for holding onto a losing position when a company disappoints. A negative earnings surprise is a hard and cold fact that says something is wrong. At the end of the year, when performance is reviewed, portfolio managers do not want to have to explain why they decided to hold a large position in a company that produced evidence that it could not deliver the goods. Day traders should be extremely wary of trying to scoop up bargains after negative earnings surprises,

---

*"Trigger-Happy: Merrill Lynch Poll Sheds Light on the Vicious Punishment." *Barron's*, December 8, 1999.

because the catalyst and panic will always be to the downside. Bottom fishing on an earnings disappointment is a fool's game and should be avoided.

A positive earnings surprise is valuable confirmation that the company is in good shape and has delivered on its promise. Portfolio managers believe that action speaks louder than words, and good news in the form of earnings is the best possible reflection of positive action. With a positive earnings surprise, the main panic that occurs is the shorts that get squeezed.

## THE NEW EARNINGS RELEASE

An area of earnings reports that creates confusion and faulty trading tactics is the new way that companies release their earnings.* An increasing number of companies today release their numbers with a twist of propaganda, including both pro forma and regular earnings numbers. Some of the different ways companies report their numbers today include pro forma, operational, adjusted, consolidated, pre-currency, diluted, and undiluted. This can slow the decision-making process for a trader who wants to trade in a split instant when the number hits the tape.

This tactic is used mainly by technology companies that have no earnings, to put a better spin on the numbers. They highlight their pro forma or operating earnings, numbers that don't include one-time charges for items such as acquisitions, goodwill, or employee-based compensation. When they exclude these costs, their overall numbers look better; but it can distort what the company is really doing and create confusion among the public.

Analysts often have to interpret these reports for ordinary clients so they can grasp what the numbers really mean. In some cases, analysts follow the lead of the tech companies by adjusting their estimates to focus on operating numbers.

For example, Amazon reported its earnings in July 1999 with multiple headlines. They reported a pro forma operating loss of $67.3 million. They reported another pro forma net loss of $82.8 mil-

---

*MacDonald, Elizabeth. "Varied Profit Reports by Firms Create Confusion." *Wall Street Journal*, Heard on the Street, CI, August 1999.

lion (this number did not include an acquisition charge); and they reported a net loss of $138 million. This slew of numbers could easily have caused traders to make mistakes if they acted before digesting the headlines. Remember that Internet companies trade off factors other than earnings, including quarter-to-quarter revenue growth, registered subscriber growth, media metrix numbers.

Before reacting to an earnings headline, take a deep breath and make sure that you understand what the headline means. Don't be fooled by numbers that look good on the surface but really tell a different story. The immediate minutes following an earnings release are filled with confusion, volatility, and a small army of winners and losers.

## EARNINGS MOMENTUM

Five-year estimates of profit growth have become popular gauges for portfolio mangers to follow because the estimates discount short-term fluctuations in earnings, focusing on longer-term earnings growth potential. With the explosion of Internet IPOs in 1999, almost all of which had not earned a penny, the five-year earnings potential brought some sort of future rationalization to extraordinarily high present valuations. One way to analyze the five-year estimates of profit growth is to examine the growth ratio, which is the ratio of a company's five-year projected earnings to its projected price-to-earnings (P/E) ratio for the next fiscal year.

Analysts and portfolio managers also examine earnings velocity indicators, which gauge the net change in a company's quarterly earnings when contrasted with the same quarter a year ago. This number is then divided by the company's stock price and used as a ratio to compare its performance with competitors in the same industry.

Another important velocity figure that the street examines is the sequential growth number for earnings, revenues, and cash flow. Portfolio managers tend to key in on sequential growth rate figures for revenues and earnings. If an Internet company has had year-to-year quarterly revenue growth of 50 percent, this may look on the surface like a stellar accomplishment. However, if revenue growth has slowed from the previous quarter on a sequential basis, red flags might go up to indicate that something in the growth model has reached a sticky point.

# CASH FLOW

In industries where the majority of the companies do not have positive earnings—such as the Internets, cable TV, telecommunication, and wireless stocks—portfolio managers and analysts focus on non-earnings-related items, such as cash flow in its various forms. Many portfolio managers and analysts believe that cash flow is an important yardstick for gauging the vitality of a company regardless of its earnings.

Investors, analysts, and portfolio managers look at cash flow in various ways. Simple cash flow is net income plus bookkeeping charges that eat into net income such as depreciation, amortization, and depletion. These charges don't physically take any cash away from the company, but they are treated that way on the books. A more important measure of cash flow is operating cash flow, which is the cash a company generates before taxes or the cost of financing. Operating cash flow is a favorite item of takeover specialists, because they can take on as much debt as the operating cash flow will pay for. Because all of the operating cash flow is used for debt payment, the company will not show any profits and will not have taxes to pay.

Free cash flow is an even tighter measure of a company's discretionary funds when compared to operating cash flow. Free cash flow is the cash that a company could tuck away without any reciprocal effects. It can use its free cash flow in any number of ways: to pay dividends, to buy back shares, to pay off debt, or to expand.

Cash flow can tell a completely different story from reported earnings. If a company has strong profits but low cash flow, it could be vulnerable to a bump in the road in the future due to an inability to pay its debts. There can be various reasons, however, for a company to have weak earnings but strong cash flow. In this case, cash flow provides a better picture of the health of a company.

The three types of cash flow measures used as a yardstick when assessing the overall financial health of a company are described here.*

Cash Flow = Net Income + Depreciation + Depletion + Amortization

**Net Income (Profit)** is the income a company reports after all its taxes and expenses have been paid. Net income is usually reported as a diluted and undiluted earnings per share figure. The

---

*Laderman, Jeffrey M., *Earnings, Schmernings—Look at the Cash*. Business Week, July 24, 1989, p. 56.

diluted figure is the bottom line number that the street focuses on. It takes into account earnings per share after tax charges due to acquisitions or other taxable items. The undiluted figure is net income before taxable items are accounted for.

**Depreciation** is a non-cash accounting charge that is deducted from revenues in determining operating income. This charge writes off the cost of an asset over its life span. When a company has assets that decline in value over time, each year that diminishing value can be written off as an expense, taking away from reported profits but saving money in taxes.

**Depletion** is an accounting charge that writes off the cost of an asset over its life span when that asset is a natural resource. Some natural resource assets are oil, gas, and minerals.

**Amortization** is a write-down of intangible or short-term assets. Some amortized items are tax deductible; others are not.

$$\text{Operating Cash Flow} = \frac{\text{Cash Flow} + \text{Interest Expense} +}{\text{Income Tax Expense}}$$

**Interest Expense**—Interest charges can be added back to cash flow for a more extensive measure of the cash that is generated by a company's operations.

**Income Tax Expense**—When a company is the target of a takeover, the debt that is generated can eat away at most if not all of the reported profits. When there are no reported profits, there are no taxes due.

**Operating Income (EBIT)**—Pretax income that a company earns, which includes all of the operating income before taxes and interest expense.

$$\text{Free Cash Flow} = \text{Cash Flow} - \text{Capital Expenditures} - \text{Dividends}$$

**Capital Expenditures**—Expenditures on new and replacement items that a company needs to function, such as property, plant, and equipment. The necessary capital expenditure items are deducted from cash flow to determine free cash flow.

**Dividends**—Dividends should be deducted from cash flow to determine free cash flow. This holds true for a company that has always paid dividends and would not eliminate them.

As a day trader, your effectiveness will increase if you have a handle on the important fundamental catalysts that move the market. With the growing number of Internet companies listed on the NASDAQ stock market, most of which have no earnings, it has become increasingly important to understand what sort of earnings report makes the largest shareholders tick. When there are no earnings to speak of, sequential revenue growth and cash flow figures become the focal point. When you understand why the largest shareholders act, you will be prepared to trade when the fundamentals and the technicals work in tandem.

# RATIO POWER

Ratios are potent mathematical tools that interpret fundamental data in order to produce a picture of a company's health. Ratios offer a simple way to evaluate a company compared to its peers and against a benchmark. Some of the fundamentals that ratios examine and integrate include equity, assets, liabilities, income, cash flow, and stock price.

Ratios allow you to examine trends within a company or an industry, highlighting when current performance diverges from past performance. As lagging, not leading, indicators, ratios look at past performance to predict future results. Past performance sheds light on fundamental trends and momentum, which is useful for developing an overall picture of the company's strengths and weaknesses.

Statistical analysis of ratios can be employed when determining the consistency of management methods and the earnings viability of the company. One statistical tool used to examine ratios is the standard deviation. The standard deviation can be useful for evaluating the volatility of management's control over operations. Used in isolation, a financial ratio is meaningless. For example, suppose a company has a P/E ratio of 35. Unless you know what the P/E ratios of that company's competitors are, you will not know if that is a high or low P/E ratio. Analysts and portfolio managers have been known to diverge in their interpretations of ratio benchmarks within various industries.

## PROFITABILITY RATIOS

Profitability ratios gauge a company's capacity to generate revenues, control costs, increase profitability, and produce results. In order to properly evaluate profitability, other areas of a company's business should be taken into account. These areas include total sales and the total capital invested. Some of the most important profitability ratios are shown in Table 8-1.*

**Table 8-1** Profitability Ratios

| Profitability Ratio | Formula | Definition |
|---|---|---|
| Gross Profit | Net Sales – Cost of Goods Sold | Gross profit is the broadest measure of the profitability of a company's output operation. |
| Gross Profit Margin | $\dfrac{\text{Net Sales} - \text{Cost of Goods Sold}}{\text{Net Sales Period 1}}$ | Gross profit margin measures gross profit as a percentage of total revenue. |
| Net Sales Growth | $\dfrac{\text{Net Sales Period 2} - \text{Net Sales Period 1}}{\text{Net Sales Period 1}}$ | Net sales growth measures how fast a company is growing in revenue from one period to the next. |

---

*Also see Griffis, Michael. *Ratio Analysis*. Stocksguide@About.com, 1998.

**Table 8-1** *(Continued)*

| Profitability Ratio | Formula | Definition |
|---|---|---|
| Net Income Growth | $$\frac{\text{Net Income Period 2} - \text{Net Income Period 1}}{\text{Net Income Period 1}}$$ | Net income growth measures how fast a company is growing in net earnings from one period to the next. |
| Operating Profit Margin | $$\frac{\text{Net Sales} - \text{Cost of Goods Sold} - \text{Operating Expense}}{\text{Net Sales}}$$ | Operating profit margin examines the operating expenses of a company in light of operating profit. |
| EBITDA Profit Margin | $$\frac{\text{Pretax Income} + \text{Interest Expense} + \text{Depreciation} + \text{Amortization}}{\text{Net Sales}}$$ | EBITDA profit margin examines the operating cash flow generated from net sales before taking into account interest, taxes, depreciation, and amortization. |
| Net Margin | $$\frac{\text{Net Income}}{\text{Net Sales}}$$ | The net margin examines the earnings generated by each dollar of sales. |
| P/E Ratio | $$\frac{\text{Stock Price}}{\text{Earnings per Share}}$$ | The P/E ratio measures a company's stock price compared to its earnings per share. The P/E ratio can be measured on a trailing or a projected basis. A higher P/E ratio indicates that the market is upbeat about a company's future earnings potential. |
| Price-to-Ratio Cash-Flow | $$\frac{\text{Stock Price}}{\text{Cash Flow per Share}}$$ | The price-to-cash-flow ratio portrays the relationship of a company's stock price to its cash flow. |
| Price-to-Book-Value Ratio | $$\frac{\text{Stock Price}}{\text{Book Value per Share}}$$ | The price-to-book-value ratio measures the relationship of a stock's price to the company's net worth. The higher the price-to book value ratio, the more optimistically the market has priced a company. |

**Table 8-1**  *(Continued)*

| Profitability Ratio | Formula | Definition |
|---|---|---|
| Price-to-Sales Ratio | $$\frac{\text{Stock Price}}{\text{Sales per Share}}$$ | The price-to-sales ratio measures the relationship of a company's stock price to its annual sales per share. This ratio is applied differently across industries. Sectors with low margins have low price-to-sales ratios, usually lower than 1. Other industries that have higher margins have higher price-to-sales ratios. |

## RETURN ON EQUITY (ROE)

The return on equity of a company (ROE) is a calculation used to examine how much the company earns on the investment of its shareholders. Dividing a company's net income by the common shareholders' equity results in the ROE figure. Portfolio managers examine return on equity very carefully and use it when deciding whether to buy or sell. ROE is used when evaluating whether a company eats up cash or creates assets. If a company makes $2,500,000 for $10,000,000 invested, then the ROE is 25 percent.

A high ROE figure can mean that the company has a high return on leverage or debt, or that it has a high return on assets. If the company does not have a lot of debt on the books and has a high ROE figure, chances are that management is earning higher profit margins on the assets. If the company is highly leveraged and has a high ROE figure, its return on assets is lower.

Like all financial ratios, the ROE is most effective when used to evaluate a company against its peers. Because return on equity is derived from earnings or net income, an earnings surprise provides a first hint of a change in the ROE trend.

## LIQUIDITY RATIOS

Liquidity ratios evaluate the capacity of a company to pay its short-term liabilities. They examine how a company converts cash to meet its obligations from the time an order is received until accounts payable and debts are met. Two of the most commonly used liquidity ratios are described in Table 8-2.

**Table 8-2**  Liquidity Ratios

| Liquidity Ratio | Formula | Definition |
|---|---|---|
| Current Ratio | $\dfrac{\text{Current Assets}}{\text{Current Liabilities}}$ | The current ratio is a short-term liquidity ratio that measures the company's ability to pay its bills. This ratio varies in scope from industry to industry. For example, companies in the retailing industry have lower acceptable current ratios than those in the manufacturing industry. |
| Quick Ratio | $\dfrac{\text{Quick Assets}}{\text{Quick Liabilities}}$ | The quick ratio examines assets that can be converted to cash quickly. This produces a short-term, conservative picture of how liquid a company is. Quick assets include cash, marketable securities, short-term cash convertible investments, and trade receivables. |

Current assets include cash, marketable securities, short-term cash convertible instruments, trade receivables, other receivables, inventories, prepaids, and miscellaneous current assets. Current liabilities include short-term claims against the company, which must be paid within 12 months. These include accounts payable, wages, salaries, dividends, taxes, and other short-term obligations, including bonds, debentures, and bank loans.

# LEVERAGE RATIOS

Leverage ratios examine how much debt a company uses for finance, and what sort of liability that debt imposes on the company's welfare. When subordinated debt exists, the ratios that are used take into account a company's senior liabilities and capital funds, or tangible capital funds. This is because subordinated debt increases a company's net worth on the books; it is considered to be capital as long as the loan exists. Some of the important leverage ratios are described in Table 8-3.

**Table 8-3** Leverage Ratios

| Leverage Ratio | Formula | Definition |
|---|---|---|
| Debt-to-Equity Ratio | $\dfrac{\text{Long-Term Debt}}{\text{Shareholders' Equity}}$ | The debt-to-equity ratio measures a company's long-term debt as a percentage of shareholders' equity. It examines how much leverage the company uses to conduct business. It is a popular measure of risk when looking at the company's longer-term viability |
| Liabilities-to Net-Worth Ratio | $\dfrac{\text{Total Liabilities}}{\text{Net Worth}}$ | This is the broadest measure of leverage, taking into account all of a company's debt and all of its net worth. Total liabilities include a company's current and long-term liabilities as well as deferred taxes. The net worth of a company is the stockholders' equity. |
| Liabilities-to-Tangible-Net-Worth Ratio | $\dfrac{\text{Total Liabilities}}{\text{Tangible Net Worth}}$ | This ratio is the most conservative measure of leverage because it takes into account only those assets that can easily be converted into cash. Tangible net worth is stockholders' equity minus intangible assets. Intangible assets are items that cannot be converted to cash easily, such as goodwill, patents, trademarks, and so forth. |

**Table 8-3** *(Continued)*

| *Leverage Ratio* | *Formula* | *Definition* |
|---|---|---|
| Liabilities-to-Capital-Funds Ratio | $$\frac{\text{Senior Liabilities}}{\text{Capital Funds}}$$ | This ratio is the most liberal measure of leverage because it takes into account only senior debt obligations, discounting shorter-term liabilities. This ratio also increases the net worth with subordinated debt, which is considered part of the company's assets for the life of the loan. Subordinated debt is the debt that is paid back after the bank is repaid what it is owed. Capital funds is net worth or stockholders' equity plus subordinated debt. |

## ACTIVITY RATIOS

Activity ratios gauge how effective a company is in utilizing its assets. These ratios compare the income of a company to its asset base. Some of the most important activity ratios are described in Table 8-4.

**Table 8-4** Activity Ratios

| *Activity Ratio* | *Formula* | *Definition* |
|---|---|---|
| Accounts Receivable Turnover | $$\frac{\text{Net Sales}}{\text{Net Accounts Receivable}}$$ | The accounts receivable turnover ratio measures how often accounts receivable turns over when compared to revenue. |

**Table 8-4** *(Continued)*

| Activity Ratio | Formula | Definition |
|---|---|---|
| Inventory Turnover | $$\frac{\text{Cost of Goods Sold per Period}}{\text{Inventory}}$$ | The inventory turnover ratio measures the number of times inventories turn over per accounting period. |
| Accounts Payable Turnover | $$\frac{\text{Cost of Goods Sold per Period}}{\text{Trade Accounts Payable}}$$ | The accounts payable turnover ratio looks at how long it takes a company to pay its suppliers. |
| Total Assets Turnover | $$\frac{\text{Net Sales}}{\text{Total Assets}}$$ | The total assets turnover ratio measures the output competency of a company's total asset base without distinguishing among various asset types. This ratio is used in examining return on equity. |

Financial ratios are tools for interpreting the financial statements of a company. Different ratios are applied across different industries because of digressing capital frameworks. Because of this divergence of use, ratios are most valuable when used in comparison to an industry benchmark or to a company's peers. The objective in using ratios is to determine if the company is profitable and if it can meet its debt obligations; how the company is doing compared to previous quarters or years; how the company compares to its competitors; and how the business performs against its benchmark.

C H A P T E R

# ECONOMIC INDICATORS AND THEIR IMPACT ON DAY TRADING

There is a broad range of economic statistics that have an impact on the financial markets. On a weekly basis, economic numbers are reported that often generate powerful undercurrents for the day's market activity. Because there are numerous indicators tracking various segments of the economy, it is easy to lose track of the significance of each report. This chapter provides a snapshot of the most important numbers and how they affect the markets.

Economic news affects stocks, bonds, the U.S. dollar, foreign currencies, and the global markets. Positive economic news suggests a growing economic climate and possible inflation on the horizon. Negative economic news suggests a slowdown in production and economic growth. The best possible bullish combination for stocks is economic growth combined with low inflation. This powerful duo was the driving force behind the great bull market of the 1990s. Technology and the Internet fueled the economic growth of the 1990s, increasing production without having an inflationary impact on prices.

A vibrant economy with strong growth tends to lead toward stronger demand, which in turn creates higher prices. Higher prices normally produce inflation, which the Federal Reserve Board is designed to avoid. At signs of inflation, the Federal Reserve Board adopts a tightening bias, which means that they take the objective of slowing down economic growth by tightening the money supply through higher interest rates.

The stock market tends to react positively when economic growth is stimulated, and negatively when economic growth is slowed. A rise in interest rates by the Fed tightens growth and generally causes stocks and bonds to fall. A lowering of interest rates loosens money supply, stimulating growth, and generally causes stocks and bonds to rally. Stocks and bonds can also rally with a rise in interest rates if the perception is that the Fed will not hike rates again in the near future; or they can fall with a drop in interest rates if the consensus is that it is the last such drop on the horizon.

Economic growth combined with inflationary pressures creates a bias for higher interest rates and lower stock prices. Economic growth combined with noninflationary pressures creates a neutral bias for interest rates and a positive bias for stock prices.

Negative economic news includes a slowdown in production and economic growth. Economic decline is associated with lower demand. When demand is slowing, prices fall because supply increases. During this environment, inflation is not a concern. In a weak economy, the Federal Reserve is more interested in stimulating economic growth. It does this by lowering interest rates in order to stimulate borrowing and spending. Weak economic news creates a bias toward lower interest rates, higher stock prices, and higher bond prices.

## ECONOMIC NEWS AND THE U.S. DOLLAR

Positive economic news, which is associated with lower bond prices and higher interest rates, rallies the U.S. dollar against other foreign currencies. The value of the U.S. dollar represents the strength of the U.S. economy. When the economy is doing well, other people want to own a piece. For example, the sharp rally of the yen against the U.S. dollar during the early fall of 1999 was the by-product of a perception of a strengthening Japanese economy.

Negative economic news, on the other hand, which is associated with higher bond prices and lower interest rates, weakens the U.S. dollar against other foreign currencies. If the U.S. economy is perceived to be weak, the dollar represents that weakness. The U.S. dollar posted its all-time post–World War II lows against the yen just before the great bull market of the 1990s kicked into full force. During this period, the American economy was in recession, just starting to come up for air.

## ECONOMIC INDICATORS AND THEIR EFFECT*

As with earnings reports, perception is key when economic numbers hit the tape before the market opens. Markets move based on the change in the number reported relative to what the expectations are on the street. The total change in the number when compared to the previous quarter or year is not important to the short-term impact. It's important to be prepared before the number hits the tape. Know what the street expectations are, and what it will mean for the market if the number exceeds or misses those expectations.

With the advent of trading around the clock, there has been an increase in pre-opening and after-hours trading by all types of traders and individual investors. The increased liquidity means additional trading opportunities immediately following economic reports.

How the market will react has a lot to do with perception about what the policy will be in the future. As already mentioned, there are instances when the Fed raises rates and stocks and bonds rally, or when it lowers rates and stocks and bonds fall. For example, on November 16, 1999 the Federal Reserve Board hiked interest rates by 1/4 of a point. Stocks rallied following this news, because the Fed concurrently adopted a neutral bias toward raising rates again in the future, allaying fears. Many times stocks and bonds move in anticipation of an event, then change directions after the event is announced, because the price action has already been accounted for in the move. Stocks and bonds can rally prior to an anticipated interest rate cut and sell off when the cut takes place.

Table 9-1 lists economic indicators and their impact on the markets, or the most likely course of action for prices, all else being equal. These reports affect prices because of uncertainty about what

---

*See also *Economic Indicators and Their Impact on the Financial Markets*. NatWest Financial Markets Group, 1995.

**Table 9-1** Economic Indicators

| Indicator | Measurement | Market Impact | Explanation |
|---|---|---|---|
| Consumer Price Index (CPI) (Monthly) | The CPI measures the change in the price of a fixed basket of products used by the average consumer, in order to determine the level of price inflation. | *Exceeds Estimate:* Stocks Fall Bonds Fall Yields Rise U.S. Dollar Stronger *Misses Estimate:* Stocks Rise Bonds Rise Yields Fall U.S. Dollar Weaker | A strong CPI points toward higher prices and rising inflation, which may induce the Fed to raise interest rates. |
| Housing Starts (Monthly) | New home construction. | *Exceeds Estimate:* Stocks Fall Bonds Fall Yields Rise U.S. Dollar Stronger *Misses Estimate:* Stocks Rise Bonds Rise Yields Fall U.S. Dollar Weaker | New home construction is generally a by-product of economic strength. Excessive building could indicate the Fed might act to slow growth. |
| Index of Leading Indicators (Monthly) | Eleven economic indicators grouped together, created to forecast broader movement within the economy. | *Exceeds Estimate:* Stocks Fall Bonds Fall Yields Rise U.S. Dollar Stronger *Misses Estimate:* Stocks Rise Bonds Rise Yields Fall U.S. Dollar Weaker | The basket of Leading Indicators that is on the rise points toward growth in the economy, which may induce the Fed to raise interest rates to stem stem inflation. |
| Industrial Production and Capacity Utilization (Monthly) | Gauges the production of the manufacturing, mining, and utility industries. | *Exceeds Estimate:* Stocks Fall Bonds Fall Yields Rise U.S. Dollar Stronger *Misses Estimate:* Stocks Rise Bonds Rise Yields Fall U.S. Dollar Weaker | Surging production in manufacturing, mining, and utility sectors suggests that the economy is strong and that the Fed may act to slow growth by increasing rates. |

**Table 9-1** (*Continued*)

| Indicator | Measurement | Market Impact | Explanation |
|---|---|---|---|
| Initial Unemployment Claims (Weekly) | This figure examines how many workers have filed initial claims for unemployment benefits. | *Exceeds Estimate:* Stocks Rise Bonds Rise Yields Fall U.S. Dollar Weaker *Misses Estimate:* Stocks Fall Bonds Fall Yields Rise U.S. Dollar Stronger | If unemployment on the rise, that indicates that the economy may be weaker because there are fewer jobs available due to less growth. In this case, the Fed may act to stimulate growth by lowering interest rates. |
| Nonfarm Payroll Employment (Monthly) | A key economic indicator. This monthly measure takes into account production across sectors to determine the overall strength of the economy. | *Exceeds Estimate:* Stocks Fall Bonds Fall Yields Rise U.S. Dollar Stronger *Misses Estimate:* Stocks Rise Bonds Rise Yields Fall U.S. Dollar Weaker | Strong employment growth suggests a growing economy, which is conducive to stronger demand and higher prices, causing inflation. The Fed may be inclined to raise interest rates because of a strong number. |
| Producer Price Index (PPI) (Monthly) | Measures wholesale inflation on a monthly basis. This number examines the change in wholesale prices of goods shipped from manufacturers. | *Exceeds Estimate:* Stocks Fall Bonds Fall Yields Rise U.S. Dollar Stronger *Misses Estimate:* Stocks Rise Bonds Rise Yields Fall U.S. Dollar Weaker | If producer prices are on the rise, the increase will be passed on to the consumer and can mean the beginning of inflation. The Fed would act to hike interest rates in order to keep inflation in check. |

**Table 9-1**  *(Continued)*

| Indicator | Measurement | Market Impact | Explanation |
|---|---|---|---|
| Real Gross Domestic Product (GDP) (Quarterly) | Measures the aggregate value of goods and services produced. | *Exceeds Estimate:* Stocks Fall Bonds Fall Yields Rise U.S. Dollar Stronger *Misses Estimate:* Stocks Rise Bonds Rise Yields Fall U.S. Dollar Weaker | If production in the U.S. is growing too fast, it could cause inflationary pressures, which in turn may cause the Fed to raise interest rates. |
| Retail Sales (Monthly) | Looks at consumer spending by measuring retail sales to consumers. Includes both durable and nondurable items. | *Exceeds Estimate:* Stocks Fall Bonds Fall Yields Rise U.S. Dollar Stronger *Misses Estimate:* Stocks Rise Bonds Rise Yields Fall U.S. Dollar Weaker | If consumers are spending more on retail items, it indicates that demand is high, which could create higher prices. The Fed may move to raise interest rates to stem inflationary pressures caused by high retail sales. |
| Unemployment Rate (Monthly) | Polls 60,000 families to see how many within those homes are looking for work. | *Exceeds Estimate:* Stocks Rise Bonds Rise Yields Fall U.S. Dollar Weaker *Misses Estimate:* Stocks Fall Bonds Fall Yields Rise U.S. Dollar Stronger | If unemployment is on the rise, the economy could be slowing down. The Fed may act to raise interest rates in order to stimulate growth and create new jobs for the unemployed. |

the Fed will do in reaction to the number. There are times when stocks and bonds do not react according to expectations, given the strength or weakness of the indicator. Many other factors can come into play when interpreting these numbers, including price action leading up to the report and biases of the Fed.

## THE FEDERAL RESERVE AND ITS MONETARY POLICY

The Federal Reserve Board's objective is to foster a strong and steady economy in the United States. It oversees the availability of money and credit, with the objective of advancing sustainable growth and price stability. The Federal Reserve is guided by a Board of Governors whose job it is to create and institute policies for regulating the money and credit flow in America. The Fed's monetary policy has a direct effect on economic growth, price inflation, and employment.

The Federal Reserve Board utilizes three main techniques for instituting its monetary policy:

1. Regulating the reserve requirements for depository institutions.
2. Adjusting the discount rate, which is the rate the Fed charges depository banks for overnight credit.
3. Buying or selling U.S. Treasuries in the open market. This activity has a direct impact on interest rates, because these operations either increase or decrease the reserves in the U.S. banking system, which affects the demand and supply relationship.

Open market operations are the devices most used by the Fed for implementing its monetary policy. The policy for open market operations is determined by the Federal Open Markets Committee.* The Federal Open market Committee is a 12-member committee that sets credit and interest rate policies for the Federal Reserve System. The FOMC sets short-term monetary policy for the country's central bank. This policy is derived from economic measurements, both domestic and international.

---

*Federal Reserve Bank of Minneapolis. http://woodrow.mpls.frb.fed.us/index.html. Minneapolis, 1999.

The FOMC's 12 members include 7 members from the Federal Reserve Board of Governors, the president of the Federal Reserve Bank of New York, and 4 alternating seats that are held by presidents of the 11 other Reserve Banks. The FOMC must meet a minimum of four times each year, in Washington, D.C. Since 1980, the FOMC has scheduled eight meetings annually, which have been held at interims of five to eight weeks.

When the FOMC meets, the main focus is whether or not they will change the short-term Federal Funds Rate. The Federal Funds Rate is the interest rate banks charge one another for overnight loans. Once the FOMC sets a target for that rate, it uses its open market operations to buy or sell government securities in order to move the Treasury market to the level it has set. A change in the Federal Funds Rate in turn moves all of the other short- and long-term interest rates.

When the Fed announces that it has increased the Federal Funds Rate, it means that it is engaging in a tightening of monetary policy. This occurs during periods of strong economic growth when the Fed is concerned about an increase in inflation. Under these circumstances, the Fed sells U.S. Treasuries, which subtracts from the reserves of the banking system and in turn causes the Federal Funds Rate to rise to the announced rate.

When the Fed announces that it has lowered the Federal Funds Rate, it means that it is engaging in an easing of monetary policy. This happens during periods of weak economic growth when the Fed is concerned about stimulating the economy. Under these conditions, the Fed buys U.S. Treasuries, which adds to the reserves of the banking system and causes the Federal Funds Rate to fall to the announced rate.

## BOND PRICES AND INTEREST RATES

The most important thing to remember about bond prices and interest rates is that they have an inverse relationship, which means that they move in the opposite direction. Positive economic news generally has the effect of causing bond prices to fall, which in turn creates a higher yield.

When bond prices rally, the yield falls; when bonds prices fall, the yield rallies. When interest rates rise, bond prices fall because the value of the present bond is worth less than the value of the new bond, which has the higher interest rate. When interest rates fall, bond prices rise because the value of the present bond is worth more than the value of the new bond, which has a lower interest rate.

The yield curve portrays the connection between the yield of bonds and their date to maturity. The yield curve has a normal upward bent representing interest rates that increase with an increase in their date to maturity. Investors receive a higher premium for holding bonds with a longer maturity, because of the risk factors involved with time, including inflation, higher interest rates, and opportunity cost.

If the marketplace expects positive economic growth in the future, then the yield curve increases. This is because higher premiums will be factored into the farther end of the yield curve due to an expected increase in interest rates and inflation associated with a stronger economy in the future.

A flat yield curve comes into play when the Fed has adopted a tightening bias and has thus increased short-term interest rates. With an increase in rates, the marketplace reduces their expectations for inflationary pressures in the future, and the premiums on the farther end of the yield curve will be lowered. The yield curve becomes flat because the shorter end rises with the rates, and the farther end falls lower with the diminished premiums.

Yield curves become inverted when long-term interest rates fall below short-term interest rates. This normally happens when the Fed has raised short-term rates consecutively, usually in a strong economy. The farther end of the yield curve falls because the marketplace believes that the increase in short-term rates is enough to slow future inflation.

Important economic numbers often dictate the market tone for the rest of the day. The Federal Reserve watches these numbers carefully and uses them to dictate future policy. Numbers that point toward strong economic growth tend to be associated with inflationary pressures, which the Fed frowns upon. If the Fed senses that inflation is on the rise, it adopts a tightening policy, which means higher interest rates and lower stock prices.

Economic indicators that point toward strong growth and low inflation are the best of both worlds for the stock market. In this scenario, the Fed has no inclination to adopt a tightening policy, so the economy can continue to grow unimpeded. Weak economic numbers point toward a slowdown and can prompt the Fed to adopt a loosening policy, which means lower interest rates and higher stock prices. Low interest rates make it cheaper for companies to borrow, which means they can spend and grow. Higher interest rates make it more expensive for companies to borrow, so growth is slowed.

The economic numbers that are reported provide insight as to which actions the Fed might take in the future. When you have a handle on these numbers before they come out, knowing which direction the Fed is most likely to take if the number exceeds or misses expectations, then you will be prepared to act quickly and more profitably.

# 10

# ORGANIZE YOUR INFORMATION FLOW

It is easy to become overwhelmed by the sea of information that every day trader is inundated with. There are thousands of Web sites alone dedicated to educating and informing investors about topics ranging from hot news on stocks to tax tips. You will be at a disadvantage if you allow your valuable time to be spent focusing on information that is not directly relevant to your goals and objectives for the current trading day. When you can effectively locate, manage, and organize the information that is available, you will be in good shape to trade unencumbered.

## UTILIZE INTERNET RESOURCES EFFECTIVELY

There are a number of financial Web sites that are extremely useful in helping to pinpoint and organize information flow that is pertinent to making informed trading decisions. The abundance of information available on the Internet today can be a mixed blessing for the day trader. On the plus side, information works to the trader's advantage when it can be managed and used as a backdrop for uncovering ideas or supporting trading decisions. On the minus side, a trader who does not really know what sort of information to look for or where to look for it can easily get lured into excessive analysis that interferes with day trading.

Information overload is a problem that many investors, traders, and portfolio managers have to deal with on a daily basis. In the spring of 1999 a number of prime-time news features discussed the information assault that has accompanied the on-line revolution. The average business executive today receives upward of 50 e-mail messages a day, 30 voice mail messages, and 10 pieces of unsolicited regular mail daily. For the day trader, the information deluge is even worse. If it is not managed, this information overload can easily encourage a dangerous trading condition known as "analysis paralysis."

Excessive analysis is a trap. Too much analyzing causes procrastination and indecision. The most successful traders have a few simple ways to determine what course of action to take. They are able to act when their entry criteria are matched—and they don't look back.

The Web sites listed later in this chapter represent a comprehensive set of investment and financial resources. The list is an aggregation of the most popular Web sites that are used most often by market makers and the financial community. They offer valuable technical and fundamental tools to enhance your decision-making process. The key to using them successfully is to know what you are looking for and avoid being sidetracked.

## THE WATCH LIST

A watch list is a powerful organizational tool that a trader should utilize in order to be prepared. A watch list is a dynamic list of stocks, updated daily, that you can track with price alerts. The price alerts will let you know when a stock you are tracking enters into your price range. When you maintain a watch list comprised of your focus stocks, you can use the list to zero in on the information that is most important to you.

Watch lists can easily be constructed on a blank monitor page contained within most software packages. Some of the Web sites listed later in this chapter offer free watch lists that will send you pertinent information by e-mail. Clearstation.com is one Web site that allows you to set up an effective and dynamic watch list. Watch lists are especially effective because they encourage you to stay with an idea until its completion. If you are scanning charts and you come up with a number of trading ideas, develop the habit of entering them onto your watch list. An idea that does not work today might still be viable tomorrow, or even a week from today. It is also worthwhile to look at stocks you placed on your watch list that never worked. These stocks can serve as valuable and inexpensive learning experiences.

Areas of support and resistance for broader sectors should also be monitored on your watch list, with limit price alerts. For example, if the daily resistance in the NDX is 4,000, a limit alert will provide you with timely information if that level is pierced and a breakout is in play.

## EMPOWERING WEB SITES FOR DAY TRADERS

The Web sites listed here are used actively by market makers and the professional trading community.

**BigCharts.com**—BigCharts is the place to go for an extensive array of efficient charting tools. BigCharts is a user-friendly investment research Web site that provides access to interactive charts, quotes, news, and analysis, with intraday stock scanning capabilities. BigCharts also provides the capacity to view up to 50 intraday quotes at one time with option pricing and dynamic charting.

**Bloomberg.com**—Bloomberg.com is a comprehensive financial news and services site that provides extensive financial information. Bloomberg furnishes its services to over 140,000 users in more than 91 countries.

**Briefing.com**—An excellent place to visit regularly for current briefings and snapshots of the most important events affecting the current day's trading action in stocks and bonds.

**Cbsmarketwatch.com**—A hot spot for premier market-moving news and award-winning analysis, research, and educational articles.

**Clearstation.com**—ClearStation focuses on trading techniques and ideas utilizing an easy-to-use and effective interface, watch list, and alert feature. ClearStation integrates three main investment viewpoints: technical analysis, fundamental analysis, and input from the trading community.

**Cnbc.com**—All the best CNBC has to offer, on-line, in a user-friendly, comprehensive, and educational format with access to past and present features.

**Cnnfn.com**—CNN's financial news site with subsections on markets and investing.

**Companysleuth.com**—Companysleuth.com tracks down hard-to-find information and e-mails the results to you on a daily basis. The site acts as a private investigator by giving you useful clues about the companies you are trading. If a stock is on the move and you do not know why, this site could be the place to go.

**Dailystocks.com**—A must-have bookmark. DailyStocks.com provides passage to prevalent Web sites for all the market information you need, including market updates, news, earnings calendars, research reports, stock screeners, IPOs, public filings, corporate changes, and much more.

**Edgar-online.com**—Provides quick access to up-to-the minute SEC filing information.

**Finance.Yahoo.com**—A comprehensive financial site covering domestic and international investing issues ranging from taxes to loans to U.S. stocks. A must-see if you are searching for a good chat room on a broad range of trading topics.

**Financialweb.com**—FinancialWeb publishes financial content, stock quotes, charts, securities data, and news. It is a conglomeration of various other financial sites, including Quote Central, Rapid Research, Stock Detective, Wall Street Guru, The SmallCap Investor, Stock Tools, The Bear Tracker, NewsVest, Mr. EDGAR, Strike Price, YourFunds.com, Strike Price, Bull Mart, Annual Reports Online, and InvesToons.

**Fool.com**—Provides financial information in an interface that specializes in educating users in an amusing way.

**Hoovers.com**—A superb information resource that provides in-depth company information, including company capsules. The content is presented in a fun and easy-to-read format. Hoovers is also an excellent source for finding and narrowing down a company's main competitors.

**Investext.com**—A division of Thomson Financial Services, the Investext Group furnishes investment research including business reports and analysis on a large electronic collection of companies throughout the world.

**Investorama.com**—A leading Internet directory for individual investors, investorama.com provides the largest collection of financial resources available on the Web. It also displays a wide array of educational material for individual investors, ranging from stocks to real estate.

**Investors.com**—The official Web site of *Investor's Business Daily* provides helpful utilities for uncovering trading ideas. The Web site is unique in that it will clue you in to stocks and sectors that are in play before they receive widespread attention. *Investor's Business Daily* pinpoints potential winning stocks through its unique tables, charts, and evaluation measures.

**IQC.com**—ICQ.com is unique because it allows its users to search for stock ideas using candlestick parameters. If you are looking for tech stocks that have formed a bullish reversal pattern, for instance, then IQC is it. IQC.com can also search for ideas using fundamentals, and has an educational section that includes topics such as candlestick charting and technical indicators.

**Justquotes.com**—Provides quotes, comprehensive company research, analysis, charts, and information on the competition.

**Marketguide.com**—A source for quality research covering areas including market commentary, quick links, real-time quotes, upgrades and downgrades, headlines, story stocks, DRIPS, and broker research.

**MarketHistory.com**—A great spot to visit if you are searching for quantitative ideas. MarketHistory.com utilizes quantitative research for delivering high-reward and low-risk trading ideas. This site is used by the professional trading community and is one of a kind. It is one of the more expensive sites for a full subscription, but well worth it.

**Money.com**—A financial strategy center covering topics including markets, news, investing, real estate, insurance, autos, retirement, taxes, and trading tools.

**Moneycentral.com**—Top-rated MoneyCentral.com provides one-stop shopping for your financial needs. MoneyCentral.com is the largest financial Web site that provides you with in-depth information on a variety of securities, funds, and investment tools. The MSN Investor section focuses on portfolio management, stock screening, investment tracking, news, investment ideas and performance, research, and e-mail notifications and alerts.

**Moneypaper.com**—A Web site and monthly publication focused on enriching the financial health of independent investors through education. This site provides specific investment recommendations about the proper course of action to take given your current strategies.

**Morningstar.net**—Morningstar.net is the leading provider of research, analysis, and investor information for mutual funds and stocks. This site walks investors through the investing process with important data, news, market information, interactive tools, and education.

**Mredgar.com**—Provides access to SEC filings, company profiles, and a watch list with e-mail notification when a new SEC filing is submitted.

**Multex.com**—A main source for garnering research reports, multex.com links brokers, investors, and institutions with investment research and information services.

**Mutualfundsinteractive.com**—Provides comprehensive educational material geared toward educating consumers focused on investing in mutual funds.

**Nasdaq.com**—The home page for the NASDAQ stock market; provides up-to-the-minute information affecting the world of NASDAQ stocks.

**Nasdaqtrader.com**—Provides information on the trading activities and regulations affecting NASDAQ stocks, including market maker trading data. This site is the place to go to gain a monthly perspective on market maker volume activities.

**Newsvest.com**—A comprehensive news source for the financial community.

**Nyse.com**—The home page for the New York Stock Exchange, providing information on the trading floor, the stock market, listed companies, members and institutions, regulations, and news affecting listed stocks.

**Professionalcity.com**—Provides expansive information on targeted professions ranging from law to investing.

**Quicken.com**—Quicken.com is a personal finance site that offers a sweeping set of virtual tools created with the goal of becoming a one-stop shopping financial network. Quicken.com and Moneycentral.com are the two main Web sites that attempt to address all your financial needs. Quicken.com has areas on the site that assist with topics ranging from insurance, home loans, and tax preparation to investment and retirement planning needs. After locating what you need on Quicken.com, you can take it a step further and complete interactive forms that will get the ball rolling.

**Quote.com**—Provides a comprehensive array of financial market data including quotes on stocks, options, commodity futures, mutual funds, and indices. Quote.com also provides news, market analysis, charts, company profiles, and fundamental data.

**Ragingbull.com**—A favorite for message boards, news and commentary, and quotes and data, provided in a fun and easy-to-use format.

**Redherring.com**—The official Web site for *Red Herring* magazine, redherring.com provides information on IPOs, insider news and analysis, venture capital, and important industry news.

**TechStocks.com (Silicon Investor)**—The main place to visit for message boards and hot topics. This site is a favorite for traders who are searching for information that is not widely available. The site includes trading tools, market insight, and a portfolio section.

**Thestreet.com**—TheStreet.com is unique for its compilation of top-notch financial journalists producing articles and editorials with a Wall Street insider perspective. TheStreet.com offers highly regarded, in-depth daily market analysis that spans markets ranging from domestic equities to international debt.

**WSJ.com (Barrons.com)**—The *Wall Street Journal* on-line provides all the goodies the newspaper has to offer in a user-friendly format for less than $10 a month. With this subscription you also get *Barrons* on-line and a comprehensive database that allows you to search for past articles. This is an inexpensive and easy way to organize and save valuable articles.

**Zacks.com**—Zacks is known as a main source for earnings information, including reports, estimates, revisions, upgrades, and downgrades.

**ZDNetinteractiveinvestor.com**—Ziff-Davis is one of the world's leading technology media companies. It is a prime Web site for gathering data on the latest trends, technology, and Internet trends affecting the economy.

The Internet has put valuable information at the fingertips of all users. Information that was previously very expensive and hard to come by is now available to anyone who knows where to look for it. The Web sites listed here can provide you with the technicals, fundamentals, tools, educational materials, and commentaries you need to enhance your trading knowledge and capacity.

# PART IV

# THE TRADE

C  H  A  P  T  E  R  11

# ENTRY

Correct entry is a crucial component of the trade. When entry is carried out properly, your odds for success increase dramatically. Most traders have experienced trades that were planned out well, only to be foiled in the moment of entry, turning a potential profit into a loss.

Successful entry is composed of three parts: price, timing, and execution. When you learn how to recognize the best entry price zone and the best time to enter, your profitability will increase. You will also develop the habit of acting more quickly and with less thought, resulting in better probabilities for success. The advantage of being prepared to act is that you have already made the decision, so you will be able to execute the trade with little hesitation.

The remaining aspect of entry is whether or not you receive a good execution. Sometimes you will receive good executions and sometimes you will not. The executions you receive are not always within your control. They depend on different factors including your speed, the broader market action, the stock's liquidity, the execution system you are using, and what is going on in the stock at that particular time.

The premium you are willing to pay for a stock when you do not receive the execution you were looking for is within your control. Paying a costly premium by chasing a stock on entry when you missed your targeted entry zone is one of the most common mistakes made by traders. Through preparation, discipline, and patience, this mistake can be avoided; we discuss entry premiums in further detail later in the chapter.

## THE SCALED ENTRY APPROACH

The scaled entry approach involves entering into a position on a scaled basis. Instead of buying or shorting the entire position in one shot, you first take part of your intended position, preferably one-half to two-thirds. After the initial entry, you add to your position only when and if it is working in your favor, thus at a higher price than you originally paid.

The scaled entry approach provides flexibility, price discovery, and a stronger risk profile. By using more than one level to enter into a position, you gain flexibility for entry, because you do not need to be entirely right on entry. Market makers often use multiple levels to trade into and out of positions.

Successful market makers have controlled the ego-based need to be absolutely correct. Because markets are constantly in motion, it is almost impossible to be exactly right on a trade by entering or exiting at the very high or low point of a move. Traders who relinquish this ego-based desire free themselves to trade more aggressively by adding to a position if it is moving in their favor, and by cutting a position if it is not. In essence, they are trading after they have received price confirmation, not before.

The price discovery that you achieve with scaled entry is a valuable commodity. It is easier to act with conviction when you have confirmation that your strategy is correct. The best confirmation is achieved only through action, after executing a trade. You'll confirm not only price action and timing, but your own strategy as well. Action is the only cure for fear and doubt. If you buy a stock and it goes in your favor, you have valid confirmation that your strategy is correct. If it turns against you, then you know your strategy was not correct. When the stock moves in your favor, you not only have confirmation but you also have a profit and the psychological advantage of a positive P&L buffer. If the stock turns against you, you have lost less than you might have because you entered with only a partial position. When you add to a winning position, always do it in increments of half or less. This way, when you add to a trade, even if it is at the worst possible time, your P&L will still be positive even if the stock suffers as much as a 50 percent retracement off its highs. When adding to a winning position, always wait for the motion to stop on the downside after a small pullback. Add to a winning position only when the pullback stops above your initial entry zone.

*A market maker wanted to go long 50,000 shares of ABCD with a scaled entry approach. It was currently quoted 40—40$^1$/$_{16}$, with 37,500 offered out loud at a 1/16. The trader used Select Net to take the offerings and immediately bought 25,000 shares at 40$^1$/$_{16}$. The stock immediately moved higher, to 40$^1$/$_4$—40$^5$/$_{16}$. After 5 minutes, ABCD pulled back and stopped at 40$^3$/$_{16}$—40$^1$/$_4$. At this point the market maker bought another 12,500 shares at 40$^1$/$_4$ and the stock moved higher again. The trader was now long 37,500 shares. After the stock moved above 40$^1$/$_2$, the trader bought the remaining 12,500 shares at 40$^9$/$_{16}$, ending up long 50,000 shares at an average price of 40$^1$/$_4$.*

Many successful day traders utilize the scaled entry technique in order to test stocks first, before they go in full blast with their normal size. For example, if your objective is to buy 25,000 shares of ABCD, first buy 10,000 to 15,000 shares. By doing this you will quickly discover if your short-term assessment about the direction, timing, and momentum is correct.

As a general principle, stocks that are hard to buy are going higher, and stocks that are hard to sell are going lower. If you bought ABCD and it immediately moved lower, you would know that something about your short-term strategy might not be correct. You could sit back and wait to see if your plan worked out with less at stake because you do not have a full position. If you get stopped out, you have successfully cut your losses because you only bought part of your intended size.

If you had a hard time buying ABCD because it quickly moved higher, then you would know that your short-term plan was correct, and you could feel confident about adding to that position, preferably in increments of half or less. If you bought 15,000 shares, your next purchase would be 7,500, or half of the 15,000. After going long the stock, if it moves more than 2½ percent in your favor, take profits before adding to your position.

Adding to a winner is different from chasing a stock. When entering into an initial position, it is important to identify at what price the motion began. Once the motion begins, refrain from chasing the initial point of entry past your buffer range. The buffer criteria depend on the price of the stock and should be used as a general benchmark, not a rigid number. Use your knowledge of the stock you are trading and your common sense to stay flexible with your entry approach, centered around the entry buffer zone (see Table 11-1).

Most of the time stocks do not move in a straight line without first consolidating and pulling back. The odds are that prices will take a breather at some point before continuing their ascent. More volatile Internet stocks have a wider entry parameter from the point where the motion began. Usually, when you chase an entry you are ignoring the fact that stocks move forward in a steplike fashion: They move, stop, and pull back; move, stop, and pull back. It is important to give yourself a buffer for entry, but if that buffer is exceeded too strongly, move on to the next trade.

If you miss your buffer entry zone, you can reenter on a pullback if the initial move does not exceed double your entry criteria. For example, if you want to buy a $50 stock, your initial buffer zone is 3/8 of a point. If the stock moves up 3/4 of a point before you bought any, you can still get in if it pulls back to within your initial 3/8 of a point area of 50—50⅜. If the stock moves higher than 3/4 of a point and then streams back in, leave it alone. Market conditions could have changed, and the initial move that you were aiming for could have been missed.

A stock that shoots significantly past your entry area and then falls back in is called a fallen star (discussed in more detail later in the chapter). Fallen stars have a difficult time regaining momentum in their original direction, because they were met with strong opposition. When this occurs, reassess market conditions and consider any entry a new trade if you still want to get in.

An advantage of scaling into a position is that you have extra buying power in reserve to use if the trade is a winner. This buying power should never be used to add to a losing position. No matter how tempting it may be, resist the urge to buy or sell stocks that are moving against you. You should only be willing to pay prices that are higher than your initial entry. Don't get lured into doing the comfortable and easy thing, like buying a stock because the price seems low or selling a stock because the price seems high.

Large mutual funds have the luxury of averaging down in order to improve their volume-weighted average price (VWAP). Day traders have different objectives than mutual funds. Remember that as a day trader, your objective is to make money today. Half of the equation of making money is not losing a lot of money. The two ways novice and professional traders alike lose the most money are averaging down and bottom fishing. Once you become aware of how dangerous and costly these faulty trading tactics are, your profitability will immediately begin to improve.

Scaled entry is a key to successful trading. Successful day traders and market makers stay profitable because they have mastered the art of keeping their losses small while maximizing their gains. If you initiate a position with half of your normal size and the position moves against you, then you have cut your losses in half. If the position moves in your favor, you have not cut your gains in half because you can still add to it. You have only cut your initial gains in half, and depending on the stock that is not the meat of the move that you are looking for anyway. Scaled entry provides you with confirmation that your initial strategy is sound, and with the ability to stay flexible in your approach.

## THE CHASE

Knowing how to enter into a position is just as important as knowing how not to enter into one. The two most common ways of botching an entry are chasing a stock past your ideal entry point and anticipating a move to an entry point too early.

When you decide to enter into a position, refrain from chasing a stock too far past your ideal entry target range. This does not mean that you cannot get into the stock; it simply means that instead of paying an immediate premium for it, you are waiting for it to pull back before getting in. You can get in on a pullback as long as the stock does not move excessively past your entry point. If it does move too far past your entry point and then falls back (a fallen star), it should be avoided. The chart in Table 11-1 can be used as a general guideline of the buffer zone ranges for entry, given the price of the stock. These ranges are meant to give you general criteria to prevent excessive chasing. They are not set in stone and should be used with a flexible approach, given the stock that you are trading or the circumstances you are trading under.

**Table 11-1**  Buffer Ranges for Stock Entry

| Stock Price | Buffer Range |
|-------------|--------------|
| $0—$25      | 1/4 point    |
| $25—$50     | 3/8 point    |
| $50—$75     | 1/2 point    |
| $75—$100    | 5/8 point    |
| $100 +      | 3/4 point    |

Most market makers are unwilling to chase a stock too far past an entry range in order to execute a customer's retail order. They prefer to short a stock to a retail buyer if the stock moves up excessively, rather than pay up for it. This is because stocks tend to pull back in a steplike fashion after moving higher.

For example, if a stock is quoted $39^{15}/_{16}$—40 and it begins to move, you should resist paying more than $40^3/_8$ to get in. If you miss the move, wait for it to pull back into your entry range before getting in. If the $40 stock moves more than $1^1/_2$ percent above $40^3/_8$, or in this case above 41, and then falls back into your initial entry zone, stay away from it. Market conditions could have changed. Your objective should be to buy stocks that are moving in your direction, not against you. The law of diminishing returns states that the higher the cost of entry, the lower the profit. When you understand this rule and abide by it, your profits will increase steadily.

Stocks that move more than $2^1/_2$ percent past your entry point without pulling back and consolidating before lifting off again are more the exception than the rule. If you have acquired the habit of chasing prices too far past the price where the motion began, then you are consistently paying a premium for entry. The disadvantage of paying a higher entry cost is evident across all businesses, not just trading. Any entity that regularly pays above the average price for its goods will have smaller margins and a tougher time earning profits.

Many traders tend to disregard entry cost. A 1/2 point move in a $20 stock is $2^1/_2$ percent; that is a stronger move in percentage terms than a 1/2 point move in a $100 stock, which is only 1/2 percent. Trading is a game of probabilities. Your chances for success in trading increase when the odds for continued motion are in your favor, not against you. Paying a premium for entry on a consistent basis after the motion has begun decreases your odds for successful continued motion under most circumstances.

The higher the price of the stock, the larger an entry buffer you should provide yourself with. For stocks that are priced at over $100, widen your entry buffer zone to roughly 3/4 of a point after the motion has begun. If your entry point is missed, you can always get back into the stock, but you should regard it as a new trade and a new short-term trend that you are attempting to catch.

Internet IPOs, for example, are not normal trading circumstances and should be considered a completely different trading ballgame. Day traders who try their hands at Internet IPOs use a different strategy than they use for most of the other stocks they trade. Because of the wild price swings with Internet IPOs, chasing the stock is often the only way to get in or out. Entry zones have to be huge, as do slippage adjustments. It is not uncommon for day traders to chase entry by 5 percent to 10 percent of the stock's price. The two most important things to watch when trading Internet IPOs are the AX, or the leading underwriter, and the spot where the motion began. These two items often go hand in hand, because the AX has the power to move the market due to a large natural customer order flow. If you trade Internet IPOs, use a predetermined limit for chasing entry and stick to it. Emotions of greed and fear run the highest with new issues. Resist the urge to hit the ball out of the park, and stay disciplined.

Traders usually chase stocks because they get emotional about having missed a move, and they want in at all costs. Buying a stock with upward momentum is a plus, but if the initial move is missed, you are better off letting it go. The chances are that another opportunity will materialize. Remember, missed money is better than lost money. Chasing stocks is the most common way to lose money when entering into positions.

Another common mistake made by professionals and novice traders alike is to anticipate a move into your entry zone before it gets there, with the motive of getting a cheaper price. When prices do not move to your level, there is usually a good reason. By anticipating the move, you are nullifying the reason for getting in.

Always wait for the price to enter into your sweet spot before acting. Use caution and refrain from anticipation. Anticipation is a dangerous quality to possess as a trader. Regardless of how tempting it may be to get onto the wave early, when you anticipate you are projecting your will onto the market. Allow the market to open the door for you before you act. Read the market's will, and refrain from imposing your own.

The problem with anticipating a move through support or resistance is that these levels are called so for a reason. The buyers or sellers of yesterday usually fortify those levels with increased resolve. The bulls or bears may be waiting in the wings to protect their territory. The very reason you are entering into the position in the first place is because of the evidence that the selling resistance or buying support has been nullified by today's stronger action. Anticipating a move to these levels is wishful thinking and has no basis in reality.

## FALLEN STARS

Fallen stars are stocks that have met your entry requirements and have proceeded to make a significant move in your direction, only to fall back into your initial entry zone. Traders who miss an original move often hope for a stock to fall back into their original entry range so they can get in and redeem themselves for having missed the move.

It is frustrating to watch a stock move significantly in your direction when you intended to get in but missed the move for one reason or another. The regret factor is one reason behind support and resistance levels. Traders and investors remember having missed a move and often try again if they get another chance. However, market conditions often change between the time the stock rises and when it falls.

Fallen stars should be avoided because they indicate that the initial move ran out of steam, and that the opposing force has counterattacked and is now in control. If there was significant buying power behind a move up, then the chances are that the stock would not fall back that easily into your original entry area. When you go long a fallen star, you are buying a stock that is moving against you. It is not a momentum play; it is rather an emotional play. As a rule of thumb, most stocks that have moved $1^1/2$ percent to $2^1/2$ percent past your initial entry area and then fallen back are fallen stars and should be avoided.

## THE SWEET SPOT FOR ENTRY

There exists a sweet spot for entry that, if acted upon, will increase your chances for a successful trade. The sweet spot is a price pattern that can be exploited on a consistent basis. Prices tend to spring through these areas when they are penetrated, so knowing where they are and how to take advantage of them will provide you with a sharp advantage.

The sweet spot for a long entry is right above the previous day's high. (Refer to Table 11-1 for targeting your entry price for longs and shorts.) The previous day's high is the shortest-term measure of resistance that, when broken, often results in a burst of momentum, clearing the path for further gains. (See Chapter 6 on the previous day's high and low.) The advantage of waiting for a stock to cross above its previous day's high before going long is that you are assuring that the short-term trend is positive. A move above yesterday's high suggests that the sellers who took a stand have succumbed to the stronger buying force of today. Once broken, the previous day's high turns into a new price support, and provides you with a floor for a tighter stop-loss point.

The sweet spot for shorts is right below the previous day's low. The previous day's low is the shortest-term measure of support. If you are trading from the short side and you wait for prices to cross beneath yesterday's low, you are assuring that the short-term trend is negative. Yesterday's low marks the point where the buyers took a stand and were able to push back the bears. A move below that line represents a victory for the bears of the current day, and represents new price resistance. A break beneath the low point means further lows are in store.

When a stock moves above the previous day's high or below the previous day's low for the first time, you have confirmation that two other powerful daily trend and entry indicators are in your favor. The two other indications that the short-term trend is in your favor are the net price and the opening price signal. (See Chapter 6.) The net price is a short-term measurement of a stock's health. It displays how the market players in that stock at any given time have rated the stock compared to the previous day's price action. A positive net price is equivalent to a green light. A negative net price is equivalent to a red light. Your probabilities for success increase when you trade in the direction of the net price. When a stock crosses from positive to negative or negative to positive it provides an excellent signal for further momentum in that direction.

The opening price signal is an even shorter-term measurement of a stock's health. It rates a stock on how it is trading when compared to its opening price. A stock that is trading above its opening price indicates that the short-term trend is positive. A stock that is trading beneath its opening price indicates that the short-term trend is negative. The best scenario is to have both the net price and the opening price signal pointing in the same direction that you want to trade from. When the opening price signal changes sides on the day for the first time it provides a trading signal that a further move is on the way.

As a day trader, it should be your goal to act quickly when your risk–reward ratio for a profitable trade is the highest. This ratio is the highest when the net price, the opening price signal, and the support or resistance levels are in your favor. These three conditions will always be in your favor when prices initially break through the previous day's high or low. If you can enter just when these support or resistance levels are pierced—the sweet spot—your chances for success increase dramatically.

## TIMING THE ENTRY

It is important to realize that your odds for catching a profitable trend increase dramatically during the first and last hour and a half of the trading day. Between 9:30 and 11 AM and between 2:30 and 4 PM, the motion in the market is the greatest. Volatility and momentum during these periods produce the maximum opportunity for profit. Day traders should stay focused on entering into new positions that are in motion during these periods.

The first 5 to 15 minutes of trading in the early morning should be avoided when entering into new positions. Just after the market opens, trading is often the most unpredictable, subject to powers not easily recognized. It is usually during this period of time that the early morning pullback occurs. This is when specialists and market makers make money the easiest, because retail investors and novice traders have a tendency to chase stocks that are being marked up or marked down on the open. When a stock is being marked up, it will open higher than the previous night's close. When a stock is being marked down, it will open lower than the previous night's close.

Market makers and professional traders like to take the opposite side of markups in the morning, which results in an early morning contra move. S&P futures that gap up in the morning often close that gap at some point throughout the trading day. This fill-in often occurs within the first half-hour of trading and is commonly referred to as the early morning contra move.

It takes time after a stock has an aggressive opening for the orders to pan out. During this period of time, unpredictable volatility can cause havoc for day traders. There is no hard-and-fast formula for pinpointing the exact window when this volatility will end. It could take 5 minutes, or it could last for half an hour. All too often stocks gap on the opening with excessive enthusiasm or pessimism, only to reverse course quickly once the professionals take the other side of the markup. By waiting patiently after the opening for a stock to settle in, you will reduce the risk of getting whipsawed, and you will have a better picture of what side the real demand or supply is on.

Amateurs usually dominate the openings, while professionals dominate the close. Amateur investors send in market opening orders after reading news that has already impacted the price of the stock. Because of this, they end up paying the highs or selling the lows of the opening.

With the dramatic increase in equity ownership by the American public, the equilibrium of buying power has shifted in part to the smaller investors. These investors like to act in the morning. When the masses act in unison with thousands of small orders, these orders become a potent force and have the strength to move stocks around and dictate openings.

The late morning and midafternoon hours of trading taper off, with lighter volume and trendless ranges. This is when traders often try to force things to happen, entering into positions that go nowhere. Instead of catching a trend in motion, they end up frustrated by losses that could have been avoided. As a day trader, you have the power to pick your time and place to trade. Exercise that right.

Profitable entry requires a combination of careful preparation, patience, and quick action. When entering into a position, wait for the stock to enter into your ideal price range before trading. Refrain from chasing the stock past your ideal price range. If you missed the trade, then so be it; another will materialize. Don't indulge yourself by looking back at what could have been.

C H A P T E R

# 12

# EXIT

When carried out properly, correct exit will make the difference between a small profit or no profit, and a large one. There are various techniques for getting into and out of positions. Traders often come up with excellent trading ideas and execute them properly upon entry, but give back or cut short their gains in the moment of exit. Correct exit is an art. The reason exiting properly takes time to master is that it requires the application of two opposing forces, which requires discipline: staying power and hard-nosed action. The key to prevailing when exiting or entering a stock is preparation. As Benjamin Disraeli once said, "The great secret of success in life is for a man to be prepared when his opportunity comes." When you are prepared to exit, your profitability will increase measurably.

# THE SCALED EXIT APPROACH

The solution to balancing the forces of greed and fear when exiting a position is the scaled exit approach. The scaled exit approach is exiting a position incrementally. Rather then selling your whole position in one shot, in a scaled exit you initially sell only part of your position, while letting the other part run. Like the scaled entry approach, the scaled exit approach provides you with flexibility, price discovery, and the potential for greater profits.

The scaled exit satisfies your urge to lock in a profit, while allowing you to maximize your gains by letting some profits run. This approach is empowering because it reduces the illusive ego-based desire to be entirely right on a trade. Another advantage of having locked in a partial profit is that you are playing with the market's money on the second half of the trade. This provides you with an emotional and psychological advantage. If after selling part of your position the stock drops back into the area where you initially bought it, you have still locked in a partial profit. If the stock rallies past the point where you made a partial sale, you can rest at ease because you still have part of your position. You always have the option of reentering the stock if you want a larger position.

Scaling into and out of positions when you believe the market is in an overbought or oversold state can allow you to take advantage of market turns while maintaining the discipline of trading the meat of your position with the trend. It is important to remember that when markets are turning, volatility increases, making it harder to get good executions. The best-case scenario is to lighten up existing positions that are working into support or resistance. Cover part of your short going into support; sell part of your long going into resistance. If you want to short at resistance or go long at support, establish a position with only half or less of your normal size, and do so only when the opening price signal (see Chapter 6) is in your direction, providing you with confirmation.

One scaled-exit criterion is to sell part of your position after it has moved at least $2\frac{1}{2}$ percent in your favor. For example, if you go long 25,000 shares of ABCD at $50, you would immediately place a partial profit-taking limit order to sell part of your position, let's say 12,500 shares, at $51\frac{1}{4}$, or $2\frac{1}{2}$ percent above your entry price of 50. If the stock continues to rally, you are still long 12,500 shares, so you have not cut your profits short. If the stock moves through $51\frac{1}{4}$ and then fails, you can rest assured because you have already taken profits off the table, so you are still making money.

Since you have already locked in a partial profit, you have increased flexibility for your remaining position. If the stock continues to move higher, you can scale out of half of your remaining long, or 6,250 shares, and keep the other 6,250 until the daily uptrend is broken (see Chapter 6). You can also use the trailing profit protective stop method (see Chapter 3). It is important to develop the habit of letting your profits run as long as possible after you have locked in an initial profit through the scaled exit method.

## MAXIMIZING YOUR GAINS

If your initial entry was successful and you have locked in the first and important part of the daily trend, you can relax and focus on letting your profits run. Successful traders focus on maximizing their gains, not on the number of times they win. Many times this is easier said than done. It is very tempting to lock in small profits for immediate gratification. This is especially true if you have acquired the habit of continuously focusing on your P&L. Knowing your P&L is important; but when you are glued to it, you are essentially glued to what it represents, which is subjective and clouds your decision-making process, encouraging greed and fear.

Rather than focusing on the profit or loss, the best traders stay focused on doing the right thing, and let the profits take care of themselves. Locking in small profits is a fear-based approach. The fear is that you'll lose what you have already gained.

The Wall Street saying that you can never go broke taking profits is false. If you consistently take small profits, commissions and slippage will eventually eat you alive. The larger profits are the ones that will make up for your smaller losses and your cost of doing business. The majority of successful traders are correct on trades just above 50 percent of the time. The reason they come out on top after paying for commissions and slippage is that they let their profits run longer than they let their losses run.

On the other hand, the greed-based approach of never locking in profits can also work to a trader's detriment. The are many occasions when a market maker or day trader enters into a position successfully and lets the profit run, only to watch it reverse and end up with nothing or a loss as a result of not taking any profits.

Giving money back in a stock because you did not take any profits is one of the most frustrating experiences for a trader. It is easy to get stubborn about a position that was working for you and is now a loser. Under these circumstances, regret runs high. Instead of getting more, you got less. Many traders who give back hard-earned gains blame themselves and reinforce their resolve not to let it happen again. If you end up holding yourself responsible in this situation, you will end up where you started by locking in small profits, because you fear giving your gains back again. Take partial profits off the table after a successful entry and let the other part ride.

## SITTING

In *Reminiscences of a Stock Operator*, Edwin Lefevre said, "It never was my thinking that made big money for me. It was always my sitting. Got that? My sitting tight!" Sitting with a position that is working is an important key to success. The main way professional traders make up for smaller losses, slippage, and commissions is through the larger gains they earn by sitting with positions that are moving in their favor.

The importance of sitting when trading also refers to sitting on your hands when a trade is missed. If the trade is missed, then wish it good riddance. The probabilities are in your favor that you will find another profitable trading opportunity. Instead of fretting about missed opportunities, use your valuable time to uncover other good possibilities. Looking back, in trading, as in life, should be avoided at all costs.

The practice of sitting will help you avoid aggressive overtrading, a practice that is expensive on three counts—the bid–ask spread, commissions, and time diverted from other winning possibilities. Statistics demonstrate that trending markets normally retrace a solid part of a move before reestablishing their trend. These mini corrections occur against the major trend, and they provide excellent opportunities to get back into the trade. When a trade is missed, be patient; the opportunity to reenter a trade generally presents itself. Having the patience to refrain from overtrading will help you become more profitable.

Exercise the practice of sitting after you have established a trade that is not yet working nor has it proved itself wrong. Give the trade a chance to demonstrate its merit. Don't be so anxious to kick out a position at the first sign of a little head fake. If the position is not immediately working, sit on it. When a trade begins to work, give it time to play itself out.

Prices will arrive at their own equilibrium regardless of the short-term head fakes and moves of the market. Maintain the conviction to sit with your position either until it makes you money or you are stopped out. If you have a position and you abandon it too early out of fear, you are second-guessing yourself and overtrading, both detrimental practices. Acting with conviction and confidence is a habit that can be developed through practice. Every time you second-guess yourself and disregard your plan, you negatively affect your development as a trader.

Once you have established a trade, give the idea an opportunity to develop. Allow yourself to be stopped out. Do not get caught up by the insignificant head fakes caused by market makers that accompany most moves. Always know where you plan to exit a position once you get in. Have two exit points before establishing the position: an initial stop-loss point and a profit-taking range. Predetermined profit-taking orders will help you to take partial or total profits when the position is moving in your favor, not against you.

Use a scaled exit approach to take advantage of trading around a position. The scaled approach will help you to relinquish the need to pick the bottom or the top of a move. When a position is moving in your favor, try to maximize your gains as much as possible. Taking a partial profit through a scaled exit will help you to do this.

# EXECUTION AND CONTROL

A good execution can make the difference in terms of profitability on a trade. Different factors determine whether you receive a good fill, a bad fill, or no fill. The increase in volatility combined with the swelling number of day traders today creates an environment in which the competition for the best executions is fierce.

The executions you receive when entering or exiting positions depend on elements in and outside of your control, including the liquidity of the stock you are trading, your speed, the execution medium you are using, the type of order you place, market conditions, and the unforeseen. Knowing the nature of the stock you are trading is crucial when determining what sort of execution you can hope to receive.

## MARKET ORDERS

When a stock enters into your ideal target range, always use a market order to attain execution. As a day trader looking to catch momentum, your objective is to buy or sell stocks that are on the move. Market orders are often the only way to get executions when a stock is in play. The risk with a market order is that you will pay a slippage premium, which means that you will pay more than you wanted to in order to get into your position. The premium, however, is often necessary to a certain degree. The degree to which you should be willing to pay a slippage premium is the maximum amount of your entry buffer zone, as explained in Chapter 11. If the price range exceeds the amount that you are willing to pay, cancel your market order immediately.

Professional traders refrain from initiating positions in the direction of a markup on the opening. As a day trader, you should resist entering market orders to buy or sell on the opening. Wait for either the early morning contra move or for confirmation that the markup or markdown is followed by institutional interest in the form of block prints, as well as a move above the important opening price.

One way to insure that the slippage you pay on a market order is kept in check is to place a marketable limit order. For example, if you have an entry buffer of 1/2 point, then you could use a variation of a market order, called a marketable limit order, taking into account your buffer range.

The NASDAQ Level II screen in Figure 13-1 shows Adobe Systems (ADBE) quoted at $95^{1}/_{8}$—$95^{5}/_{16}$. Your buffer zone is 1/2 point and you want to buy 5,000 shares. You think that the stock is about to move because it just broke through resistance. To go long, you would enter an order to buy 5,000 at $95^{13}/_{16}$. If you have access to Select Net, you can execute by sweeping the offerings right through your target price of $95^{13}/_{16}$, bidding for a total of 5,000 shares. This is a combination of a market order and a limit order.

## SHADOWING THE AX

A popular entry and exit tactic that day traders employ is a technique called shadowing the AX. The AX is the market maker who has the dominant order flow in a particular stock. On the Discovery

| Symbol | ADBE |

| | | | | | | | | | |
|---|---|---|---|---|---|---|---|---|---|
| INCA# | 95 1/8 | 96 1/4 | 5 | 9 | REDI# | | 0 | 95 5/16 | 0 | 2 |
| p PKJC | 95 | 97 | 1 | 1 | ISLD# | 94 3/16 | 95 5/16 | 15 | 2 |
| p CANT | 95 | 96 5/8 | 1 | 1 | BTRD# | 95 | 95 3/8 | 1 | 2 |
| p MONT | 95 | 96 | 1 | 1 | p SNDV | 94 | 95 3/8 | 1 | 1 |
| p WARR | 95 | 96 3/4 | 1 | 1 | p SHMD | 94 1/4 | 95 3/8 | 5 | 5 |
| p PERT | 95 | 97 3/8 | 1 | 1 | p NITE | 92 | 95 7/16 | 1 | 5 |
| p DBKS | 95 | 96 1/16 | 1 | 4 | p SBSH | 94 7/8 | 95 1/2 | 1 | 1 |
| p LEHM | 95 | 96 | 1 | 1 | p MASH | 94 5/8 | 95 5/8 | 1 | 1 |
| p SLKC | 95 | 95 11/16 | 1 | 1 | p SLKC | 95 | 95 11/16 | 1 | 1 |
| p JEFF | 95 | 98 | 1 | 1 | p PRUS | 94 3/4 | 95 3/4 | 1 | 1 |
| BTRD# | 95 | 95 3/8 | 1 | 2 | p MLCO | 94 3/8 | 96 | 1 | 1 |
| p JPHS | 94 15/16 | 96 3/16 | 1 | 1 | p USCT | 92 | 96 | 1 | 1 |
| p SBSH | 94 7/8 | 95 1/2 | 1 | 1 | p MONT | 95 | 96 | 1 | 1 |

**Figure 13-1**  Adobe Systems Quotes on a NASDAQ Level II Screen

channel, when you watch a large whale swimming under the sea, you always see a group of smaller fish that are latched onto the whale. These fish are feeding off the whale while catching a free ride in the process. This is the same principle day traders use when they shadow the AX.

If you have spotted the AX in a stock and that stock trades with a wide spread of 3/8 point or more, you can use an ECN to place a bid 1/16 above the AX's best bid. When you buy the stock 1/16 in front of the market maker, you can immediately offer the stock 1/16 below the best inside offer. This technique takes patience and works better with stocks that have a larger spread. It can also be employed when you are not sure who the AX is, but nevertheless you feel confident that you have identified the short-term trend in a stock with a wide spread. Always establish your position in the direction of the trend first, before attempting to shadow the AX and trade for a spread profit.

## THE SLIPPAGE FACTOR

Slippage refers to the difference between where you would like to have a trade executed and where it actually gets filled. The difference can be vast in some cases, given the extraordinary volatility of many Internet-related issues today. These stocks move faster than the broader market and can be up or down points in a heartbeat.

| Symbol | EBAY | Order: | | | | | | | |
|---|---|---|---|---|---|---|---|---|---|
| Last 127 3/8 01:28 | Chg +9 5/8 | Vol 7389700 | HiLo 128 7/16 120 1/4 | pCl 117 3/4 | | | | | |
| Ins: ↓ 127 3/8- 127 7/16- | 5-27 | S5 E: (126)/100/1 | (129 1/2)/500/1 | | | | | | |
| Your: | R: | | | | | | | | |
| Res: | NMS EBAY INC | | | | | | | | |
| Price: 1/4 | Size: 2 | B&A: | B: | A: | | | | | |

| p | MLCO | 127 3/8 | 127 1/2 | 1 | 1 | | ISLD* | 127 5/16 | 127 7/16 | 5 | 27 |
|---|---|---|---|---|---|---|---|---|---|---|---|
| p | PERT | 127 3/8 | 128 | 1 | 5 | p | MASH | 127 1/4 | 127 7/16 | 2 | 1 |
| | INCA* | 127 3/8 | 127 1/2 | 5 | 10 | p | COST | 101 | 127 1/2 | 1 | 1 |
| p | HMQT | 127 3/8 | 134 1/8 | 5 | 1 | p | HRZG | 127 | 127 1/2 | 4 | 1 |
| | BRUT* | 127 5/16 | 127 3/4 | 5 | 2 | p | GSCO | 124 1/2 | 127 1/2 | 5 | 5 |
| | ISLD* | 127 5/16 | 127 7/16 | 5 | 27 | p | MLCO | 127 3/8 | 127 1/2 | 1 | 1 |
| p | MASH | 127 1/4 | 127 7/16 | 2 | 1 | p | NITE | 127 | 127 1/2 | 10 | 2 |
| p | SLKC | 127 3/16 | 128 3/16 | 1 | 1 | | INCA* | 127 3/8 | 127 1/2 | 5 | 10 |
| | ARCA* | 127 1/16 | 128 1/4 | 1 | 10 | | | | | | |
| p | USCT | 127 | 128 | 1 | 1 | | BRUT* | 127 5/16 | 127 3/4 | 5 | 2 |
| | MNSE | 127 | 127 3/4 | 2 | 1 | | MNSE | 127 | 127 3/4 | 2 | 1 |
| p | HRZG | 127 | 127 1/2 | 4 | 1 | p | SHMD | 126 | 127 3/4 | 1 | 5 |
| p | NITE | 127 | 127 1/2 | 10 | 2 | | REDI* | 126 7/8 | 127 3/4 | 1 | 7 |
| | REDI* | 126 7/8 | 127 3/4 | 1 | 7 | p | PRUS | 125 | 127 7/8 | 1 | 1 |
| | | | | | | p | SBSH | 126 1/2 | 127 7/8 | 2 | 2 |

**Figure 13-2**   EBay Selling Off from Its Daily High

*On August 18, 1999 at 3:53 PM, EBAY was up 9⁵/₈, trading at 127³/₈—
its high of the day. (See Figure 13-2.) Believing that the upward momentum would carry it to even higher prices into the close, Ron decided to go
long 5,000 shares. He bought them with ease in Instinet, usually a bad
omen. When a stock is easy to buy, it means that short-term supply is
greater than short-term demand. Suddenly, a vicious sell program kicked
in. Within 2 minutes, EBAY sold off almost 3 points, to 124³/₈, where it
closed. After going long the stock, Ron realized almost immediately that
he was wrong but hesitated for too long before doing anything. By the
time he started to try to sell his position, 5 minutes after he entered, it was
already down 2 points. He ended up selling the position for a loss of
$12,500 in less than 5 minutes.*

Ron experienced slippage the hard way on his long position in
EBAY. More than 35 percent of the volume in Internet stocks trades
through Electronic Communication Networks (ECNs). This requires
traders to get in and out of positions when they can, usually by bidding for or offering stock. This means that in the short term, they may
be wrong because someone else is hitting or lifting the stock.

It takes patience and awareness to ascertain what sort of slippage you may experience in any given stock. In some very liquid
names on the NASDAQ market, it's not uncommon to see 100,000
shares or more, out loud, being bid for or offered. Generally as you
approach the "round" number in these stocks, which refers to the

whole numbers without fractions, the size gets even larger due to psychological stop-loss points.

On the NASDAQ Level II screen shown in Figure 13-3, on August 18, 1999, Dell Computer was the most active, trading more than 100 million shares. At any given time during the day, you could have bought or sold large sizes on the inside market. On that same day, as displayed in Figure 13-4, at certain times you would have

**Figure 13-3**  Dell Computer Quotes on a NASDAQ Level II Screen

**Figure 13-4**  Inktomi Quotes on a NASDAQ Level II Screen

been lucky to buy or sell 1,000 shares of Inktomi (INKT), another Internet stock, on the inside market.

It is crucial for a trader to factor into the 2 percent maximum loss risk profile, the worst-case scenario for poor executions. If you were trading DELL on August 18th, with all of the liquidity, factoring in 1/8 point for slippage would be reasonable. On the other hand, if you were trading EBAY or INKT on the same day, anywhere from 1 to even 3 points of slippage would be more reasonable to factor in, depending on the size of the position.

Liquidity refers to the density of volume traded in a given stock on a given day. Stocks that have a larger market float, or more shares outstanding, usually trade with thicker volume. Heavier volume allows institutions and traders to take larger positions, because they can enter and exit with less slippage or market impact.

Every stock has its own personality, subject to various outside influences. The more influences the trader is aware of, the better equipped you will be to correctly judge and size the market. Some of the influences that impact a stock's personality include market capitalization, float, average daily volume, institutional ownership, sector correlation, beta, standard deviation or volatility, which market maker has the AX, ECN volume percentage, and other fundamental and technical factors.

It is unrealistic to believe you will be able to get out of a losing position in a stock that is not liquid. A large part of day traders' losses are attributed to slippage. This is one reason paper trading is unrealistic. This is a crucial component of risk evaluation, because many traders fail to properly factor in the possibility of poor executions. It is always better to err on the smaller side with positions, expecting the worst executions; that way you'll be pleasantly surprised when you get the best.

The reason thinly capitalized names are susceptible to large slippage is that market makers move stocks single-handedly in order to achieve price discovery.

A trader's position size should always be smaller if the stock you are trading is less liquid. Your stop-loss point should also be wider, given the hit-or-miss nature of illiquid stocks. If you are trading a stock that you are unfamiliar with, evaluate the average daily volume for the last 20 days. If the stock begins to trade with more volume, you can always add to an initial smaller position if the stock is moving your way.

## SHORT SELLING

The NASDAQ short sale rule is in force between the normal market hours of 9:30 AM and 4 PM EST. NASDAQ members and the customers they represent are not allowed to short a NASDAQ stock on the bid when that bid is a down tick. To short a NASDAQ stock when the bid is a down tick, the trade must be executed at least 1/16th above the inside bid. Market makers who are conducting bona fide market-making activity are deemed qualified by the NASD and are exempt from the NASDAQ short sale rule. This means that market makers can short a NASDAQ stock on a down bid, but a day trader cannot.

Many day traders are biased toward trading from the long side because it is easier for them to get executions, due to the NASDAQ short sale rule. Market makers, on the other hand, have more of a neutral bias toward long or short positions. A long side bias works well in times of a bull market. Because many day traders today have only experienced a bull market, trading from the long side has been the profitable thing to do. However, in a bear market, trading from the short side is obviously the more profitable endeavor. If you are biased toward trading from the long side, the odds are that in a bear market you will have more difficulty trading profitably.

For example, day traders were shaken out of the stock market in droves during the short-lived bear market in Internet stocks of the spring and summer of 1999. Many day traders have never witnessed such consistent selling pressure as the Internet stocks experienced during this period of time, and they lacked the experience and flexibility to take advantage of the sell-off from the short side.

When you short stock during a bull market, or into strength, you are fighting the trend. If the trend is positive and you short into it, the chances of that stock rising against you increase considerably. When you short during a bear market, or into weakness, your odds for a successful trade increase because you are trading with the underlying force and trend.

Shorting a stock because the price is high is a losing game. The greatest gains in terms of percentage of a move occur at the end of the move. The last 10 percent of a bull move has been known to encompass as much as 50 percent of that move. The price that might look high to you right now can actually be the starting point at which the stock begins to make its greatest move forward.

Short interest is the total number of shares that have been sold short and are still outstanding. Stocks that have greater short interest are susceptible to panic buying on the upside when they break above resistance, especially on the way to new all-time highs. The short interest ratio measures the number of days of average trading volume it would take to cover the short interest. It is measured by dividing the outstanding short interest by the average daily trading volume.

Always be mindful of the type of stock you are shorting. When you short a stock with a high short interest ratio or one that is thinly capitalized, you are at the mercy of larger market forces that can move the stock on a whim. All it might take for you to be squeezed is one phone call from a large institution in a thin name. A stock that might have looked weak on the charts could be up a number of points in a heartbeat. If you are shorting illiquid names, you should anticipate maximum slippage, and accordingly enter with a wider stop and a smaller position.

## SEC ORDER HANDLING RULES

The SEC implemented two new order handling rules in January 1997 that changed the way investors' and traders' orders are reflected to the general market. The first rule changed the way limit orders are displayed, and the second changed the quoting standards. The new order handling rules have worked to improve prices and narrow spreads, creating increased transparency and liquidity for individual investors and traders. With the move to quoting stock prices in sixteenths, the average spreads have shrunk, by some estimates, 40 percent or more. The new order handling rules affected both traders and individual investors.

First, the limit order handling rule requires market makers to change the way they had historically handled customer limit orders.

Under the new rule, market makers who receive and accept customer limit orders have to either fill the order, display the order at the improved price through their quote, or send the order to an ECN and have it displayed there.

This rule requires market makers to reflect the actual size and price at which they are willing to execute customer limit orders that are on the inside of the market and are not greater than 10,000 shares or more than $200,000 in value. If a market maker receives an execution at or better than the customer's price, the customer will receive execution first.

All market-making firms have the obligation to protect their customer limit orders by giving them equal or improved price executions before executing orders for themselves. Market-making firms are not required to accept limit orders; but if they do, they must abide by the NASDAQ limit order handling rule.

Under the limit order handling rule, when a market maker has a limit order on the books, that order will receive a partial or complete fill when the market maker trades any stock at that price or through that price. For example, if a market maker has a customer limit order to buy 1,000 shares at $50^{1}/_{8}$, the market maker cannot buy any stock personally at $50^{1}/_{8}$ or lower without first giving the customer the execution.

The second order handling rule instituted by NASDAQ was the quote rule. The quote rule requires market makers to publicly display their most competitive quotes in a consolidated format. Under this rule, traders and investors have access to the best price at which market makers or other individuals are willing to trade. The quote display rule prohibits market makers from displaying two separate quotes on more than one trading system. This rule requires ECNs to collectively post their internal order books to the public, to insure that the best quotes are available on one screen for all to see. Day traders using ECNs, like Island, can now have their orders reflected. This means that if a trader is willing to buy or sell a stock at a more competitive price than a market maker, the trader's order will be displayed first and get filled first. This has put individual traders on par with market makers, because they can display their orders similarly.

## SELECT NET

Select Net is an electronic execution system sponsored by NAS-DAQ, and is the main instrument used by market makers to trade with each other and with other traders. The system replaced the telephone as the main execution medium for transacting trades. Tools of the Trade was the first widely implemented software package designed for market makers to use with Select Net. With Tools of the Trade, market makers were able to quickly buy and sell stock without taking the time to make a telephone call. There are now numerous software packages that incorporate Select Net and allow market makers to buy or sell stock with the click of a button.

## FRAGMENTATION VERSUS CENTRALIZATION

The current market structure, in which orders are executed within NASDAQ and the New York Stock Exchange, has become increasingly fragmented. The onslaught of competing ECNs and various exchanges has resulted in a segmented system in which the customer who enters the most competitive order may not be the one to receive execution. This occurs because other broker-dealers can use a customer's posted order as a reference point to internally match their own orders, or to trade in front of an order. This scenario has become increasingly common with the explosion in volume of orders from on-line brokers who route their orders to specific market makers.

In response to the increasing fragmentation of executions in the marketplace, five powerful Wall Street firms approached the SEC in February 2000 with a proposal to move toward a centralized order system that would include a central display of all quotes and be operated by one self-regulating group. A centralized order system would route all orders to one execution system where customers' orders would be filled in price–time priority. This means that an order to buy or sell stock at a specific price would be executed in the order it was received, across all markets, regardless of which execution system it was entered on.

Some argue that a centralized order book would provide a disincentive for market makers to compete for order flow, resulting in a lack of innovation. However, with customer interests and efficiency as the objectives, the structure of the market is quickly moving toward consolidation and centralization, and away from fragmentation. In February 2000, NASDAQ and the New York Stock Exchange reported that they had held merger talks, with the objective of preserving a central and primary role in the abruptly changing marketplace. It was also reported that the two largest ECNs, Instinet and Island (a division of Datek), had held merger talks with the goal of preserving their role as the largest contenders among ECNs. These rounds of merger talks indicate that consolidation and centralization are on the horizon. The form the new marketplace will take, however, is still open to debate.

Another signal pointing toward a unified exchange or a single execution medium came in December 1999, when the New York Stock Exchange's board of directors repealed Rule 390. Rule 390 prohibited NYSE member firms from trading stocks listed before April 26, 1979 on anything other than a national exchange. While the rule was in effect, NASDAQ broker-dealers could not act as principles on these stocks by trading them on their own exchange. Stocks listed before April 26, 1979 account for 23 percent of NYSE-listed issues, producing 46 percent of its volume.

In the short term, the revocation of Rule 390 will serve to increase the competition for and fragmentation of executions in listed stocks among competing exchanges. For the longer term, however, it is a significant step toward the centralization of executions. The move sends a message that the barriers between exchanges are being broken down and that establishing one centralized execution medium makes more sense now than ever.

## NASDAQ SUPER MONTAGE

The introduction of Super Montage will be the next major change in the NASDAQ architecture. Super Montage will replace the NASDAQ Level II and III screens with a dual-mode display. On the top of the screen, Super Montage will anonymously display the aggregate size and three-tier depth of a quote. Priority in execution of limit orders will be determined based on displayed interest, not on reserve interest. Only at the time of execution will market makers' identification be displayed, not before. On the bottom of the screen, Super Montage's display will allow market makers and ECNs to line up their orders and interest as they did on Levels II and III.

The NASDAQ Super Montage is designed with the objective of improving electronic access to the best prices. It will enhance the display of trading interest with greater transparency and depth of liquidity. The Super Montage should also reduce the locked and crossed markets and trade through orders.*

**Super Montage Display Window**

*Top Part:* Shows aggregate size and multiple price levels

| BID | TOTAL | ASK | TOTAL |
|-----|-------|-----|-------|
| $30.00 | 7,000 | $30.05 | 5,400 |
| $29.95 | 10,000 | $30.10 | 14,000 |
| $29.90 | 15,000 | $30.15 | 23,000 |

*Middle Part:* Shows inside quote information
Inside $30.00 – $30.05        7,000 – 5,400
Last $30.00        +.70        12:30        Vol. 15,300,000   Hi $31   Low $29.75

*Bottom Part:* Sow market maker proprietary and agency quotes along with ECN orders in a price/time priority.

| MMID | BID | SIZE | MMID | ASK | SIZE |
|------|-----|------|------|-----|------|
| SBSH | $30.00 | 5,000 | HRZG | $30.05 | 5,400 |
| MLCO | $30.00 | 2,000 | SBSH | $30.10 | 3,000 |
| MSCO | $29.95 | 3,000 | GSCO | $30.10 | 6,000 |

*The NASDAQ Stock Market, Inc. March 2000

**Figure 13-5** NASDAQ Super Montage

Super Montage was created with the objective of providing greater transparency by rewarding liquidity. For example, if you want to buy 5,000 shares and you are willing to bid for them out loud at the most competitive price, you will be able to buy the shares before another trader who wants to buy the same amount but is only wiling to show 1,000 shares. Super Montage will provide reserve size accessibility at all levels, which will allow market makers and traders to display a limited amount while keeping a larger size in reserve.

With accessibility to Super Montage in mind, NASDAQ is currently making modifications to the antiquated SOES and Select Net execution mediums. The modifications will reduce the current dual liability of market makers to SOES and Select Net by routing both mediums through one pipeline. This will increase the speed with which you can access Super Montage by reducing message traffic. Also, negotiating for executions will be automatic, so traders who enter orders will know immediately whether their orders were executed. The market maker receiving the order will be forced to either execute or move immediately. This will eliminate the frustrating time delay that is currently permitted to give market makers a window to decide whether or not to execute. NASDAQ will also implement the decimalization of quotes by the fourth quarter of 2000. Quotes will appear on NASDAQ in nickel increments, as they do now on NYSE. Executions will be possible in penny increments. This change will act to further narrow spreads, benefiting customers.

## ELECTRONIC COMMUNICATION NETWORKS (ECNS)

Electronic Communication Networks are broker-dealers that facilitate two-sided order flow through an electronic medium. An ECN is a privately maintained market, employing various methods of electronically matching orders. The popularity and liquidity of ECNs exploded in the late 1990s, after NASDAQ changed its order handling rules in 1997 requiring increased visibility, which is the ECNs' specialty. ECNs today account for almost 30 percent of the total volume traded on NASDAQ. It is estimated that by the year 2001, more than half of the total volume traded on NASDAQ will emanate from ECN order flow.

With the limit order regulatory changes imposed by NASDAQ, ECNs have become a popular way for on-line investors and traders to display their orders. Institutions and market makers often frequent ECNs for anonymity and liquidity, resulting in less market impact cost.

The NASDAQ stock market is primarily a dealer-driven market that requires human involvement in order to facilitate order flow. ECNs are automated systems that match orders on an electronic book. NASDAQ is electronic, but it is decentralized, acting as an electronic messaging system dependent upon market makers.

The long-term viability of ECNs is questionable, however, because of the inevitable move of NASDAQ away from fragmentation and toward centralization and automation. If NASDAQ has its own central order book, then the need for the fragmented ECNs will disappear.

When a market maker receives an institutional order, the first objective is to buy or sell the stock discreetly, so as not to attract any unwanted attention. Institutions are best served when their orders are executed without any market impact cost. Institutions prefer to trade their merchandise with other "natural" merchandise, so they receive better prices without affecting the natural price of the market. Market makers are increasingly using ECNs to lessen the market impact of an order.

The advantage of a market maker using an ECN instead of its own name is that it will have less of a chance to alarm other players. If a market maker who is a known AX in a relatively illiquid stock suddenly moves the market to the inside bid, other market makers and traders may scramble to buy the stock first.

Market makers utilize all the tools at their disposal, including ECNs, to get the job done effectively for their clients or for themselves.

## (SOES) COMMISSIONS AND SCALPERS

Scalping is a day trading tactic used to capture small discrepancies in price, as little as 1/16. Scalping for small fractions has become an increasingly hazardous path toward successful day trading. Popularized through the SOES day trading tactics of the late 1980s and early 1990s, scalping for fractions was less complicated then than it is today. At first, all a SOES day trader had to do was pick off a market maker and offer the stock back out to the street at a better price. This tactic was easy and profitable when competition for the prime executions was minimal because of the smaller number of SOES traders. Market makers also displayed larger sizes on the inside market, and were slower to react to an SOES trade because of antiquated technology.

Today, however, scalping for fractions is much harder. Now there are thousands of traders using SOES, many competing for the same print from a single market maker. It has also become increasingly difficult for SOES scalpers to receive 1,000-share executions, because market makers on NASDAQ can now represent the inside market with as few as 100 shares. If an SOES scalper is being charged $25 per one-way execution, then SOES prints for fewer than 1,000 shares, which are common today, are not cost-effective.

For the day traders who do pay up to $25 for a one-way trade, proper entry is extremely important, because a break-even trade is really a loss of $50. Assuming the SOES trader is using 1,000-share lots to trade, a gain of 1/8 on a trade is only a $75 win, while a loss of 1/8 on a trade is a $175 loss. Just like in a casino, with these odds, the probabilities clearly favor the house. Actively trading with the objective of scalping for small fractions is a losing proposition over time.

If you are focused on scalping for small fractions, make sure that your commissions are as small as possible. Remember that every battle is won before it is ever fought. Take pains to insure that the odds are in your favor before going into battle.


The combination of enhanced visibility brought on with the SEC's order handling rules and ECNs, together with the explosion of competition among on-line brokers for customer order flow, has created a dynamic and rapidly progressing execution environment that benefits day traders. Day traders can now pay under $10 to have a limit order reflected through an ECN or a market maker with the click of a button. As little as five years ago, this ease of access at such a low cost would have been unfathomable.

For day traders, this means that the execution tools are at their disposal to trade on par with market makers—and it's only going to get better. With the increase in consolidation among ECNs today, by the year 2002, only a few will be left standing. The consolidation will act to increase liquidity even further.

P A R T

# TECHNICAL ANALYSIS

# CANDLESTICK CHARTING TECHNIQUES

There is no question that mass psychology has an impact on a stock's price: Prices are driven by emotions, mainly fear and greed. Perception is reality for the day trader, and charts reflect this. Technical analysis incorporates price action and volume to produce a blueprint of where a stock has been and where it may go. It traces the emotional extremes of the bulls and the bears to produce clues as to where the greed or fear is the strongest. Knowing how to spot repeating price patterns in the market will provide you with a valuable advantage.

Technical analysis works because investor psychology has a massive impact on price action. Traders and investors remember what a stock did in the past, and that memory often causes pain or regret because of missed opportunities. The emotional attachment to missed opportunity increases a trader's resolve not to miss the trade the next time around.

When you become familiar with important support and resistance levels and recurring patterns, you will be able to take advantage of significant technical events in your market and in related markets. For example, a breakdown in the long bond or a drop in the U.S. dollar below an important level of price support can result in related selling in the equity market.

*On May 2, 1999 at 10:30 AM, the equity market sold off sharply for no apparent reason. Savvy traders, however, knew what was going on: The bond market was in a free fall after slipping through a technically significant 120 mark, which served as a major prior support. The technical break was a perceptual catalyst that caused related selling in the stock market.*

There are a number of fundamental, technical, and emotional catalysts that cause individual stocks and the market as a whole to move with force. Research analysts and value-type investors have been known to discount the value of technical analysis. They believe that technical analysis is an art that attempts to neutralize the importance of a company's fundamentals; this is false. Technical analysis traces, confirms, and makes evident the underlying fundamentals that cause prices to move. Whether or not the public knows these fundamentals, they must be reflected through price and volume. Price action displays the true hand of the fundamentals.

Charts provide significant leverage when used in conjunction with fundamental analysis. Value-oriented investing focuses on stocks that are cheap based on fundamentals alone. Value investors pick stocks that have "good value" based on the theory that a stock's price will rise in due time to match its earnings and book value. However, it could be years before a value stock climbs to meet expectations. Investors who pick stocks on value alone could fight a trend for a long time, while adding to a losing position unnecessarily.

Technical analysis supplements fundamental investing by incorporating price action and volume to produce a comprehensive picture of a stock's health. By integrating basic charting tools such as candlesticks, moving averages, oscillators, and support and resistance levels, technical analysis provides value investors with a sharp edge, encouraging them to trade with the trend, which will save them time and money. Technical analysis supplements a fundamental approach that can narrow down the choice between a few stocks, and it could provide levels for profit taking.

With access to charts easier than ever today, almost anyone can learn to read and understand them. Many people are intimidated by technical analysis, believing it to be complicated and hard to decipher. This is far from the truth. There are some very basic techniques that can provide a trader with insight and ammunition for successfully entering and exiting trades. Some of the very best traders have the simplest trading plans. Trading should not be made complicated. Technical analysis helps to block out the noise when used with basic principles and a few choice indicators.

One problem with technical analysis is that because there are so many charts and indicators easily available, many traders are overwhelmed and develop what's known on Wall Street as "analysis paralysis." They become paralyzed with indecision by attempting to trade off multiple indicators, some of which may be producing conflicting signals. A trader who is prone to indecision in the first place could easily find a reason to procrastinate by overanalyzing charts or indicators. All the colors and interesting patterns can have a hypnotizing effect, acting like candy for the brain.

Every stock has its own character. A chart can be used as an objective reflection of the stock's trading character, or, if you are not careful, as a mirror of your own character. It is easy to look for confirmation of an inflexible opinion by interpreting charts to fit your need. When you develop a consistent game plan for trading with charts, it will help you to maintain discipline. As you spend more time watching charts throughout the day, you will develop increased conviction for making decisions.

Charts can be displayed in multiple time frames, ranging from monthly to tick by tick. The guidelines applied to one time frame can generally be applied to another. There are groups of time periods that can produce multiple confirmation of a pattern when used together. Daily charts are the most common and are used to generate daily ideas before, during, and after market hours.

Intraday charts are powerful tools used to reflect the short-term intraday pattern of a stock or the market. Weekly charts allow a trader to step back a little longer in order to determine the longer-term trend with less noise or daily interference. Monthly charts are interesting for a longer-term perspective, but are hard to integrate into a short-term trading plan.

# CANDLESTICK CHARTS

Candlestick charts were developed in Japan in the eighteenth century. Munehisa Homma developed these charting principles to amass a huge fortune trading rice coupons. Homma used candlestick techniques to trade unconventionally as a warrior; he had a ruthless ability to seize opportunity and take action, due in part to candlestick conviction. Eventually Homma won the honorary title of Samurai because of his demonstrated mastery.*

Many credit Steve Nison, author of the groundbreaking book, *Japanese Candlestick Charting Techniques*, with introducing candlestick charts to the United States in the 1980s. In his book, Steve provides a comprehensive, easy-to-understand guide to reading and applying candlestick charts.

Japanese candlestick charting techniques provide a fun, simple, and extremely effective means for charting stocks. Once you become familiar with candlestick charts, you'll have a difficult time looking at bar charts. Candlesticks provide a fresh, powerful dimension for traders and charting enthusiasts.

Candlestick charts display a stock's price action in a multidimensional view, utilizing color and symmetry. Candlesticks allow the viewer to take into account the important opening price, as well as the high, low, and close.

Japanese candlesticks utilize the opening price, the closing price, the high price, and the low price to form a pattern. Each candlestick has a body and a wick. The color of the body reflects the relationship between the opening and the closing price, and is one of the most important characteristics.

A white body is formed when the closing price is above the opening price. White bodies are bullish, illustrating that the bulls won the battle for the day. A black body is formed when the closing price is lower than the opening price. Black bodies are bearish, illustrating that the bears won the day's battle. The wick or shadow is the high or low range outside of the body.

Candlestick charts produce potent reversal patterns as well as valid continuation patterns. When combined with Western charting techniques, candlestick charts provide a potent one-two combination for increased decision-making leverage.

---

*Nison, Steve. *Japanese Candlestick Charting Techniques*. Simon & Schuster, 1991.

**Figure 14-1** Candlestick Construction

## THE OPENING PRICE

The opening price is the starting gate in candlestick trend analysis, and is more important than the previous night's close. A lot can change between the previous day's close and the current day's opening. By using the opening price as the starting point for the color of the candle, candlesticks place more emphasis on the here-and-now aspect of the market.

The opening price is especially important for market makers, because it is often determined by the emotional extreme reflected in nonprofessional order flow. (See Chapters 6 and 21 on the opening price signal and gaps.) Because of this emotional extreme, the opening price is often close to the high or low of a stock's price action for the day. Market makers who have buy or sell orders that have accumulated from the night before and from the early morning dictate the market's opening. These orders are usually the product of novice investors or panicky traders who are acting on old news from the previous night or from the early morning.

Market makers enjoy a unique advantage at the opening, because they have an inside look as to the real demand or supply for a stock. Specialists or market makers gap a stock on the opening when they have one-sided order flow affecting the supply-demand relationship.

If the markup or markdown is due to small order flow with no institutional demand behind it, market makers may deem it to be artificial and will often sell or "fade" the opening. This means taking a position on the opposite side of the gap. (See Chapter 21 on artificial gaps.) For example, if a stock is marked up 2 points on non-institutional order flow, market makers may short the stock on the opening for their own inventory. The same holds true if the stock is marked down on noninstitutional order flow, in which case market makers would buy it for their own inventory.

New York Stock Exchange specialists are the sole proprietors of the order flow for their stocks, so they have single-handed control of the opening price. Market makers on the NASDAQ have to compete with one another for order flow, so they do not have a complete picture for the pre-opening demand. In many instances the opening price is close to the high or low point of the day because it was dictated by the emotional capitulation of amateur players at the opening bell.

## THE CLOSING PRICE

While the opening price is often the product of retail investors and novice traders, the closing price is often the product of the professionals and the institutional heavyweights. Candlestick bodies reflect that the closing price is often the opposite extreme of the opening price.

Part of the reason professionals dominate the close is that many buy-side institutional traders are compensated on their ability to meet or beat the almighty VWAP (Volume Weighted Average Price). As the name suggests, the volume weighted average price is the average price at which the stock traded for the day when volume is weighted. If institutional traders can beat the VWAP, their performance benchmark is raised and at year-end they are compensated better. The institutional traders usually save part of their orders until the end of the day so they can improve their VWAPs if they have the chance to do so. If a stock has been better to buy all day and then falls back a little during the early afternoon hours on light volume, the stage could be set for a rally into the close, as long as the market holds. A buy-side trader who was unable to attain price improvement will have to buy the stock anyway, thus forcing prices higher and dictating the close.

## THE HIGH PRICE

The high price in candlestick charting is the top end of the upper wick, or the top part of the body if there is no wick. The high price represents the maximum strength of the bulls for the day. This is the point of short-term resistance because it represents sellers who managed to hold their line of defense.

Stop-loss orders for shorts tend to accumulate just above the high price of the day. The previous day's high is the first point of resistance for the current day's trading action. Trade either from the long side or the flat side when a stock is trading above the previous day's high. Refrain from shorting short stocks that are trading above the previous day's high or at the current day's high.

## THE LOW PRICE

The low price in candlestick charting is the bottom of the lower wick, or the bottom part of the body if there is no wick. It represents the lowest point at which the bears were able to force a stock down before the bulls halted the onslaught and fought back.

The low of the previous day serves as the first area of short-term price support. Stop-losses for longs often accumulate just beneath the low price of the previous and current trading day. New lows for longs represent new losses, some of which may be intolerable to traders, forcing them to liquidate their positions.

## CANDLESTICK REVERSAL PATTERNS

Candlestick charts produce effective reversal signals on a daily and intraday basis. Reversal patterns provide two-sided clues: what to do and what not to do or selection and negative selection.

The reversal patterns imply that a trend has run its course. Trends can and do turn around quickly. However, the goal of astute day traders should be to seize the middle of the move, not the top or bottom. Always wait for prices to confirm that the reversal pattern was authentic. The short-term risk of waiting for this confirmation is that you'll miss the top or bottom part of a trend. This part of the trend has the highest risk. When you stick to trading the middle of the move, your risk profile is lowered.

You'll know that a pattern is confirmed if prices follow in the direction of the reversal. As a day trading entry rule, when prices move above the high price of the bullish reversal pattern, use that as a signal to go long, using 1/8 of a point below the low of the pattern as a stop-loss point. When prices move below the low for bearish reversal patterns, use that as a signal to go short, using 1/8 of a point above the high of the pattern as a stop-loss point. For example, suppose you spot a hammer, which is a bullish reversal pattern that occurs at the bottom of a downtrend. If the hammer was formed on day 1, with a high price of 21 and a low price of 20, on day 2 you should wait for the price to move above 21 before initiating a long. Once the long is initiated, your initial stop-loss should be placed 1/8 of a point below the low point of the hammer on day 1, or at 19⅞.

A danger when trading based on reversal patterns is the temptation to anticipate a change in the trend without waiting for confirmation. This is the equivalent of bottom or top fishing and should be avoided. It is more prudent to use the reversal pattern to take profits from an existing position if there is no confirmation. For example, if you are short 10,000 shares of an NDX stock and the NDX sector puts in an intraday hammer on the 15-minute chart, use that as a sign to cut your short position in half rather than to go long. If prices close above the intraday hammer and your other entry criteria are met, then go long. Remember to wait for confirmation before initiating trades based on reversal patterns. Confirmation means price action taking place above a bullish pattern or below a bearish pattern.

You will increase your risk–reward ratio when you check the intraday sector action with candlesticks before you trade. You will lose less because you will refrain from trading against the odds by going long against bearish reversal patterns, or by going short against bullish reversal patterns. This is negative selection. Develop the habit of watching the NDX 100 and the SPX on intraday candlestick charts. This practice will almost immediately increase your effectiveness as a day trader, because you will have a better view of the mood of the market knowing where your risk–reward is the greatest.

The intraday 15-minute NDX chart in Figure 14-2 shows a bullish reversal pattern. On December 1, 1999, the NDX formed a triple bottom accompanied by three bullish candlestick reversal patterns: a morning star, a bullish engulfing pattern, and a hammer.

Figures 14-3 through 14-15 depict the candlestick patterns described here.

Figure 14-2 Candlestick Reversal Patterns on NDX 100

**Figure 14-3** Abandoned Baby

**Figure 14-4** Dojis

**Figure 14-5** Engulfing Patterns

**Abandoned baby**—This is the most powerful variation of the morning or evening star patterns. It occurs when the second day of the pattern is a doji or small body that has gapped away from both bodies; thus, it's abandoned. The gap that the small body has formed is closed by the third part of the pattern, which is a long body. This gap or window in candlestick terms indicates important resistance or support.

**Doji**—Dojis are reversal patterns that represent an equal tug of war between the bulls and the bears. A doji is formed when the opening and closing prices are the same. The wicks outside of the opening and close could vary in size, ranging from very long to nonexistent. The doji reversal signal is most effective when it is formed near the top or bottom of a trend.

**Dragonfly doji**—This doji has a long lower wick with the opening and close at the top of the formation. This is a bullish reversal pattern when formed at the bottom of a move and is similar to a hammer. When formed at the top of a move, it is bearish and is similar to a hangman.

**Gravestone doji**—This pattern is the opposite of a dragonfly doji. It has a long upper wick with the opening and close at the low price of the day. The gravestone doji is a bearish pattern when formed at the top of a move, especially after a breakout, similar to a shooting star. If the pattern is formed at the bottom of a move, it is similar to an inverted hammer and is bullish.

**Engulfing patterns**—An engulfing pattern is a reversal pattern that is formed at the bottom of a downtrend or at the top of an uptrend. An engulfing pattern occurs when the current day's body engulfs the previous day's body. When this occurs, the opening and close must be wider than the previous day's opening and close.

**Bullish engulfing**—This pattern forms when a large white body engulfs a black body at the bottom of a downtrend. The low point of the white engulfing candle becomes the new price support.

**Bearish engulfing**—This pattern forms when a large black body engulfs a white body at the top of an uptrend. The high point of the black engulfing candle becomes the new price resistance.

**Hammer**—A hammer is a bullish reversal pattern that is formed at the bottom of a downtrend. The name comes from the concept of hammering out the bottom of a move. Hammers have a long lower wick with a small upper body. The wick should be at least two to three times the size of the body. The body can be any color. The hammer is a powerful and popular reversal pattern. The chart of Microsoft (MSFT) in Figure 14-6a shows the stock putting in a daily hammer on the last trading day of January, at an area of support. MSFT rallied powerfully after the hammer was put in.

**Inverted hammer**—This formation is a hammer turned upside down at the bottom of a downtrend. It has a long upper wick that is two to three times the size of the small lower body. It is an excellent reversal indicator, and is especially useful in intraday charting. The inverted hammer looks like a shooting star at the bottom of a downtrend. It represents that the bears lost the battle to the bulls early in the session, and only through a last-ditch effort were they able to force prices down again.

**Hangman**—A hangman is a bearish pattern that is formed at the top of a move. It has the same look and feel as a hammer, except that it's at the top of an uptrend. Hangman patterns have small upper bodies with long lower wicks that are at least two to three times the size of the bodies.

A hangman shows that the bears were able to knock the stock lower before the bulls managed to muster their last bit of strength to bring the stock back to its opening. This is significant when it is the first time after the uptrend that the bears were able to take control; it could be an indication for future activity. The color of the body is insignificant.

**Figure 14-6**  Hammer

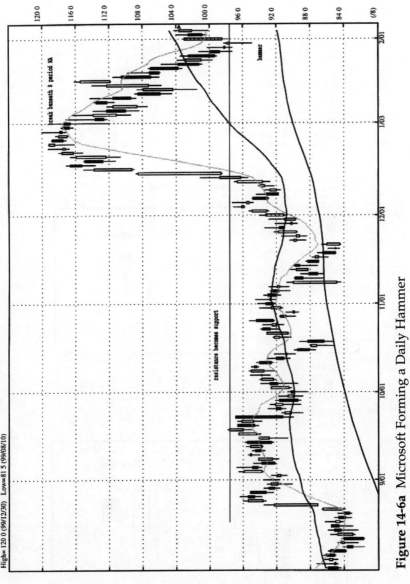

2000/02/03 16:18

msft.q.1.3 129Days 1999/08/03-2000/02/03 MA(Close.50) 104.815 MA(Close.200) 91.882
Lastn 103 5 PC=20.67% AV=29145445
High= 120 0 (99/12/30) Low=81 5 (99/08/10)

break beneath 8 period MA

resistance become support

hammer

120 0
116 0
112 0
108 0
104 0
100 0
96 0
92 0
88 0
84 0
(/8)

9/01 10/01 11/01 12/01 1/03 2/01

**Figure 14-6a** Microsoft Forming a Daily Hammer

149

**Figure 14-7** Inverted Hammer

**Figure 14-8** Hangman

**Figure 14-9** Harami

**Harami**—A harami is a reversal pattern that is the opposite of an engulfing pattern. A small opposite color body is within a larger body at the top or bottom of a move. It indicates that the trend has lost momentum.

**Bullish harami**—A short white body formed within a large black body at the bottom of a downtrend.

**Bearish harami**—A short black body formed within a large white body at the top of an uptrend.

**Harami cross**—This pattern occurs when a doji is formed within a larger body at the top or bottom of a trend. It represents indecision at the top or bottom of a move and is a potent sign that the trend has halted.

**Marubozu**—Marubozus have long bodies with no wicks. In Japanese, *marubozu* means bald head. This pattern is formed when there is a large discrepancy between the opening and the close, and there is no high or low range outside of the opening or close.

A white marubozu is a bullish continuation pattern and points toward higher gains. This is formed when the stock opened at its low and closed at its high. A white marubozu at the bottom of a trend is a bullish reversal signal.

A black Marubozu is a bearish continuation pattern and points toward lower price action. It is formed when the stock opened at its high and closed at its low. A black marubozu at the top of a trend is a bearish reversal signal.

**Figure 14-10** Harami Cross

**Figure 14-11**  Marubozu

**Figure 14-12**  Morning and Evening Stars

**Figure 14-13**  Piercing Line and Black Cloud Cover

**Morning star**—The morning star is a powerful bullish reversal pattern. It is a long black body followed by a small white or black body, followed by a long white body. The small body on the second day ideally would have gapped down from the black body. The morning star is usually followed by a small pullback toward the middle of the long white body, before the reversal pattern continues upward. The small body represents the waning of momentum after a down move, while the long white body represents confirmation of the reversal.

**Evening star**—The evening star is the opposite of the morning star. It occurs at the top of an uptrend and is composed of a long white body followed by a small black or white body, followed by a long black body. Ideally the small body would have gapped up from the long white body. The small body represents stalled uptrend momentum, while the long black body provides confirmation that the trend is reversing. The long black body is usually followed by a small pullback toward the middle of that body before downward momentum kicks in.

There are variations of the morning and evening star patterns in which the smaller body could be a doji or a spinning top, or could be placed at various distances from the first long body.

**Piercing formation**—This is a bullish reversal pattern that has a long white body that pierces through the midpoint or higher of a long black body. This occurs after a downtrend. It is similar to a bullish engulfing pattern except that the bulls did not show up in complete force to completely engulf the previous day's move.

**Dark cloud cover**—The opposite of a piercing formation, this bearish reversal pattern occurs at the top of an uptrend. It is a long black body that covers half or more of a long white body. It is similar to a bearish engulfing pattern except that the bears did not force prices down far enough to cover the previous day's up move.

**Shooting star**—This is a bearish reversal pattern that forms at the top of an uptrend. It has a long upper wick that is two to three times the size of the small lower body.

The shooting star in Figure 14-4a shows that the bears attacked in force and rescinded most of the gains that the bulls had made for that session. The shooting star represents the first change in sentiment since the uptrend began.

The chart in Figure 14-14b shows the NDX forming a daily shooting star on November 26, 1999. This short-term bearish reversal pattern would be confirmed once the low just above 3100 was broken.

**Spinning top**—Spinning tops have small bodies with large wicks on both sides. The body can be white or black. This is a reversal pattern, similar to a doji, representing indecision. A spinning top at the top of a trend is a bearish reversal signal. A spinning top at the bottom of a trend is a bullish reversal signal.

The chart of BJ Services (BJS) in Figure 14-16 shows a number of candlestick reversal patterns with support and resistance levels:

1. hammer (bullish engulfing);
2. piercing (second part of 1 – 2 double bottom);
3. breakout (continuation pattern);
4. resistance turned into support;
5. resistance;
6. spinning top;
7. breakdown gap;
8. abandoned baby, hammer;
9. piercing pattern.

The chart of Dell Computer in Figure 14-17 shows a solid hammer formed in the beginning of June on strong volume, which

**Figure 14-14a** Shooting Star

Page Title : F8.pg

ndx.masr.1.1    128Days    1999/06/01-1999/11/30    MA(Close,50) 2642.30    MA(Close,200) 2308.95
Last= 2966.73    PC=1.97%    AV=0
High= 3151.77 (99/11/26)  Low= 1987.40 (99/06/02)

1999/11/30 16:15

shooting star

**Figure 14-14b** Shooting Star Pattern on the NDX

155

**Figure 14-15**  Spinning Top

formed an interim bottom. DELL formed another hammer in the beginning of August, which marked another low. After reaching a high toward the beginning of September, DELL formed a number of spinning tops and sold off from there. In October, two dojis marked the high and low of the channel that was formed.

## CANDLESTICK CONTINUATION PATTERNS

As a general principle, when trading off of candlestick charts, the color of the candle represents the side of the market you should be trading on. Simply put, if the candlestick is white, then trade from the long side—don't be caught short. If the candlestick is black, then trade from the short side—don't be caught long. This holds true for overnight as well as intraday positions.

For overnight positions, if the body of the candlestick closed as white, then either be long or flat into the next trading day, but don't be short. If the body of the candlestick closed as black, then either be short or flat into the next trading day, but don't be long. This simple and effective short-term trend indicator works like a charm from a risk-control perspective. Regardless of your thoughts about a stock, it will force you to listen to the market's vote for the short-term trend and will keep you from getting into trouble by fighting the trend.

A long body represents a forceful continuation pattern. A long white body represents that the trend is likely to continue higher, at least overnight. A long black body indicates that the trend is likely to continue lower, at least overnight. The long body indication holds

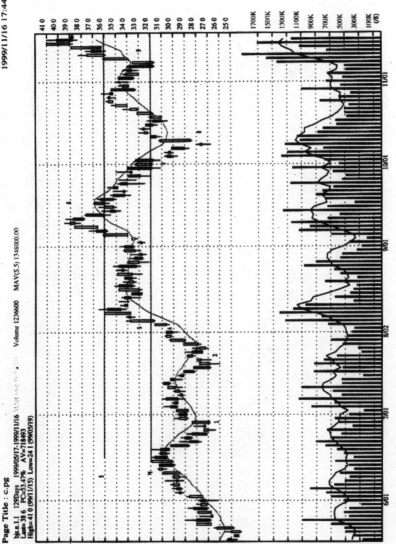

Figure 14-16  Candlestick Reversal Patterns in BJS

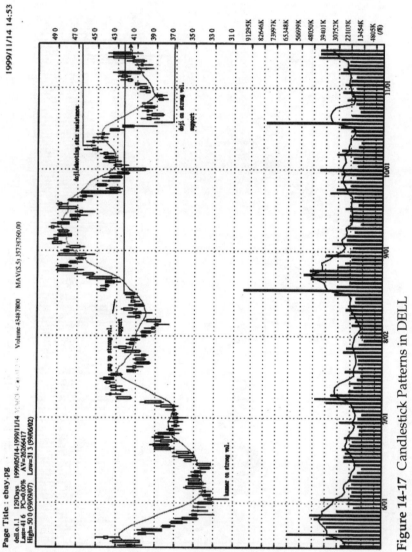

Figure 14-17 Candlestick Patterns in DELL

true intraday as well. When you trade on the side of the opening price signal, you insure that you are on the correct side of the color of the candlestick.

Rising and falling windows make up another powerful continuation pattern. If a stock is in an uptrend and gaps higher, it means that the trend is a powerful one and should continue higher yet. If a stock is in a downtrend and it gaps lower, then the downtrend is gaining force to the downside. Always trade in the direction of continuation windows. Long white or black bodies often precede continuation windows.

In the chart in Figure 14-18, JDS Uniphase (JDSU) broke out above resistance on October 2. After breaking out, it pulled back and consolidated before marching forward to gain 80 points in less than a month. During this uptrend, it formed a number of continuation patterns, including three rising windows and a number of long white bodies. If you had caught just the middle of this move, you would have profited handsomely.

Technical analysis is the footprint of the market. It takes into account the rational as well as irrational components of price action. Price levels of support and resistance as displayed through technical analysis can become self-fulfilling prophecies. Stocks often move fast because of technical breaks through support or resistance levels. Traders who are keyed into these levels have an advantage, because they understand why the stock is moving.

Candlestick charts are powerful tools when used in conjunction with basic chart formations. Candlestick charts provide a simple, quick, and effective way to utilize technical analysis when making trading decisions. Candlestick charts provide a multi-dimensional view, utilizing color and symmetry to highlight reversal indicators and continuation patterns. Candlesticks incorporate the important opening price, the closing price, and the high and low price ranges to help you interpret a stock's path of least resistance. Candlesticks are effective trading tools from a daily and an intraday standpoint. The more you watch candlestick price patterns develop on an intraday basis, the more effective you will become as a trader.

Under certain conditions, human beings act similarly and predictably. If you develop the habit of watching these patterns as reflected through charts, you will become more effective at spotting those recurring human tendencies.

Figure 14-18 Candlestick Patterns in JDSU

160

C  H  A  P  T  E  R

# SUPPORT AND RESISTANCE LEVELS

Support and resistance levels are prices at which stocks or futures lose momentum due to previous buying or selling pressure. These levels can be spotted on weekly, daily, and intraday charts. Support and resistance levels are important in determining the risk–reward ratio of a trade.

Support and resistance levels can be used in two basic ways: Buy at support and sell at resistance; or buy when resistance has been broken and sell when support has been breached. If prices break through resistance, the old resistance becomes new price support. If prices break through support, the old support becomes new resistance.

It is important to know the price levels for support and resistance for the broader market, the sector in which you have positions, and the individual stock you are trading. For example, if you are trading Yahoo (YHOO), it is important to know where the support and resistance levels are for the NDX, the Internet index (DOT), and the individual stock.

Significant support and resistance levels cause prices to reverse. They mark the end of a trend and are usually accompanied by above-average volume. The volume in many cases can be climactic, marking a grand finale of a battle waged between the bulls and the bears at that price. These battles provide important signals to the shrewd trader who knows how to spot them. You will be able to increase your trading effectiveness should those levels hold or be violated.

## SUPPORT

Support is the price level at which the buyers have turned the tide on the sellers, causing a stock's or sector's downward momentum to halt. The low point of this move serves as support because the buyers who missed the low point of the rally feel regret. They remember the price and will be waiting to buy the stock—thus supporting it— if it dips back.

Significant levels of support have large numbers of buyers waiting to get back in. Less important levels of support have smaller buy interest. Sell orders usually accumulate just beneath areas of support. The first level of short-term support for a stock is usually the previous day's low price. The previous day's low is also the first level of support for the broader market.

The daily Amazon (AMZN) chart in Figure 15-1 shows resistance and support that were formed in September. Once resistance is broken, it turns into the first level of support. AMZN broke above resistance toward the end of September, and then fell back beneath the first level of support to stop at the second level of support toward the beginning of November. After reaching the second area of support, AMZN rallied.

## RESISTANCE

Resistance is the price level at which the sell orders have overwhelmed the buy orders, causing rallies to fail. Resistance causes buyers to stumble and to reassess where they think prices are headed. Traders who were long and did not sell at the high point of the rally will be anxious to unload their positions if prices rise back

**Figure 15-1** Resistance and Support Levels in AMZN

up to the levels that they missed—causing resistance. Also, sellers who wanted to short the stock or sector when it was higher feel regret for having missed the opportunity and will be waiting to sell at the higher price if it gets back up there. The previous day's high price is short-term resistance for stocks and the broader market.

Sharp market makers use levels of price support and resistance to take the other side of order flow by selling incoming buy orders at areas of price resistance, or buying incoming sell orders at levels of price support. The incoming buy or sell orders that reach the market maker's desk when a move has just about run its course near resistance or support is usually retail-driven. Retail order flow generally comes from nonprofessionals, who normally chase stocks if they missed their ideal entry points, due to a spate of greed or fear.

It is not uncommon for market makers to see orders originate from the same source when a move has just about completed its course. These orders tend to be predictable contrarian indicators because the traders who are entering them are driven by their emotions. Emotion-driven traders have the habit of panicking at the same recurring price patterns.

When market makers take a stand at levels of support or resistance, they use short-term sentiment indicators to confirm that the market may be holding and reversing. They watch fair value to see if the futures are trading at a discount or premium. They watch the tape to see what size prints are hitting the tape: Are they block prints or smaller retail prints? If the market is falling to a level of support, a market maker may test the bids to see what sort of buy interest is out there before going long. It is not uncommon for a market maker to hit the street with anywhere from 5,000 to 25,000 shares, depending on the liquidity of the stock, simply to see if there are any real buyers out there. If the bids fade and no one buys the market maker's stock, then chances are that the support level was not valid. If buyers in the street step up to buy the market maker's stock, then the market maker knows that the support level is valid at least for the short term, and can quickly reverse the position, using the support area as a stop-loss point.

## PRICE CONFIRMATION

Support and resistance levels are not always exact. Attempting to trade off them by shorting into strength or buying weakness without first receiving confirmation that prices have halted should be avoided. When the price level that you have pinpointed as support or resistance is tagged, watch the broader market sentiment indicators to see how the market is reacting. Allow the market to be your guide.

By watching fair value, the TICK, and the AX (see Chapter 19), you can put together a realistic picture of whether the support or resistance zone is a valid one. These three leading indicators lead price action. If support is reached and the S&P futures suddenly start to trade at a premium to fair value, and the TICK turns positive, then the support level is probably a valid one at least for the short term. If the market maker with the main institutional order in the stock moves to the bid while the market is touching support, this can provide additional confirmation that support has been reached.

*After falling in a steady downturn for the better part of the morning hours, the NDX was down 53 points, trading at 4525. A stronger than expected PPI number at 8:30 AM had spooked traders, causing them to fear that the Fed would adopt a tightening bias. The previous day's low in the NDX was 4522, so it looked like the first level of price support for tech stocks.*

*The S&P futures were trading at a consistent discount to fair value throughout the morning, trading between 7.5 and 8.5. Fair value for the day was 10, with sell programs kicking in below 8.5 and buy programs kicking in above 11.5.*

*The S&P futures suddenly moved from 7.5 above cash to 12 above cash, and the TICK steadily climbed from −500 to +300.*

*A market maker in MSFT was short 50,000 shares and noticed that the S&P futures were in a rally mode, trading at a premium to fair value for the first time since the morning sell-off. The market maker also recognized that the NDX had halted at an area of support, producing the first intraday 15-minute white candle. At this point, MSFT reached 90 or 1/4 point above the previous day's low, which served as support.*

*Taking these factors into consideration the market maker bought 100,000 shares of MSFT at 90, covering a 50,000-share short position and going long 50,000. It turned out that 90 was the low point in MSFT for the day.*

Establishing a position at support and resistance levels is different from trading around one, or from taking profits off the table. The difference is in the risk–reward ratio: If you are buying stock at prices you think could be support in order to cover or trade around a short position, the very worst that can happen is that you cut part of your profits short. On the other hand, when you initiate a long or short position at prices that you think could be support or resistance, you risk losing your own money, not just the market's. The market maker who bought the 100,000 shares of MSFT used support to cover a short and to go long. The market maker had a positive P&L from a successful short, and so had the psychological advantage of trading with the market's money, not the market maker's own money. The market maker also received price confirmation that the support level had held. The NDX and MSFT had rallied off their low points of the day.

When you initiate a position by buying low or shorting high without price confirmation, your psychological edge diminishes. The correct way to use support and resistance to initiate a position is to wait patiently for prices to break through these levels, and then establish a position in the direction of the momentum and trend. Remember that, as a day trader, your goal should be to trade stocks that are moving in your direction, not against you. Refrain from bottom or top fishing by trying to cherry pick support and resistance prices.

Support and resistance levels provide a trader who has a position with a target price for taking some profits off the table. Once you have established a position, immediately offer part of the position if you are long or bid for part of the position if you are short, at a price that you have identified as resistance or support. This forces you to maintain the discipline of creating realistic trading goals by scaling out of positions when your objectives have been reached. Remember that you can always reenter a position if you scaled out of it too easily.

By scaling out of a long at resistance, you are trading with the trend. If resistance breaks and prices move higher, you are in good shape because either you have a partial long position or you are flat. If you short into resistance without price confirmation, you are attempting to pick the top, disregarding the meat of the move. When significant resistance or support levels are split, stocks burst through them like a punctured dam. In this case, the risk–reward ratio is not in your favor because you stand to lose more from being short at resistance should prices continue higher than you do if prices turn lower.

The first confirmation of support or resistance should come from the price action of the sector you have an interest in. If you are considering covering a short in a hardware stock such as DELL Computer at support, first look to see what the hardware index is doing on an intraday chart, using more than one time frame. The 8-period moving average on a 15-minute intraday chart works well as a short-term trend-following tool (see Chapter 6). If the HWI index moves above its 8-period moving average for the first time during the session, then the short-term market sentiment has changed. If the HWI sector is net down on the day, and the 15-minute candlestick chart moves above the 8-period moving average, use that as a signal to cover part or all of your short position, but not to go long. If the HWI sector is net positive on the day, and the 15-minute candlestick chart moves below the 8-period moving average, use that as a signal to sell part or all of your long position, but not to go short.

The best way to identify levels of support and resistance is through a multiple time frame approach (see Chapters 5 and 6), integrating daily and intraday charts. For example, you might use a 5-minute, a 15-minute, a 60-minute, and a daily chart to provide a manifold evaluation of consequential price levels. All four of these charts can be viewed on one charting page that is divided into four segments.

Support and resistance levels often become self-fulfilling prophecies. They exist because buyers and sellers remember where they bought or sold something, or where prices stopped before. Many feel regret or pain for having missed the prior move and are waiting for the opportunity to get back on board if they have another chance to do so.

Traders who bought stocks at the highs, which is resistance, feel anguish for having top-ticked the move. They are upset because they were wrong, and they would do anything to get out flat. They stubbornly hold onto their long positions, hoping to unload them if prices rally back.

Those who shorted at resistance just before the stock sold off—nailed the trade—wish that they had shorted more. If prices rise back to the original area, they tend to use that as an opportunity to lay off more stock. Whether it's from being right or wrong at price levels that hold and reverse those areas become emotional firestorms where traders look to make amends for past action.

Support and resistance regions come in many shapes and sizes. Some areas are significant, established by heavy volume and massive congestion over an extended period; other areas are shorter-term and less substantial in nature. Massive support might come from prices that have held a level for years or have never traded through certain prices before, such as a stock's all-time high or low. Shorter-term support comes from intraday price action with a time frame as small as 15 minutes.

If prices linger and churn within tight density zones for an extended period, then those territories become more meaningful support or resistance areas. An intraday example of an extended congestion zone is the NDX on Thursday, August 19, 1999. The NDX quietly traded within a very narrow range for most of the day after having swung around in the morning. As the day wore on, the odds increased that when prices broke this congestion area, they were going to move big.

This was especially true because the NDX whipped around wildly on the previous day's close and on the morning's opening. During the last half-hour of trading, after a couple of short-lived head fakes, the NDX broke beneath its range with a vengeance, selling off hard into the close and throughout the following morning. Traders who shorted into this move were rewarded generously for their patience and discipline.

Longer-term charts display the best support or resistance, while shorter-term charts provide less significant levels of support or resistance. The best way to get a broad view of the playing field is to examine multiple time frame charts, starting with the weekly, the daily, and intraday—on at least two multiple time frames. If you receive confirmation from all time frames, the probabilities for a successful trade increase dramatically.

The weekly chart should be the first time frame you look at. It will provide you with a wider snapshot of what the longer-term underlying force is behind the current move. If you like a stock from the long side and the daily chart is confirming your opinion, but the weekly chart is telling you that the trend is down, be cautious: Look for a different trade, or take a smaller position than you normally would and use tighter stops.

If the daily chart is a screaming buy, but the intraday chart says that the market is running into some resistance and should sell off, be cautious: Take some profits off the table, or wait until the intraday price action confirms the broader daily picture to the upside. On an intraday basis, look for confirmation from at least two various time periods. The 60-minute and the 15-minute work very well together.

Many day traders are accustomed to monitoring short intraday time periods, such as a tick chart or a 2-minute or 5-minute time period. The problem with shorter intraday charts is that they are prone to noise and head fakes. The most effective way to integrate shorter intraday time periods is to combine them with the longer time periods. For example, integrate the 2-minute, the 5-minute, the 15-minute, and the 60-minute on one page with four windows. Most charting packages allow traders to watch at least four charts on one page. As the standard page, you should have a daily, an hourly, a 15-minute, and a 5-minute chart. Your weekly chart could be on a separate page, because its intraday movements will not usually affect the weekly trend to the point that you need to monitor it constantly throughout the day.

The right way to use support levels is:

1.  Use support as a stop-loss point on long positions; sell a long position after support has broken, not before.

2.  Go short after support has been broken, using the support level that was broken as resistance for your new stop-loss point on the short.

3.  Take profits if you have a short position headed into support, while keeping part of your position.

4.  Wait for upward price confirmation that support has held, then go long with half your normal size, using support as a stop-loss point.

The wrong way to use support is to bottom fish by going long when prices have fallen to support, and hoping that the level holds, without first receiving price confirmation that the support region is valid.

The right way to use resistance levels is:

1.  Use resistance as a stop-loss point on short positions; cover a short position after resistance has broken, not before.

2.  Go long after resistance has been broken, using the resistance level that was broken as new support for your stop-loss point on the long.

3.  Take profits if you have a long position headed into resistance, while staying long part of your position.

4.  Wait for price confirmation that resistance has held, then go
    short with half of your normal size, using resistance as a stop-
    loss point.

The wrong way to use resistance is to top fish by going short
when prices have risen to resistance, anticipating that the price level
will hold, without waiting for downward confirmation.

If you become familiar with spotting support and resistance levels, you will increase your profitability on different fronts. You will
refrain from initiating trades from the wrong side when these levels
are reached; you will hold back from going long at resistance or
going short at support. You will also hold onto positions longer,
instead of trading out of them for a loss when they should hold; you
will keep your long at support, and keep your short at resistance.

You will also become adept at spotting breakouts sooner, which
will provide you with an edge for going long when resistance has
been broken, and from going short when support has been broken.

# 16

# BASIC CHART
# PATTERNS

There are basic chart patterns that produce potent reversal signals that all traders should be aware of. These patterns can be used in combination with candlestick patterns, volume, and oscillators to produce buy and sell signals. They display emotional extremes that have been subdued by the opposing sentiment. These patterns are often accompanied by heavy volume, because the optimistic and pessimistic forces battling for right of way are usually defending their turf in full force. These patterns will help you to recognize and exploit a move more quickly. They will also help you to take profits sooner if you are on the wrong side of the formation.

## BREAKOUTS

Breakout patterns are continuation patterns that occur at important levels of support and resistance. Many times the resistance or support levels that the price is breaking away from are the all-time highs or all-time lows. Pinpointing breakout areas before they occur will prepare you to take advantage of the move when it happens. Knowing where breakout areas are will also warn you what side of the market you should not be on.

Breakouts occur when prices move forcefully through price resistance on above-average volume. The more significant the price resistance, the more powerful the breakout. Volume and the length of the trading range prior to a move are the two important facets to watch when determining whether a breakout is real. An ideal breakout has an opening and close above price resistance. The more often a stock tests price resistance, the more bullish that price action becomes. Stocks usually hold price resistance on the second and third tries. When prices test resistance more than three times, it is more likely that a breakout will occur.

The longer prices have been channeling in a range, the more significant the price resistance or support tends to become. A stock that has been channeling within a trading range for weeks or even months is prone to false breakouts. On the other hand, a stock that has been channeling in a tight trading range for less than five days has weaker price resistance or support, so a breakout above that range will occur more easily but might not last as long.

The market has become prone to false breakouts today because of the increase in the number of day traders who artificially move stocks through levels and then attempt to take profits, resulting in knocking the stock back down. If day traders are the ones responsible for moving a stock through a breakout zone, those same traders will be the ones looking to take profits once the momentum has waned. When a breakout above a trading range occurs on light volume, market makers have the tendency to take the other side of the breakout by selling into the short-term strength once the move has retraced off its highs.

It is important to understand what forces are behind the price action that causes a breakout. If a market maker has the main institutional order and is driving the breakout above resistance with institutional block prints, chances are that the move is legitimate. Short sellers who step in front of such a breakout tend to be squeezed easily, forced to cover at a loss and driving the price up even higher. Often before stocks break out they consolidate in a tight trading range just beneath a previous high or an important area of price resistance. When the breakout occurs, it often takes place within the first 15 minutes of trading, led by a strong broader market, a strong sector that the stock is a member of, and institutional demand. Fundamental news on the stock or sector is often the catalyst for pumping the stock through important price levels, creating breakouts.

When you are tuned in to important price resistance levels of stocks that you are following, and are prepared to act, especially if the broader market looks poised to rally, your chances for success increase dramatically. Immediately after the breakout occurs, there is usually a small pullback before the stock explodes upward. Prior resistance levels quickly become price support after the breakout. The small pullback should not fall back beneath the support zone.

The chart in Figure 16-1 pictures the NDX breaking out above resistance on October 29, 1999. This breakout occurred on strong volume; after a small breather the next day, NDX resumed its climb upward and never looked back.

Figure 16-2 pictures Amazon (AMZN) breaking out after channeling in a tight range for most of September. This breakout occurred on powerful volume. Note that the Bollinger bands (see Chapter 17) were contracted and very narrow at the time. When Bollinger bands contract into a narrow channel, they act like a spring after prices break out of that range.

Figure 16-3 shows that Oracle (ORCL) broke out above a long, narrow trading range, first in the beginning of September 1999 and again in the beginning of November 1999. Both breakouts occurred on above-average volume.

## BREAKDOWNS

Breakdowns occur when prices move forcefully below price support on above-average volume. The more significant the prior price support, the more powerful the breakdown will be. Volume and the length of the trading range prior to the move are the two important facets to watch to determine if a breakdown is real. An ideal breakdown has an opening and close beneath price support.

Breakdowns can occur on regular price moves or on gaps. The longer a stock has consolidated (traded in a narrow range on light volume) before the breakdown, the more important the lower move on heavy volume will be. Stocks tend to consolidate immediately

Figure 16-1 NDX Breaking Out Above Resistance

Figure 16-2 AMZN Breaking Out Above Resistance

175

Page Title : msft.pg

orcl 4.1.1    252Days    1998/11/16-1999/11/14    Volume 1743310u    MAV(5,5) 1392807020.00
Last= 65 1    PC=194.35%    AV=15662938
High= 66 6 (99/11/12)    Low= 21 0 (99/04/07)

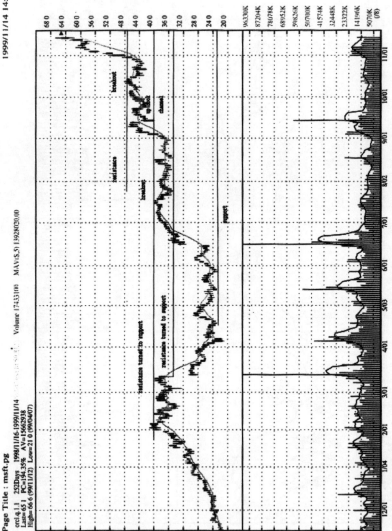

Figure 16-3 ORCL Breaking Out Above Resistance

above price support for two or three days before breaking below. The more often a stock tests price support, the more bearish that price action becomes. Stocks usually hold price support the second and third times they touch that level. After a stock tests price support more than three times, the chances for a breakdown are better.

Similar to a breakout, the best place to short a breakdown is always after the stock price has pierced through its support zone. Depending on the price of the stock, always provide yourself with an entry buffer zone. (See Chapter 11, Entry, and Chapter 12, Exit.) With a $50 stock, your buffer zone should be about 1/2 point. If this price zone is missed when you attempt to short the stock and the stock moves more than $2^1/_2$ percent beneath the breakdown zone and lingers there for a period of time before roaring back to the initial entry zone, leave it alone. It could be a rising star (the opposite of a fallen star), which means that market conditions and sentiment about the stock have changed, and you're better off forgetting about this particular trade.

The chart in Figure 16-4 shows Microsoft (MSFT) breaking down on two separate occasions. The first breakdown occurred on October 15, 1999, when prices ratcheted beneath 90, which was price support. After rallying back through that level, MSFT broke down through 90 again on November 8, on negative fundamental news.

## DOUBLE BOTTOM

The double bottom is one of the most powerful reversal formations, after which stocks and indices tend to advance formidably. They are powerful patterns because stocks or sectors have retested lows but have failed to break through on the downside, indicating that the selling pressure has subsided. At this point, shorts stop pressing and start covering—sometimes in a panic. Buyers who missed the last dip become aggressive because they're worried that they may miss the new buying opportunity. Bottom fishers also jump on board because they smell a "bargain" and want to be on board for the ride.

The first leg of the double bottom is usually accompanied by above-average volume; prices hold and then rally. After the initial rally, the prices retest the lows of the first leg of the move on lighter volume, then hold and rally from there, producing a solid double bottom foundation.

Page Title : F8.pg

Figure 16-4 MSFT Breaking Down on Two Occasions

The mass psychology after a double bottom has been formed switches from panic on the downside to exuberance on the upside, creating an emotional pendulum. Double bottoms are often accompanied by engulfing patterns, hammers, or morning stars. Double bottoms can be spotted on different time frames, especially on daily and intraday charts. They are confirmed when the second rally crosses above the peak of the first rally. Look for bullish divergence signals with oscillators to confirm double bottoms.

Figure 16-5 shows America Online (AOL) forming a double bottom. The first part of the double bottom took place on August 4, 1999. It occurred on record volume of more than 33 million shares, representing a volume capitulation (see Chapter 18) at the low of a move. It also formed a hammer on that day, which is a bullish reversal pattern. After briefly pulling back two days later, AOL rallied and then retested its low in mid to late September, forming the second part of the double bottom. The second part of the double bottom was formed on lighter volume. AOL rallied from that point on, gaining more than 70 points in two months.

Another example of a double bottom is shown in Figure 16-6, formed in the Internet Index (DOT) on a 60-minute intraday chart. The first part of this formation occurred on August 5, coinciding with a piercing and bullish engulfing reversal pattern. On August 10, the DOT retested its low and held, forming a bullish engulfing pattern. After the second part of the double bottom was formed, the DOT rallied above its 60-minute, 8-period moving average, and stayed above that moving average for the next 9 trading days. (See Chapter 5 on trend spotting.)

## DOUBLE TOP

The double top, which is the opposite of a double bottom, occurs at the top of a trend, with the first leg occurring on above-average volume. It is a powerful indication that the uptrend has stopped and that a large sell-off is likely. The second leg of a double top is another attempt by the bulls in their exuberant state to lift a stock or sector

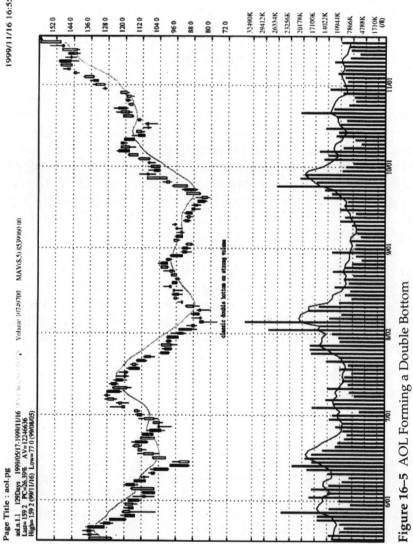

Figure 16–5 AOL Forming a Double Bottom

Page Title : F5.pg

dot.us.1.1   60min
T=566.43    +0.00   16:30   A=0.00   B=0.00
H=580.33    L=452.90   V=0   TS=0   PC=2.53%   AV=0

double bottom

Figure 16-6  A Double Bottom Formation in DOT

back to new highs. On the second try, however, the bulls are weary and have diminished willpower and less cash to buy with, so the volume is lighter and the attempt fizzles out. When the double top fails to breach the previous high, traders and investors who are long decide to take profits, and they bail out. Shorts who missed the first move wait with increased resolve to short on the second try. The selling momentum picks up, and pretty soon the mass psychology has changed from bullish optimism to bearish pessimism. Double tops are often accompanied by shooting stars, bearish engulfing patterns, or evening stars. Look for bearish divergence signals with oscillators to confirm double tops.

The chart in Figure 16-7 shows a daily picture of IBM forming a double top. The first part of the double top formed in mid-July 1999. The second part formed in the beginning of September, and was accompanied by a bearish marubozu (see Chapter 14), a candlestick reversal pattern. After the second part of the double top was formed, IBM moved beneath its 8-period moving average, and stayed below it for 95 percent of the move down.

Figure 16-8 depicts an intraday double top formed in the DOT during the end of September 1999. The page has four charting time frames—a daily, a 60-minute, a 15-minute, and a 5-minute. Looking first at the daily chart, the first part of the double top took place with a bearish engulfing pattern occurring in mid-September. The high of this move occurred at the 650 level, marking that point as short-term resistance. Four trading days later, the DOT retested the highs of this move and failed.

Looking at the 60-minute chart, you can see that the DOT was unable to close above the high that took place on September 23. The DOT formed a shooting star on the 60-minute chart during the second test, which is a short-term bearish reversal pattern. The 5-minute and the 15-minute charts both formed intraday double tops on September 29. What we have here are two intraday double tops within the context of a wider double top, with the first part occurring on September 23 and the second occurring on September 29.

When the price action broke beneath the 8-period moving average on the 15-minute chart, that was a signal to sell longs, and not to go long. Because the net price was still positive on the day, and the last price was above the opening price, traders would not want to go short yet.

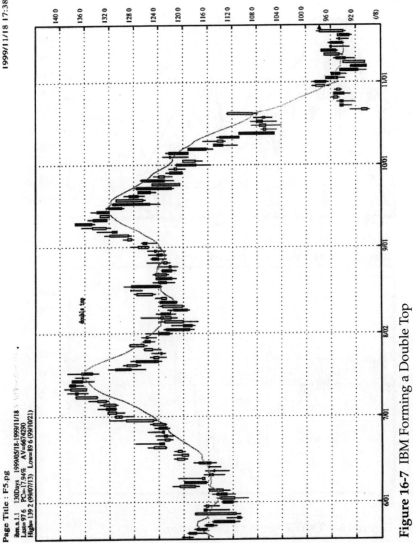

**Figure 16-7** IBM Forming a Double Top

183

**Figure 16-8** DOT Forming a Double Top

**Figure 16-8** *(Continued)*

# HEAD AND SHOULDERS TOP

A classic bearish reversal pattern, the head-and-shoulders pattern forms at the top of a trend. It is composed of a left shoulder, a head, a right shoulder, and a neckline. It is similar to a double top, except that it has a peaking formation, which juts up between the right and left shoulders on high volume. The right shoulder should be slightly lower than the left and usually occurs on lighter volume.

The best time to sell short following this pattern is after a bounce upward toward the middle of the right shoulder and then a reverse downward through the neckline. A head-and-shoulders top produces heavy resistance and a change in sentiment. Refrain from trading from the long side until price action clears above the top of the head-and-shoulders pattern. This pattern can be spotted on a weekly, daily, and intraday basis.

The chart in Figure 16-9 shows a head-and-shoulders top formed in EBAY. Remember that charting is part art and part science. Patterns do not always look picture-perfect, and they are open to interpretation. Once you have the basic concept down, you will be able to spot patterns that portray the same messages as the classic formations. This chart of EBAY is a good example of a head-and-shoulders pattern that could be interpreted as having two right shoulders.

# REVERSE HEAD-AND-SHOULDERS BOTTOM

This is a classic bullish reversal pattern formed at the bottom of a trend. It is composed of a left shoulder, a lower middle head, a slightly higher right shoulder, and a neckline. The right shoulder normally occurs on lighter volume than the left shoulder. This pattern resembles a double bottom, except that in the middle is a lower formation that occurs on high volume.

The best time to go long following a reverse head-and-shoulders bottom is after a retracement toward the middle of the right shoulder and then a bounce upward through the neckline. This pattern can be found on a daily and an intraday basis.

The chart in Figure 16-10 pictures the Dow Jones Industrial Average forming a reverse head-and-shoulders pattern. The pattern displayed in this daily chart took a month to form. Reverse head-and-shoulders patterns, like all charting patterns, vary in time and scope. They can take months to form, or they can develop in a shorter time period, such as on the intraday 5-minute chart.

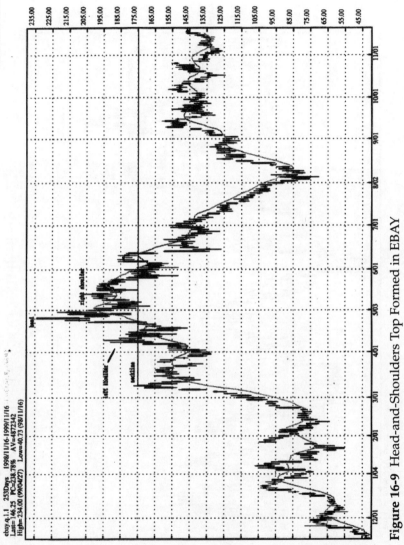

**Figure 16-9** Head-and-Shoulders Top Formed in EBAY

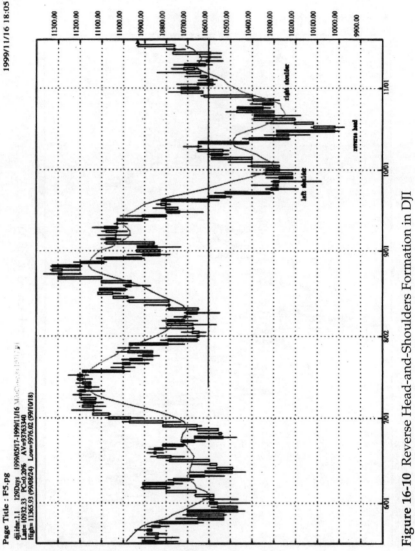

Figure 16-10 Reverse Head-and-Shoulders Formation in DJI

Chart formations that develop with price support and resistance levels leave traces and can be exploited consistently. When you become familiar with spotting these basic chart patterns, you will increase your profitability on three fronts. First, you will take profits at better price levels because you will know that there is support or resistance. Second, you will refrain from entering into new positions when the risk–reward ratio is not in your favor. Third, you will be able to take advantage of chart patterns in order to enter and exit new positions in the right direction, after you have price confirmation. This will allow you to catch trends sooner and to increase your profits.

# OSCILLATORS AND REVERSAL INDICATORS

Oscillators and trend-following indicators are valuable tools that help traders to locate trading ideas and to find additional confirmation of what they're seeing in the charts. Technical indicators are broken down into two areas: trend-following tools and oscillators. Both will help you to identify trending markets, overbought and oversold conditions, pullbacks, and turning points. You'll find that certain indicators resonate with you, while others don't. The object of using them is to help you narrow down an idea, not for confirmation alone. Price action and volume are the only factual confirmations available to a trader. Indicators will help you locate the potential for price action.

Combining charting with indicators will provide you with additional objective confirmation of what you see. Charting is part art and part science. If your charts and indicators point toward the same conclusion, you will be able to trade with more conviction.

This will give you the impetus to stick to your game plan. The best way to get the most out of indicators is to find one or two that you like, and combine them with another indicator from a different area. For example, the Relative Strength Index is a popular oscillator that is a leading indicator. It measures overbought and oversold conditions by tracking the changes in a stock's closing price. Bollinger bands are statistical tools that use a 21-day moving average and two standard deviations to produce overbought and oversold signals. You can increase your conviction by combining these two separate measurement sources to see if they confirm one another.

Oscillators are powerful tools for confirming a pullback during a trend. It is during the period of time when trends consolidate that oscillators produce potent signals for reentry onto the trend. Going long during a pullback within an uptrend is referred to as trading the up hook. The up hook is a second chance to enter a move that you might have missed earlier. If a stock is in an uptrend and the oscillator pulls back beneath its lower oversold line and then crosses above it, you have a potential signal to trade the trend from the long side. During a downtrend, if the oscillator pops up above the overbought line and then crosses beneath it, you have a potential signal to trade from the short side.

Many traders mistakenly believe that oscillators work best when stocks are caught within a trading range. They may go short with an overbought signal or go long with an oversold signal, and hope to hang on until the stock reaches the other side of the range. This technique is simply bottom or top fishing a range because it looks like prices are either low or high. This sort of trading mentality should be avoided. A trader's objective should be to buy or sell stocks that are moving in your direction, not against you.

Oscillators can be used to produce overbought and oversold signals within a range; but the danger is that sooner or later the range will be broken, and you'll be caught on the wrong side of the trade. Oscillators produce overbought and oversold signals when prices are in a trend and pull back within that trend.

Oscillators also produce potent overbought and oversold signals when they diverge from price action. Some of the strongest reversal patterns oscillators produce are with divergence signals. When prices continue to move toward new highs or new lows, and the oscillator indicators do not confirm that price action, you have price divergence.

Illustration 17-1 presents diagrams of the different types of divergence that occur between prices and the indicators.*

Be careful not to get overwhelmed by using multiple indicators. The simpler your trading rules the better. Trading is not meant to be a complicated endeavor. The best traders are successful because they have a high degree of confidence in their particular trading plans. If a trader is constantly looking at various indicators and jumping from one to the next, then it will be difficult to develop the conviction and belief necessary to win.

If you get overwhelmed by indicators, you'll increase the odds for procrastination, indecision, and overall analysis paralysis. Remember that trading is a game of action, not thought. Too much tinkering and thinking inhibits a trader. Soon after you enter into a position, you'll know whether you're right or wrong. Distractions are a trader's enemy and should be avoided at all costs. Select only a few simple indicators that you understand and believe in.

## BOLLINGER BANDS

Bollinger bands form a standard deviation channel in which the width changes with price volatility. The upper and lower bands are two standard deviations away from the 21-day moving average. This means that 95 percent of all price action would be contained within those bands. Bollinger bands can be used as momentum indicators or as overbought and oversold indicators.

When stocks are channeling with light volatility, the Bollinger band channel contracts and can be used as a momentum signal. In this situation, wait for prices to pierce the upper band to go long, or to pierce the lower band to go short. This is usually a short-term momentum play.

Bollinger bands can also be used effectively as overbought and oversold indicators. During times of increased volatility, the bands expand. During this period, when prices pierce the upper band, wait for confirmation in the form of a pullback beneath the upper band, and then go short. Place your stop-loss just above the high point of the move above the upper band.

---

*Elder, Alexander. *Trading for a Living*. Wiley, New York, 1993.

| Bullish Divergence | Bearish Divergence | Bullish Divergence | Bearish Divergence |
|---|---|---|---|
| Price | Price | Price | Price |
| Oscillator | Oscillator | Oscillator | Oscillator |
| Prices make a new low while the oscillator makes a higher bottom. | Prices make a new high wile the oscillator makes a lower top. | Prices make a new low while the oscillator makes a double bottom. | Prices make a new high while the oscillator makes a double top. |

| Bullish Divergence | Bearish Divergence |
|---|---|
| Price | Price |
| Oscillator | Oscillator |
| Prices make a double bottom and the oscillator makes a higher bottom. | Prices make a double top and the oscillator makes a lower top. |

**Illustration 17-1**   Types of Divergence that Occur Between Prices and Indicators

If prices break below the lower band, wait for a bounce above the lower band, and then go long. Place your stop just below the low price of the move beneath the band.

Candlestick patterns can be used effectively when Bollinger bands are brought into the picture. For overbought conditions, wait for the first red candle to dip beneath the upper band before you go short. For oversold conditions, wait until the first white candle appears before you go long. Reversal patterns often form above or below the Bollinger bands. These patterns provide additional confirmation that a reversal is at hand.

The right way to use Bollinger bands is:

1.  After prices cross above the expanded upper Bollinger band, wait for them to fall back beneath the upper band, then trade from the short side, using a stop-loss on the short just above the high point of the move.

2.  After prices cross below the expanded lower Bollinger band, wait for them to rise back above the lower band; then trade from the long side, using a stop-loss on the long just below the low point of the move.

3.  When Bollinger bands have contracted to a narrow range, wait for prices to break above the upper band; then trade from the long side, using a stop-loss on the long just below the upper band.

4.  When Bollinger bands have contracted to a narrow range, wait for prices to break beneath the lower band; then trade from the short side, using a stop-loss on the short just above the lower band.

The chart in Figure 16-2 (page 175) shows Amazon (AMZN) piercing its upper Bollinger band toward the end of April 1999. During this period, the Bollinger bands for AMZN were in an expanded state, representing volatile trading activity. After piercing its upper Bollinger band with a large white candle, AMZN formed a spinning top followed by a dark cloud cover (see Chapter 14), a bearish candlestick reversal pattern. Afterward AMZN pulled back beneath its upper Bollinger band, representing a sell signal and confirming the bearish candlestick reversal patterns.

On the same chart, in late September 1999, AMZN channeled in a tight range for almost a month, creating contracted Bollinger bands in the form of a bottleneck. When Bollinger bands are contracted like this, they produce excellent signals for getting long volatility, or for trading a breakout. Option traders can use Bollinger bands to buy contracts that will increase in value with volatility when the bands are contracted, or to sell options that will increase in value when volatility decreases when the bands are expanded.

Figure 17-1 shows an example of Bollinger bands working well as an overbought and oversold indicator in Cost Plus Inc. (CPWM), used in conjunction with candlestick charting reversal patterns. At the end of October, CPWM broke above the upper Bollinger band and formed a shooting star reversal pattern. The next day CPWM formed a bearish engulfing pattern, falling beneath the upper Bollinger band. This confirmed the shooting star reversal pattern above the upper Bollinger band and created a sell signal. After CPWM sold off, it reached its low toward the beginning of November, beneath the lower Bollinger band, forming a hammer followed by a bullish engulfing pattern and a morning star pattern. The day after the hammer was formed, the large white candle produced a buy signal when it crossed above 30¾, which was above the lower Bollinger band and above the high point of the hammer formed the day before.

## MOVING AVERAGE CONVERGENCE-DIVERGENCE (MACD)

This leading trend-following indicator consists of three exponential moving averages that give buy or sell signals when they cross. The MACD consists of a solid line and a dashed line. The solid line is the MACD line and the dashed line is the signal line. When the fast MACD line crosses above or below the slower signal line, then a buy or sell signal kicks in.

The MACD line is the difference between two exponential moving averages (EMAs). The standard moving averages used are the 26-day EMA and the 12-day EMA. The difference between these two averages produces the fast line. To calculate the slow line or signal line, use the 9-day EMA of the fast line. The advantage of using the MACD is that it will provide a bullish or bearish consensus with less choppiness than plain moving averages do.

The right way to use MACD is:

1.  Trade from the long side when the fast line crosses above the slow line, and when it stays above the slow line.

2.  Trade from the short side when the fast line crosses beneath the slow line, and when it stays beneath the slow line.

Figure 17-1  Bollinger Bands in CPWM

# MACD HISTOGRAM

Subtracting the slow line (signal line) from the fast line (MACD line) creates the MACD histogram. Plot the difference in the form of histogram bars. When the fast line is above the slow line, the histogram bar is plotted above the zero line. When the fast line is beneath the slow line, the bar is beneath the zero line. The slope of the histogram depends on the difference between the fast line and the slow line. Stronger bull action will cause the fast line to be farther above the slow line; thus the histogram will have longer lines above zero. The same holds true to the downside when the bears take control.

The right way to use the MACD histogram is:

1.  Trade in the direction of the slope of the histogram. If the slope is positive, trade from the long side; if it is negative, trade from the short side.

2.  Sell longs or trade from the short side when the histogram is above the zero line and the slope heads downward. This indicates that the bulls have lost steam and a reversal is in the making.

3.  Cover shorts or trade from the long side when the histogram is below zero and the slope turns upward. This indicates that the bears are out of gas and the bulls are taking back the reins.

4.  Go long with bullish divergence between lower prices and a higher histogram.

5.  Go short with bearish divergence between higher prices and a lower histogram.

Figure 17-2 shows a chart of Dell Computer (DELL) with MACD lines superimposed on top of the chart, and with an MACD histogram displayed beneath the chart. The chart also has an 8-period moving average. Toward the end of July and the beginning of August, DELL formed bullish divergence with the MACD histogram. On the second higher bottom of the MACD histogram, DELL also formed a hammer followed by a bullish engulfing pattern. During this period, the fast line on the MACD crossed above the slow line.

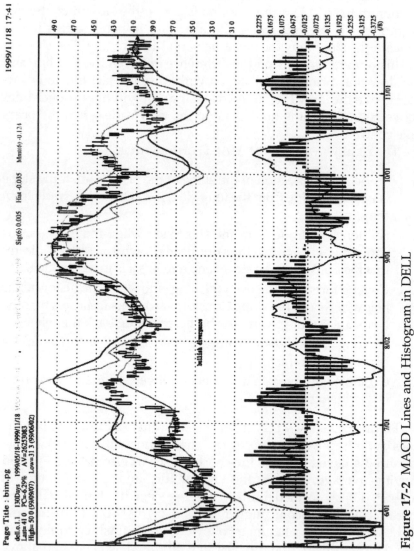

Page Title : bim.pg

dell.o.1.1    130Days   1999/05/18-1999/11/18   Wav...    Sig(6) 0.005    Hist -0.035    Mmt(6) -0.124
Lam=41 0   PC=-6.29%    AV=26253083
High= 50 0 (9909/07)   Low=31 3 (99/06/02)

bullish divergence

Figure 17-2  MACD Lines and Histogram in DELL

198

## STOCHASTICS

Stochastics trace the correlation between the closing price and the recent price range. They track the power of the bulls or bears, represented by their ability to close a stock near the extreme end of the high-low range. If the bulls are strong, they will be able to close prices at or close to the highs. If the bears are strong, they will force prices lower and will be able to close them at or near the low end of the range.

If stochastics rise and then turn down, it shows that the bulls attacked but had to retreat due to a stronger force, so a sell signal lights up. When stochastics turn upward after prices were beaten down, it shows that the bears are now the ones running for cover, and produces a buy signal.

There are two types of stochastics that traders can follow: the fast stochastic, which is comprised of the %K and the %D lines; and the slow stochastic, which is a smoothed function of the fast stochastic. Stochastics are plotted between 0 and 100, with reference lines usually drawn at the 30 and 70 percent levels to mark overbought and oversold conditions.

Five days is the default in most charting packages for plotting %K. The fast line (%K) is calculated by taking today's close and subtracting it from the low price for the 5-day period. Let's say that today's close is 50, and the low price for the 5-day period was 45; the result is 5. Divide that number by the high price for the 5-day period subtracted by the low price for the 5-day period. If the high price for the 5-day period is 55 and the low price is 45, the result is 10; 5 divided by 10 is .5. Multiply the result by 100. (.5 × 100 = 50) The current day's level for the fast line (%K) is 50. The slow line (%D) is calculated by smoothing the fast (%K) line. Taking the 3-day sum of the %K equation and multiplying that number by 100 will smooth the %K.

The fast stochastic calls market turns faster than the slow stochastic, but also produces more false signals due to noise and interference. The slow stochastic eliminates the hullabaloo of the market, removing the head fakes associated with the fast stochastic. The slow stochastic is calculated by taking the slow line (%D) of the fast stochastic and making it the fast line (%K) of the slow stochastic.

The right way to use stochastics for bullish signals is:

1. If prices make a new low, but the stochastics do not confirm that low by making a higher bottom, cover shorts or go long. This indicates bullish price divergence.

2. If prices are in an uptrend and the stochastic lines move below the oversold 30 line, and then cross above the 30 line, cover shorts or go long. This indicates a pullback within the context of an uptrend and presents the opportunity to reenter the uptrend from the long side.

The right way to use stochastics for bearish signals is:

1. If prices make a new high, but the stochastics do not confirm that high by making a lower top, then sell long or go short. This indicates bearish price divergence.

2. If prices are in a downtrend and the stochastic lines move above the overbought 70 line, and then cross below the 70 line, sell longs or go short. This indicates a bounce within the context of a downtrend, and offers an opportunity to reenter the downtrend from the short side.

The chart in Figure 17-3 is a weekly picture of Adobe Systems (ADBE) with stochastic lines. In the middle of February, the fast line crossed above the slow line when the stochastics were in an oversold state, trading beneath the 30 line. After the fast line crossed above the slow line, both lines moved above the lower reference line. ADBE formed a bullish engulfing pattern and moved above the weekly 8-period moving average.

ADBE also formed weekly bullish divergence with the stochastic lines. The first bottom in the stochastic lines occurred on June 12, and the second one occurred in the beginning of August, when prices made a lower bottom but the stochastic lines made an equal bottom to the June 12th low.

## RELATIVE STRENGTH INDEX (RSI)

The RSI is a leading indicator that measures the overbought and oversold condition of a stock by tracking the changes in its closing price. RSI is plotted between 0 and 100, with 30 as the default oversold line and 70 as the default overbought line. When the RSI line dips beneath 30 and then crosses back up above it, that represents

adbe.q.1.1  106 Weeks  1997/11/21-1999/11/22  全始末値方式  Stoch(S)  %5.0±62.5±0±5  D(3) 91.44%
Last=76 1  PC=210.71%  AV=10137066
High=79 0 (99/11/19)  Low=11 7 (98/09/04)

bullish divergence

Figure 17-3  Stochastics on an ADBE Chart

an oversold condition that is about to bounce. When it extends above the overbought 70 line and then crosses beneath it, that marks an overbought condition that is about to sell off.

When calculating the RSI, use the formula:

RSI = 100 – 100 / 1 + RS

where RS equals the average of net up closing changes for a specific number of days, divided by the average of net down closing changes for the same number of days. The common default number of days used is 7.

The right way to use the RSI for bullish signals is:

1.  If prices make a new low, but the RSI does not confirm that low and instead makes a higher bottom, cover shorts or go long. This indicates bullish price divergence.

2.  If prices are in an uptrend and the RSI line moves below the oversold 30 line, and then crosses back above the 30 line, cover shorts or go long. This indicates a pullback within an uptrend, and presents the opportunity to reenter the uptrend from the long side.

The right way to use the RSI for bearish signals is:

1.  If prices make a new high, but the RSI does not confirm that high and instead makes a lower top, then sell long or go short. This indicates bearish price divergence.

2.  If prices are in a downtrend and the RSI line moves above the overbought 70 line, and then crosses back below the 70 line, sell longs or go short. This indicates a bounce within a downtrend, and offers an opportunity to reenter the downtrend from the short side.

The chart in Figure 17-4 shows that EBAY formed a bullish engulfing pattern in the beginning of August with the RSI line crossing above the oversold 30 line for the first time since mid-June. This took place with strong volume and a move above the daily 8-period moving average.

## MOMENTUM

Momentum can be defined as a speedometer for price change. The speedometer gauge of momentum measures the trend accelera-

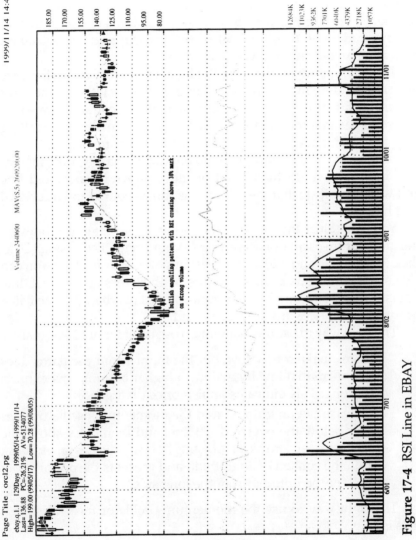

1999/11/14 14:41

Volume:2440600    MAV(S,5) 7695760.00

ebay.q.1.1  129Days  1999/05/14-1999/1/14
Last= 136.88  PC=-26.21%  AV=5134077
High= 199.00 (99/05/17)  Low=70.28 (99/08/05)

bullish engulfing pattern with RSI crossing above 30% mark
on strong volume

**Figure 17-4  RSI Line in EBAY**

203

tion—the rate and quantity of change—not the actual value. Momentum is measured as the difference between the closing price today and the closing price X number of days ago; 7 is usually the default value for X. When the momentum of price has run its course, it indicates that a stock or sector has reached its overbought or oversold level. During this period of time, oscillators are useful in cautioning traders as to a reversal of price at support or resistance, indicating an oncoming reversal in trend.

The momentum oscillator will rally when price changes increase at an accelerating rate from X number of days ago. If the momentum indicator flattens out as prices continue to rise, it could indicate that the trend has matured and prices will reverse. If prices were falling at an escalating pace, then the momentum indicator would be in a downtrend. If prices continue to fall but not as sharply, the momentum indicator would flatten out or move above the oversold line and would indicate that the sell-off has run its course and a reversal is at hand.

You can adjust the overbought and oversold reference lines on the momentum oscillator according to your preference. Using –20 as the oversold line and +20 as the overbought line is effective. You can also use the 0 line as a crossover line, with a cross above the 0 line bullish when prices are in an uptrend, and a cross beneath the 0 line bearish when prices are in a downtrend.

The right way to use the momentum oscillator for bullish signals is:

1.    If prices make a new low, but the momentum oscillator does not confirm that low by making a higher bottom, cover shorts or go long. This indicates bullish price divergence.

2.    If prices are in an uptrend and the momentum oscillator lines moves below the oversold -20 line, and then cross above the -20 line, cover shorts or go long. This indicates a pullback within the context of an uptrend and presents the opportunity to reenter the uptrend from the long side.

The right way to use the momentum oscillator for bearish signals is:

1.    If prices make a new high, but the momentum oscillator does not confirm that high by making a lower top, then sell long or go short. This indicates bearish price divergence.

1999/11/18 17:43

yhoo.1.1    130Days    1999/05/18-1999/11/18
Last=113.7    PC=34.20%    AV=8675513
High= 215.4 (99/11/18)    Low=110.0 (99/08/05)

Figure 17-5 Momentum Oscillator in YHOO

205

2.  If prices are in a downtrend and the momentum oscillator lines move above the overbought 20 line, and then cross below the 20 line, sell longs or go short. This indicates a bounce within the context of a downtrend, and offers an opportunity to reenter the downtrend from the short side.

In the daily Yahoo (YHOO) chart in Figure 17-5, the momentum oscillator formed a double top above the overbought 20 line in late June and then crossed beneath the 20 line, with prices crossing below the 8-period moving average. Then, in early August, the momentum oscillator formed bullish price divergence in conjunction with a bullish engulfing pattern before moving above the 8-period moving average. When the price action moved above the 8-period moving average and the momentum oscillator crossed above the 0 reference line, that was a buy signal.

Oscillators can be used as a supplement to charting to help you uncover overbought and oversold conditions. They work most effectively to uncover oversold pullbacks within the context of uptrends, or overbought bounces within the context of downtrends. Oscillators are also excellent tools for spotting bullish or bearish divergence. Divergence occurs between the price of the stock and the reading of the oscillator. The most popular oscillators are leading indicators that will give you the first clue that a stock or sector is ripe to enter or exit. When using oscillators to enter a position, abide by your overall trading plan, utilizing price confirmation and stop-loss areas.

P A R T

VI

# THE PULSE OF
# THE MARKET

C  H  A  P  T  E  R

# VOLUME

Volume is the second dimension of technical analysis. It indicates the active interest in a stock at any given time. If charts represent a map of the territory you are planning to embark upon, then volume measures the depth of that territory. Just as it is impossible for elephants to tread in the jungle without leaving footprints, it is also hard for institutional accounts to enter or exit positions without leaving traces through volume.

Volume provides traders with clues. Significant levels of support and resistance are often marked by high volume. High volume represents intense emotional and monetary interest. This conviction in the form of volume creates memories for future reference points. For example, if a stock trades to its all-time high on heavy volume and then sells off, there will be winners and losers. The winners are the ones who sold a long position, or shorted close to the top. The losers are the ones who went long, covered their short, or didn't sell close to the top. If and when the stock rallies back up toward its all-time high, the losers will be waiting with a vengeance for another opportunity to sell. When significant volume reference points are retested, emotions resurface and the buyers or sellers come back, attempting to amend past actions.

Volume spikes are often the result of numerous buyers or sellers reacting to some significant piece of fundamental news. Volume tends to attract volume. Large holders of stocks do not want to miss the opportunity to scale around a position if the stock is in play and is trading actively. The largest institutions are usually active in their largest positions most of the time, either adding to them, scaling them back, selling them, or just day trading them for short-term profits. When stocks move on volume that is above the 20-day moving average, price action and chart patterns have increased validity.

## BLOCK PRINTS

A block print is defined as a trade of 10,000 shares or more. Depending on the average daily volume, block prints of at least 25,000 shares represent meaningful institutional interest that could dictate a stock's movement in the short term. Volume of 25,000 shares is a significant number, because if there is a large order, the institution with that order will be able to buy or sell at least 25,000 shares—or more—from an institutional market maker, in order to work the rest of the order.

Block prints should be monitored closely throughout the day, because they can easily tip the hand of a large buyer or seller, alerting traders to market-moving institutional interest. As a general rule, block prints that go up on the offering side indicate buy interest, and block prints that go up on the bid side indicate sell interest. Block prints that go up on both sides mean that stock was crossed between buyers and sellers. Multiple block prints on the same side of the market denote that more than one institutional buyer or seller is working through the same market maker. Multiple block prints on the same side of the market provide an excellent sign that the stock should continue to move in the same direction the prints went on the tape.

Market makers who are working two large orders simultaneously on the same side of the market will give both accounts equal prints. If an institutional account knows that there is additional buy or sell interest in a stock, the institutional trader will be more aggressive about getting the order done, because he knows that he is participating with other volume. The institutional trader is the representative from the institutional fund who gives the market-making firm the order, with instructions. At the market-making firm, there is a sales trader who is the intermediary between the market maker and the institutional trader.

Mutual funds, hedge funds, and pension funds are considered to be buy-side institutions. These funds give market makers, who facilitate institutional order flow, orders to buy or sell stock. There are market makers who specialize in institutional order flow; and there are market makers who specialize in noninstitutional order flow, or what is called retail and Internet-driven order flow. The market makers who specialize in institutional order flow put up initial risk capital in order to get the order in the door. If a stock is quoted 50—50$^1/_8$, and an institution calls an institutional market maker with 100,000 shares to buy, the market maker would normally sell that account at least 25,000 shares at 50$^1/_8$ in order to work the rest of the order. This means that the market maker is at risk on the first print, or is now short 25,000 shares. If the stock moves in his favor after this print, he will make money; if it moves against him, he will lose money. If the stock is liquid, the market maker would likely sell the institution the entire 100,000 shares at 50$^1/_8$.

Prints of less than 25,000 shares in relatively liquid stocks are not as meaningful as larger prints, because they are not generally followed up with more stock coming from the same source. If a large institution had a lot of stock to buy in a liquid name, then the market maker would put up a larger print for the institution to get the order started.

After a market maker puts up risk capital for an institution, the institution normally leaves a working order with that market maker to buy or sell more stock. In our example, if the market maker sold an institution 25,000 shares at 50$^1/_8$ to work 75,000 shares behind it, the market maker now has the objective of eliminating risk. In order to eliminate risk, the market maker wants to buy back stock for a small profit, flat, or for a small loss. Once he eliminates his risk, his objective is to trade the remaining 75,000 shares for the bid–ask spread of 1/16 or 1/8 of a point. If he buys back 12,500 shares at 50$^1/_{16}$ and 12,500 shares at 50$^1/_8$, he is now free to participate with volume at zero risk in order to trade the rest of the order for a profit.

He may do this by sitting on the 50⅛ bid and buying stock there, and then selling it to the institution at 50³/₁₆ or 50¼. This means that although he made a marginal profit or zero profit on the first 25,000 shares, he will now make 1/16th to 1/8th of a point profit on the remaining 75,000 shares.

Institutional traders who have market orders have the objective of participating with volume in order to complete their orders. This means that if volume trades outside of the market maker with the order, then the institutional trader will expect to also have part of her order completed. In our example, after the market maker sold an institution 25,000 shares at 50⅛ to work 75,000, if the volume on the stock increases by 100,000 shares or so, the institutional trader will expect to have bought more stock. Depending on the liquidity of the stock, and what kind of volume is printing (whether block prints or smaller volume), the trader will expect more volume because the market maker has had ample opportunity to cover his short and to buy more stock.

In another example, WXYZ is 40 bid and has an average daily volume of 1.5 million shares—a semiliquid name. A market maker is long 25,000 shares at 40 after buying stock from an institutional seller in order to work a larger order. The institutional trader who sold the market maker the 25,000 shares has 75,000 shares for sale behind it, and she wants to get her order completed at the market as quickly as possible. After the market maker prints the 25,000 shares at 40, the 40 bids start to fade because the block print hitting the tape on the bid spooked other players.

The market maker who is long the 25,000 at 40 has two choices: Sit and do nothing and watch the stock drop; or participate with volume by selling stock lower than the price where it was bought. When market makers want to sell stock in a semiliquid name, they often have to lead the price to a level at which other buyers might care to step in. When a market maker puts up risk in a semiliquid name, he wants to cut his loss as quickly as possible, if stock is trading lower, and if he knows he has more stock for sale behind it.

The market maker who sits and watches a stock fall if he has it for sale, without acting, runs the risk of being shut out from the additional volume that might trade. This would be negative for the market maker on two fronts: First, the market maker would lose money from a long position, which he inherited to work the order; second, the institutional trader who has more stock for sale would be angry because of not selling any more stock with the increase in volume. Because the market maker has more stock for sale at the market from the institutional seller, it would not make any sense to hold onto the initial long position without acting.

Like all successful traders, the best market makers act quickly to cut their losses without hoping for things to be different. Good market makers do not fight a losing position with hope by watching it or by adding to it. Instead they cut out the loss as quickly as possible and move on to the next trade. In the case of WXYZ, the market maker could always roll the 25,000-share long position again on a clean-up after cutting his initial loss at a lower price.

## CLEAN-UP PRINTS

Clean-up prints are large block prints that mark the end of a short-term move. They represent the end of an institutional order that caused a market to move to a certain level. Because the order is complete, it alleviates the pressure, allowing the stock to reverse course.

It takes patience and a trained eye to spot a clean-up print. They take the form of many shapes and sizes. Clean-up prints occur at the extreme end of a trading range, and occur after an institution has been applying consistent buying or selling pressure that could last minutes, hours, or even days, depending on the liquidity and size of an order. Many times market makers take the opposite side of a clean up print. Clean-up prints occur after a market maker with the large order has walked the stock up or down multiple levels with numerous block prints. For example, if there are 50,000 shares left for sale out of a total of a million shares when the order began, the market maker may go long the 50,000 shares for his own position to clean up the order.

Because the market maker has completed the order, and because the order was the reason the stock moved to the oversold or overbought level, the stock should change directions after the final print. Stocks reverse hard off a clean-up print, especially when the institutional buyer or seller was too aggressive about completing the order.

When you have identified an AX forcing a stock in one direction, and then notice a large print at the high or low end of the intermediate move followed by a sharp price reversal, chances are that is a clean-up print. The market maker will fade out of the picture after the clean-up print, sliding away from the inside market. If it was a clean-up print from an institutional seller, then the market maker will fade off the offering, not having any more stock for sale. If it was a clean-up print from an institutional buyer, then the market maker will fade off the bid as a result of no longer being a buyer.

## VOLUME CAPITULATION

Volume capitulation is a volume crescendo that occurs at the top or bottom of a trend and marks the end of that trend. It is caused by emotional exuberance that has reached an extreme, resulting in a washout of buyers or sellers. If the volume capitulation occurs at the top of a trend, the buyers are washed out, with no one left to buy. If the volume capitulation occurs at the bottom of a trend, the sellers are washed out, with no one left to sell.

Volume capitulation creates a top or bottom and a new level of significant support or resistance. The reason an eruption of volume at the high or low end of a move may signal an end to that move is that the bulk of traders who either missed the move or had a position in the wrong direction threw in the towel and ran for the hills. The financial and emotional pain was too severe for those who let their losers run too long or who missed the move for too long.

Price-volume divergence is a potent reversal indicator that often kicks in when prices retest previous volume capitulation levels. Prices that were created on a volume climax are usually retested. When prices retest previous tops on lighter volume, an excellent opportunity arises to go short. When prices retest previous lows on lighter volume, an excellent opportunity arises to go long. Watch volume carefully with double tops and double bottoms. Always look for the second leg to be lighter than the first.

## VOLUME BREAKOUTS

Volume breakouts are price moves through significant support or resistance levels that are accompanied by above-average volume. Price breakouts that are accompanied by institutional interest in the form of block prints have significant staying power. The way to identify a valid breakout is to watch the volume that accompanies the move. Legitimate breakouts should be forged with an eye-popping increase in volume. Without institutional interest, a stock that breaks through a level can fall back quickly, because the traders who pushed it through the level are going to push it back by taking profits. If a large account is moving a stock through an important technical level, then the volume accompanying the break will spark the interest of other large players, who may also want in or out. If above-average volume accompanies an uptrend, then prices are likely to go higher. If above-average volume accompanies a downtrend, then prices should proceed lower. A descent in prices can endure longer on lower volume than an ascent in prices. Remember that stocks need buyers to rise, but tend to fall easier on their own accord because more people are long the market than short it, so fear tends to be magnified to the downside.

## ON-BALANCE VOLUME (OBV)

On-balance volume is a volume indicator created by Joseph Granville. It is a cumulative total of volume that tracks the relationship between the volume of a stock and its net change on the day. If a stock closes higher than the previous session, the volume for that day is added to a running total of OBV. If a stock closes lower than the previous session, the volume for the day is subtracted from the running total of OBV. If prices close unchanged from the previous day's session, the OBV remains static. When the trend of the OBV line confirms price action, it indicates that the trend in prices should continue. An effective way to use OBV as an indicator is when the OBV line diverges from price action.

The right way to use OBV for bullish signals is:

1. When prices make a new low but the OBV line makes a higher top, that is bullish divergence and should be used to cover shorts or initiate longs. The divergence shows that the bears are losing their selling power because the volume does not confirm the lower price action.

2. When prices are in an uptrend or make a new high and the OBV line confirms this price action, trade from the long side.

The right way to use OBV for bearish signals is:

1. When prices make a new high but the OBV line makes a lower top, that is bearish divergence and should be used to

sell longs or initiate shorts. The divergence shows that the bulls are losing their buying power because the volume does not confirm the higher price action.

2. When prices are in a downtrend or make a new low and the OBV line confirms this price action, trade from the short side.

The chart in Figure 18-1 shows the OBV line of Yahoo forming a double bottom in early August 1999, and then turning upward into a steady uptrend, confirming YHOO's price action above its 8-period moving average.

## ACCUMULATION/DISTRIBUTION

The accumulation/distribution (A/D) line, created by Larry Williams, adds a portion of the current day's volume to a bullish or bearish side in order to calculate its signal. The A/D line uses the opening price of a stock as the benchmark to calculate the winner, rather than using the previous night's close. The A/D line is calculated by subtracting the previous night's close from the current day's open, and dividing that figure by the range of the day (high minus low), then multiplying the result by the volume.

What's interesting about the A/D line is that it only attributes a portion of the day's volume to the winning side, based on the net difference between the opening and close, compared to the entire range for the day. In candlestick charting terms, the A/D line compares the body of the candle to the wick, and uses the body's percentage of the move to calculate the volume weighting.

The right way to use the A/D line for bullish signals is:

1. When prices make a new low but the A/D line makes a higher top, it indicates bullish divergence and should be used to cover shorts or initiate longs. The divergence shows that the bears are losing their selling power because the volume does not confirm the lower price action.

2. When prices are in an uptrend or make a new high and the A/D line confirms this price action, trade from the long side.

The right way to use the A/D line for bearish signals is:

1. When prices make a new high but the A/D line makes a lower top, it indicates bearish divergence and should be

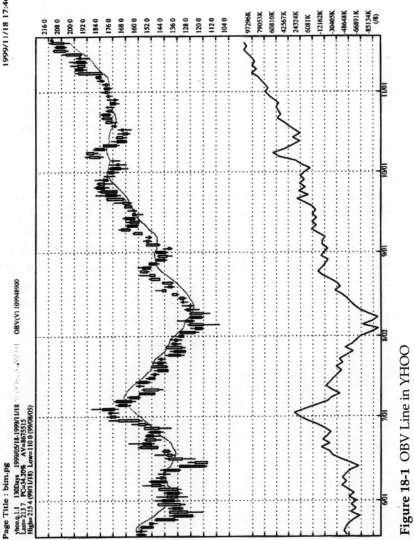

Figure 18-1 OBV Line in YHOO

used to sell longs or initiate shorts. The divergence shows that the bulls are losing their buying power because the volume does not confirm the higher price action.

2.  When prices are in a downtrend or make a new low and the A/D line confirms this price action, trade from the short side.

The chart in Figure 18-2 shows a picture of Intel Corp. (INTC) breaking above its short-term, 8-period moving average beginning in June of 1999. The A/D line formed a triple bottom during the same period and then broke above resistance toward the end of June, climbing in an uptrend and confirming INTC's positive price action.

Volume represents an integral part of a stock's price action throughout the day. By carefully tracking a stock's volume, you will acquire insight as to important support and resistance levels, and on which side the path of least resistance lies. Throughout the day, monitor the quantity and location of block prints and use that information to confirm price action. Above-average volume usually confirms a stock's price movements. Below-average volume usually indicates that price movements are inconsequential.

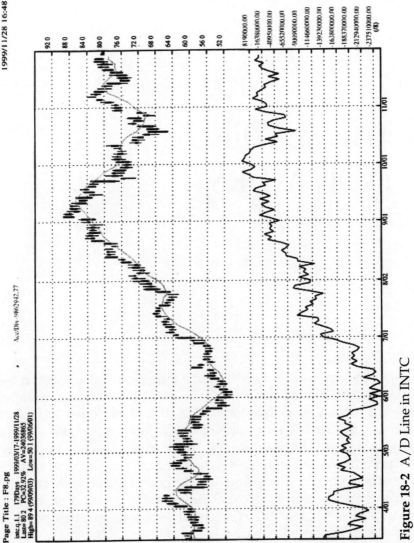

Figure 18-2 A/D Line in INTC

# THE LEADING INDICATORS

Short-term day traders need to have a quick, reliable method for tracking the intraday pulse of the market. There are many times when a widely watched index like the Dow Jones Industrial Average, the S&P 500, or the NASDAQ Composite could show a large gain or loss in one direction, when in reality some important market internals are telling a different story. When the panic reaches an extreme, it is usually a sign that the end of the move is at hand, and the market should do just the opposite. When a short-term trader knows what to look at, you will be able to use other people's panic as an opportunity to cash in.

There are a handful of market gauges that will tell you which direction the intraday market sentiment is pointing in and when it is about to change. When these internal market measures are used in conjunction with charting, you will be able to judge quickly on which side of the market your best risk–reward ratio lies. These intraday timing tools provide the first green lights for entry and exit.

## TICK

The TICK measures the net number of stocks that are upticking versus the net number of stocks that are downticking. If a stock is trading with an uptick, someone is paying for the offer to buy it. If a stock is trading with a downtick, someone is selling the stock on the bid.

The TICK reading is available for the NYSE composite index, which represents all of the stocks traded on the New York Stock Exchange. The TICK is also available for other sectors, including the Dow Jones Industrial Average, the NASDAQ 100, and the S&P 500. The NYSE TICK reading is one of the most widely used. All of them are valuable measures.

For example, if the TICK reading on the NYSE is +500, it means that 500 more stocks are being bought than are being sold. This number is meaningless as an absolute value, but it is useful as a relative number when compared to the net number of upticks or downticks preceding the measurement.

The TICK identifies overbought and oversold conditions when it diverges from broader market measures. When prices have reached their highs or lows and are about to reverse, the TICK is a leading indicator. You can plot the TICK, which will point toward that reversal, on a chart using a short-term moving average, such as the 8-period, to identify changes in market sentiment and the trend.

If the broader market has been selling off all morning with the TICK in negative territory, a jump into positive territory indicates that a short-term rally is under way. A change in sentiment displayed by a rally in the TICK can be plotted on a chart using an 8-period moving average. A move above the 8-period moving average indicates positive sentiment; a move below the average indicates negative sentiment.

Excessive enthusiasm or gloom is associated with market tops and bottoms. When the NYSE TICK reaches an extreme reading of +1,000 or –1,000, it is a sign that a rally or sell-off is reaching a capitulation point, and an overbought or oversold condition may be in place. An extreme reading indicates that frantic bulls or bears have thrown in the towel and have either sold their longs at the bottom or covered their shorts at the top in an emotional frenzy. It is usually when the pain is the greatest that most people tend to give up. After these people give up, things start to turn around because all the weak hands are washed up.

## TRIN

The Trader's Index (TRIN) is a leading indicator that is effective in measuring overbought and oversold conditions that are the result of emotional extremes. The TRIN measures the ratio of advancing stocks to declining stocks and compares it to the ratio of advancing volume to declining volume. The TRIN changes dynamically and can be tracked with the symbol TRIN on most market minders. It can also be plotted on an inverse overbought or oversold scale, with upper and lower reference lines, included with most charting packages.

The formula for the Trader's Index is:

$$\text{TRIN} = \left(\frac{\text{Advancing Issues}}{\text{Declining Issues}}\right) \left(\frac{\text{Advancing Volume}}{\text{Declining Volume}}\right)$$

The objective of the TRIN is to produce a dynamic snapshot of volume and price action to assess the market's health. The TRIN has a reading of 1 when the advancers move proportionately with advancing volume and when the decliners move proportionately with declining volume. For example, if 10 issues advance on 100,000 shares, and 5 issues decline on 50,000 shares, then the TRIN has a reading of 1. If 5 issues advance on 50,000 shares and 10 issues decline on 100,000 shares, the TRIN still has a reading of 1.

A TRIN reading below 1 is considered bullish, and a TRIN reading above 1 is considered bearish. As the TRIN widens from the neutral 1 reading, it indicates that the bulls or bears are gaining force. The TRIN declines beneath 1 when the volume of the advancers is greater in proportion to the number of stocks that are advancing. Bulls tend to become exceedingly optimistic at market highs, and the increase in volume without an increase in prices reflects this bullish sentiment. For the day trader it is important to remember that a dropping TRIN is considered bullish.

For example, if advancers are outpacing decliners by 3 to 2, and if advancing volume is outpacing declining volume by 3 to 1—a higher proportion—then the TRIN will have a bullish reading of .50. In this case, the price action is not keeping pace with the strong volume. A low TRIN can produce an overbought signal on an inverted scale. It produces a sell signal when it crosses below its upper reference line.

The TRIN rises above 1 when the declining volume is greater in proportion to the decliners. Excessive pessimism is reflected at market lows, when the bears want out and are selling stock without a correlated number of issues declining. If decliners are beating advancers by 3 to 2 and declining volume is leading advancing volume by 3 to 1, the TRIN has a bearish reading of 2. A high TRIN can produce an oversold signal on an inverted scale. It produces a buy signal when it crosses above its lower reference line.

The right way to use the TRIN for bullish signals is:

1.   When the TRIN crosses above its lower oversold reference line, it indicates that the bears have lost power, and a bullish reversal could be at hand.

2.   When prices make a new low but the TRIN makes a higher low, it represents bullish price divergence.

3.   A falling TRIN is considered bullish.

The right way to use the TRIN for bearish signals is:

1.   When the TRIN crosses below its upper overbought reference line, it means that the bulls have lost power, and a bearish reversal could be at hand.

2.   When prices make a new high but the TRIN makes a lower high, it represents bearish price divergence.

3.   A rising TRIN is considered bearish.

## FAIR VALUE

The fair value spread is monitored by subtracting the S&P cash from the S&P futures. For example, if the S&P futures were trading at 1,500 and the S&P cash was trading at 1,490, the spread would be +10. If fair value is calculated for the day to be 10, with the upper bound at 11 and the lower bound at 9, buy programs will kick in when the futures are trading at more than 11 points above cash. Sell programs will kick in when the futures are trading at less than 9 points above cash.

If the S&P futures have been trading at a consistent discount to fair value throughout the morning, and then suddenly they trade at a consistent premium, chances are that a short-term bottom has been reached and a rally is under way. The validity of this change in sentiment would be reinforced if it occurred at a support level.

If the S&P futures are trading at 1,500 and the S&P cash is trading at 1,488, the spread is +12, one point above the upper bound, so the market is in a short-term rally mode. (See Table 19-1.) If the S&P futures are trading at 1,496 and the S&P cash is trading at 1,488, the spread is +8, one point below the lower bound, so the market is in a short-term sell mode.(See Table 19-2.) Most software programs allow traders to monitor the fair value spread dynamically with a symbol.

Certain trading packages have the futures-cash spread built into their market minders. When the futures are trading at a premium above the upper bound, a green light signals it is time to buy. When the futures are trading at a discount to the lower bound, a red light signals it is time to sell for a short-term move.

**Table 19-1**  S&P Futures in a Buy Mode

| | |
|---|---|
| Spread (Futures – Cash) | 12 |
| S&P Futures Last | 1,500 |
| S&P Cash Last | 1,488 |
| Fair Value | 10 |
| Upper Bound | 11 |
| Lower Bound | 9 |

**Table 19-2**  S&P Futures in a Sell Mode

| | |
|---|---|
| Spread (Futures – Cash) | 8 |
| S&P Futures Last | 1,496 |
| S&P Cash Last | 1,488 |
| Fair Value | 10 |
| Upper Bound | 11 |
| Lower Bound | 9 |

Fair value interprets the relationship between the S&P futures and the S&P cash. This relationship is important, because the S&P 500 index is the main benchmark for portfolio managers and is the most widely used measure for broader market sentiment. The S&P futures is the main derivatives instrument used to put large amounts of money to work quickly and efficiently when institutions or traders want to own or hedge the S&P cash.

The S&P futures leads the S&P cash in price action, because traders go there first when they need to increase or decrease their broader market exposure. The S&P futures are popular because they are equivalent to a one-stop shopping deal for a trader wanting to buy or sell the broader market quickly and efficiently. They are extremely liquid, the cost of entry is significantly less than the underlying cash due to spreads and commissions, they can be shorted on a downtick, and there are lower margin requirements for trading them.

Because the S&P futures trade at a premium or discount to the S&P 500 cash index throughout the day, a fair value for the spread is calculated daily. The fair value determines the appropriate distance that the futures should be trading above the cash. The fair value spread is determined by applying a formula that calculates the dividend payments of the S&P 500, the short-term interest rate (using either the T-bill or the LIBOR [London Interbank Offered Rate])and time decay (the time descent until the quarterly expiration) for the futures contract.

When the premium or discount of the futures to the cash becomes overextended, buy and sell programs kick in to take advantage of the discrepancy in price. Traders attempt to sell the futures and buy the underlying cash when the futures are trading at a premium to fair value, above the upper bound. They attempt to buy the futures and sell the cash when the futures are trading at a discount to fair value, beneath the lower bound.

The spread between the S&P futures and S&P cash is the best short-term directional indicator available to day traders. When the S&P futures trade at a premium to fair value, a flurry of buy orders kicks in and the market rallies. When the S&P futures trade at a discount to fair value a flurry of sell orders kick in and the market falls. Bulls are showing a burst of optimism when the premium is high, and bears are showing extreme disenchantment when the discount is low.

As a word of caution, when the futures are trading at an excessive premium or discount to cash it becomes tough to get good executions. It will also be hard to buy stock by bidding for it, if in a buy mode or to sell stock by offering it, if in a sell mode. Trading off fair value requires a quick, aggressive market order. Depending on your speed and the liquidity of the stock, sometimes you'll get good fills and at other times you won't.

Fair value is used most effectively in conjunction with other entry criteria. Going long or short just because the spread jumps above or below the upper or lower bound is faulty trading. Because it is a leading indicator, fair value is susceptible to false moves and can jump around easily when the market is quiet, especially during lunchtime.

## THE LONG BOND AND FINANCIAL STOCKS

The long bond, or the 30-year Treasury, provides a backdrop and a pulse for the fixed income markets. The long bond net and yield are important to monitor when you are trading interest-sensitive sectors such as bank and brokerage stocks, insurance stocks, Internet stocks, and any other sectors that rely heavily on interest rates. (See Chapter 9.)

Interest-rate-sensitive sectors favor a low interest rate environment because that makes money cheaper to borrow. Because bond prices and interest rates move with an inverse relationship, as bond prices fall, yields rise; the perception is that the interest-rate-sensitive stocks will fare worse. As bond prices rise and yields fall, the perception is that interest-rate-sensitive stocks will fare better.

The banking and brokerage stocks are interest-rate-sensitive and are important elements when assessing the internal strength of the broader market. When the financial sector is performing well, the S&P 500 tends to rally. If banks and brokers are fairing poorly, then the S&P 500 has difficulty holding its ground.

The financial stocks are key indicators because they have a pulse on the financial and economic health of America. When financial stocks are doing well, the perception is that America is in good shape because more people are borrowing money, investing in stocks, and spending. When interest rates are low, money is cheaper; so the demand for loans increases, which is followed by an increase in spending. A low interest rate environment is associated with a bias on the part of the Fed toward stimulating economic growth, which bodes well for financial stocks. A strong financial sector should stimulate the S&P 500 sector, because it is comprised of America's largest companies, who borrow from the banks to spend more.

When financial stocks are performing poorly, they tend to drag down the broader market. This happens when the Fed has a tightening bias toward interest rates, usually due to inflationary fears. If interest rates are high, banks will not loan as much money because it is more expensive and demand decreases. With fewer loans being made, the spending level of the S&P 500 companies decreases and growth slows.

**Table 19-3** Banks and Brokers in Two Key Indices

*Philadelphia Bank Index (BKX)*

| Symbol | Name | Weight |
|--------|------|--------|
| C | Citigroup | 22% |
| BAC | Bank of America | 13% |
| WFC | Wells Fargo | 9% |
| CMB | Chase Manhattan | 8% |
| ONE | Bank One | 5% |

*Brokerage Index (XBD)*

| Symbol | Name | Weight |
|--------|------|--------|
| MER | Merrill Lynch | 22% |
| MWD | Morgan Stanley Dean Witter | 13% |
| GSC | Goldman Sachs | 9% |

Perception of future action by the Fed can determine the short-term price action of the financial sector. If interest rates are raised, with a neutral bias toward raising them again in the future, financial stocks could stage a relief rally. If interest rates are lowered, with a neutral bias toward lowering them again in the future, financial stocks could stage a sell-off.

There are a few key financial institutions that you can monitor intraday and that will key you in to whether a strong or weak foundation is supporting the day's price action for the broader market. Table 19-3, shown on page 227, lists some of the heaviest-weighted banks and brokers in two key indices.

Leading indicators can be used the way a lighthouse is used in a storm: They can guide you toward your goal. They allow you to keep your eye on the prize without getting distracted by the flood of incoming information that every trader is besieged with. The arsenal of leading indicators provides you with a first look at the market internals, and alerts you to the fact that a trend you are looking for is about to begin or is about to reverse. The leading indicators tell you when not to enter into a position as well as when to enter one. With a quick glance, they can provide you with the quickest measure of short-term market direction.

PART

VII

# ADVANCED TRADING TACTICS

# ADVANCED CHART PATTERNS

When scouring for day trading ideas, certain recurring chart patterns produce excellent opportunities to profit. These chart patterns work well because they provide entry points that occur within the context of a trend. When you uncover these chart patterns, you can feel confident that the risk–reward ratio leans in your favor. These patterns occur just above or below important support and resistance levels after a trend has started. They provide you with a chance to time the entry as well as an ideal place to enter your initial stop-loss.

## THE DEAD CAT BOUNCE

The dead cat bounce is a short-lived bounce that occurs when a stock has gapped down excessively—usually at least 10 percent or more—due to a piece of disenchanting fundamental news affecting the company or industry. The gap down is accompanied by heavy volume and creates a gap or window between the previous night's close and the current day's opening.

The dead cat bounce is a knee-jerk reaction that kicks in off the stock's lows and offers an opportunity to go short the stock when the bounce stops on the upside. Profit takers and amateur investors are lured into buying the short-lived bounce because they think that the low prices make it a bargain. Market makers and professional traders recognize this bounce as an opportunity to sell or short the stock.

Knowing when and how a dead cat bounce rears its head will help a trader to take advantage of it from the right side of the market. It is very easy to get sucked into bottom fishing a stock that has had a large move down in a single day. Investors smell a bargain and rush in, sometimes without regard for what they are buying. The people who buy a stock after the price has corrected sharply are usually the ones who were thinking about buying it at higher levels, before the stock fell. Now that the stock is much cheaper, they jump on board, believing they are getting a deal.

Institutional investors, however, see a different story. When a stock has had bad news, and that news is reflected in its sharply lower price, many of the big holders want to partially or completely cut back their long exposure. The mutual funds do not want losers on their books at the end of the year. They may have already realized a significant gain in the stock and see this piece of news as a reason to take profits. Stocks that are battered down in a single session tend to stay down for a long time after a dead cat bounce, depending on how negative the news was.

Stocks that make new lows on heavy volume and bounce almost always retest those lows. The holders who are long the stock and witnessed a sharp reduction in the value of their holdings regret that they did not foresee that the company had problems. These holders would be eager to have the opportunity to sell their holdings at prices close to where they were before the correction. Any bounce that approaches those levels is normally met with renewed selling interest.

The dead cat bounce provides an ideal low-risk, high-reward trading opportunity. The way to trade a dead cat bounce is not to buy it for the bounce, but rather to short it after the bounce, knowing that stocks normally continue on the downward path after bad news. It is a favorite tactic of professional traders to short the dead cat bounce, because they know that it was mainly bought by bargain hunters and shorts covering their positions.

As the dead cat bounce approaches levels closer to the previous night's close, the risk–reward ratio favors the shorts. Logically, this makes a great deal of sense. If a stock has had negative fundamental news and has moved sharply lower because of it, but then bounces to a price close to where it was before it fell, what would make it a better buy now than it was before the negative news came out? Unless the fundamental news was incorrect and refuted, it would not make much sense for the stock to be priced equal to or higher than where it was before the news came out.

A dead cat bounce begins after the stock that has gapped down has stopped making new lows. There are usually two dead cat bounces after the big move down. The first happens right away, usually on the same day as or the morning after the initial decline. This bounce reaches for the price at which the stock opened on the gap-down day. This opening price serves as resistance, and often halts the bounce dead in its tracks. After the stock bounces and halts at resistance, it reverses course and heads south again. The reversal downward after the first bounce is similar to an aftershock following an earthquake: Just when everyone thinks the worse is over, another quake hits.

The second dead cat bounce takes a little bit longer to develop, but fails nonetheless. After the sell-off following the first bounce, the stock usually forms an interim bottom. After this short-term bottom, the stock catches a second wind and attempts to rally back toward the high point of the gap-down day. This second bounce normally takes place one to three days after the initial sell-off. It is met with heavy selling from the longs who missed their first chance to sell at a better price, and from the shorts who regret not having shorted the stock on the first bounce up.

The charts in Figures 20-1 and 20-2 display a daily and an intraday picture of a dead cat bounce in EBAY. EBAY gapped down on June 14, 1999 on heavy volume after negative news over the weekend. After EBAY gapped down, the first dead cat bounce occurred in the morning during the first hour of trading. EBAY briefly rallied, as displayed in Figure 20-2 by the white intraday 60-minute candle marked 1. After this rally failed, three trading days later, on June 18, the second dead cat bounce occurred, when EBAY rallied to test the high of the gap-down day and then failed, 2 on the chart.

Figure 20-1 Dead Cat Bounce in EBAY

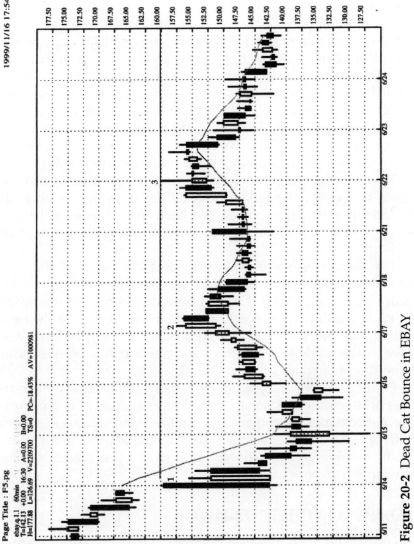

Page Title : F5.pg

1999/11/16 17:54

**Figure 20-2** Dead Cat Bounce in EBAY

Three days later, on June 22, EBAY once again attempted to rally and stopped dead in its tracks at resistance, which is the top of the gap-down day. This rally is marked 3 on the chart. After one more attempt at a rally on July 1, EBAY failed and went into a downward spiral lasting 80 points.

The opening price signal and candlestick charts (see Chapters 6 and 14) are superb trading tools for tracking and taking advantage of the dead cat bounce. The first dead cat bounce that occurs during the day of the gap down can be followed using the opening price signal. Day traders should look for the first negative opening price signal at the highs of the gap-down day after a bounce to confirm that the bounce is coming to an end. When the opening price signal is negative, you have the clearance to short the dead cat bounce.

The second dead cat bounce takes place a number of days after the initial decline. After the initial decline, stocks usually gravitate higher, as displayed on candlestick charts as short white daily bodies. After the daily white bodies have been formed, look for the first daily black candlestick body, usually at an area of resistance, then go short.

The chart in Figure 20-3 shows a daily picture of a gap down in Nike (NKE) followed by a dead cat bounce. The gap down occurred on November 3. The first dead cat bounce occurred during the same day. The second dead cat bounce occurred the next trading day, November 6. The high point of the gap-down day serves as the first area of resistance and can be used as a zone for an initial stop-loss point.

Earnings surprises represent the single largest reason why institutional investors mercilessly unload stock. Earnings is the hardcore performance benchmark that mutual fund managers watch. Managers have little tolerance for companies that disappoint. During earnings season, you will find more opportunities to pinpoint and to short dead cat bounces.

## GOING LONG THE UP-HOOK

The up-hook is a chart pattern that provides an excellent opportunity to trade from the long side during a pullback within the context of a breakout. Breakouts that occur above resistance on heavy volume usually pull back on light volume toward the initial breakout zone due to profit taking. These pullbacks usually occur during the

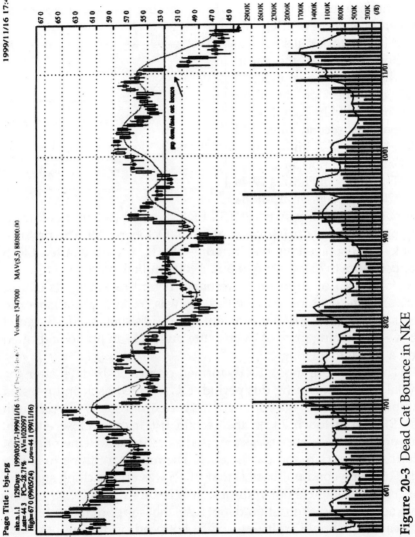

Page Title : bjs.pg

**Figure 20-3** Dead Cat Bounce in NKE

same day, and again a few days later, after the initial breakout. Both pullbacks create excellent opportunities for going long after the pullback bounces off support. The ideal area to go long an up-hook is when the hook begins to turn upward.

The base of the up-hook, which was the previous price resistance, becomes new price support.

After a stock pulls back to support for the first time, it usually halts, regains confidence, and continues on its prior upward path. Up-hook traders go long this second wave and place a stop-loss immediately beneath the support area.

Price breaks above resistance on strong volume then falls back to old resistance on lighter volume, which becomes new support. After the price falls back it regains its ascent.

The charts in Figures 20-4a and 20-4b picture an up-hook formed in Electronic Arts (ERTS). ERTS created two up-hook trading opportunities during its breakout in October 1999. The first up-hook, as displayed in the intraday charts, occurred after ERTS gapped above 75 on a breakout. ERTS pulled back to retest the breakout area of 75 in mid-afternoon, before resuming its course upward. The opening price on this day was 76. After pulling back to test support at 75, ERTS resumed its climb. As soon as ERTS traded above its opening price of 76 after the pullback, an up-hook formed and a signal to go long.

The second up-hook ERTS formed occurred six days after the initial breakout. During this period, ERTS pulled back and retested support, which was the bottom of the breakout zone at 75. Although ERTS did not touch 75 on the second try, it came close enough. Support and resistance areas are used as estimates. Remember that charting is part art and part science. The important thing to recognize on the second pullback is that ERTS was approaching support. As a day trader, it is not your objective to buy stocks that are moving against you. You should not use the support to buy ERTS; instead you should wait until ERTS bounced off the support area and started to climb higher, and then go in. This occurred on November 4, as demonstrated by the first white candle body after the pullback in Figure 20-5. Figure 20-5 is a 60-minute chart that shows why the pattern is called an up-hook. The 60-minute chart shows the first up-hook pattern occurring on November 4.

Figure 20-4a  Up-Hook in ERTS

239

Page Title : F8.pg

erts.q.1.1  130Days  1999/05/05-1999/11/05  Volume N/A  * MAV(5,5) 152174000
Last= 81 7  PC=63.34%  AV=828043
High= 84 4 (99/11/01)  Low=45 4 (99/05/07)

Figure 20-4b  Up-Hook in ERTS

Page Title : F9.pg

1999/11/04 10:51

erts.q.1.1　60min
T=78 6　+1 2　10:50　A=78 7　B=78 5
H=84 4　L=65 6　V=253500　TS=100　PC=19.09%　AV=197471

Figure 20-5 Up-Hook in ERTS

241

Oscillators can be used in conjunction with the up-hook pattern, creating confirmation that the light sell-off after the breakout was really a pullback within the context of an uptrend. With oscillators, a dip beneath the oversold line and then a move up above it produces the signal that the up-hook has been confirmed and it's time to go long.

Let's say ABCD breaks out above 50 on double the normal volume. Over the next two days, ABCD climbs to reach a high of 55. At 55 the profit takers and the short sellers start selling the stock. ABCD eventually falls back down to $50^3/4$ on relatively light volume and a weaker broader market. The $50 price, which was previous resistance, is now solid support. After closing at $50^3/4$, the next day ABCD starts to climb higher again. Up-hook traders now go long ABCD, using a stop-loss $1/4$ point beneath the support area of 50.

Trying to buy ABCD at 50 is bottom fishing. Support areas are not always clear-cut. Broader market forces could be contributing to the sell-off with a temporary disregard for the $50 price support and could force the stock down lower. Remember that, as a day trader, your objective is to make money today, not tomorrow or the next day. Always wait for the market to confirm your view through price action. This will tell you that your opinion has been acknowledged and it's time to act.

The ideal spot to buy the up-hook pattern is not when the preceding pullback is on the way down, but rather after the stock's downward momentum has stopped. When the stock bounces off support and marches higher once again, the up-hook is formed and it's time to go long.

Candlestick charts provide a clear picture for recognizing when the trend has turned in your direction after bouncing off support. This is portrayed in the color of the candlestick. A black candlestick indicates that the momentum for the day is down. A white candlestick indicates that the momentum for the day is up.

When a candlestick turns white for the first time after testing a level of support, you have price confirmation that the support area is a valid one. When the last price crosses above the opening price, it will produce the first white candlestick body since the pullback. This is your signal to go long.

There are two entry points you can use to go long the up-hook. The first entry point is when the last price crosses above the opening price, after prices bounce off support. This is the more aggressive entry point, because there is still short-term resistance emanating from the previous day's high. When a move up occurs above the opening price and above the previous day's high, you will have dual confirmation for going long.

When the last price crosses above the opening price, you receive a positive opening price signal that tells you to go long. Remember that you should monitor the opening price signal dynamically to give you intraday signals. A positive opening price signal is the first clue that your stock is on the move upward above resistance and that it is time to go long. When the opening price signal turns positive after the base has been formed, jump on the long side.

Your initial stop-loss can be placed in one of three areas: 1/4 point beneath the opening price, 1/8 point beneath the low price of the day, or 1/4 point beneath the support zone where the initial breakout took place. All three points are valid areas. You can use a scaled stop-loss approach if the stock you are trading is more volatile, using a combination of the stop-loss points.

The second entry point to use when going long the up-hook is when the stock trades above the previous session's high. By waiting for the up-hook to move above this point, you will have confirmation that short-term resistance has been cleared. You will also know that both the net price and the opening price signal are in your favor. One effective scaled-entry approach is to buy half of your position when the last price moves above the opening price, and buy the other half when the last price moves above the previous day's high.

The chart in Figure 20-6 is another example of an up-hook formed after Chrysler gapped above resistance on October 28. Chrysler pulled back to test support 9 trading days later and then resumed its climb, forming an up-hook. The large white candle body that formed after the up-hook above 53 was the signal to go long. When the last price crossed above the opening price at 53, it was a positive opening price signal and a signal to go long the stock.

The chart in Figure 20-7 is depicts an up-hook formed in the NDX on a 5-minute intraday chart. Up-hook patterns can be captured across various time periods.

## SHORTING THE REVERSE HOOK

A reverse hook is the opposite pattern of an up-hook. It occurs after a stock has broken down through support, and then bounces back to the original breakdown area. The reverse hook is formed when a stock that has sold off on heavy volume bounces back toward the

Page Title : intc.pg

c.n.1.1 129Days 1999/05/17.1999/11/16  Volume 1398340  MAViS,5),9771160.00
Last= 58 1 PC=24.66%  AV=9035313
High= 58 2 (99/11/16)  Low=40 1 (99/06/02)

Figure 20-6  Up-Hook Formed in Chrysler

**Figure 20-7** Up-Hook Formed in the NDX

old support range, which is new price resistance, on lighter volume. The new resistance area causes the stock to halt and reverse course back downward, creating a reverse hook. The bounce back toward old price support is a short-covering and bottom-fishing rally within the context of a downtrend, and it is usually short-lived.

Oscillators can help to clue you in as to when a stock has reached this overbought condition within the context of a downtrend. An oscillator that climbs above the overbought line and then turns beneath it, when a stock has recently broke through significant support on heavy volume, produces a sell signal that allows you to spot and take advantage of a reverse hook.

Breakdowns that occur on above-average volume tend to bounce back toward the initial breakdown point on lighter volume over the next two to ten days. The bounce back to the initial breakdown level is normally met with heavy selling from the longs, who missed the first opportunity to sell their positions, and the short sellers, who regret not having taken advantage of the break in price earlier.

The first clue that the stock is rolling over to produce a reverse hook can be found using candlestick charting techniques. The rally on lighter volume toward previous price support after a breakdown produces smaller white candlestick bodies. The first black candlestick body to form after the white candlestick bodies is the sign that the reverse hook is forming.

Price breaks below support on strong volume then rises back to the old support zone on lighter volume, which becomes new resistance. After the price rises it regains its descent.

After momentum has stopped at the area of resistance, wait for the last price to cross beneath the opening price, then go short. This is the first negative opening price signal since the bounce began. When you have a short position, place a stop-loss in one of three places: 1/4 point above the opening price, 1/8 point above the high of the trading day, or 1/4 point above previous price support. All three areas are good spots to choose. You can select a combination of them to set a stop-loss on a scaled basis.

For example, WXYZ broke down beneath 35 and sold off to 32 within a day. Over the next two days it managed to rally back toward the old price support of 35, to close at 34$\frac{1}{4}$. The next morning the stock opened for trading at 34¹/₂ and then sold off to 34, producing a negative opening price signal of –1/2 point. In this case, you should short WXYZ as soon as the opening price signal turns negative by 1/4 point, anywhere beneath 34¹/₄. Your first stop-loss should be 1/4 point above the opening price, or 34³/₄.

For examples of reverse hooks after gap downs see Figures 20-1, 20-2, and 20-3.

After you have identified a potential pattern, it is crucial that you enter the stock on a watch list and follow it to its completion. It will do you no good to uncover a potential pattern only to lose track of what the stock is doing a few days later because you were focused on a different situation. Always follow up on your ideas; you can learn from them whether or not they pan out.

When you become seasoned at spotting chart patterns, you will be able to act more quickly with increased confidence. Your risk will be lower while your potential for reward will be higher. Stocks that make strong moves usually fall back within two to five days on profit taking and light volume. When this sort of pullback or bounce occurs within the context of a defined trend, it produces an opportunity for prepared traders to catch the move.

# TRADING THE GAP

A gap or window is a chart pattern that is created after a stock has broken away from the previous session's close. Gaps form the best levels of support or resistance. When gaps are accompanied by strong volume, the support or resistance becomes increasingly significant. When a stock gaps higher, the low point of that gap or window becomes price support. When a stock gaps lower, the high point of that gap or window becomes resistance.

The larger the gap, the more significant the support or resistance tends to become. Aside from providing support and resistance levels, gaps also furnish continuation, breakaway, and exhaustion patterns. The continuation gap occurs in the direction of the current trend and points toward further gains in an uptrend or losses in a downtrend. The breakaway gap is a sharp breakaway from a current channel or trend and indicates a new trend in the making. Exhaustion gaps occur when a trend has run its course. They represent capitulation and a reversal of the current trend.

## BREAKAWAY GAPS

Breakaway gaps are created in response to overwhelming supply or demand for a stock triggered by fundamental news that came out overnight or early in the morning. Breakaway gaps usually occur after a stock has been range-bound for a period of time. The longer the stock has been caught in the range, the greater the significance of a breakaway gap outside that range. Breakaway gaps create a new level of support or resistance that could remain valid for an extended period of time. They can be spotted when a large gap is accompanied by a huge increase in volume and a significant piece of news that propels a stock into a new price range, creating a new trend.

The chart in Figure 21-1 shows Placer Dome Inc. (PDG) breaking above resistance at 18 with a large breakaway gap. PDG gapped up to open at $20^1/_8$, and then traded above its opening price to gain another 2 points. Once PDG traded above its opening price after the early morning pullback, you would have a signal to go long. On the day after the breakaway gap, PDG gapped up again to open above 25. This gap, however, closed quickly. The opening price signal (see Chapter 6) turned negative quickly after the opening, producing a sell signal. (See Figure 20-6 for another example of a breakaway gap.)

## CONTINUATION GAP

A continuation gap takes place during the middle of a trend and confirms that the trend is a strong one and likely to continue. A continuation gap occurs when a trend is picking up momentum and exuberance is running high. The bulls or bears, worried that they may miss the move in this stock or sector, may pile on in force. Volume increases above its average volume on the day of the continuation gap, and new highs or lows within that trend should follow. When a trend is strong, it is not uncommon for a number of

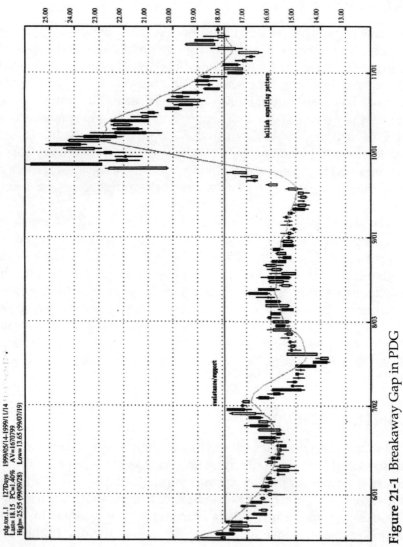

Page Title : cpwm.pg

pdg.tot.l.1    127Days    1999/05/14-1999/11/14
Last= 18.15    PC≈1.46%    AV=1670799
High= 25.95 (99/09/28)    Low=13.65 (99/07/19)

1999/11/14 15:58

Figure 21-1  Breakaway Gap in PDG

250

continuation gaps to occur within that trend. Never short into continuation gaps. (See Figure 14-16 for an example of a continuation gap.)

## EXHAUSTION GAPS

Exhaustion gaps represent the end of a move. They occur at the top of an uptrend or at the bottom of a downtrend on heavier-than-normal volume. They represent a grand finale and final exuberant push of the forces behind them. Exhaustion gaps are often the product of amateurs who are late to the party. They also occur because of panic shorts in response to an up exhaustion gap, or panic longs in response to a down exhaustion gap.

Exhaustion gaps can be spotted easily with candlestick charts, because they often take the form of island tops or bottoms, rising or falling dojis, or abandoned babies. All of these patterns are reversal patterns with gaps. Exhaustion gaps also take place at levels of support and resistance. Exhaustion gaps are often accompanied by strong moves in the stock's sector, which adds fuel to the fire.

## ARTIFICIAL GAPS

Artificial gaps occur when everything about the stock is status quo: The volume is average, the price patterns are inconsequential, and the fundamentals are the same as the day before. Many stocks have an artificial gap up or down in the morning because market makers are moving the price in conjunction with what the S&P futures are doing, and because of smaller order flow. Usually, when the S&P futures have a large gap up or down opening, they pull back or bounce to fill in the gap partially or completely. Many S&P traders like to fade this sort of gap opening, counting on an early morning pullback.

As a day trader, you can take advantage of artificial gaps by fading them like the market makers do. When fading artificial gaps, it is imperative to keep your eye on the opening price signal. Artificial gaps occur mostly with a mark up or down in the S&P futures in the morning. If the morning markup is overdone short-term, then you will receive that confirmation with the direction of your opening price signal within the first 15 minutes of trading. If a stock gaps up on an artificial markup, it will usually pull back to below the price where it opened within the first 15 minutes of trading.

You can take advantage of an artificial markup by shorting the stock when the opening price signal turns negative. You can also go long artificial markdowns by buying the stock when the opening price signal turns positive. This is a short-term trading tactic that is used to take advantage of volatility in the early morning.

Many software packages today have data displays that list the ten leading stocks that have gapped up and gapped down on the NYSE and the NASDAQ markets. The gap listings can be displayed in terms of absolute points or in percentage terms. Both are worth looking at, but the gap movement in terms of points is more effective for day traders. A stock that is low-priced could be listed as one of the highest gap openings in terms of percentage if it has gapped up small in terms of fractions. The largest gap-up and gap-down listing can be used to produce trading ideas.

## GAP-UP SHORT

When a stock gaps up in the morning more than 1 point above its previous session's close with no important news pumping it as a catalyst, it may be a shorting opportunity. There are five facets to monitor to determine whether the gap-up is real or artificial. The five facets to monitor are volume, price resistance or support, time, the opening price, and the AX.

As discussed earlier, artificial gaps have a tendency to be short-lived and are often the highs of the trading day. Gap-ups that are valid are the product of large institutional buyers. Positive fundamental news or important breakouts through technical resistance usually signify breakaway gaps that are not artificial.

If a stock gaps up and then sells off and remains beneath its opening price after the morning pullback has stabilized, it's possible that the stock has reached its high of the day. However, if a stock gaps up and pulls back during the morning pullback, but then rallies to break above its opening price, the markup was probably not artificial and the stock should make new intraday highs.

Monitoring time, especially the first half-hour of the trading day, is tricky. Specialists on the New York Stock Exchange and market makers on NASDAQ make a good part of their profits during market openings. Many stocks pull back after a gap-up within the first 15 minutes of trading. This is because, after the initial exuberance, the smaller nonprofessional orders and the panic short covers are flushed out.

Refrain from shorting a gap-up on the opening bell. Wait for at least 5 minutes, until the market flushes out the nonprofessional buy orders and the panic short covers. When this period of time has elapsed, you'll have a clearer picture of what kind of order flow has caused the initial markup. After the first 5 minutes have elapsed, wait for a negative opening price signal (see Chapter 5) to provide you with short-term confirmation that the markup was artificial and that the short-term trend is pointing downward. Remember shorting an artificial gap up is an aggressive trading tactic, employed to capture the contra-move associated with markups on the opening.

After the first 5 minutes of trading, if the opening price signal turns from a positive signal to a negative one by at least 1/4 point, this is the go-ahead to go short, using a tight stop-loss point. The reason a buffer of 1/4 point is used for confirmation of the opening price signal is that trading with the opening price signal is not an exact science.

The best spot to place your stop-loss on the short is 1/8 point above the high of the day. If you are trading a volatile stock, use two areas to place protective stops when shorting an artificial markup. The first is 1/4 point above the opening price, for half of your short position; the second stop is 1/8 point above the high of the day. Traders who want to fade gap-up openings on Internet stocks should adhere to 1/4 point above or below the opening price as the first stop-loss point. Internet stocks often swing around wildly on an opening markup, so it is prudent to provide yourself with additional leeway by picking two spots for a scaled stop-loss.

A common fault of amateurs and professionals alike is impatience when it comes to putting on a position when the market opens. Order flow is all over the place in the first minutes of the opening, and market makers are often trading defensively, negotiating to unload unwanted positions and get orders off their desks as soon as possible.

Depending on the market-making firm, each market maker might have as few as 10 or more than 100 stocks that he and an assistant are responsible for trading. During a busy opening, a market maker and his assistant have their hands full with market orders emanating from various sources, including buy-side institutions, retail brokers, agency orders, the Internet, option firms, internal orders, and other broker-dealers. This early morning order flow causes choppiness, volatility, an undefined trend, and small inefficiencies in price. Don't let these false movements lure you into believing that something is happening when it really isn't. Choose to trade when the timing is working in your favor, not against you.

It is important to watch the volume carefully, when determining if a gap is valid. If a stock has gapped up high, ask yourself what kind of volume is printing on the tape at these levels? Does the volume warrant a move in price this high? If a stock has gapped up high, institutional block prints should hit the tape to confirm that the move is real. If institutional block prints do hit the tape and the price of the stock remains above its opening price after the early morning pullback, which usually occurs within the first 15 to 30 minutes of trading, it is an excellent sign that the stock has further to go on the upside.

On the other hand, if the stock has gapped up high but then slips beneath its opening price with no large prints hitting the tape, chances are that the markup was artificial, with the institutional players on the sidelines, waiting and watching.

During a gap-up it is important to keep your eye on the AX of the previous day to see if he is accumulating stock on the bid. Depending on the liquidity of the stock, it could take institutions with large orders several days to buy all the stock they intend to. These institutions normally give the order back to the same market maker until the order is complete.

If the stock was strong on the previous day and you identified the market maker who traded most of the volume, that market maker was the AX for that day. If that same market maker is back the next morning accumulating stock on the bid after it has gapped up, it is possible that the institution has given the market maker more stock to buy.

One of the best risk–reward trades available for a day trader during a gap-up situation occurs when a large institution takes advantage of an artificial markup to sell a large chunk of stock on the opening bell to the market maker. Market makers dread this situation, but are nonetheless placed at risk this way at one point or another. This happens when a stock is marked up and an institution offers a large block of stock to the market maker within a 5-minute window before or after the market opens.

Market makers advertise themselves as large buyers or sellers pre-opening in their largest and most active stocks. They do this through the electronic medium of Autex, Bridge, and the FIX for natural customer merchandise. When a stock gaps in the morning, the market maker often has to determine which side he wants to advertise on pre-opening. The market maker's objective is to identify the side where he thinks the institutional interest will be the greatest, and to take the opposite side in order to get the order.

If the market maker thinks that the stock will be better to buy, he will advertise himself as a seller. If he thinks that the stock will be better for sale, then he will advertise himself as a buyer. This is a risky way of capturing order flow, because it forces the market maker to take the opposite side of the short-term trend. If he misprices the merchandise, or if he is wrong in his evaluation of the trend, then he will lose money quickly. When the market maker is caught on the wrong side of the market on an artificial gap, the gap closes very quickly.

*AMAT opened up 2¹/₂ at 64¹/₈ bid, with the S&P futures trading 10 handles above fair value. A market maker who trades AMAT wanted to get involved. He had buyers the day before and he believed that the stock would be better for sale, so he advertised himself as a buyer on Autex pre-opening. An institution called his firm with a large order., "Dan, I see that you're out as a large buyer of AMAT this morning. I'll sell you 250,000 shares at 64 to work 500,000 behind it."*

*The market maker is now going to be long 250,000 shares of AMAT,*
*regardless of the final price that is negotiated. The market maker coun-*
*tered with a 63⁷/₈ bid for the 250,000 shares, and the institution sold it to*
*him. After the print hit the tape at 63⁷/₈, the bids faded, and AMAT sold*
*off 1 in a hurry, to 62⁷/₈. The market maker was able to sell 100,000 shares*
*to the street along the way, but still ended up with a large loss.*

If a sizable print hits the tape after a gap-up and the stock immediately comes under selling pressure, chances are that this print was
a seller. If a large print hits the tape in a gap-up situation and the
stock runs higher, then chances are that it was a buyer—probably
the reason for the gap-up in the first place. The market maker will
support the stock if he has the buyer, or he will sell stock in a hurry
if he has the seller. Institutions do not generally chase stocks in the
direction of the gap in the early morning unless there is a fundamental reason for doing so.

## GAP-UP LONG

A stock that gaps up on the opening on positive news and heavy
volume should continue to go higher. A gap-up that is accompanied
by institutional buying provides an excellent opportunity to trade
from the long side.

The way to tell if a gap-up is real is to wait and see if the stock
trades above its opening price after the morning pullback. The
morning pullback takes place sometime within the first 15 to 30
minutes of trading. If a stock that has gapped up trades above its
opening price after the pullback, this produces a positive opening
price signal. An opening price signal that is positive by at least 1/4
point or more after the morning pullback usually bespeaks further
gains. Block prints taking place above the opening price in this case
provide excellent confirmation that the institutionals wants to own
a piece of the stock and that the gap-up is legitimate.

In a gap-up situation, when the opening price signal is positive,
after the first 15 to 30 minutes of trading, go long and use a stop-loss
at 1/8 point beneath the low of the day. If the stock is a high-priced
volatile issue, you can use two stop-losses in case it sells off. The
first should be placed 1/4 point beneath the opening price, for half

the position; the second should be placed 1/8 below the low of the day. Remember that the best way to trade volatile stocks is on a scaled basis.

In Figure 19-1, on the first day after PDG gapped up through resistance, the opening price signal was positive, as represented by the white candlestick. On the second day after the initial breakout, PDG gapped up again, but produced a negative opening price signal almost immediately on the opening and throughout the day, as represented by the long dark candlestick. The second day after the initial gap up was a gap-up short.

## GAP-DOWN LONG

Unlike the dead cat bounce, the gap-down long provides an opportunity to go long after an artificial gap-down. The artificial gap-downs usually occur with light volume, and usually when the S&P futures or the NDX 100 futures are marked down excessively. Market makers gap stocks lower in this situation due to nonprofessional order flow piling up on the sell side, usually the product of panicky longs selling their positions or eager shorts chasing a stock down on the opening.

Artificial gap-downs are not associated with negative fundamental news or a move through heavy technical support. When the S&P futures are trading at a steep discount to fair value in the morning, the broader market acts as a drag, bringing other stocks down with it. This synthetic markdown furnishes day traders with a chance to buy the opening when the opening price signal turns positive.

The timing objective in trading a gap-down from the long side is to catch the morning rally, which occurs within the first 15 to 30 minutes of trading after the market has been marked down excessively. To buy an artificial gap-down, wait at least 5 minutes for the market opening orders to pan out, then watch for the last price to cross above the opening price by at least 1/4 point. When it does, go long, using a stop-loss that is 1/8 point beneath the low of the day.

If the stock is extremely volatile, use two prices for your stop-loss. The first should be 1/4 point below the opening price, for half of your position; the second should be 1/8 of a point beneath the low price of the day, for the other half of your position.

In Figure 16-4, MSFT gapped down on November 11, opening at its lows and rallying almost 7 points from there. MSFT produced a positive opening price signal after the opening, as represented by the large white candle. This was a gap-down long opportunity.

## GAP-DOWN SHORT

A gap-down short provides an opportunity to short a stock after it has gapped down in the morning. Stocks that gap down on heavy volume and negative fundamental news usually have further to go on the downside. The gap-down short is associated with institutional selling pressure in the form of block prints, which normally demonstrate that there is more force behind it.

Gap-downs that are real occur because of negative fundamental news, a technical break beneath support, an identified AX that is sitting on the offer, or some other reason. Why a gap-down occurs is not as important as knowing how to identify whether the gap is real or artificial. As a trader, you should not concern yourself with analyzing and thinking about why stocks are moving where they are moving. Instead, you should develop quick, simple methods for identifying trends and trading signals, and then take action.

To trade a real gap-down from the short side, wait for the stock to trade beneath the opening price by at least 1/4 point after the morning bounce. When the opening price signal turns negative, go short using a stop-loss 1/8 point above the high of the day.

If the stock is a high-priced volatile mover, use two points for a stop-loss to encourage a scaled method. The first stop-loss should be placed 1/4 point above the opening price, for half of your short position; the second stop-loss should be placed 1/8 point above the high of the day, for the second half of your short position.

In Figure 17-4, EBAY gapped down on June 14, and immediately produced a negative opening price signal, as represented by the long dark candlestick body. This was a gap-down short opportunity.

Gaps provide numerous day trading opportunities. They clue a trader in to new and important support and resistance levels, to trends that have picked up strength, to price inefficiencies on the opening, and to forceful breakouts and breakdowns. Gaps that occur on important fundamental news indicate that a new trend is in the making. When used correctly, gaps provide some of the best risk–reward opportunities available to day traders. Gaps provide a discernible picture that is easy to spot on a chart. When used correctly, they will increase your profitability.

# EVENT-DRIVEN TRADES

Event-driven trades represent fundamental ideas that produce opportunities to profit. Fundamental ideas always work best when price action confirms the underlying event. At times it is confusing to interpret how fundamental news will affect a stock's price. Day traders should avoid subjective interpretations and excessive analysis. If your fundamental interpretation is valid, then others will see what you're seeing and the price of the stock will change in accordance with mass perception. When the price begins to change, you will have the confirmation you are looking for. As a day trader, you do not want to be too early or too late to the party. You want to enter the party when it is in full swing, so you can quickly enjoy the best part of it.

## THE EARNINGS RELEASE

Earnings announcements often provide pockets of volatility that traders can take advantage of. The volatility usually begins a day or two before the company announces, and ends a day or two after the report. A common error made by novice traders is to enter in an opening market order to buy a stock after a positive earnings announcement has hit the tape. If a stock is expected to beat the street earnings estimates, and more importantly the whisper number, then this positive news is usually factored into the opening price by the time the report is made public.

Professional traders and market makers buy the rumor and sell the news. Rumors of positive earnings start to circulate a few days or more before the news actually hits the tape. The pros trade the stock from the long side before the report, and sell their positions to the public after the report comes out on the tape.

After a positive earnings report, stocks tend to gap-up in the morning, because buy orders stack up on the market makers' desks from smaller nonprofessional investors and from traders who are short the stock in anticipation of a poor report, and are subsequently getting squeezed. A stock that has had a significant move up in price the day prior to an earnings report, and gaps higher still the morning after the report is out, could be forming an exhaustion gap that signals the end of the interim move. In many cases this is considered to be a sellable event, and profits can be taken if you are long or shorts can be initiated.

To short an exhaustion gap-up opening on a positive earnings report that had a strong run-up on the preceding day, wait for at least 5 minutes to elapse and then keep your eye on how the stock trades compared to its opening price. When the stock crosses beneath its opening price by at least 1/4 point, go short using stop-losses at 1/4 point above the opening price and 1/8 point above the high of the day.

If the earnings report blows away the whisper number and the stock did not move up much in price prior to the report, this could mean that the report has caught people off guard. Under these circumstances, the stock will usually move forcefully above its opening price after a gap opening. In this case, if the stock gaps up and trades above its opening price after the initial morning pullback, you should go long, and use stop-losses at 1/4 point beneath the opening price and 1/8 point beneath the low price. On gap-up earnings scenarios, always watch how the last price trades in regard to the opening price within the first half-hour or so of trading. Remember that it is during the first half-hour of trading that the morning pullback usually occurs. If a stock can trade above its opening price on a gap-up after the morning pullback, then it is a winner.

Many times the conference call following the earnings release is even more important than the number itself. Many professional traders wait for the conference call to hear what management has to say. There are numerous occasions when stocks trade higher or lower following the immediate number, only to change direction in a heartbeat after the conference call. Sometimes the conference call is available to the public and sometimes not. Either way, after the call is under way, headlines will light up the tape, explaining what is being said. The best indication as to how the call is going is how the stock is trading on Instinet during and after the call. Remember to let the market confirm your opinion through price action. Refrain from imposing your opinion of what the stock price should do after the number is released.

EBAY's earnings release in July 1999 is a prime example of the havoc, panic, and loss that can follow a convoluted earnings release. On the day prior to the earnings release, EBAY closed at $103^5/_8$. After the number was reported, the stock traded as high as 110, only to reverse course to trade below 100 within minutes following the conference call. This sort of volatility is dangerous for short term traders.

Institutions generally unload a good part of their positions when a company disappoints with earnings.

Market makers who want to get involved in a big way are willing to put up sizable risk in order to get a large order in the door. When a company disappoints, market makers begin the bidding process in the late afternoon, after the report hits the tape through early morning. The market makers put out indications in Autex, showing where they are willing to buy a large piece. Market makers base their indications on where stock is currently trading in an ECN, if it is, or where price support appears to be on a chart.

*ABCD closed at 30 the night before it announced a negative earnings surprise of 10 cents per share, when the mean estimate for street was at 15 cents per share. After being halted, the stock reopened for trading at 5:30 PM, and offers immediately appeared in an ECN at 27. The following morning, 10,000 shares traded in Instinet at $26^1/_2$, with current bids* *appearing at 26¹/₄ and offers at 26³/₄. Prior price support was 26. With the intention of capturing a buy order, a market maker put out a menu of buy indications. Because the stock had high average liquidity, the buy indications the market maker entered were: 26¹/₂ for 100,000; 26¹/₄ for 250,000; 26 for 500,000; and 25¹/₂ for 1,000,000. After seeing the indications, an institution called and sold the market maker 250,000 shares at 26¹/₄, with an order to sell 750,000 shares behind it.*

Institutions that want to unload stock may go to the market maker with the best bid, sell stock pre-opening, and then give the sell order for the rest of the day to the same market maker. The market maker may take a hit on the first risk bid, but will usually make it back and more with the remaining sell order.

## INITIAL PUBLIC OFFERINGS (IPOS)

Internet Initial Public Offerings (IPOs) have created some of the most volatile trading opportunities available today. The extraordinary price swings occur so quickly that only the most flexible and seasoned of traders should consider trading them. The spreads on IPOs are often treacherous and can cause an enormous amount of slippage. Some day traders focus mainly on trading IPOs. If you are going to be trading these new issues, make sure that you have access to the best technology, and that your executions are quick and reliable.

The main way to enter or exit these issues is to do it when you can, not when you have to. This often involves bidding for them in an ECN if you want to buy, or offering them in an ECN if you want to sell. When you do bid and buy, it means that the stock will be moving against you in the short term because someone is out there hitting the bids. If you are long an Internet IPO and it starts to gain momentum on the downside, it is not uncommon for it to take several points before you can sell your position. Traders should expect the maximum amount of slippage on IPOs, and always begin with smaller positions than normal.

Because the AX is the one with the institutional buy orders, many traders attempt to shadow the AX's movements on the bid side if they want to buy, or shadow movements on the offering side if they want to sell. (See Chapter 13.) A favorite day trading tactic is to wait for the IPO to sell off after the opening and then wait for it to stabilize with the lead underwriter on the bid. When the bids stabilize and the market begins to move higher again, many day traders try to pile on from the long side, attempting to front-run the AX by taking the offerings or bidding through an ECN.

Because the spreads are normally so wide and the pockets of volatility and momentum are so vicious, if you do go long you should immediately put out an offering in an ECN up a certain number of levels. That way, when the stock moves in your direction, you will sell it when you can, into strength.

Using a scaled approach for entry and exit is important when you are trading an Internet IPO. Rather than attempting to pick a spot and hold on for dear life, you should constantly scale into and out of your position. Maintain the discipline to immediately put out an offering once you are long. This might mean that you are putting out part of your position up 1/2 point, part of it up 2 points, part up 4 points, and so on. The last thing you want to worry about when trading Internet IPOs is the commission for entry and exit. Commissions when trading Internet IPOs can be minuscule compared to the cost of slippage and spreads.

The lead underwriter has the institutional order book coming from clients who received allocations, and so can accurately judge where the large demand lines up. These market makers are not the ones who gap the stocks up to sky-high levels before the opening. The noninstitutional market makers who specialize in Internet and retail order flow are often the ones who bid up the IPO pre-opening, so they can short the market opening orders at a high price and thus earn greater profits.

A large markup is often followed by a sharp retracement off the stock's highs. This sell-off often ends up at a lower level, where the AX, who is the lead underwriting firm, is waiting with the larger institutional buy orders.

## SECONDARY OFFERINGS

Secondary offerings occur when companies issue additional stock to the public. Companies do this because they want or need to raise additional capital. Secondary offerings increase the public float and can be perceived as a positive or negative move for the company issuing the shares. If the company is doing well, with consistent earnings growth in a positive market environment, then the secondary offering could be well received. If the company is doing well fundamentally, and moves forward with a large secondary offering in a weak market environment, investors may question why the company was in such a rush to unload its stock, and it could be taken as a negative sign. If the company has negative fundamentals in a weak market environment, a secondary offering could be a favorite for the shorts, and the stock might be in for a double whammy to the downside.

Profit takers and shorts love to take a shot at companies that have large secondary offerings on a day when the market is under a lot of pressure. In a situation of this sort, the investment bank that is leading the books on the secondary will do everything in its power to stabilize the offering at its issue price. This involves invoking what is called the green shoe option, which provides the underwriter with a predetermined quantity of shares to use in order to stabilize the stock at or below the offering price. It is up to the investment bank whether to invoke the green shoe, and how much of the green shoe to use.

In a weak market environment, sellers hit the stabilizing bid with size, using the liquidity to take advantage of what they believe to be an artificially high price. In a well-received secondary that opens in a strong market environment, buyers go long, using the spot where the secondary was priced as a stop-loss, knowing that the stabilizing bid should be there to defend the stock.

## STOCK SPLITS

Going long a stock that has announced a stock split has gained so much popularity for retail investors in the bull market that a markup the morning after the news has become a self-fulfilling prophecy. Stock splits are usually announced after the close, along with an earnings release, when a stock has been performing well. A stock split is a marketing strategy utilized by the company to create the impression that its stock is more affordable for the average individual investor. A stock split, however, does not create any additional value whatsoever.

Shorting the markup following a stock split announcement is a risky and dangerous move. Stocks are usually better to buy up until the actual day or two following the split. If you want to short a stock split, wait until after the split has occurred and then use a stop-loss 1/4 point above the opening price. If the stock is volatile, use two stop-losses: the first at 1/4 point above the opening price, and the second at 1/8 of a point above the high of the day.

The best time to trade a stock split from the long side is after the stock has pulled back following the initial markup. The most important thing to remember when trading a stock split from the long side following an announcement is to wait for the opening price signal to be positive. This will be your first clue to go long. The opening price signal may not be positive for a day or two after the announcement, if the initial markup was too extreme. The lower part of the window caused by the gap-up should serve as the first area of price support and can be used as a potential target for entry. (See gap-up long and up-hook techniques in Chapters 20 and 21.)

To trade a stock split announcement from the long side, wait for the last price to cross above the opening price by at least 1/4 point or more; then go long, using a stop-loss 1/4 point beneath the opening price. If the stock you are trading is volatile, choose two places for stop-losses. The first is 1/4 point beneath the opening price, and the second is 1/8 point beneath the low of the day.

The best time to trade a stock split from the long side is after the announcement but a day or two immediately preceding the split. At this time, the stock has normally already pulled back from the initial exuberance following the announcement, and it is ready for a second wave of buyers leading into the split, especially if the broader market is strong.

On the day of the actual split, the stock can act weak due to traders taking profits or shorting the stock. Often, the split is old news on the day it takes place. Remember that the professional traders tend to buy the rumors and sell the news. Let price action confirm your opinion, regardless of the fundamental news.

Over the long term, stocks that split normally trade higher because there already exists a strong underlying force that bid up the stock in the first place, allowing it to declare a split.

Splits occur during periods of high demand. However, if a company delivers numerous splits within a relatively short period of time, it is not necessarily positive news for the company. It can indicate that the company is splitting its price as much as it can quickly because it believes that the run-up is coming to an end. This phenomenon was witnessed during the Internet run-up preceding the sell-off of the spring and summer of 1999. Many of the split announcements took place rapidly, one after the next, and were eventually met with a strong selling force because they were perceived as indications that a top was near.

Always rely on technicals and a game plan to provide you with an assessment of what to do. It is easy to get lured into a trading situation because of news or rumors. A common mistake made by professional traders is to buy or sell a stock because the story was great, when in fact under normal circumstances they would not be in the stock to begin with because the price action and volume did not confirm the trading idea. Price action will always tell you how the public perceives a fundamental event such as a stock split. Refrain from doing the obvious and comfortable thing when trading off fundamental news. Whenever you can, trade when the technicals and fundamentals work together in harmony.

PART

# PSYCHOLOGY

C H A P T E R

# THE TRADING MIND

All the great traders attest to the impact psychology has on trading. Many believe that psychology has the greatest impact on trading decisions. Crucial psychological elements, both conscious and unconscious, affect the decision-making process for traders. Many of these mental elements and psychological profiles are ingrained from childhood, and traders are unaware of them. Prices move with emotional extremes, triggered by psychological associations with gain and loss. The first step toward successful trading is developing an awareness of the influence of psychological and emotional factors on your actions.

## NO FEAR

> *There is only one thing that makes a dream impossible to achieve—the fear of failure.*
>
> THE ALCHEMIST

Fear is perhaps the most debilitating emotion a trader can experience. Painful memories produce fear, which warps a trader's focus. When you are afraid to lose for one reason or another, you will end up focusing on loss and, by doing so, will attract precisely the opposite of what you hope to avoid.

When you operate out of the fear of being wrong, you are focusing your energies in a losing direction. Fear is the main reason traders cut their profits short and let their losses run. With winning positions, traders fear that they will lose what they have gained. Because of the fear of loss, they look for signs that indicate that the trade will reverse course, instead of looking for reasons why it should work out. They eventually find a reason that confirms their fears, so they cut profits short instead of letting them run.

The fear of loss is a double-edged sword that will convince a trader to do the wrong thing not only when you have a winning position, but also when you have a losing position. If you have a position that is going against you and is losing money, your fear of loss will cause you to look for signals that the trade will work, because you do not want to accept the fact that you are experiencing loss. Because of this fear, you will let the loss run instead of accepting it and quickly cutting it short.

The Reticular Activating System* (RAS) is a mechanism in your brain that determines what you observe and how you pay attention to it. The RAS attracts information to support what you are focusing on and alters your conscious experience. An example of the RAS in action is when you suddenly notice an item that you just purchased everywhere.

If you believe that you will win at trading and you focus on where you want to go, then the RAS will attract information that supports your focus and belief. On the other hand, if you continually harbor fear in your heart about losing money on a position, your RAS will draw pieces of information that support your fear. If you enter into a trade that is working but you are afraid to lose what you have gained, the RAS will feed off the emotional intensity of fear, and will attract you to information on why the trade might not work, encouraging you to cut your profits short.

Because your brain can only focus on a limited number of items at once, the RAS blocks out whatever it does not hold important. It

---

*Robbins, Anthony. *Awaken the Giant Within*. Fireside, New York City, 1991, p. 287.

filters out the noise it believes to be unimportant to your priorities. When you are trading stocks, innumerable tidbits of information about the market come streaming in, all of which require your interpretation. Because it is impossible for your brain to absorb all of the information coming at you at once, your RAS will determine what you will notice. When you focus on where you want to go, the RAS will block out information that is nonessential for you to achieve your objective.

Anthony Robbins describes fear as "...the anticipation that something that's going to happen soon needs to be prepared for." Regardless of whether the event ever takes place, fearful anticipation is a reality. Preparing for the anticipated event beforehand is a crucial step toward managing fear. The worst thing a trader can do is deny that fear exists. Fear delivers a message that will not disappear until it is acted on. *Action cures all fear.*

If you relinquish control to fear, then you allow it to increase its grip over your actions. If you ignore fear completely, then you are not respecting the potential value behind its message. The first step toward managing fear is to acknowledge that it exists. Be aware of its presence and determine what steps you need to take in order to diminish its power.

Fearful emotions in trading range from small quantities of worry, unease, and apprehension to extreme levels of anxiety, panic, and horror. The associations a trader has developed about what a loss means to you on a personal, professional, or financial level will dictate your various levels of fear. The very best traders are comfortable with the notion that they can lose it all. This acceptance of and detachment from loss eliminates a large part of their fear. Because their fear is managed, they have the mental freedom to focus their energies on winning.

One of the best recipes for conquering the fear of loss is to prepare for the loss beforehand with proper risk control. Detachment from loss comes with the knowledge that you can financially withstand to lose everything you have riding on your current positions. If your liquid net worth is $500,000, and you have a large percentage of that riding on a few positions without an adequate stop-loss risk profile, the fear of loss will be magnified dramatically. This holds true especially if you are trading stocks that are volatile and less liquid, with a large slippage factor.

When a day trader is trading with high levels of margin in volatile stocks, and the lion's share of his portfolio is riding on a few positions, his level of fear will be magnified because a loss under these circumstances will mean a lot. If he loses under these circumstances, it will be easy for him to get caught up in a losing cycle. Desperation may set in and he will trade emotionally and subjectively to win back what he lost. The emotions he will experience at this point are not just fear of financial ruin, but also feelings of guilt, shame, and unworthiness. Under these circumstances, his confidence and conviction will be close to zero, which just happens to be the very worst time to be trading.

When you invoke the financial discipline to trade with only a portion of your liquid net worth, and use a stop-loss risk profile of about 2 percent of your portfolio, then your fear of loss will be substantially reduced because you can afford to lose. This requires keeping expectations realistic about the amount you can expect to earn from trading, especially when you are just beginning.

If you have $500,000 in liquid assets and you earmark 20 percent or $100,000 to trading, using a $2,000 maximum stop-loss level per day, you have made a realistic preemptive strike against fear of loss. As you trade this money and if you are successful, you can reinvest your gains and use the profits to expand your base for larger trades.

Managing and reducing the fear of loss also requires a willingness to understand and accept the fact that the money you have invested in day trading is money that you may never see again. When you come to this understanding beforehand and you are willing to lose the money, then you will not be attached to or afraid of loss. When you trade in this state of mind, your chances for success increase because you are free to act objectively, without hesitation or inhibition. When you reach this state, you are levels ahead of most of the other traders. Don't be afraid of the worst-case scenario when you are trading. If you understand that failure is a natural and necessary part of the trading process, you will have increased confidence to take risks and to cut losses quickly.

## LISTEN TO THE MARKET

The current price of the market represents the belief and perception of all the traders who are participating in the market at the current time. The last price represents the emotional unanimity of the masses that are currently acting on their perceptions. The reason a stock or the market has reached a certain price level is irrelevant. Price action represents the interpretations of all the players, whether they are valid or not. If someone has inside information about a stock and acts on this information, the price action will be portrayed for all to see. Information that is acted upon cannot be hidden, because price and volume will always uncover it.

Being right and making money when you are trading can be two separate issues. Your goal as a day trader is to make money, not to be right. Prices move in the direction of the strongest energy behind them. When you listen to the force behind the prices and jump on board for the ride, your actions will not conflict with the market's opinion. For example, suppose you have done research on a company and you know that it is undervalued relative to its peers. Because of your conclusion, you buy 5,000 or 10,000 shares, only to watch it drop two points. Who was right—you or the market?

Waiting for the market to confirm your initial opinion is crucial. The market provides clear signals for the best course of action, regardless of your opinion. You must let go of any preconceptions about what the market is going to do, and instead remain focused on what the market is doing here and now. The clues and signals about what is happening are readily available to all who are willing to put aside their opinions and listen to the market instead.

To increase your ability to listen to the signals of the market objectively, you should develop a mental state of mind that Deepak Chopra calls detached awareness. Detached awareness occurs when you observe what's going on with little at stake to your ego. Detached awareness occurs when you step outside of yourself and calmly observe your actions. For the trader, this detachment means abandoning your associations about what a stock's move will mean for you emotionally, financially, and personally.

## ACCEPT RESPONSIBILITY

Taking responsibility for all your actions and all your trades at all times, regardless of the rhyme or reason, takes a great deal of maturity and can be a hard thing to do. Even if something happened that was outside your control, act as though you alone were responsible for the outcome.

You alone are in control of your mind, and therefore your actions and your results. When you accept responsibility for all your actions, you will be empowered with the ability to choose how you want things to be. You alone will be the cause and effect for your outcomes.

Time and again, traders rationalize their actions by passing the buck for something that went awry onto someone or something outside of themselves. Rationalization has a corrupting influence on a trader, because it encourages you to dodge responsibility. There will always be excuses and reasons why a trade or anything in your life did not work out the way you planned or hoped for. The strongest traders are the ones who recognize that excuses and rationalizations are folly.

As soon as you relinquish responsibility by rationalizing your actions, you lose the power to learn from your mistakes, which is the best way to learn. You can always think up reasons for holding on to a loser or adding to a losing position. Even when your reason for doing the wrong thing is sensible and learned, if you do not accept responsibility for the loss, you will not learn from it.

Rationalization forms a barrier between what you know is the right thing to do and what you hope will ultimately happen. It indicates that you are having trouble admitting that you are wrong. When you catch yourself making excuses for things that went wrong, it is a sure sign that your ego is swelling up and getting in the way of your improved future performance.

You immediately empower yourself as a trader when you accept the consequences of all your actions, regardless of how painful it might be to do so. Trade with the belief that you are the cause in your universe of trading results. Do not believe for a second that there is such a thing as an accident in trading. When you accept the principle of cause and effect, you will be empowered to take responsibility for everything that happens on your trading pad and in your life.

There will be many times when you are faced with a situation you do not want to take responsibility for, one that may not be your fault. Some common excuses in trading include faulty trading systems, slow executions, backing away, an assistant who made a mistake, misinformation, false rumors, listening to others' opinions, and fuzzy thinking. Many of these could be valid, but resist the urge to fall back on them.

When you do not accept responsibility, you relinquish the power to make things different in the future. This is a short-term fix used to alleviate discomfort, but a long-term blunder. When you accept responsibility for everything that happens in your life, you empower yourself to create the trading world you would like. By accepting responsibility for your trades, you empower yourself to consistently improve your performance in the future.

## GREED IS AN OBSTACLE

Webster's dictionary defines greed as excessive or reprehensible acquisitiveness. The problem with greed is that it feeds on itself and fosters a state of lack: the opposite of what you are trying to achieve by being greedy. When you are driven by greed, as you attain more you want more, so you have less instead.

Wanting can actually be defined as a state of lacking. When you want something badly, your brain is sending you signals of destitution. If you live in a state of wanting something, then you will attract scarcity. Whatever you focus on and attach emotional significance to expands in your life. If you are driven by greed, then you are trading in a state in which you are constantly aware of what you do not have. This is called poverty consciousness, and it will work against your goals of creating abundance in your life.

Greed indicates that your attachment to money is ironclad. It arises from the belief that you lack something because there is not enough to go around. This belief is destructive and false. The universe's natural state is one of abundance and wealth. Deep down, if you did not believe this was true, then you would not be trading with the objective of fulfilling your potential. Greed is unfulfilling because there will never be enough to satisfy what you believe you lack, so the more you get, the more you believe you need.

Greedy traders are attached to what money represents to them on a personal level. Most people go through life with the belief that money and the material objects that it secures represent the acknowledgment, approval, and validation of others. The thirst for approval is one of the strongest emotions human beings experience. These feelings are ingrained from early childhood and are dominant in the subconscious.

The quest for approval causes traders to act in all sorts of weird ways, disregarding their trading plans in the search for the stronger desire to attain approval in all forms—from their peers, their parents, their childhood teachers, themselves; the list goes on. Acknowledging the fact that you are seeking approval and recognition in a given situation is the first step toward releasing that emotion, which will provide you with freedom to trade objectively and without greed.

## CONQUER FRUSTRATION

Traders make some of the worst decisions when they are frustrated. Frustration clouds thought and destroys objectivity. Frustration is a state of insecurity or discontent stemming from unconcluded problems or needs that have not been fulfilled. This dissatisfaction can be commonplace among traders who are experiencing losses. It is very easy to become frustrated when you are trading. Hundreds of factors in trading can leave a door wide open to feelings of frustration.

Trading is one of the most intense and physically demanding occupations. With so much dependent upon technology, and with so much at stake, little mishaps can pile up to create a state of agitation and frustration. Frustration is a common emotion in trading because so much effort is put into preparing for the moment when it's time to trade. Because loss in trading is natural and common, a trader can get frustrated quickly if you experience a string of losses without experiencing any reward.

The perpetual motion of markets and prices causes discrepancies in price that will often test a trader's mettle and conviction. If you let yourself become frustrated due to a lack of immediate results, you are setting yourself up for a blurred subjective vision. When you experience frustration, realize that it is a sign for you to complement your approach to trading with increased flexibility and patience.

Your success as a trader at times hinges on your ability to conquer frustration. Frustration will always appear on your path toward greatness. Some will triumph over it, while others succumb to its pettiness. When you encounter obstacles on your trail toward achievement, remind yourself that they were placed there in order for you to overcome them, so you can learn from them and become better than you were before. Remember, little things affect little minds.

## DON'T LOOK BACK

Regret is a poisonous emotion that traders experience all too often. It can be very painful to watch a stock move forcefully in your direction after you missed the chance to get on board for one reason or another. Because of the vast number of trading opportunities in the market, it is impossible not to miss many of them.

Let go of regret and instead treat yourself kindly when trading. Do not beat yourself up for having missed an opportunity. Remember that there will be many, many more chances for winning trades. Regret is toxic because it encourages you to look back and to focus your energies on the past, when you should be using your valuable time and energy to focus on the here and now in order to uncover trading opportunities.

When you acknowledge that you are feeling regret, then you have taken the first step toward diminishing its power over you. Regret can serve a purpose when you admit that it exists, learn quickly from its message by accepting responsibility, and then pardon yourself and move on.

Rather than living in the past by regretting what could have been, resolve to live here and now, in the present. Remind yourself that if you could have taken action, you would have. Excuses have no place in trading, because in the end they never make a difference anyway. Admit to yourself that for some reason, something within you prevented you from action. Only you know what it was, and only you can fix it. By accepting responsibility without blaming yourself, you will learn from the experience and develop into a stronger trader, without regret. Growth in trading is a continuous process. There is always room to become better, so give yourself the space to breathe and to learn unencumbered by feelings of regret.

## EXUDE CONFIDENCE

The best traders are successful because they are able to maintain unshakable confidence in themselves and in their decisions. This serene self-confidence creates a positive state of mind and the will to act.

There is an old saying: "If you would be powerful, pretend to be powerful." One technique for developing confidence when you are trading is to role-play. Think of a confident role model, preferably a successful trader whom you look up to, and pretend to be that trader. Imagine that you have the power to act decisively when trading, without hesitation, letting your winners run and cutting your losses short. This will transform the way you perceive yourself and how you make your decisions.

We communicate more with our body language and tone of voice than with our words. When your body language and voice portray a confident person, then people will respond to you as if you were a confident person. Practice sitting, talking, and acting confidently in everyday life and watch your conviction and decision-making process on the trading desk improve.

Exercise also substantially boosts your confidence. When you feel positive about yourself and how you look, you are more inclined to act confidently. Exercise also has a number of other positive side effects for traders, including alleviating stress and reducing anxiety. Because trading is such a physically demanding occupation, you owe it to yourself to exercise as often as possible. Consider exercise an investment in your trading career.

Dress well when trading, because looking good will increase your self-esteem. High self-esteem will positively affect your everyday decisions and help you feel more optimistic in general.

Developing confidence in yourself and in your actions is a continuous, lifelong process. This is an area that you should devote time to every single day. As your confidence increases, you will feel better about yourself and the world around you. As you practice using a confident tone of voice and body language on a regular basis, that confidence will be readily accessible when you need to use it in your decision-making process. When you look, sound, and act confident, you yourself will believe that you are. Others also react to you as a confident person, which in turn will empower you.

## MAINTAIN PROSPERITY CONSCIOUSNESS

Deepak Chopra says that "all relationship is a reflection of your relationship with yourself." If you feel guilty or insecure about hav-

---

*Chopra, Deepak. *The Seven Spiritual Laws of Success*. New World Library, 1994, p. 19.

ing wealth or good things in your life, those feelings are a part of your character that you have to address. Profitable trades will not solve these issues. As a trader, an important question to ask yourself is whether you feel that you truly deserve to be wealthy. This question must be answered honestly. If you do not believe you deserve to be wealthy, sooner or later you will sabotage your chances for success.

Many people carry around feelings of unworthiness ingrained from childhood. These feelings often stem from the association parents or a religion attaches to money. The first step toward changing these destructive and unrealistic feelings is awareness. Only when you allow these feelings to surface consciously can you address them, release them, and let them go.

You are your own harshest critic. The feelings of guilt and shame that people carry around have no bearing on reality. People may have distorted memories of how they injured or hurt someone else, when in fact that was not the case. To achieve success in life, you have to learn to have compassion for yourself. Feelings of self-worth translate into positive outer manifestations in all areas of your life. Those who feel that they deserve only the best in life attract other people and circumstances to themselves that will confirm those beliefs. When you understand that abundance and wealth are the natural states of the universe, and you recognize that you deserve to be wealthy, your actions will begin to model your inner beliefs.

## SECURITY IS AN ILLUSION

Are you trading for security? If you are, you may be in the wrong business. If a trader is trading with the objective of being secure, you are juggling two opposing forces. You are attempting to derive stability and safety from market forces that are inherently unstable and insecure.

Is there such a thing as security? Helen Keller said, "Life is either a daring adventure or nothing at all." If you are attached to the concept of security, it will have the effect of making you feel insecure. An attachment to something outside of yourself is unfulfilling, because you feel empty without it.

There is no security in the markets. Time and again, some of the so-called smartest names in trading have gone bust practically overnight.

When you are trading for security, you are attempting to keep what you have because you are afraid to lose. This fear will inhibit your actions and will make you a less effective trader. When you fear losing, you will actually create losses. You will be unable to cut your losses when they are small, and you will miss great trading opportunities because you are afraid to lose.

The same fear of loss infects the actions of people in everyday life, holding them back from living the lives that they always dreamed of. Security is a very fleeting thing and can never come from money itself. Attachment to money or profits creates anxiety and a feeling of lack. This attachment means that your sense of well-being is dependent upon something outside of yourself, which there could never be enough of. If a person cannot afford to lose, fear and attachment will always reign.

A good question to ask yourself is what is the worst that could possibly happen to you, the worst outcome that you can imagine? You've managed to live up until now. You've always been provided for and cared for, or else you would not be reading this book. There has always been enough food on the table. Life will go on. You will be okay.

The acceptance of loss puts into perspective the fact that each trade is only a single trade in the design of things to come. Ten years from now, when you look back at the loss, it will seem like an insignificant speck, a learning experience that happened for the best. The only thing that is sure in trading is that you'll win some and you'll lose some. The markets will always change. Nothing is permanent.

The samurai lived by the code of the warrior, or Bushido. Bushido dictated their lives and provided a discipline and philosophy for them to live by. A famous samurai of the seventeenth century named Yamamoto Tsunenori wrote a book called *Ha Gakure* or *Hidden Leaves*,* in which he summed up the Way of the Warrior as resolute acceptance of death, or as we'll call it, resolute acceptance of loss. Tsunenori said the way of the warrior *is* death. What does this mean? Tsunenori said that "...to die having failed is not a shameful thing. It means that if you keep your spirit correct from morning to evening, accustomed to the idea of death, and resolved on death, and consider yourself as a dead body, thus becoming one with the Way of

---

*Musashi, Miyamoto. *The Book of Five Rings*. Bantum Doubleday Dell, 1992.

the Warrior, you can pass through life with no possibility of failure and perform your office properly." When the possibility of death or failure is accepted, which everyone will face eventually, then what is the worst that could happen to you? If you are trading with money that you can afford to lose, then you have accepted the worst-case possibility up front. Anticipation of failure or loss is worse than loss itself. Not being afraid to fail or to lose is true freedom.

> *To foster life all must be killed.*
> *Once all is killed you can dwell at ease.*
> *If you understand this meaning,*
> *an iron boat will float across water.*
>
> ZEN SAYING

## WRITE DOWN WHAT YOU WANT

> *You have to be specific with your goals because the universe will deliver what you want. The universe will give you what you dwell upon. If you dwell upon ambiguity it will give you just that.*
>
> TAD JAMES

Write down your trading goals, and be as specific as possible. The goals need to be measurable, so when you achieve them you will know it. Remember to be very specific. Once your brain has the target, it can begin to figure out ways to best achieve it. Your profit and loss objectives should be broken down into yearly, monthly, weekly, and daily goals.

Develop goals for all areas of your trading development. Focusing on the reward aspect of trading alone is a faulty approach. Certain areas of your trading approach will require more development than others. Only you know what you need to work on the most. This requires honest introspection and diligent analysis.

You may be an expert at letting your profits run, but you may have trouble cutting your losses or taking profits. Perhaps you chase stocks past your ideal entry point too often, or it could be that you are not aggressive enough at executing trades. At the end of the day, record in a journal the correct and incorrect trades you made throughout the day, so you can learn from them. Keeping a daily journal is a potent way to zoom in on your strong and weak points as a trader. Once you are aware of shortcomings as a trader, you can convert them into positive written goals.

All your goals should be written down in the present, as if you have already achieved them. When working with goals, act and feel as if you already have that which you are seeking. When you act and feel and believe that you have achieved your goal, your confident state of mind will reject the obstacles that stand in your way. If your objective is to earn $100,000 a month, write down the goal as follows: "I now earn $100,000 a month trading." If your objective is to stick to your stop-loss criteria, then your written goal could be: "I always stick to my prearranged stop-loss points." Read these goals out loud in the evening before you go to sleep and in the morning when you wake up. When reading them, use as much emotion as possible so you can work yourself into a state of experiencing the outcome.

Your trading goals should be as realistic as possible. If you do not believe inside that you can accomplish the result, then it will be hard for you to internalize it. A goal that is unrealistic is discouraging. The way to make your goals realistic is to start where you are today. Decide what specific action you can take and what sort of results you can expect to receive from that action. Begin with a more conservative goal for the near term. Use your past achievements as the immediate benchmark for what you can expect in the future.

Your goals need to be timed toward your objectives. Setting specific dates is very important. Once you write down and commit to a deadline, your brain takes over, sometimes in mysterious ways. We use only a very small part of our brains consciously. Having a written goal accomplishes amazing things. Write out your goals as far as possible into the future, with as much detail as possible.

Remember that you should always judge yourself by your goals only, not by anyone else's. What others are doing or have done should be of no concern to you. Financial goals in day trading can range from as little as $200 a day to over $1,000,000 a day. Just remember that it is important to maintain realistic expectations about your abilities and your resources.

Psychology has a powerful impact on trading results. It is impossible to separate your psychological makeup from your results. Being aware of the way your mind works is the first step. You must know your own strengths and weaknesses before you can hope to grow stronger and to overcome the obstacles that will inevitably appear in your path toward trading greatness.

# CONCLUSION

This book was written with the goal of carefully laying out the various ingredients it takes to trade successfully. As you practice applying its principles and techniques, your profitability will increase and you will develop progressively as a trader. This book's themes are applicable to all traders, not just NASDAQ market makers or day traders.

Trading on the right side of the market and profiting from it requires a different set of talents and traits than intellectual brainpower. The traits and talents required to succeed as a day trader involve using your brain in a different way. The internal qualities necessary are often hard to develop and to maintain, because they are often the opposite of what most people have acquired growing up. They require constant maintenance and fine-tuning for the rest of your trading days. Some of the qualities are mental discipline, courage, confidence and conviction, detachment from the outcome, a small ego, acceptance of loss, patience, acceptance of responsibility for all your actions, open-mindedness, and a strong belief that you deserve to prosper.

Thinking too much when day trading will only confuse you. Intellectuals are usually poor traders. For example, if you use your brain to think about the great bull market of the 1990s, do you come to the conclusion that the astronomical valuations really make sense? Would you have surmised that it is rational for people to be paying hundreds, even thousands, of times what a company earns because of future speculation? Maybe you would have thought it rational and maybe not.

If you spent your time thinking about it too much, you probably would have had a hard time deciding to trade—thus you would have ended up missing a large part of the most profitable bull market in history. Even worse, those who did not think that the valuations were reasonable and acted on those thoughts by shorting the roaring bull at the wrong time ended up losing fortunes—because they allowed their doubts to creep up and to cloud their objective day trading vision as confined by price action.

The characteristics that make a market maker or any trader successful are grown and nurtured from within. It is rare to find a successful trader who started out successful. The best way to learn is by making mistakes, often more than once. Many of the greatest traders started out by losing all they had. Many of them were able to ride out the storm in the beginning, only to lose everything once again because they allowed old bad habits to disrupt their game plans. The process of learning to trade requires action in the form of capital commitment. Many beginning traders do not last because they do not have the funds to survive after learning the lessons the hard way, without proper risk control.

The qualities that make a trader successful will work for you whether you are a market maker trading NASDAQ stocks or a day trader trading S&P futures. Just as success is an attitude, trading is a discipline.

Learning to trade is like tuning a piano. Piano tuners don't simply tune a piano once and then leave it for complete. They tune it once a week for a number of weeks. After that, they tune it once every two weeks, then once a month, then once every six months for the rest of its life. Through consistent application, piano tuners refine and reinforce the tunes they taught the piano on the first try.

A successful trader has to do the same thing. The fine-tuning process never ends. You must always strive to develop profitable trading habits. This can be accomplished through the application of discipline and patience, combined with open-mindedness. Trading is a way of life, not just an occupation. It is impossible to separate who you are as a person, including your thoughts and beliefs, from your results as a trader. As you make the effort, there will always be new insights. The way to success is through continuous training.

# INDEX

## About the Author

Josh Lukeman is an institutional NASDAQ market maker at Morgan Stanley Dean Witter, concentrating on technology stocks. He produces a daily technical analysis bulletin, incorporating candlestick charting methods, which analyzes and interprets the movement of sectors for Morgan Stanley's OTC group. Josh was previously employed at Buffalo Partners, where he traded listed stocks and futures.

# Business Lessons from a
# Radical Industrialist

**Also by Ray C. Anderson**

*Mid-Course Correction:*
*Toward a Sustainable Enterprise*

# Business Lessons from a Radical Industrialist

**Ray C. Anderson**
with Robin White

ST. MARTIN'S GRIFFIN
NEW YORK

BUSINESS LESSONS FROM A RADICAL INDUSTRIALIST. Copyright © 2009, 2010 by Ray C. Anderson. All rights reserved. Printed in the United States of America. For information, address St. Martin's Press, 175 Fifth Avenue, New York, N.Y. 10010.

www.stmartins.com

The Library of Congress has cataloged the hardcover edition as follows:

Anderson, Ray C.
     Confessions of a radical industrialist: profits, people, purpose—doing business by respecting the earth / Ray C. Anderson with Robin White.—1st ed.
          p. cm.
     ISBN 978-0-312-54349-5
     1. Industrial management—Environmental aspects.   2. Social responsibility of business.   3. Entrepreneurship.   I. White, Robin A.   II. Title.
     HD30.255.A53 2009
     338.7'6989—dc22

                                                                                          2009013189

ISBN 978-0-312-54455-3 (trade paperback)

Originally published by St. Martin's Press in hardcover format under the title
*Confessions of a Radical Industrialist*

First St. Martin's Griffin Edition: April 2011

10  9  8  7  6  5  4  3  2  1

# Dedication

This book is dedicated to the people of Interface, Inc., the company I founded in 1973 and which has prospered and grown to dominate its field—carpet tile production—globally.

Carpet tiles, often called modular carpet, were new in America in 1973 and had hardly dented the market, though they were well established in Europe. But at that moment a revolution was taking place in the design of American office interiors. The "Open Plan" was being adopted: Interior walls were disappearing; the private office was giving way to systems furniture that came with its own partitions; and power and telecommunication wiring, with no walls to house them, were being routed beneath the office floor. This interior demanded modular carpet to provide an acoustical treatment of the floor that also permitted easy access to the wiring beneath the floor.

Interface was a start-up from scratch—from just an idea to produce carpet tiles in America for the emerging "Office of the Future."

After a harrowing experience raising the initial capital, I brought on four very special people: Joe Kyle to head up manufacturing, Don Russell to lead sales and marketing, Don Lee to head up administration, and Albert Ayers to assist Joe in building a factory and installing production equipment. Soon after, they were joined by Graham Scott, who moved to Georgia from England with some of the first European technology that we acquired.

This was our first nucleus of people. Without them, I feel safe in saying, there would be no Interface today.

Thirty-six years later, the numbers have grown to some four thousand people (at one time eight thousand, before a series of divestitures of acquired businesses). When I published *Mid-Course Correction* (Chelsea Green) in 1998, the number stood at approximately five thousand.

*Mid-Course Correction* was dedicated to environmentalists everywhere. This book is dedicated to the four thousand environmentalists of Interface, without whose commitment, one mind at a time, to the vision of a sustainable Interface, this extraordinary journey to the symbolic top of a very high mountain—Mount Sustainability—would not be happening.

Yet it is happening, and my heartfelt appreciation goes to each of my fellow "mountain climbers." Without them all, this radical industrialist would be out on a thin ledge all by himself.

# Contents

# Acknowledgments

Patricia Adams Anderson (Pat), my wife of twenty-five years, leads this list for so patiently supporting me in my personal mission to tell the Interface story far and wide. I can't count the nights I have spent away—leaving her alone at home—over the last fifteen years as I have given more than 1,300 speeches and interviews. Those have provided much of the substantive content of this book. So, thank you, my dearest wife and best friend, for your sacrifices that made this book possible.

Others whose significant contributions I want to acknowledge are:

Lisa Lilienthal, Interface's publicist, and Jo Ann Bachman, my scheduling assistant, who have been constant and dedicated teammates in helping me tell the Interface story around the world, evaluating speaking and interview opportunities, and getting me there and back safely and successfully.

Linda Sutton and Sheila Shealey, who have typed seemingly endless versions of speeches and the many generations of manuscripts that culminated in this book.

Barney Karpfinger, my agent and friend, whose wise guidance through the process of identifying and engaging a publisher has been indispensable, as has been his advice on myriad day-to-day issues around engaging the publishing world.

Robin White, my co-author, whose research into the depths of Interface's initiatives, and those of other companies as well, required patience I never would have summoned.

George Witte, of St. Martin's Press, who saw and appreciated the uniqueness of the Interface story, put his company's money on the line, and personally performed the editing of the manuscript.

These people, along with the people of Interface to whom this book is dedicated, are the reason this book exists. Without them, I could never have come close.

Thank you all.

Finally, I want to acknowledge the primary source of my motivation for pursuing sustainability for Interface: my daughters, Mary Anne Anderson Lanier and Harriet Adelaide Anderson Langford, and their children (my grandchildren), James Augustus Lanier III (Jay), John Anderson Lanier, Patrick William Lanier, Harriet Melissa Langford Heflin, and Cameron McCall Langford. Assuring a healthy future for them and their progeny is what this book is about.

# Foreword

**A**s I sit down to write this foreword, I have a lot on my mind. My company, Interface, Inc., has just marked an important milestone—ten years until our target year for Mission Zero, for zero environmental footprint, a goal for which we have set 2020 as our deadline. I'm immensely proud of Interface, and encouraged about our future. At the same time, I have spent the last year dealing with cancer, thankfully holding my own—barely.

You may be familiar with my story (before cancer)—the epiphany I experienced in 1994 when I read Paul Hawken's book, *The Ecology of Commerce,* seeking inspiration for a speech to a task force that was organizing at Interface to answer customer concerns about the environment. That change of worldview led me down a road I had never imagined for myself or my petroleum-intensive company—eventually to get off oil.

Distancing ourselves from the wellhead requires that we reimagine the antiquated, linear, take-make-waste industrial system of which we are all a part. And instead, to become part of a thoughtful, cooperative, cyclical system that mimics nature in the way that we design, source, manufacture, sell, install—and eventually reclaim and recycle—our products. This ambitious undertaking requires new technology, new inputs, and new thinking. It is intensely complicated and, at the same time, completely liberating to think outside the traditional confines of design and manufacturing. Somewhere along the way, the idea that what we were doing was so right—so right, and so smart—emerged to propel us forward. At Interface, this new way of thinking is working—our products are better than ever, our employees are more engaged than ever, customers are extraordinarily loyal; and, importantly, costs are down, not up, dispelling the myth that sustainability is expensive. That's the story you'll find in more detail in this book.

I've always believed that there was something nagging at the back of my mind in 1994—something that caused me not only to pick up Paul Hawken's book, but also to be taken so forcefully by his ideas. I was, at the time, sixty years old. Ego may say that the nagging sense was a search for my personal legacy, but maybe it was actually conscience—the thing in us that inherently knows right from wrong. Can it possibly be right that we humans are burning up more than a cubic mile of oil each year, as well as mountains of coal, to power our homes, our cars, our offices, and our factories; fuels that took millions upon millions of years to create, and only a few hundred years to exhaust? Inherently, we must know that this is wrong—and stupid. A wise farmer would shake his head and say we were eating our own seed corn. Some capitalists would say we can't afford to do it differently.

But what if those capitalists took into account the value of the services that nature provides? What if the balance sheet and profit-and-loss statement required that we account for the cost of creating air; water purification and distribution (the hydrologic cycle); soil creation and maintenance, thus food; energy and raw materials (at their full costs); climate regulation; pollination; seed dispersal; nutrient cycling; an ultraviolet radiation shield; flood and insect control; and net primary production, the product of photosynthesis? Surely, even the capitalists will know that without any of these, there would be no economy in the first place.

At Interface, the pursuit of sustainability has opened our eyes, not only to how wrong we had it before, but also to the enormous opportunity that new thinking provides.

As we begin the next leg of our journey, looking at the ten years to go and the path before us, one thing is even more clear to me. If we capitalists intend to go on, if we aspire to thrive in a carbon-constrained world and to put down multiple threats—global climate disruption, species extinction, resource depletion, and environmental degradation—we need a new way, a better way, of thinking and acting. Wrong thinking got us into this mess. Eating our own seed corn, as it were, is unsustainable.

The unrepentant capitalist might say, "Business can't afford to have a conscience." But I am here to tell you, the farmer was right, and business can't afford not to have a conscience.

So we have the business case—which I detail in this book—and we have our collective conscience: society's need to distinguish right from wrong on a local and a global scale.

If that's not persuasive enough, let's get personal. Cancer is no fun. If you don't receive the right treatment, you die; and even with the very best treatment, you can still die. I seem to be receiving the right treatment; though the very best results one can hope for, complete remission (which I am nowhere near yet), leave one knowing it can recur, maybe in a different part of the body as a metastasis, or maybe in a mutated form. It's difficult not to let cancer take over your life.

As you can imagine, I find some interesting analogies in this experience.

In cancer, it's often not clear whether the original cause was hereditary or environmental—nature or nurture. My mother was one of seven siblings. My father, too, was one of seven. Not one of those fourteen people who were the generation before mine had cancer. In my generation, my two brothers, one of our first cousins, and I have had cancer. One would tend to think that the probable cause is nurture—something in the environment, not inherited, that got to us. And, of course, "the environment" is, in this case, paradoxically, nurture, not nature. Nurture is what we are exposed to that, perhaps throughout the branch of human evolution that led to us—my generation, our forebears—were never exposed to, at least not in deadly amounts. My forebears, therefore, never had the need to evolve immunity to cancer; so my generation has no inherited immunity—we have the cancer.

But these are not intended to be comments about *my* cancer. These comments—and this book—are about the "cancer" that is attacking the earth, for lack of the right treatment: sincere exercise of responsibility from those responsible for the industrial system. And like human cancer, industrial cancer can take over our lives.

Like my siblings, our cousin, and me, life on the earth is "seeing," i.e., being exposed to hazards it has not seen in the earth's entire existence: manmade substances—chemical compounds—that are completely unnatural. Even substances the earth put away in its crust millions, even billions, of years ago through sedimentation and sequestration, allowing a sweet environment conducive to life to evolve up here, are being dug up or drilled up, processed and reintroduced into our surroundings. And the earth's fragile ecological balances are constantly abused. By whom? By *homo sapiens*—modern man, doubly wise man, man who knows and knows he knows, and who ought to know better. Conscience again—we cannot afford to ignore its nagging.

So this brings me to the central point of this book; I'll make it now and flesh it out in the book. Irresponsible business—the diggers, the drillers, the processors of poison, all of whom ought to know better—they and their abusive industries—are a cancer on society. Humankind cries out for responsibility to be taken seriously by them and, in fact, by all of industry. To me sixteen years ago, that meant starting with my own company. This book is our story, our response to the imperative: Start here.

It's high time we all started the right treatment of this hateful disease that is inflicted on the earth by us humans before it takes us all down. It's time for the public—the revered marketplace—to say to the institution of business: "You think you can not afford to exercise responsibility and remain competitive. The truth is, you can no longer afford *not* to act responsibly; stop your companies' crimes against nature, for we will run you out of business if you don't. That's the "stick."

I'll end on a positive note, with an update on Interface's climb up Mount Sustainability—the latest metrics on our eco-odyssey (as of year-end 2009), and a restatement of my central thesis. This is the "carrot":

- **80 percent** reduction in the landfill waste per unit of production since 1996
- Water intake, down **80 percent** per unit of production since 1996
- Total energy, down by **43 percent** per unit of production since 1996
- With changing energy mix to include renewables, fossil fuel intensity reduced by **60 percent**
- With verified offsets, net GHG reduced **94 percent** (absolute)
- **30 percent** of global energy is from renewable sources
- **36 percent** of total raw materials (by weight) is recycled or bio-based materials
- **100 percent** renewable electricity in Europe (89 percent worldwide) in our factories
- **111 million square yards** of climate-neutral carpet produced since 2003: "Cool Carpet"

- **100,000 tons** (200 million pounds) of reclaimed product via Re-Entry, our reverse logistics carpet reclamation program
- **200 million** airline passenger miles offset by some **106,000 trees**
- Overall footprint reduction, more than **60 percent**
- Cumulative avoided waste costs totaling **$433 million** since 1994—costs down, not up—waste elimination paying for the entire mountain climb

If we can do it, anybody can. If anybody can, everybody can. That includes you.

RAY C. ANDERSON

# Prologue

This is a book about the future of business and industry, a future driven by a new and powerful idea: sustainability. Specifically, it deals with what it takes to run a profitable, modern business with the environment in mind, doing no harm *to* the earth and taking *from* the earth nothing that cannot be renewed naturally and rapidly *by* the earth. It is about a new business model that can generate not just bigger profits, but better, more legitimate ones, too.

But as I sit here today, October 10, 2008, writing while I vacation in the ancient town of Brugge, Belgium, a global financial meltdown seems to be under way, putting into question whether the economic system can survive.

Here's a snapshot at this moment in time. While it's 7:05 P.M. in Belgium, it is 1:05 P.M. in Atlanta, where I live. The Dow Jones Industrial Average is down 345 points, following seven consecutive days of decline. It appears to be moving toward 8,000, or lower. The Federal Trade Commission has just approved Wells Fargo's acquisition of Wachovia for $11.7 billion. Venerable Merrill Lynch is in the process of disappearing into Bank of America, a route Countrywide Financial has already taken. Lehman Brothers, a longtime pillar of stability in the investment banking world, has failed; only its brokerage and mutual fund businesses survive under the banners of Barclays of the United Kingdom and Neuberger Investment Management, respectively. Fannie Mae and Freddie Mac have gone into federal government "conservatorship." Washington Mutual, the largest savings bank in the United States, is being gobbled up by JPMorgan Chase, out of the receivership of the Federal Deposit Insurance Corporation (FDIC). Bear Stearns, the first really big shoe to fall, is already being absorbed by JPMorgan Chase in a deal brokered by the U.S. Treasury Department over a weekend.

Goldman Sachs and Morgan Stanley, for so long dominant forces in the investment banking world, have opted to change their very nature and become regulated commercial banks. They were the last of the mega–investment banks once Bear Stearns, Merrill Lynch, and Lehman Brothers were gone. Mitsubishi UFJ, a Japanese bank, is taking a $9 billion equity position in Morgan Stanley to shore up MS's capital structure and prepare it for the role of acquirer in the turmoil ahead, portending more consolidation to come. American International Group (AIG), said to be too big to be allowed to fail, is being propped up by the Federal Reserve to the tune of more than $100 billion.

And the U.S. Treasury Department is trying to determine just how to "invest" $700 billion of taxpayers' money to jump-start the "clogged up" (Secretary of the Treasury Henry Paulson's term) American credit markets. "Clogged up" means banks have stopped making loans, even among themselves, and credit is drying up, even for borrowers with impeccable credit standing. Meanwhile, European central banks are undertaking their own forms of rescue with capital infusions of more than a trillion dollars.

A year ago the Dow Jones Industrial Average was above 14,000. The Dow is an important number on Wall Street. It is an important number on Main Street, too. Wealth worth trillions of dollars has evaporated, taking with it the savings of millions of people. While the much-touted benefits of a "trickle down" economy have always been hard to document, the trickle-down hurt of a freeze in capital, in short-term lending and in mortgages and auto loans, is now painfully apparent to just about everyone.

I look into my laptop's screen and see a financial industry in turmoil. It seems as if the financial world we have known for three quarters of a century is changing before my eyes. The underlying culprit is said to be the bursting of the subprime home loan bubble in the United States, which precipitated a whole new set of consequences: many trillions of dollars lost in arcane derivatives that few people even understand.

Watching this unfold from afar is truly surreal. Personal, too, as I watch my own investment portfolio shrink. I think that all my holdings are in sound companies, but who really knows? Even those who have the responsibility of running those banks don't seem to know what to do or where to turn. One wonders who or what is "running" whom.

However, another kind of sustainability is on my mind. My company, Interface, has become nearly synonymous with corporate environmental sustainability. But can we sustain sustainability, or will the economic storm sweeping over the world force us to put our efforts on the back burner?

I answer myself: No way! We *will* continue. You see, while environmental and financial sustainability have often (and mistakenly) been seen as opposite goals, they are, in truth, one and the very same. We have seen that for ourselves. We know it to be absolutely true.

Oil's price is down today to less than $80 a barrel, the lowest in a year. Not long ago oil was $147 a barrel and reaching for more. Down $67 a barrel! Is that good? Or bad?

The book that follows this introduction was largely written while the Dow was falling from around 13,000 to around 10,000, oil's price was rising, and gasoline was topping $4 a gallon in the United States. But concern for the future of the American banking system, and the unprecedented entry of government institutions into the world of private finance—to rescue it, no less—never once entered my mind, though smart people I know and talk with regularly have been saying financial upheaval was coming.

Yet, quite intentionally, I was writing about the future, the future of the real economy—the place where real stuff gets made and sold, and real services are rendered. It is quite distinct from the financial economy, with its stock market and its various indexes, altogether a sort of imperfect analogue of the real economy.

The point of my story is deceptively simple. Business and industry—not just American business and industry, but global business and industry—must change their ways to survive. Some people have been saying this for a long time. Many more are saying it today.

I make no claim to prescience, only to conviction. And by survive, I do not mean maintain identity and integrity within the context of a financial system in meltdown, either. By survive, I mean business must be steered through a transition from an old and dangerously dysfunctional model to a far better one that will operate in balance and harmony with nature—thrive in a carbon-constrained world, and put down the threats of global climate disruption, species extinction, resource depletion, and environmental degradation. In a word, develop a business model that is *sustainable*.

Even as I write this introduction I have not yet settled on a title for the book. But I think it should somehow mention "hubris." (It probably won't because it's not catchy enough.) For there's nothing quite like staring apocalypse in the eye to humble oneself or a society. To know that nobody has control over events puts the limitation of power into a new perspective. Puffed-up hubris is run out of town on a rail by something just as useless: unthinking fear.

What we need instead of hubris or fear, and what this book offers, is a new and better way forward. And yes, hope, a hope learned from my own, personal experiences running a company that is reaching for sustainability.

There is a chance that on the other side of this financial meltdown a new sanity will overtake the world of business, industry, and finance, and its analogue, the stock market. Then this book can assume relevance for newly opened minds and become a map for change.

Therefore, I am altering as few of the words already written as possible, though it is tempting to rewrite some passages that are predicated on high prices for oil. But I take the view that the upheavals in finance will be followed by slowing business and declining demand, therefore falling oil prices—for a while. Then this too will pass away, but the fundamentals of supply and demand will still be there. So I let stand unchanged those passages, in the conviction that their relevance will become clear on the next leg up of the real economy.

The story you will read has grown out of real-life experiences—mine and those of the people of my company, Interface, Inc. We're not some small, boutique manufacturer of green widgets. We make and sell carpet tiles—more than a billion dollars' worth in the most recent year. We also make broadloom carpets—about a hundred million dollars' worth in a year. Our sales force covers the world, selling our products in 110 or more countries in any given year.

Almost all our products are made for commercial and institutional interiors. A relatively small but growing portion is made for home use. Interior designers and architects are extremely important to us. It is their choices of our products for their projects that keep the wheels turning in our factories in six countries on four continents—with more to be built in time, always close to their markets, not for cheap labor, but for sensitivity to customer needs and to shorten transportation pipelines.

We are a company that is highly dependent for our raw materials on petrochemical products produced by big chemical companies. We use a lot of energy, too. All of it used to come from burning fossil fuels. Not so anymore. But I get ahead of myself.

In 1998, I published *Mid-Course Correction*, an autobiographical account of my formative years and some forty-two years (at that point) in the business world. The last twenty-five of those years had been invested in the founding of my company, its growth and development and survival. But the last four of those twenty-five years were the primary focus of *Mid-Course Correction*.

Those were the four years that followed my 1994 epiphanal reading of Paul Hawken's *The Ecology of Commerce* (HarperCollins, 1993), four years that had seen the literal "mid-course correction" of Interface away from the extractive, abusive path of business as usual and toward a renewable, cyclical, and benign business model—a model of sustainability. The plan for executing our course correction—a wide-ranging and astonishingly successful program we now call Mission Zero—was the heart of *Mid-Course Correction*.

Ten years have passed since *Mid-Course Correction*'s publication. A lot has happened at Interface during those ten years, but Mission Zero is still the plan. Given the progress we have made in executing it, I thought it was not only time for an update but for a how-to manual to more clearly show others the way.

For the reader who has not read *Mid-Course Correction*, I have rewritten its essential story, so you need not feel something important is missing from this account. For the reader who has read *Mid-Course Correction*, you may read some passages that seem familiar, but they are expressed more expansively here. I hope not to bore anyone with repetition. As with *Mid-Course Correction*, I make no effort to prove anything. This is not an academic book. It is a real life story of real people doing real, if extraordinary, things.

Today, as many CEOs are wondering how they will weather the financial storm, the step-by-step plan that we crafted at Interface assumes greater importance than I imagined when I set out to formulate it. As you read this book, you will see that the choices—the trade-offs—we are told we must make between financial success and environmental success, between doing well and doing good, are just plain false.

I began by saying that this is a book about the future of business and industry; I should say it's about the *necessary* future of business and industry, if we are to choose the survival option and lead humankind away from the environmental abyss toward which we are rushing headlong. Conversely, if the institutions of business and industry fail in their own mid-course correction toward ecological survival, the financial meltdown I am observing from Brugge will seem like a tea party by comparison.

That is a very large burden for the institutions of business and industry to bear. This book is about lightening that burden. It offers a template for a better, more benign business model. It also makes the business case for sustainability in pure business terms.

If you have better ideas, I hope you will share them with me; for as long as I live, I will be looking for a better way. That's what sent me and my company on a quest to achieve the very sustainability that some really knowledgeable people said was just plain impossible.

Of course, many of those same people were the ones who brought us subprime mortgages, overleveraged hedge funds, and credit default swaps, and a traditional framework of financial "values" that appears to be collapsing before our eyes.

Meanwhile, the value of nature's services to all of humanity—clean air, fresh water, arable land, pollination, seed dispersal, and climate regulation, just to name a few—has not lost a cent. They are, they will be, and always were the real gold standard. Investing to conserve and protect them has been a winner for us. As you read this book, I think you will see that investing in the earth's future—the earth that all business, all life, utterly depends upon—can be a winner for you, too.

RAY C. ANDERSON
*October 10, 2008*
*Brugge, Belgium*

# Business Lessons from a
# Radical Industrialist

*I would not give a fig for simplicity this side of complexity; but I would give my right arm for simplicity on the far side of complexity.*

—Oliver Wendell Holmes, Jr. (1841–1935),
American jurist

*Cicero spoke and people marveled. Caesar spoke and people marched.*

—Cato the Younger (95–46 b.c.),
Roman statesman

# 1 | Mission Zero

am Ray Anderson, and in addition to being a husband, a father, and a grandfather, I'm an industrialist. Some would say a radical industrialist. *Time* magazine called me a "Hero of the Environment." *U.S. News & World Report* said I was "America's Greenest CEO." *Fortune* magazine was kind and astute enough to include my company, Interface, in its annual list of the "100 Best Companies to Work For"—twice. The GlobeScan (2007) Survey of Sustainability Experts listed Interface, Inc., as leading the list of global companies with the greatest commitment to sustainability. Following Interface, in order of ranking, were: Toyota, GE, BP, and DuPont.

But I've also been called a hypocrite and a dreamer who pours his time, energy, and stockholder money into lofty ideas about ecology and sustainability instead of the bottom line. Yet I would reply that I'm as profit-minded and competitive as anyone you're likely to meet.

I grew up in a small Georgia town during the tail end of the Great Depression and the Second World War. My father worked in the post office. My mother was a retired schoolteacher. I attended college on a football scholarship, graduated with highest honors, and spent seventeen years in industry working for someone else.

Then, in 1973, I took the entrepreneurial plunge and founded a company, Interface, with nothing more than a good idea, my life's savings, and the faith of a few brave investors. We grew that company from scratch into the world leader in carpet tiles (modular carpet) with annual sales of more than a billion dollars.

In 1994, at age sixty and in my company's twenty-second year, I steered Interface on a new course—one designed to reduce our environmental footprint while increasing our profits. I wanted Interface, a company so oil-intensive you could think of it as an extension of the petrochemical industry, to be the first enterprise in history to become truly sustainable—to shut down its smokestacks, close off its effluent pipes, to do no harm to the environment, and to take nothing *from* the earth not easily renewed *by* the earth. Believe me when I say that that goal is one enormous challenge.

But as I said, I'm profit-minded and extremely competitive. I thought "going green" would definitely enhance our standing with our customers and maybe give us some good press, too. But I *also* thought it just might be a way to earn bigger profits from doing what was right by the earth. No one had ever attempted that kind of transformation on such a large scale before. We aimed to turn the myth that you could do well in business or do good, but not both, on its head. Our goal was to prove—by example—that you could run a big business both profitably and in an environmentally responsible way. And we succeeded beyond my own high aspirations.

Not everyone at my company was happy with this in August 1994. It had been a very good year at Interface. We had weathered a deep recession, we were growing again and very profitable. Why should we conduct this grand experiment when nobody, not even I, knew how it would come out? It was a reasonable question.

We caught plenty of flak from outside the company, too. Wall Street heard "environment" and thought "costs." Even after we showed them how reaching for sustainability could take a big bite out of waste and save us real money, even after we discovered that running a billion-dollar corporation with the earth in mind was a terrific new business model, there was still a lot of skepticism. There still is some, even though we now have over a decade of hard numbers that prove—beyond a doubt—that our course was both right *and* smart. Why, then, all the resistance?

I think it's because our transformation flew in the face of all the old rules that still drive the "take-make-waste" economy, old rules that we inherited from the steam-driven days of the first industrial revolution and (many of us) unthinkingly accept as true. That old way of doing business seemed to work just fine when we thought the earth could provide endless resources, endless energy, and endless room to throw away all the stuff we make and waste.

But those rules don't work anymore. Daniel Quinn, in his book *Ishmael*, said that they're like those badly designed wings of the early aircraft at the dawn of human flight. Our civilization is like that would-be "aeronaut" who jumps off a high cliff in his misbegotten craft. He's pedaling away, wings flapping like mad; the wind is in his face, and the poor fool thinks he's flying when he's really in free fall. Though the ground seems far away at first, his flight is doomed because the design of his wings has ignored the laws of aerodynamics.

Like that high cliff, the vast resources available to our industrial civilization—the oceans, forests, fossil fuels, even the air we breathe—make the "ground" seem far away to us. But as sure as gravity, it's rushing up fast. Our flight will end up no better than his. Why? Because our industrial civilization has ignored the laws of sustainability, laws that would enable humanity to pull out of our terminal dive and "fly."

Whichever way we look, from global warming to deforestation, from empty water reservoirs to vanishing species, to the price of a gallon of gas at the pump, the evidence is all around us. The earth is finite and fragile, and we ignore these plain physical facts at our peril. That's why we need a new industrial revolution and a new set of wings, ones properly designed according to the laws of "aerodynamics." Wings that will allow our civilization—and our grandchildren's—to fly, sustainably. To soar, not crash.

But conventional wisdom and the status quo are powerful sedatives. Like opiates, they dim our vision and blur our minds. They whisper, *Maybe all those arguing experts are wrong. Maybe there's nothing to worry about. Or, okay, so there's a problem, but I surely can't solve it. Why even try?*

Maybe that's why conventional wisdom, wed to the status quo, was certain there was no business case for sustainability, that what we started at Interface was misguided, tangential, and doomed to fail.

Conventional wisdom was wrong. Consider a few facts. Remember the Kyoto Protocol? It was designed to reduce greenhouse gas (GHG) emissions by about 7 percent by 2012 here in the United States. Though a small reduction like that doesn't even begin to address the problem of climate disruption, a lot of my peers in industry were sure that if the United States signed on to Kyoto, it would drive them right out of business. Really?

From 1996, our baseline year, through 2008, my business has cut its net greenhouse gas emissions not by 7 percent, but by 71 percent (in absolute tons), while our sales increased by two-thirds and our earnings doubled. Profit margins expanded, not contracted, while GHG intensity, relative to sales, declined some 82 percent.

No business case for sustainability?

While some businesses fret and sweat over rising fuel bills, renewable energy, limitless and available right now, provides electricity to power eight of our ten factories. The electrical power for seven of them comes *entirely* from renewables. Our consumption of fossil fuels per square yard of carpet is down 60 percent. As I write this, the price of oil has broken all previous records. Will it stay up there? Will it keep on rising, or fall back? I don't know. But go take a look at some of *your* recent fuel bills. Think you could make the case for reducing them by over half?

Our companywide waste elimination measures have put a cumulative $405 million of avoided costs back into our pockets. Not only have these measures paid for themselves, they helped us ride out the deepest, longest marketplace decline—the "perfect storm" of Y2K's diversion of capital to computer systems, the bursting of the dot-com bubble, and 9/11—in our industry's history.

Even better, taking a sledgehammer to conventional wisdom has thrown innovation into overdrive. We've patented machines, processes, and products that do a whole lot more with a whole lot less, and better, too. Each year, more of our products take their inspiration from nature, exhibiting nature's beauty as well as benefiting from her genius for design that has been perfected over billions of years.

We're making more of our carpets from recycled materials, too; at last count, we've kept 175 million pounds of carpet out of landfills and trimmed the scrap we generate and send to the landfills by 78 percent. Now, what used to be waste for the landfill goes back into our factories as feedstock. Valuable organic molecules are salvaged to be used again and again, with less fresh oil required each year, emulating nature in our industrial processes. After all, in nature, one organism's waste becomes another organism's food.

We haven't used our final drop of oil quite yet, but I can see that day coming, and I hope to be around when it arrives. Just think about what that could mean for your business, your family, and your country. And if enough people did it, the planet.

In fact, since 2003, we've manufactured and sold over eighty-three million square yards of carpet with no net global-warming effect—*zero*—to the earth. We call these climate-neutral products "Cool Carpet,™" and they have been runaway bestsellers. That's competitive advantage at its best—doing well by doing good.

Here's the thing: Sustainability has given my company a competitive edge in more ways than one. It has proven to be the most powerful marketplace differentiator I have known in my long career. Our costs are down, our profits are up, and our products are the best they've ever been. It has rewarded us with more positive visibility and goodwill among our customers than the slickest, most expensive advertising or marketing campaign could possibly have generated. And a strong environmental ethic has no equal for attracting and motivating good people, galvanizing them around a shared higher purpose, and giving them a powerful reason to join and to stay.

Sometimes even they are surprised. Some of our best engineers and managers from top-tier universities have come up and told me, *Ray, I never thought I'd be working for a carpet company.* They come and they stay, because we aren't just making carpets. We're making history.

The business case for sustainability is crystal clear, and we're just beginning. You see, there's a mountain out there that we call "Mount Sustainability." It is higher than Everest, but we have a plan to climb it—all the way to the top—by the year 2020. We call this initiative Mission Zero.

We will reach the summit when we have cut our last umbilical cord to the mines and the oil wells, when we no longer dump any waste into the landfills or pollution into the air or water. When we no longer take anything from the earth that the earth cannot renew rapidly and naturally.

But Mount Sustainability is a high, high mountain—higher than Everest. There isn't just one path up but at least seven, and we know we must climb them all. Yet, if a company like mine can get there, any company can get there. And I believe that this book will help others—from CEOs to suburban homeowners—find their own way to their own summits, too.

Mind you, striving for the top will require nothing short of a vast, ethically driven redesign of our industrial system, a new industrial revolution that corrects the many things the first one got wrong. But can we do it in time?

I think we can, though I can't promise the climb will be easy or painless. But there certainly is reason for hope. As physicist Amory Lovins likes to say, "If something exists, it must be possible." We at Interface have committed

*One day while explaining our plan for achieving sustainability, I drew a simple illustration of Mount Sustainability, with the point at the summit representing zero footprint and a stick figure (us) climbing the mountain. This has become a simple, but clear and widely understood, depiction of our vision and mission.*

ourselves to bringing sustainability fully into existence, to proving that it is not only possible, but profitable—a better way to bigger, more legitimate profits.

Based on our experiences since 1994, I can promise this: Done right, sustainability doesn't cost. It pays. And the view from that summit—looking out on a clean, healthy world for which our children and grandchildren will thank us—will make every step you and I take today for ourselves, and for them, worthwhile.

# 2 | The Power of One Good Question

*I stood indicted as a plunderer, a destroyer of the earth, a thief of my grandchildren's future. And I thought, My God, someday what I do here will be illegal. Someday they'll send people like me to jail.*

—RAY C. ANDERSON

So how did a man who had spent his whole working life in business—fifty-two years as I sit here writing—suddenly decide that modern industry (his own included) had it all wrong? That the old rules were not just financially foolish, but dangerous? In a word, reluctantly. Let me explain.

I'd like to invite you to imagine a pretty big corporation about to have a head-on collision with an even bigger problem, a problem that had nothing at all to do with cash flow, profit margins, or losing business to cheaper competitors. By those measures—by just about any business metric you could name—the corporation, Interface, was successful. In just twenty-one years it had grown from a dreamer's idea to nearly a billion dollars in annual sales, from one factory and no orders on the books to factories on four continents and sales in 110 countries.

You may be thinking, if that's Anderson's problem, it's one a lot of businesses would like to have, especially these days. And it's true. I was—and remain—extremely proud of everything we've accomplished. Why not? It was a Horatio Alger story come true. I was the founder, the chairman of the board, and the CEO, the man behind the wheel, driving a substantial twentieth-century corporation full speed down the road. Then the future showed up in our headlights, and I saw a very worrisome problem coming at us. I didn't like the looks of it one bit, but we couldn't stop, and it wouldn't move.

I founded Interface in 1973 to equip the emerging, technology-driven "office of the future" with a new kind of carpet, a floor covering that could change along with its owner's needs and offer the versatility that traditional wall-to-wall carpet could never provide. But carpet tiles, modular and infinitely adaptable, could.

Carpet tiles were already well established in European offices, and though they were starting to catch on here in the United States, they hadn't made much of a dent. In fact, when experts in the field heard we were cutting up perfectly good broadloom carpet into little pieces and selling them for twice the going price, I expect some of them chuckled and thought I'd gone around the bend.

By conventional standards they were right. But going around the bend is sometimes the very essence of leadership. Someone has to see what is out there. So when I traveled to England in 1969 and saw carpet tiles for the very first time, I knew I was looking at the future. I fell in love with the idea. I knew they were smart. I knew they were right. I *had* gone around the bend (and not for the last time, either), and I liked what I saw.

Sure enough, making carpet tiles turned out to be a very good idea. I watched my company, this "third child" (after my two natural daughters), grow into a dynamic and profitable organization with five thousand employees and global dominance in a highly competitive market.

As its founder, I was a local hero. I had quit a good, secure job with a major corporation and taken the entrepreneurial plunge to start Interface. I bet all my chips—my life savings, my reputation, even my marriage—on a new idea, and just look what we had accomplished in twenty-one years! Not many other boys who grew up in West Point, Georgia, during the Depression had become captains of industry.

And so, after two decades of what can only be called spectacular success, it didn't bother me a bit that Interface consumed enough energy each year to light and heat a city. Or that we and our suppliers transformed more than a billion pounds of petroleum-derived raw materials into carpet tiles for offices and hospitals, airports and hotels, schools, universities, and stores all around the world. So what, if each day just one of my plants sent *six tons* of carpet trimmings to the local landfill? What happened to it there? I had no idea. Why should I? It was someone else's problem, not mine. That's what landfills were for.

In fact, our belching smokestacks, our gushing effluent pipes, our mountains of waste (all completely legal), were tangible proof that business was

*someone else's problem*

good. They meant jobs. They meant orders coming in, products going out, and money in the bank.

Keep all that energy, those smokestacks, pipes, and mountains of waste in mind. We'll return to them shortly.

Our head-on collision with that worrisome future loomed when a short memo was dropped on my desk in the summer of 1994. It was a handwritten note passed along by Jim Hartzfeld, then an associate in our research division. It had been sent to him by a sales associate out on the West Coast. On it was this simple question: "Some customers want to know what Interface is doing for the environment. How should we answer?"

This was not exactly breaking news. I had already heard from that West Coast sales manager about a potential customer who had told her that when it came to the environment, Interface "just doesn't get it." We stood to lose a pretty important sale, and I was not happy. My only thought was, Interface doesn't get *what*? Of course, by asking that question I only confirmed the customer's observation, but I didn't realize it at the time. That would come later.

You see, making carpet tiles demands so many petroleum-derived chemicals that we weren't just dependent on the oil companies, we were like an extension of them. But we had not broken one environmental rule. Not even bent one. We were legal, in compliance—100 percent.

Didn't get *what*?

But remember, I am extremely competitive. I will never, ever forget the day Interface's first factory opened for business. Our equipment was installed, raw materials had been bought and paid for, people had been hired and trained, and our first product line was ready to go. And there was not a single order on the books. Not one. It was a defining moment, and it branded my brain for a lifetime with the ruthless fact that a business is always just one order away from being out of business. It's like a heartbeat. If you don't get that next order, that next heartbeat, you are dead.

From that day to this, the single most important person in our company has been the customer, the source of that next heartbeat. We learned to listen very carefully to each of them. I wasn't about to ignore any customer's concerns or to turn my back on any piece of business. If we didn't answer the question Jim had relayed, I knew we stood to lose other sales. How many? I had no idea. But I did know that telling our customers, "We comply with all environmental laws," wasn't going to cut it. We had already tried that.

Jim suggested that we convene an environmental task force to frame a better response. It would bring together representatives from all of our divisions around the world to see what we were doing for the environment. "Sounds good to me. Go for it," I said, and sat back, relieved that somebody else would tackle the problem.

But Jim didn't go away. He took up the cause, and asked me to give the kickoff speech, to launch the task force, and share my "environmental vision" with them. The trouble was, other than obeying the law, I did not have an environmental vision. In all my working life—thirty-eight years at the time—I had never given a thought to what I or my company were taking from the earth, or doing to it, except to comply with all the many rules and regulations that government agencies seemed to love to send our way.

The task force was going to meet on August 31, 1994—just four weeks away—and I had no idea what I should tell them. To say that I was reluctant is putting it way too mildly. I did not want to make that speech. I dragged my feet; I hemmed and hawed. But Jim stayed on my case. Finally I relented. The middle of August came; I had not a clue what to say. I was sweating. I could not get beyond, "We obey the law, we comply." I kept searching for something better. I knew "complying" was not a vision.

It was a propitious moment. Then, as if by pure serendipity, a book, *The Ecology of Commerce* by Paul Hawken, arrived on my desk. I'd never heard of Paul Hawken. I was in crisis mode, looking for inspiration, but Hawken's book didn't seem like one at the time.

I looked at the cover. Ecology and commerce? To me ecology was just a source for raw materials and the place to (legally) flush our wastes; ecology, nature, was just a component of a larger entity—the economy. You know, the "pollution part." And anyway, who was this guy? What business did he build up from scratch?

Then I started to thumb through the book, and on page 19 I came to an arresting chapter title: The Death of Birth. Hmmm . . . Now what could that mean? I started reading, hoping to find something beyond compliance, maybe even some inspiration I could pass along to that task force.

What I found was an indictment.

According to Hawken (who had built a business, the Smith and Hawken garden supply firm, from scratch), our planet—the one you and I and all our children and millions of other species call home—was in terrible danger. Every place you looked—the oceans, the air, the forests, the farmland, and all the living systems in and on them—were in decline. This was what Hawken meant by the death of birth: species disappearing, falling into extinction, never to be born again.

The prime suspect? The culprit? Why, it was business. It was industry. It was corporations just like mine, taking from the earth, using resources inefficiently, generating pollution, sending more and more stuff out of our factories into the world just to end up buried in landfills or burned up in incinerators. Forcing the earth to absorb (sometimes over the course of thousands of years) things we used only briefly, and then threw away.

And it was more than just one industry's fault, too. It was the entire linear, take-make-waste industrial system. Fundamentally, it was a way of thinking about the world that assumed unlimited resources, unlimited energy, and unlimited space. It assumed sources that were able to provide whatever we wanted, and sinks (the oceans, the air, the land) able to absorb whatever poison we might send their away.

According to Hawken, we didn't own the earth. We were part of it. And there was no place called "away" for throwing things, either. Thinking there was had put us on a collision course with two of nature's iron laws of thermodynamics that we have been slow to realize: Nothing goes away or ceases to exist, it just disperses; and everything is connected—that what we do to the earth, we also do to ourselves.

Well, to be honest, if that had been the book's only message, I might have stopped reading right there. I do know a few things about business and industry. Bad as we might seem to some, industry hooked up to a free market is the most efficient engine for generating wealth that the world has ever seen. If you don't believe it, just look at all the failed alternatives. Perhaps some might look at the global financial consternation set in motion by Bear Stearns's demise, and say the jury is still out, but not me.

It is an article of faith, bred into every industrialist's DNA, that as technology improves we'll get better and more efficient at supplying whatever the market demands. Did it really matter how many mouths we had to feed? The American farm was the envy of the world, and would surely respond. Who cared how many cars we drove, or how big they were? If gas became expensive, Detroit would figure out an answer. And if it didn't, Toyota would. The market is absolutely ruthless when it comes to picking winners and tossing out losers.

Then Hawken told the story of St. Matthew Island, a little speck of rock up in the Bering Sea off Alaska. It only took a few moments for me to read, but when I finished, I was stopped dead in my tracks.

You see, during World War II, the U.S. Coast Guard operated a radio station on St. Matthew Island. The weather was awful, and keeping the base supplied with food was chancy. Someone decided to stock the island with an emergency supply of food by importing and releasing twenty-nine reindeer—a number a Fish and Game biologist had calculated to be well within the island's "carrying capacity."

Every farmer understands carrying capacity: Graze too many cows on your pasture and pretty soon you won't have a pasture anymore (or any cows, for that matter). It is in his self-interest to keep the balance going between his herd and the rain and the grass. So long as he does, he's got a sustainable source of milk and meat.

It was the same for those reindeer on St. Matthew Island. Keep the balance going between animals and the stuff they eat—lichens and willow bushes, mainly—and you've stocked the island with a bottomless meat locker. If storms kept the supply ships away, the men could shoot a reindeer for dinner.

Barged over from Nunivak Island, these twenty-nine animals found themselves in reindeer paradise—dense stands of willow bushes and vast, unbroken carpets of lichen four inches thick. There were no wolves, no bears. No predators at all, except for the men of the Coast Guard station. When the war ended, the base was shut down and the last predator left.

That same Fish and Game biologist returned to the island twelve years later and found those original 29 reindeer had become 1,350; just a little short of the number his colleagues had calculated as the island's ultimate carrying capacity. The animals were fat and seemed to be in excellent health. But he also noticed that the lichen mats were starting to look a little thin.

St. Matthew Island is so far off any beaten track he didn't return for six more years. When a Coast Guard cutter dropped him off again in the summer of 1963, as his boots hit the shore he saw reindeer tracks, reindeer droppings, and trampled willows. And everywhere he looked, wall-to-wall reindeer. In just six years those 1,350 animals had become 6,000—far more than the island could ever hope to carry. The lichens were sparse, and large areas of tundra were bare. Not surprisingly, the animals didn't look so fat and healthy anymore.

Other commitments kept him from returning for three more years. When he did, in 1966, the island he found was just about unrecognizable. The willows were gone. The last patches of lichen were gone, too, chewed down to gravel. Reindeer skeletons were scattered over the tundra. He found only 42 animals left alive.

What on earth had happened? In biological terms, it was a classic case of "overshoot." A population that had exploded far beyond the island's natural carrying capacity had collided head-on with another one of nature's iron laws: You can't go on consuming more than your environment is able to renew. It might take a while, but there will come a terrible day of reckoning, a catastrophe that biologists call "collapse."

And collapse it had. Those reindeer had destroyed a predator-free paradise. The accidental experiment was over, and there have been no living reindeer there for more than thirty years. Today the only sound you hear on St. Matthew Island is the wind howling over barren rocks, bare, muddy ground, and bleached bones.

I put that book down. I've often described the moment I finished reading that story as a spear in the chest. I don't know a better way of describing it. It was an epiphany, a rude awakening, an eye-opening experience, and the point of that story felt just like the point of a spear driven straight into my heart.

Reading Hawken's abbreviated account, I knew intuitively that what had happened on a small scale to that little island was the same thing we were doing on a vast scale to our whole world, with, as Hawken wrote, one key difference: "The resources used by the reindeer were grasses, trees, and shrubs. They will eventually return. Many of the resources we are exploiting will not."

Here was an ominous metaphor for the earth as well as for humankind. Just like those reindeer, our civilization was chewing up resources faster than the earth could renew them. We were poisoning the biosphere, killing it off species by species, forest by forest, farm by farm, ocean by ocean. And like those reindeer, there would come a time when our civilization—you, me, and everyone else—would collide with the same law of nature, a law as sure as gravity: Overshoot—consuming more than the earth can renew—ends in collapse.

I went to the tall bank of windows that grace my big corner office. I could see Stone Mountain on the horizon, rising up out of the brown crud of Atlanta's summertime air. Hawken's words haunted me as I thought about our factories, the smokestacks, the discharge pipes, the receiving docks stacked with raw materials made from oil, and the truckloads of scrap heading for the landfill, where they'd sit for something like the next twenty thousand years.

I stood indicted as a plunderer, a destroyer of the earth, a thief, stealing my own grandchildren's future. And I thought, *My God, someday what I do here will be illegal. Someday they'll send people like me to jail.*

Here was a bleak future, that worrisome problem in the headlights. I did not want to look, but I couldn't take my eyes off it either.

Well, I sure wasn't going to make *that* gloomy speech in front of the task force. So I took Hawken's book home that night. My wife of ten years, Pat, could see I was upset, and she was right. It was like being trapped in a car skidding on ice, headed straight for a cliff. You know what's coming but you can't turn, you can't stop. I read the story of St. Matthew Island to her, and we talked about its deeper meaning. I'm not ashamed to say that I wept. Then I went to bed, still reading, still confused, still without a vision for that speech.

Then, about midnight, I found something I wasn't expecting.

According to Hawken, not only was business and industry the principal instrument of global destruction, it was also the only institution large enough, wealthy enough, and pervasive and powerful enough to lead humankind out of the mess we were making.

Not government. Government never seems to lead; it always seems to follow. Not religious institutions, either. Until very recently many churches helped perpetuate the myth that the earth was ours to conquer and subdue, to abuse as we pleased. And sadly, not colleges and universities; they could train the next generation, but we needed action here and *now*. Who, then?

Hawken's answer was business and industry. Companies like mine. People like me.

Those of you who have studied some chemistry know about supersaturated solutions. You've prepared your experiment, mixed your chemicals correctly; the temperature is right. Everything is perfect. And yet the beaker refuses to change color; the crystals fail to form. Then you tap the glass with your pen, and suddenly everything changes.

*The only institution large enough, wealthy enough, and pervasive and powerful enough to lead humankind out of the mess we were making . . .*

Paul Hawken had just given me one hell of a tap.

Looking back, I realize now that so much was "in solution" in my mind. I was nearing the point in my career where smart founders start stepping back from day-to-day operations. In fact, I'd already recruited the management team I hoped would eventually take over the reins. But I was still uneasy. Some big, nagging questions were pushing that "inner solution" in my head in the direction of change.

What was I going to do next? Retire to the mountains or the seashore? Travel? Chase a little white ball up and down green fairways? What would this company, this precocious third child of mine, grow up to be? What kind of world would it see? What would my legacy be?

To those questions, add one more: What kind of world would my grandchildren inherit from me? If I can be allowed to borrow something Thoreau once said: "What use is a house if you haven't got a tolerable planet to put it on?"

The equation was simple and disturbing: Overconsumption and overshoot end in collapse. Sustainability means survival—as a company, as a nation, maybe even as a species. What business strategy could be more important than that? What about all the ingredients that go into making commercial carpets—the nylon face, the polymeric backings, all those billions of pounds of fossil fuels? You can pretty much sum them up with one word: oil. If a petro-intensive business like mine could start the sustainability ball rolling, the world might just sit up and pay attention. What, then?

In a flash, this supersaturated solution precipitated a true vision for me and for Interface. It was more than a speech for an environmental task force. It was a lot more than the "greenwash" we've seen so much of lately. You know what I mean: the transparent, self-serving green veneer with which some companies paint themselves in the hope that no one will take a closer look.

It was a vision that absolutely transcended compliance. It would be so much more than an answer to reassure our customers, and more than just a call to arms. It was a call to lead and a call to hope, loud and clear and powerful enough to energize a corporation and, with any luck, start a chain reaction throughout industry—not just ours, all of industry. A vision certainly big enough to give me a new purpose in life.

I got up from bed to get a glass of water and stopped in front of a mirror. I looked at myself long and hard, and I thought, Why not?

August 31 came and I stepped into that off-site conference room. Outside, the air was muggy and hot. Thunderstorms were in the forecast. Inside, the air-conditioning made the room temperature so cold you could almost see your breath. I saw familiar faces from our operations from around the world. Men and women who'd bet their futures on the same revolutionary idea for a revolutionary product that I had. As they quieted down and turned their attention my way, I thought, *If you thought carpet tiles were revolutionary, just wait.*

"Jim requested over a month ago that I make the keynote remarks for this conference," I began. "He wanted me to share my environmental vision with you. I accepted reluctantly because, frankly, I did not feel in my heart of hearts that I had one. Now I do."

I launched into my speech, using Hawken's material shamelessly, and described the epiphany I'd had from reading his book. I told them the story of St. Matthew Island, hoping they would see the same metaphor and draw the same conclusions I had. "An ecological crash will happen," I told them. "And hundreds of thousands, maybe millions, of species will be lost—forever. The 'death of birth,' Hawken calls it, for countless species never again to experience the miracle of birth."

My colleagues were looking a little nervous. I knew they were expecting a talk about legal compliance, about how to keep our corporate reputation clean. I could tell some of them were wondering where all of this was going and what it had to do with making carpet tiles.

"What happened on St. Matthew Island is a metaphor for the world," I told them. "Look around and you'll see many of the same signs. World grain production has already peaked and is in decline. So is the world's fish catch. Forests are disappearing. Aquifers are dropping. Deserts are growing. Oil is getting more expensive and harder to find. Nobody can predict what the implications might be for our business or our civilization. But I do know that, like those reindeer, we are far exceeding the carrying capacity of this good earth. Unless somebody does something to arrest and reverse the tide, catastrophe *will* strike. Now, what somebody am I talking about? The strongest institution in the world has to take the lead. That is not the church, it is not education, and it is not the government, either. It is business and industry. It is people just like us. Us."

No one said a word. It is not too strong a word to say they looked stunned. And with good reason. They were engineers, finance people, marketing experts, people who knew our business as well as I did.

"Look," I said, hoping to reassure them, "we're going to keep making carpet tiles. But we're going to shoulder our ecological responsibilities, too. What are they? Every business has three big issues to face: what we take from the earth; what we make with all that energy and material; and what we waste along the way. We're going to push the envelope until we no longer take anything the earth can't easily renew. We're going to keep pushing until all our products are made from recycled or renewable materials. And we're not going to *stop* pushing until all our waste is biodegradable or recyclable, until nothing we make ends up as pollution. No gases up a smokestack, no dirty water out a pipe, no piles of carpet scraps to the dump. *Nothing.*"

In the silence that followed I could actually hear the whisper of cold air flowing from the ceiling diffusers.

"I don't mean to quit doing business. I won't give up a single order, not one bit of market share. But I'm convinced that being a good steward of the earth can be good business, too."

I admit I said that with more confidence than I felt. And I could tell that some of my audience that day was, to say the very least, skeptical. But I had the same feeling about sustainability that I'd had when I first encountered carpet tiles. It was so right, so smart.

"The past belonged to the labor efficient—replacing people with machines. But the future is going to belong to the resource-efficient," I told them. "And that's what Interface must become. If our competitors copy us, fine. The earth wins. If they don't, *we'll* kick tail in the marketplace. Either way, we *will* win."

I waited for some reaction, some indication they were getting it. But all I saw was a room full of determinedly blank faces. What were they thinking?

"Listen," I said, "we all know quality doesn't cost, it pays. We're going to see if being good stewards of the earth works the same way. Our customers say they want it. Will they pay for it? Let's give them the chance to tell us. So let us commit today to doing more than just sitting here talking. Let's *act.* Let's see if we can be the first company in history to achieve real sustainability.

"So here's the vision that Jim asked me to share with you today: I want Interface to be the first name in industrial ecology, and here's my challenge to you. I want to know how long it's going to take us to get there. Then, I want to know what we'll need to do to push that envelope and make Interface a *restorative* enterprise. To *put back more than we take from the earth* and *to do good for the earth, not just no harm.* How do we leave the world better with every square yard of carpet we make and sell? We'll reconvene in two days and you can tell me. And yes, I know it's a huge technical challenge, and a big management challenge, too. But if Hawken is right, and industry must take the lead, who will lead industry? Unless *somebody* leads, *nobody* will. Why not us?"

Before they could tell me any of the dozens of good reasons that came to mind, I thanked them, turned on my heel, and left. And it was a good thing that I did.

Jim Hartzfeld, who now heads InterfaceRAISE, our corporation's sustainability consulting arm, told me what happened next. "The first reaction was one of confusion," he said. "And maybe fear, too. Here was our founder, our CEO, talking what we all knew was technical nonsense. We all knew that generating waste was part of doing business. We even had written standards for it: *expected* waste and *expected* off quality. And there was no source of, or market for, recycled carpet. Even if there were, recycled material would be too expensive, too contaminated to use. Virgin nylon is made from oil. PVC and bitumen come from oil. The electricity that runs our machinery is generated by coal, oil, and natural gas. Our trucks run on diesel. How were we going to stop using fossil fuels and stay in business? I sure didn't know.

"Then some pretty pointed remarks started popping out," said Hartzfeld. "We aren't in the conservation business. We make carpet tiles. What did this sustainability stuff even mean? Zero waste? Any engineer knows that violates simple physics. And even I thought the whole restorative thing sounded like some kind of green perpetual-motion machine. How can you make carpets out of nylon, which is oil, and add *anything* good back to the earth? Then it got down to the core questions on everyone's mind: Is he really serious? Does he really mean it? Can we put our heads down and wait for this all to blow over?"

Jim told me that that task force was on the thin edge of failure when Graham Scott stood up. He'd come over from England with some of the very first production machinery. I was Interface employee number one; Graham was number six.

"I know what it means to make compromises," he told the others. "As the head of a family, as the provider, I've had to go along with things I didn't agree with. We've all made compromises like that, haven't we?"

Heads nodded. "Compromise" sounded pretty good after the bomb I had just dropped. I guess they figured Graham was talking about pretending to go along with my plan to turn Interface sustainable, to make a few minor changes, maybe update our sales brochures with some pretty pictures of trees, and call it done.

If so, they were mistaken.

"If we can make these changes," Graham told them, "if we can transform a company that uses so much energy, so much oil, that wastes so much—if we can do all that profitably, then *any* business can do it. *No one* will have an excuse. And if we can show that to the world, I think it will make up for all the compromises we've had to make in our lives. Every one of them." And then he sat down.

There was another moment of silence, and finally Jim Hartzfeld said, "I guess we've got two days to design ourselves a perpetual-motion machine. Let's get started."

And so they did. I think what they came up with surprised them. I know it surprised me.

# 3 | One Small Digression and Six Lessons

*There is always a better way.*

DEAN FRANK GROSCLOSE, Georgia Tech, 1954

It doesn't make the news when the owner of a coal mine comes out against regulations that he thinks will take money out of his pocket. Or when a farmer growing designer lettuce pledges to go organic. And when some boys up in Vermont say they're going to make ice cream with milk from pampered, hand-raised cows, well, most folks just shake their heads and say, *What would you expect?*

But when the CEO of a sizable industrial enterprise like mine declares, with a bit of a Georgia accent, that he intends to eliminate his company's environmental footprint and become sustainable, and then restorative, it does raise some questions. Believe me, I've heard most of them.

*I thought Anderson was a cold-eyed capitalist. I thought he was one of us. What is going on here? Who is he and what planet did he come from?*

So if you'll permit me to introduce myself in my own way, here goes. I was born and grew up in the small Georgia town of West Point, the third of three sons: Bill Jr., Wiley, and I, "Baby Ray." My mother, Ruth McGinty Anderson, was a schoolteacher until she married. She had to retire, because even in the middle of the Great Depression, married ladies weren't allowed to teach school in West Point, Georgia.

My father, William, was the assistant postmaster in town, a secure government job in those hard, hard times. As the oldest of seven children, he had had to quit school after the eighth grade and go to work to help support his family. He did it because it was expected of him. He was plenty smart—especially in math—and with an education he could have done just about anything. I never heard him complain about it, though I knew it was a waste. I think he did, too.

Maybe that's why my father was bound and determined not to let the same thing happen to his three boys. He made sure that we all got good educations. Bill Jr. became a medical doctor; my other brother, Wiley, grew up to be an award-winning science teacher. What about me?

Well, I was the youngest, so I guess I knew there wasn't going to be much money left after my brothers' college bills got paid. It was a good thing I grew up with a football in one hand and a book in the other. While my mother made sure I studied hard, my father made sure I played even harder. He knew a college football scholarship would make it a whole lot easier (for him) for me to follow in my brothers' footsteps.

West Point High School's varsity football team was on its way to the state championships when their coach, Carlton Lewis, threw an eighth-grader named Ray Anderson into a scrimmage with them one afternoon. Though I was big and strong for my age, I quickly learned that quantity had a quality all its own. The lesson was hammered home that afternoon when I tackled a big, hard-charging running back who would go on to become a high school all-state and college-level player. My head and his knee collided in a bone-rattling crash that ended the day's practice for us both.

Well, that was enough for me. My head was spinning and I could feel a lump throbbing on my forehead. I could even see it rise. No scholarship was worth getting run down by a truck. So naturally enough, I didn't show up for practice the next day.

But Coach Lewis would have none of it. He left the field, found a telephone, and had a little talk with my father.

William Anderson listened to the coach, then hung up the phone. My father had never before—ever—left work in the middle of the day. But he did that day. He found someone to cover for him and stalked outside with but one purpose on his mind: finding me.

West Point is small, so it didn't take him long to walk up and down the streets, hunt me down, and deliver the tongue-lashing of my life. When he was finished I returned to the football field, sore and chastened, but also determined to *never* again be called a quitter, to never say die.

From then on I threw myself into every game I played, even when it hurt, even when injuries made it dumb to be out on the field at all, even though I *hated* football. But quit? Never. My father had made sure I got that message loud and clear. That's a memory—and a lesson—I carry with me to this day. Coach Lewis taught me to rise above all the obstacles—mental and physical—that get thrown in your path and to *compete*, and by competing to achieve more than you ever thought possible. That was another vital lesson. From founding a company to instilling its sales force with a never-say-die approach to business, they both have paid off in too many ways to count.

I also have a favorite childhood memory of sitting on the back steps of my home on a crisp, clear November afternoon, eating a pomegranate from the bush in our backyard and listening to the Georgia Tech football game on the radio. In 1945 I was an eager eleven-year-old, listening in as Tech's linebacker, Johnny McIntosh, tackled the Navy ball carrier at Tech's five-yard line. The football popped up in the air and freshman defensive sideback George Matthews grabbed it and returned it ninety-five yards for a touchdown.

A successful onside kick gave Tech the ball back, and Tech went on to win the game. I was listening again two years later when "Dinky" Bowen kicked a fourth-quarter field goal to beat Navy again, 17–14. I guess I've loved Georgia Tech for as long as I can remember.

Four years later I sat on those same steps polishing my football shoes for West Point's Friday night game, captain and all-star member of a team headed for another state championship game. An assistant to Georgia Tech's coach, Bobby Dodd, was right there with me, recruiting me to come to Atlanta as an offensive running back. When other scholarship offers arrived from Wally Butts of the University of Georgia, Shug Jordan of Auburn, and Bear Bryant of Kentucky, there was never one doubt in my mind where I was going to college. Now, with a scholarship in my pocket and a college education at hand, there was nothing that could hold me back. I was proud and happy. So was my father, who was also more than a little relieved.

But what to study? I'd always been interested in how things worked, I was good at math, and I love ideas. Engineering appealed to me, but what kind? When I showed up at Tech, I thought I'd give aeronautical engineering a try. But a couple of weeks of classes convinced me that I didn't want to design airplanes.

Civil engineering? Again, I figured out pretty quickly that laying out concrete retaining walls and designing bridges and sewers was not for me. How about textiles?

That made some sense. There were plenty of mills around West Point when I was growing up. A summer job at one of them after my freshman year at Tech taught me a lot of practical things about textiles but left me covered in sweat and lint at the end of every workday. For generations textile workers had been called "lint heads," and now I knew why. By summer's end I swore I would never to go back inside a mill again.

As I rotated through Tech's excellent engineering courses, I found them all interesting and surely challenging, but somehow they were focused too narrowly for me. I wanted to play on a wider field. And so, after my summer in the mills I gravitated to industrial engineering. Though the other kids— the "real" engineers—called IE "imaginary engineering," because it lacked a specialist's depth, its broader focus felt just right to me.

There I could study calculus, physics, electricity, chemistry, thermodynamics, fluid flow, strength of materials, and machine design. But I also learned how all those things worked together, how to make the man-machine system run efficiently, how to build something new—and market it, too. For electives I took public speaking. I took letter writing. I took a class in salesmanship.

I didn't know it at the time, but I was preparing myself for the work of an entrepreneur.

And very soon I encountered something new and very different from the hard-core engineering courses I had been taking. It didn't matter if the course was in electrical, mechanical, or chemical engineering. One got the idea that the professor *knew* there was just one good way to solve a design problem— the way it had always been done—and the sooner you learned that way the better.

Not so in industrial engineering. There my professors made sure we learned one thing first and foremost: "There's always a better way." That's another lesson imprinted on my brain for as long as I shall live. And for a lover of ideas, it's one to live by.

I played football until the NCAA ruled out two-platoon football in favor of one platoon, forcing Tech to combine its offense and defense teams into one. That was a problem for me. I was fast enough on offense. I could carry and catch the ball, even throw it. But an old injury to my shoulder meant I couldn't take a hit the way the other boys could, and playing defense meant taking lots of hits. I was one hard tackle away from a lifelong disabling injury.

Sure enough, a dislocated shoulder in my sophomore year sidelined me. I didn't quit; I was forced to "retire." But my faith in Coach Dodd was repaid in spades. Though I had to do menial work around the locker room instead of carrying the ball on the field, he honored my full scholarship. Coach Dodd's word was his bond, pure and simple. It was the measure of him as a man, and I will always remember that as a lesson, and with tremendous gratitude, too.

I know the assistant postmaster in West Point, Georgia, was certainly grateful.

I was more relieved. I figured I now had it made—a free ride at Tech on a bum shoulder. But when I said that to my father, he about took my head off and warned me to never, *ever* say those words again. What if that remark got back to Coach Dodd? Didn't I understand how lucky I was? Didn't I appreciate what I was getting?

Well, I got his message, and he calmed down. And for the next three years I did odd jobs around the locker room, handing out and picking up "socks and jocks," managing the athletic department's bookstore, and showing up every day for practice in sweats. But no more pads, no more brain-rattling collisions.

I couldn't play hard anymore, but I threw my energies into studying even harder than before. I made the Tau Beta Pi engineering honor society (a technical university's equivalent of Phi Beta Kappa), and graduated in 1956 with highest honors. It was a golden year, because this newly minted Bachelor of Science in industrial engineering found himself smack in the middle of an incredible economic boom. Finding a job was no problem at all. Picking one from the many offers on hand was the challenge.

After graduating, I worked for a major food company in a succession of engineering jobs. Then, despite my experiences in that dusty textile mill, wouldn't you know it? I found myself working for one of the biggest textiles companies in America, Deering-Milliken. My wife, Sug, had hoped I'd find something that would allow us to stay in the South, and I had. But it was like jumping into cold water after those wide-ranging, question-everything classes at Tech.

Very little was questioned at Milliken, except by Mr. Milliken himself. Everything went to him through well-worn channels as dark and dusty as the mills themselves. Mr. Milliken had all the ideas. He made all the decisions. Our only job was to carry them out. It was stultifying and frustrating. I worked hard and succeeded, but I surely was not happy.

When a position opened up at another textile company, Callaway Mills Company in LaGrange, Georgia (near my hometown of West Point), I jumped at it. Callaway was smaller, more flexible, and best of all it was in the middle of a big reorganization and revitalization, with lots of new talent being brought in. It was a good place to go for someone who thought a company should always be on the lookout for that better way of doing things.

The CEO, Fuller Callaway, after "restocking" the ranks with us new hires, gave everyone a daylong battery of intelligence and aptitude tests to see where they might best fit into his brand-new management team. I came out on top and was handed all the authority any twenty-five-year-old executive could hope for. Four years later I was vice president in charge of all nonfinancial staff functions at a company with $80 million in annual sales.

By any normal standard that was a meteoric rise. But as I climbed the corporate ladder I was aware, sometimes consciously, sometimes not, that working for someone else was not what I was cut out for. As the years went by and I gained more business experience, I became determined to build something of my own and find my own way—to do it *my* way.

That personal search got kicked into high gear when I was passed over for a job I not only deserved, but I really *wanted*—to head one of Callaway's three operating divisions. The smooth arc of my rising career had taken an unexpected sideways detour. I was stung and angry about it, too. I'd already resolved to take my fate into my own hands. A small nudge would have been enough, and this was a kick in the pants. But an even bigger one was coming.

On April 1, 1968 (yes, that's right, April Fool's Day), Mr. Callaway sold the whole company. Who bought it? Milliken. I was back in those rigid, hierarchical channels again. Some of the boxes on the organization chart had been shifted but very little had actually changed. Mr. Milliken still called all the shots. Soon, all my staff functions at Callaway were absorbed into the much larger, top-down corporate structure I'd been so glad to leave once before.

But serendipity can trump all the plans, all the expectations you make for yourself, even the disappointments. In 1969, I was assigned to be the director of development of Milliken's Floor Coverings Division. There I made the acquaintance of a brand-new product: carpet tiles. They had been invented in Holland and perfected in England. From the minute I saw them, it was love at first sight. Here (at last) was something *really* new and different. Or as my IE professors at Tech might say, *a better way.*

Carpet tile was a product tailor-made for the new offices I saw going into buildings all around me, offices that needed to retool and reconfigure themselves every few years—even every few months—with new computers, copiers, and telecommunications technology. An office landscape that was forever evolving and changing needed a floor covering that could evolve right along with it. Broadloom couldn't hack it. Tiles could. It just seemed so right to me, so obviously smart.

And so I took a leading role at Milliken in bringing carpet tiles from Europe to the United States. Though Milliken was not the first company to sell them here (no surprise there), the company was a fast follower, and its size and market dominance put this new product on the map. But I could see there was a huge opportunity out there, bigger than Milliken could ever satisfy. It was obvious to anyone who cared to look, and as I said, I was definitely looking. This was an idea with a tremendous future.

So, in 1973, after seventeen years of climbing the corporate ladder with major corporations, I cut the corporate umbilical cord. I took the entrepreneurial plunge and founded a company to produce free-lay carpet tiles in the United States. To compete. I knew it was right, but it meant making two of the hardest decisions of my life: risking my entire life's savings on a new idea a lot of smart guys thought was crazy; and putting a tremendous strain on my marriage to Sug, the mother of our two wonderful daughters.

We had married early, between my sophomore and junior years at Tech, and only with Coach Dodd's permission. We told our parents. We had to *ask* the coach. Sug had grown up in Atlanta, and we had met as teenagers when she visited her grandmother in West Point one summer. Sug's father had just died from his second cerebral hemorrhage in ten years, and her mother was drawn back to her own roots in West Point. We began to date that summer, and four years later we were married.

She was as ambitious for us as I was, though I came to believe the insecurities that stemmed from her father's early death haunted her. As a result, Sug was steadfastly opposed to the idea of my leaving a good, established job with a good, established corporation. I could see her point. Our daughters, Mary Anne and Harriet, would soon be going away to college. That would cost a lot of money. Didn't I have a dependable job? Why couldn't I just be content with that? They were good questions then, and they're good questions still.

But I was driven to seize the opportunity to build something of my own, to escape the frustrations that came from working inside a rigid hierarchy, to succeed on my own terms, and to never, ever work for someone else again if I could help it. I remember learning a poem in seventh grade. It was William Ernest Henley's "Invictus":

> *Out of the night that covers me,*
> *Black as the Pit from pole to pole,*
> *I thank whatever gods may be*
> *For my unconquerable soul.*
>
> *In the fell clutch of circumstance*
> *I have not winced nor cried aloud.*
> *Under the bludgeonings of chance*
> *My head is bloody, but unbowed.*
>
> *Beyond this place of wrath and tears*
> *Looms but the horror of the shade,*
> *And yet the menace of the years*
> *Finds, and shall find me, unafraid.*
>
> *It matters not how strait the gate,*
> *How charged with punishments the scroll,*
> *I am the master of my fate;*
> *I am the captain of my soul.*

When I learned the poem in the seventh grade it had seemed like only words. But those words had stuck deep in my psyche. Now they were taking on even deeper meaning. Being the "master of my fate" did not mean taking the easy way, the comfortable, secure path. How could I be the captain of my soul and acquiesce to another person's insecurities and fears, or to my own? This was my first real crisis of identity, and it was not easy to deal with.

I remember one particularly heated argument with Sug, while I was still wrestling with the go/no-go decision. I turned away from her, stormed into an adjacent room, slammed the door shut, and fell down to the floor in abject anguish, beset by the plague of unknowns (and fears) that accompany most major, life-changing decisions. Should I do it, or not? What if Sug is right? My God, what if I fail?

Even if everything I hoped for came to pass, even if carpet tiles really were a better mousetrap, it felt like stepping off a cliff in the dark, not knowing if my foot would land on solid ground or thin air. But one thing I knew: If I took that step, my fate—good, bad, or indifferent—would at last rest in my own hands. I would be, perhaps for only a short while, the captain of my fate.

Wasn't that worth it?

I think there comes a moment in every entrepreneur's life when all the data you're likely to get are in, all the opinions sought and heard, all the equations, all the cash flows are laid out on paper, and it is still not enough to know if you're doing the right thing. There is a gap between here and there. A wide chasm of pure unknowns that you've either got to leap over or turn away from. It is the moment when the data fall away and you're all alone, listening to your inner voice. Call it instinct, call it irrational compulsion. You might even call it hope, though I knew hope was generally a poor strategy. But what good were all the strategies in the world without it?

Well, I got up off that floor and shouted out to no one but myself, *"By God, I'm going to do it!"*

I faced that gap, that chasm. It was frightening, but I did not turn away. Despite all the uncertainties, despite the fact that Milliken claimed I was taking proprietary secrets and one of my biggest backers was forced to withdraw his support, I took the jump.

The proprietary information issue was resolved. The financing came through. I landed on the other side of my personal Rubicon, and I was on my feet. Though I found the start-up stress of founding Interface was really hurting Sug, I could only push ahead. We grew apart because of our disagreements, which opened a gap that neither of us could bridge. Ten years later, we divorced.

Interface was born in a maelstrom, and came close to not being born at all. Creating it was as costly as hell, both financially and emotionally. This is why its past, its present, but also its future are all so precious to me. I trust you can now see why I want this precocious third child to grow up healthy and strong, to thrive as a virtuoso in a healthy world where all my hopes for it can come to pass.

# 4 | Mountain Climbing

*I studied "quantum change" in business school. I didn't realize it at
the time, but "quantum change" is just a bump in the sidewalk
compared to changing Interface into a sustainable corporation.*

JIM HARTZFELD, Interface, Inc.

So, just what was that big surprise Jim Hartzfeld came up with back in
August 1994? Here it is: Two days after I gave my kickoff speech he
came back and told me that Interface could be the world's first sustainable corporation by the year 2000. That's right: In just six years, at the dawn
of the new millennium, 100 percent of our raw materials and energy could
be derived from renewable sources. We could be waste- and pollution-free,
the first name in industrial ecology, and doing business globally with no
environmental footprint. Zero.

In just six years? Ridiculous! When I asked them how long, I certainly
did not expect this.

In retrospect, I think that task force was looking at the low foothills of
Mount Sustainability and mistaking them for the summit. Their initial skepticism had turned into exuberance that, combined with a generous measure
of naïveté, had led them to an overly optimistic date. I knew in a general
sense where we should be headed, but none of us knew how to get there, or
how long it might really take. After all, corporate sustainability was unexplored terrain back then, terra incognita. For sure there was no how-to book
(like this one) to turn to for guidance.

How do you even start to think about sustainability? How do you define
it? And just as important, how do you communicate a vision of it to the
people who work with and for you, most of whom have never heard the word

*sustainability* before? These were daunting questions for us then, and good answers were hard to come by.

We knew that sustainability was not just the green branch of philanthropy, nor some pixie dust to sprinkle over a PR campaign to win market share. But did it mean throwing out the whole way we did business, or could it be something less drastic?

I knew intuitively that achieving sustainability would be more than a minor shift. It would not allow us to keep doing next year pretty much what we had done the year before. But how do you sell something like that, so new, so hard to grasp, to your associates? Your board? Your stockholders and the folks on Wall Street?

One thing I *did* know: As I immersed myself in researching the subject of sustainability, the more folks I talked to the more complicated and demanding it seemed. Profits, losses, and returns on investment are fairly simple concepts. But what in heaven's name is sustainability? How do you measure it? Where do you measure it? Where are the boundaries? What are the key variables?

Does sustainability start and stop at the factory door? Does it reach upstream to your suppliers? Downstream to your customers? Does it extend all the way from the mines and the oil wells to the landfill? What about reclamation? Does the technology even exist? What must be invented? How could we keep our people focused on the objective?

I am sure that some folks will be tempted to look at all of this complexity and throw up their hands and decide it's too much to think about. Others see an opportunity to "go green" on the cheap, either to make a quick buck, deflect public criticism, or keep regulators at bay. Take a look around today and you'll find the word used in some very odd places.

You'll come across oil companies talking about their "sustainability programs," though some of them have spent a lot more time, effort, and money trying to confuse folks about climate change. But a sustainable oil field? A sustainable refinery? You can argue about when oil production is going to peak, in five years or five hundred, but most honest people, no matter their politics, will agree that fossil fuels aren't going to be regenerated any time soon. How about sustainable tobacco? Or sustainable land-mine production?

Leaving aside the fact that some things should not be made at all, those are two very strange combinations. When the word is used in pesticide ads, you know something's really not right. Like green, everyone is for it, but what does sustainable actually mean?

In some ways, it's easier to define the word in the negative. To be unsustainable is to engage in business practices that destroy the very conditions upon which the practices depend. You can come up with your own list of examples, but here are a few:

- the water company that draws down its aquifer so far that seawater percolates in and contaminates it;
- the fishing industry that overfishes the cod population to collapse;
- the car company that stubbornly builds inefficient vehicles their customers shun;
- the logger who clear-cuts a forest and leaves a muddy wasteland where nothing—not even replanted seedlings—can grow.

And so on. But sustainability isn't just about aesthetics or fairness either. It's certainly not a box for some compliance officer to check off (Done!). And it is not a label to stick on a product, hoping to fool someone into buying it, though plenty of companies keep trying. A recent study by TerraChoice Environmental Marketing, Inc., showed that of 1,018 consumer products bearing 1,753 environmental claims, all but one was demonstrably false, or risked misleading their intended audiences. Being sustainable is more than just being environmentally "friendly," too; and sorry, but pretty pictures and superficial fluff don't pass the smell test.

If you're looking for a good, workable definition, this one comes to my mind: In business, sustainability is all about coming up with ways to meet our needs (not wants—needs) today without undermining the ability of other folks to meet their needs tomorrow. The Brundtland Commission of the United Nations says it a bit more elegantly, but the message is the same: "Sustainable development is development that meets the needs of this generation without sacrificing the ability of future generations to meet their needs."

But how many future generations is that, anyway? One? Seven? A thousand? You can discuss that forever and never get a thing done. Instead, we elected to sidestep the question by defining sustainability in our own way, and we set the bar very high:

To operate this petroleum-intensive business in a manner that takes from the earth only that which is naturally and rapidly renewable—not one fresh drop of new oil—and to do no harm to the biosphere.

In short, *Take nothing. Do no harm.* The utility of that definition is that it works today and all the way out into the indefinite future, to any number of unborn generations, and focuses us on our business and what we must do better today, and day after day.

But it is also very ambitious. And getting there will require us to think about doing business—and our place in the world—in entirely new ways.

On the societal level, we'll have to start setting ecologically honest prices that reflect the damage we do to innocent third parties—society in general—who are neither buyers nor sellers in the transactions that damage them. Only when all these "externalities" appear in prices, profits, and losses can an honest free market function responsibly.

At the corporate level, we'll need new tools to help us evaluate choices and trade-offs, tools that look far deeper than we're accustomed to and measure results beyond the immediate dollars and cents—certainly beyond the immediate financial quarter. We'll need new ways to analyze our operations in what I like to call "God's currency," the nonfinancial costs and benefits that accrue to the living world as a result of everything we do to the land, sea, and air around us.

I'll give you an example. We first recognized the need for a metric like God's currency when we faced this dilemma: Our chemists at Interface recognized a way to reduce the amount of oil-derived, nonrenewable material in our carpets by 40 percent. We could substitute benign, abundant inorganic material in place of all that precious oil-based material if we introduced a chlorinated hydrocarbon into the mix. Sounds great, doesn't it?

Except that the chlorine component, in an oxygen-starved incinerator or backyard fire, could send small amounts of toxic dioxins up with the smoke. What's the right thing to do? Save a lot of oil and risk generating a small amount of toxic gas under certain rare and unusual circumstances? Or do nothing?

We would need ten years of searching before God's currency came into focus, but we decided to follow our common sense, save enormous quantities of oil today, and simultaneously reduce our environmental footprint while tackling recycling to avoid the problems that accompany incineration.

You can see from that one example that we've got to consciously start taking responsibility for the kind of world we want to live in now, as well as for the kind we hope to hand to our children and grandchildren.

You are probably getting the idea that running a business that aspires to sustainability demands a new paradigm for running our whole industrial civilization, and you are right. It is like Daniel Quinn's new set of wings that I mentioned before, wings designed to honor, respect, and protect nature. Only they can carry us on a sustainable flight into the indefinite future.

A brief aside. I sometimes find myself talking about this to business leaders across the country, even across the globe. I've been accused of preaching to the choir, and it is true that most audiences are friendly and receptive. But not everyone in all those audiences agrees with me. Every once in a while I run into a businessman who gets red-in-the-face angry when I suggest we need to make this paradigm shift. He is dead sure I want to shackle the free market with regulations and impose limits on the way he does business. There's some real irony here, because the truth is that adopting sustainable practices is all about protecting the goose that lays all his golden eggs, for that's what nature is all about. Running his business sustainably *removes* the limits with which he has unconsciously shackled himself.

A big part of the problem is that we don't keep honest books. Just because nature provides us with services that don't appear (yet) on a balance sheet or in a profit-and-loss statement doesn't mean we can ignore them. As some large corporations have discovered, ignorance can be extremely costly.

Back in the 1980s Vittel, a mineral water company that is part of Nestlé Waters, discovered pesticides and nitrates in the spring that fed their bottling plant. It turned out that farmers had cleared native vegetation that once filtered the water that recharged Vittel's aquifer. Without that filter Vittel's mineral water, and their entire business, were suddenly at risk.

Unilever, an international corporation with brands like Lipton, Surf, and Vaseline, discovered the North Atlantic cod fishery that they depended upon for their premium frozen fish division was in real trouble. Why was that? Because those cod had been overfished to the point of collapse. This pushed Unilever's costs up dramatically and, since they could only pass some of those added costs along to the consumer, it cut their margins—by 30 percent.

Energia Global (now Enel Latin America), was a hydropower company that was literally losing its source of power—and revenue. Landowners upstream of their dams were clearing off forests for livestock and agriculture. When the rains came there were no trees left to keep the rivers from eroding their banks and filling the reservoirs with silt and mud, and you can't run silt and mud through a turbine.

In these three examples, nature was providing a service that the blind hunt for privatized profits, aided by externalized costs, had threatened. After all, why shouldn't those farmers clear their land? Use nitrates and pesticides? Cut their trees? Why shouldn't those fishing boats sweep the ocean clean of fish? Nestlé, Unilever, and Enel Latin America certainly found out why.

Here's another example, and one that hit very close to my home.

Ask yourself this question: What is the value of a forest? Traditional thinking would say that X board feet of lumber at Y dollars per board foot, less the cost of harvesting the trees, equals the value of that forest. But is that an accurate reckoning? Not by a long shot.

I'll tell you a story about a small town on the banks of the Chattahoochee River in west central Georgia. In the first hundred years of its existence, this small town never experienced a flood. Then one year the banks of the river overflowed, causing $5 million worth of damage. So the city fathers commissioned a dike to be built at a cost of about $3 million. The dike was good enough to prevent another flood for the next five years. But then came a season of especially hard rains, the dike was breached, and this time the flood damage came to $10 million.

And so they rebuilt that dike even higher, though the cost of construction—$8 million—had risen even faster than those floodwaters. The new dike protected the city for another seven years, and then, wouldn't you know it, the river flooded again, the dikes were breached, and finally someone asked, "What is going on here?"

So a team of experts was engaged to analyze the problem and find some answers. One of those experts was an ecologist, and he, with brilliant insight, looked at the problem from a different perspective. He didn't research rainfall records, or the details of the dike constructions, or the laminar or turbulent flow of rivers. No, he looked upstream. What did he find?

He found that over a period of twenty years, the forests through which the Chattahoochee ran had been clear-cut for fifty miles upstream, drastically changing the hydrology of the region. Root systems were no longer there to hold the rainfall. It ran off into the streams and rivers, eroding the land, filling the riverbed with silt, and flooding the unfortunate city downstream.

And killing the fish, too, depriving the poor people of the area an important source of sustenance. I know my father used to catch twenty-pound channel catfish in that river. Our family could eat off it for a week. Those big channel catfish are gone now.

Ultimately, our federal government, in its dubious wisdom, built a dam to control the Chattahoochee River, at a cost of $100 million. That dam destroyed twenty-eight thousand acres of forests and prime agricultural land, not to mention the habitats of all the living things that once called those acres home. Today that lake is a polluted cesspool, collecting Atlanta's occasional sewage overflow and destroying the lake's recreational value—the other justification for building the dam in the first place.

So now ask yourself that question again: What is the value of a forest? The board feet are gone, enriching but a few, but leaving the externalities for many others to deal with. The shortsightedness of traditional economics lies pretty much exposed, does it not? And I have not even mentioned the value of a forest in sequestering carbon or producing oxygen, nor the songs of birds no longer heard where those forests used to be. Neither have I mentioned the disease-spreading insects that now proliferate unchecked because the birds, their predators, are gone. Nor the children who come down with encephalitis as a direct result.

You can see what I mean when I say we need to look at the world through a different, wider angle lens. As Albert Einstein once said, "Problems cannot be solved by the same thinking used to create them." In other words, we need new thinking from a higher level of awareness. So how do we begin? The truth of a new paradigm doesn't just spring into existence. It will have been there all along, obscured by the old, flawed views of reality. After all, the earth was round even when everybody knew it was flat.

I like to say that the shift to sustainability will happen one mind, one company, one technology, one university curriculum, one industry, one community at a time. And I've seen it happen. I remember the first time I spoke before the United States Green Building Council (USGBC), back in 1995 in Big Sky, Montana. I counted heads in the audience; there were just 135 people in that room. When I shared the opening plenary at the USGBC meeting in Atlanta with Paul Hawken and Janine Benyus ten years later, there were 12,000! Two years after that, in Chicago, over 22,000 registered and an estimated 40,000 showed up. In business, that is a growth curve to die for. Today, USGBC's Leadership in Energy and Environmental Design (LEED) rating system is emerging as the global model for green building standards.

Clearly there's a broad awakening under way. Something is happening, and every business person would be wise to pay attention to it. Here in America the number of families who have some regular affiliation with companies and organizations involved with sustainability is already in the millions, and growing every year. They already have a very strong presence in the market where my company does business, and without a doubt, sooner or later, the same will be true for yours.

But there's no denying that there is also a fair amount of resistance to change. Why? Well, I think there's more than just inertia or perverse incentives at work. Our culture is very much in the grip of some old, flawed views that stand in direct and violent contrast to sustainability. Flawed views that are reflected in, and fueled by, consumerism, our insatiable infatuation with *stuff*.

There is the flawed view that treats the earth as though it were an infinite source of raw materials to feed our industrial system, stock our shelves, fill our houses, crowd our garages, and spill out into rented storage units or in landfills, waterways, oceans, and the air.

There is the flawed view that adopts the annual (or quarterly) time frame to measure the worth of an idea. There is the flawed view that forgets to ask one simple question when assessing the environmental costs of a business decision: What if everyone did it?

What if everyone discharged untreated wastewater into the local river? What if everyone sent hazardous waste to be buried in the local landfill? What if everyone left their office lights burning, or truck engines running, or thermostats set too high or too low?

What if everyone did it?

There is the flawed view that assumes this world is ours to conquer and rule, that we can take what we want from it without regard for all the other species that depend on—and comprise—nature itself. The selfsame natural world that we depend on and are part of, too.

There is the flawed view that when accumulating all that stuff gets us into trouble technology will see us through, even though it's the extractive, abusive attributes of technology—especially when coupled with numbers-driven, unemotional, results-oriented, left brain intelligence—that got us into the fix to begin with.

And there is the flawed view that relies on the invisible hand of the market to be an honest broker, even though we know the market can be very dishonest. Does the price of a pack of cigarettes reflect its true cost? Not even close! How about the price tag on a lead-tainted toy from China? A box of contaminated infant formula? I don't think so.

And the price of a barrel of oil? Last time I looked the oil companies weren't deploying armies or naval forces to the Middle East to protect the oil fields and tankers. You and I are doing that with our taxes. Our sons and our daughters are doing it with their lives. The oil companies aren't paying the medical bills for all those folks breathing smog, either. Nor are they building the seawalls our coastal cities will need to keep the warming, rising ocean from drowning them. Let all those be somebody else's problem. Let our grandchildren foot the bill.

Talk about innocent third parties!

Add up all the costs the oil companies are happy to have someone else pay on their behalf, and the price of a barrel of oil—even by today's measure—is too low by $150, and maybe $200. It is infinitely too low if you've lost a son, a daughter, a husband, or a wife to war.

Here's the thing. While a few of us might enjoy the fruits of what we think is a free market, we all suffer the consequences of a rigged one, a market that is very good at setting prices but has no concept at all of costs. A market that's rigged to get someone else to pay the bills whenever and wherever a gullible or unwary public allows it to happen. A system of economics that idealizes the so-called *Basic Economic Problem* as the driver of all economic progress. The "problem"? The gap between what we have and what we *want*; not *need*, want.

So how should we look at the world, and ourselves, from the point of view of sustainability? How do we reshape the linear take-make-waste conveyor belt we're stuck on and bend it into a closed loop circle? Let me tell you another quick story.

Right after I made that kickoff speech in 1994, one of my colleagues came up and said, "Isn't it strange how we call our factories 'plants'? They don't look like plants and they don't work like plants. A plant runs off solar power, rain, and soil. All renewable. Its waste (e.g., dropped leaves) is 100 percent biodegradable. In fact, some other plant probably uses its waste as food and turns it right back into soil, and more plants. It also gives off oxygen, so it is even restorative to the animal kingdom. What if our plants worked more like that? Isn't that what you're really talking about?"

My first thought was that this irony was an interesting, amusing observation but not a direction we could follow. What did plants have to do with making carpet tiles? But as we got down into the details of transforming our corporation, this casual observation began to take on the weight of a deeper truth. I know now that that associate was starting to get it.

In this same vein, someone once said that a computer is nothing special. If you want to see some *real* technology, study a tree. When we understand how a healthy tree works, how a healthy forest works, and emulate those myriad symbiotic processes and relationships in the way we do business, I think we'll be on the right track to a healthy corporation, a healthy industrial system, and a sustainable world.

Okay, you say, that may be the pretty view from thirty thousand feet. What am I supposed to do down in the trenches where businesses compete? Where budgets have to be set, and met? If Paul Hawken was right, and business and industry have to take the lead in creating a sustainable world, how do I do it?

When I first asked that question I was pretty much alone, and considered "around the bend." Today other CEOs have come to realize that achieving true sustainability is not just nice to have; it is a mission-critical business move (Wal-Mart, GE, PepsiCo, Patagonia, Stonyfield Farm, STMicroelectronics, and Google come to mind). But we can't wait for all the others to come to their own epiphanies the way I did. And most people in the business world shudder at the very thought of government mandates.

But there is another way, a third way, in which we can turn to move our businesses toward sustainability. A way that unleashes a force even greater than our passion for wants, powerful enough to move mountains and overcome just about any inertia. What is that force?

It's something we used to be pretty good at—good old capitalist, enlightened self-interest, the irresistible magnetic force that in a free society draws innovation and capital straight to opportunity. Economists like to say there can be no twenty-dollar bills lying in the street, because someone would surely have noticed all that cash and already picked it up. Well, when it comes to sustainability, they're partially correct.

There aren't many twenties in the street, but there's a regular blizzard of thousands! Going after them might be called "good greed," and I think it's exactly the force that will compel business and industry to charge right to the top of Mount Sustainability.

Look, I know we're not going to get this job done in just a few years. I know that bringing our companies, our universities, our governments, our families, and ourselves into balance with the earth's natural systems is a huge challenge. But the payoff is nothing short of survival—while earning a solid, honest, ethical profit. It is one of the key things we hope to accomplish at Interface: to prove this new and better business model works, to demonstrate by our own example that reaching for sustainability can lead to bigger and more legitimate profits; and by doing so, to attract other companies around the world to the model.

The good news is that we can do it one small, smart step at a time, each one paying its own way and laying the groundwork for the next. Each step will make us a little less *un*sustainable, and simultaneously more profitable. There is nothing much we need to discover and not much new technology that we still have to invent. We know just about everything that's necessary. Let me be specific.

In that kickoff speech, borrowing from Hawken, I said that every company has to face three ecological challenges honestly and head-on:

1. What we **take** from the earth.
2. What we **make**, and what collateral damage we do in the making of it (pollution of all kinds).
3. What we **waste** along the way (in all forms), from the wellhead to the landfill.

What do we take from the earth? Right now we humans are burning up something like a cubic mile of oil each year, as well as mountains of coal, to power our homes, our cars, our offices, and our factories, fuels that took millions upon millions of years to create—and only a few hundred to exhaust. A wise farmer would shake his head and say we were eating our own seed corn.

Eventually, the sustainable path will enable us to operate our factories— our plants—just like real plants, on renewable energy. A company can take a halfway step that might mean using fuel cells or gas turbines, or running the plants off reclaimed methane from our overburdened landfills. But ultimately we'll have to learn how to operate off current "energy income" the way a tree does, or, for that matter, the way we do already (or should) in our businesses and households with financial income. Not off stored natural capital like oil, coal, or gas, but off current energy income—wind, hydro, and solar.

What do we make? Right now what we make at Interface comes mostly from fossil fuels. But virgin raw materials from the mines or from forests work just about the same way. Harvest all the old-growth forest and it is gone. Mine all the metals and minerals, use them once and throw them away, and, for all practical purposes, they're gone, too. Remember the lesson of St. Matthew Island: Overconsumption (overshoot) leads to collapse.

The sustainable path will have us feeding our factories with recycled raw materials, in our case, harvesting the billions of square yards of carpets and textiles already made. As oil prices rise, the payoff will grow. Nylon-face pile will be reborn as new carpet, old vinyl backing into new carpet backing, old polyester fabric into new polyester fiber, using those precious organic molecules again and again in an endless cycle. Once through, linear processes are by definition unsustainable. Cycles are nature's way of getting the job done efficiently and right—and forever.

Of course, the recycling operations have to be run off renewable energy, too, or else we come out on the short end of the equation, consuming more fossil fuels than we save by displacing virgin petrochemicals in the first place. We must develop and apply those new tools I wrote about, seeking the wisdom of God's currency to solve the equation for a net gain, not a loss.

At Interface we've gotten the closest to understanding God's currency through our process of life cycle assessments (LCA). I'll talk about them in greater detail a bit later on, but through them we can measure comparative impacts (product versus product, process versus process, business versus business) in many dimensions of sustainability. Drawing on the best peer-reviewed science available, we can actually see the impacts and tradeoffs inherent in almost every business decision.

What do we waste? Right now, if you measured honestly, you'd discover that the overall efficiency of American industry is plain pathetic. How bad is it? Try this metric on for size: Ninety-seven percent of all the energy and material that goes into manufacturing our society's products is wasted. Mountains of tailings pile up at the mines. Energy goes up the smokestack, leaks out the wires, and ends up as waste heat. Year after year we send a tsunami of scrap to inundate our landfills. Only about 3 percent ends up as a finished product that still has any value six months later. Three percent!

We are operating an industrial system that is, in fact, first and foremost a waste-making machine. Ask yourself this analogous question: If you had a division in your company that wasted nearly everything it got its hands on, how long would you allow it to continue? I know how I would answer that question. And yet this is happening throughout industry, and is seen not only as normal, but successful!

And they said that *I* was impractical.

Eventually, the sustainable path will enable us to operate without emitting anything into the air or water that hurts the biosphere. We've come a long way with this at Interface, but we still have a way to go. Even after years of seeking alternatives, some of the materials coming into our factories still contain substances that should never have been taken from the earth in the first place. Nature spent eons removing them from up here and sequestering them down there. And down there is where they should remain. Why? Because we, like nature itself, could not have evolved in their toxic presence. One by one we're finding substitutes for them. All of them must go.

Can you imagine your factories—plants—running without creating any pollution? I can, because at Interface, we've already shut down one third of our smokestacks and 71 percent of our wastewater pipes. They've been turned into unused relics, obviated by process changes, by our relentless pursuit of that better *way*, and by working upstream with our suppliers to rid their products (our raw materials) of the bad actors.

We are determined that our trail up Mount Sustainability will not be strewn with waste. We are learning how to hunt down that waste wherever it may be hiding. We've already eliminated 78 percent of the scrap that used to be sent off to the landfill. It really bugs me that this is not 100 percent yet, but it will be one day.

The sustainable path will enable us to get our people and products from point A to point B in resource-efficient fashions. In my company, at any hour of any given day, hundreds, even thousands, of people are on the move. We've got trucks, trains, ships, and even aircraft delivering our products across the globe. We have always understood the financial costs of transportation. Now we're recognizing and assuming responsibility for the ecological costs, too.

Taking. Making. Wasting. Think of them as a three-sided prism. Looking at your business through it transforms undifferentiated white light into a spectrum of vivid colors. But instead of a red, orange, yellow, green, blue, and violet, now you see the seven paths to sustainability in sharp focus:

1. moving toward zero waste;
2. increasingly benign emissions, working up the supply chain;
3. increasing efficiency and using more and more renewable energy;

4. closed-loop recycling, copying nature's way of turning waste into food;

5. resource-efficient transportation, from commuting to logistics to plant siting;

6. sensitivity hook-up, changing minds and getting employees, suppliers, customers, and our own communities on the same page; creating a corporate "ecosystem," to borrow a term from nature, with cooperation replacing confrontation;

7. redesigning commerce, teaching a new Economics 101 that puts it all together and assesses accurate costs, sets real prices, and maximizes resource-efficiency.

These are the seven faces of Mount Sustainability. Each one must be challenged and climbed. I'll explore them separately in later chapters, using our own experiences at Interface as a model. There is a scoreboard at the end showing what we have done, what it has cost us, what the results have been, and how much we have profited by it. I will also examine what some other folks have done to scrutinize their own operations through that prism, and what they've discovered.

Underlying all of this is a new sense of the *Basic Economic Problem*: It is the gap between what we have and what we *need*. I speak a lot to audiences all over the world who want to hear the story of Interface's transformation. Usually there is a question and answer period after I speak. The most unusual (and difficult) question I ever received was this: "In a sustainable world, do you think there will be a need for carpets?" I was caught completely off guard and mumbled some incoherent reply. Only later did I think of what I wish I had said: "Yes, we are in the business of making and selling beauty to lift human spirits. That is a genuine need, and if we can do that sustainably (and only if) then, yes, there will be a place and a need for carpets."

Make no mistake. Mission Zero is hard, hard work. It is not a "program of the month." And nobody is making us do it. We're under no pressure from our competitors to achieve sustainability. Actually, I think *they* are the ones who feel a competitive pressure from *us*. Thus an entire industry inches toward sustainability.

Nor is it some unfunded mandate from the government. We're doing it because it is smart, because it is right. And when we succeed, we'll never again need another drop of oil for our petro-intensive industrial processes. We'll be doing very well by doing good.

That epitomizes my vision for Interface, and I know—just the way I knew carpet tiles were a good idea, just as I knew that what happened on St. Matthew Island was a metaphor for earth itself—that if we can get there, you can get there, too.

William Hutchinson Murray, a Scottish mountaineer who led an expedition into the high Himalayas, borrowed (and freely adapted) from Goethe's writings, when he wrote:

> Until one is committed, there is hesitancy, the chance to draw back. Concerning all acts of initiative (and creation), there is one elementary truth, the ignorance of which kills countless ideas and splendid plans: that the moment one definitely commits oneself, then Providence moves too. All sorts of things occur to help one that would never otherwise have occurred. A whole stream of events issues from the decision, raising in one's favor all manner of unforeseen incidents and meetings and material assistance, which no man could have dreamed would have come his way. Whatever you can do, or dream you can do, begin it. Boldness has genius, power, and magic in it. Begin it now.

This is so true! Genius. Power. And yes, even magic. I know from my own experiences, beginning with starting Interface from scratch, to committing it to its improbable mid-course correction twenty-one years later, that Goethe and Murray were right. I also know that the time for hesitancy and drawing back has passed. Providence and vast opportunities await us. Our grandchildren's grandchildren demand boldness from us.

Once again, it is time to stand on the edge of what might seem like a great unknown and, buoyed with vision, knowledge, hope, and, yes, confidence, to begin.

# 5 | Zero Waste: The First Face of Mount Sustainability

> *Our sustainability metrics are our reputation. If we exaggerate or mislead—even just a little bit—we could undo all the good work that's gone into them. Nothing is more important than getting the numbers right.*
>
> BUDDY HAY, assistant vice president for sustainable strategies, Interface, Inc.

When I talk about the drive to achieve real sustainability—putting what we take, make, and waste under a powerful microscope—waste always seems to hang at the tail end of things, like a caboose. But it really doesn't belong there.

The truth is, attacking waste is the engine that will pull the whole train. If you're looking for a quick, profitable ascent up one of those seven faces of Mount Sustainability, going after waste is the natural place to begin.

First, in contrast to introducing renewable energy and recycled materials into your factory, your university, or even your home, cutting back on waste is familiar territory. No CEO likes the idea of leaving profits on the factory floor. No facilities manager wants to toss good money into the Dumpster. No homeowner looks forward to writing unnecessary checks. Especially these days.

Most of us already know and accept all the whys of cutting back on waste even if we don't always know the hows. It is this familiarity that will make getting serious about it an easier sell to your employees, your board, your investors. Even to your family.

Second, really putting the screws to waste can generate cash savings that not only pay for themselves, but will also help to underwrite the more ambitious projects to come. Cutting waste is the first place where the economic risks of a bloated environmental footprint can be transformed into profitable opportunities.

That has most certainly been our experience at Interface, where our war on waste—like our pursuit of efficiency—has freed up hundreds of millions of hard dollars. This money now funds research and development, renewable energy, recycling, and new products—not to mention new designs that are inherently more efficient, less wasteful, more beautiful, and more profitable. It is a virtuous circle where you, your company, your customers, your stockholders, and the earth all come out ahead.

Third, as I said in the opening chapter, when it comes to running your operation with the earth and sustainability in mind, you will have no trouble finding skeptics. You'll find them among your friends, your colleagues, your board. The bold ones will take you aside and say, *Don't you know that all this environmental, global warming, peak-oil stuff is just*————. (You can fill in the blank.) Even if they're not quite that bold they might still ignore—or undermine—your efforts.

You might even run into resistance in some corners of Wall Street, though there has truly been a dramatic shift in attitudes there. But it surely wasn't that way back in 1994, when a man by the name of Dan Hendrix had the unenviable job of convincing the investor community that even if Interface's founder and CEO had gone round the bend, the company was still a good place to invest. But I ought to let him tell you what happened.

"I was the CFO—the finance guy—back in 1994," said Hendrix, who is now the CEO of Interface. "I had to take Ray's vision and sell it to Wall Street. It was not an easy job. The bankers and brokers heard 'sustainability' and equated it with cost, pure and simple. They did not like all this green talk one bit.

"But when I could go back to them with hard numbers and show that sustainability was about reducing waste and cutting costs while pumping up profits, they started to pay attention. When I could prove that Ray's vision had rewarded Interface with more sales, more market share, more profits, and better margins, they forgot their early objections and became our allies. They might not have understood sustainability, but when our stock went from $6.75 in 1994 to $15 three years later, they sure could understand *that*."

Today, finding "green investors" is not the uphill battle Dan experienced fourteen years ago. Now there are lots of folks on and off Wall Street who understand that the early mover corporations that start the climb to sustainability today are going to be the big winners tomorrow. And the ones that don't? Between the oncoming train of government regulation and the shift in the marketplace to environmentally responsible products, they're just going to be left in the dust. That prospect is beginning to soak in, too.

But no question, you will still encounter skeptics close to home. Gearing up to attack waste and turning environmental liabilities into a demonstrable cash flow is probably the most effective way to bring them on board.

Finally, shedding waste, like shedding pounds from your backpack, makes every subsequent step you take up Mount Sustainability that much easier. After all, no one should think of covering the roof of an office building with (expensive) photovoltaic panels (the technical term for solar panels) just to keep hundreds of incandescent lightbulbs burning. No trucking company should invest in a biodiesel fuel plant and not make sure that all the tires are properly inflated first. No college campus should buy a highly efficient heating and cooling system without insulating its buildings. Cutting waste first, then tapping into alternative supplies, is the right way to go.

Above all, remember:

- the greenest kilowatt-hour is the one you don't use;
- the greenest gallon of gas, diesel, heating oil, or ton of coal is the one you don't burn;
- the greenest Dumpster is the one you never fill.

So then, how should you think about what constitutes waste? Fortunately, it's a whole lot easier to define than sustainability. Here's the one that worked well for us:

*Waste is any measurable cost that goes into our product that doesn't add value for our customer.*

At Interface that means not only off-quality carpet and scrap, but anything we don't do right the first time: a misdirected shipment; a wrong invoice; a missed delivery date. Anything. Then, in 1998, we added this little kicker to our own definition: *All fossil fuel we use will be counted as waste to be eliminated.*

Think about that for a moment. All fossil fuel used—natural gas, oil, diesel, or electric power from a coal-fired plant—is treated in our metrics as pure waste. That was a revolutionary idea then, and I think it still is. And we kept pushing the envelope.

In 1999, we turned the spotlight on our yarn recycling program, folding it into our companywide waste-control campaign. Consequently, treating our most important, most expensive, and most energy-intensive raw material with great care moved onto everyone's radar screen. As we uncovered more and more ways to save on yarn, we pushed the envelope again and went after packaging. From 2001 on, 50 percent of all company packaging (generally cardboard cartons filled with yarn or carpet tile) has counted as waste. It would have been 100 percent, but those cartons do serve some useful purposes.

I love this story. The facility manager from a very large corporation, doing his due diligence, came to visit us to see if we were for real on all this "sustainability stuff." He took a tour of our factory in West Point, with an Interface guide, and when he saw stacks and stacks of old, used cartons, his face just fell. He was incredulous. I admit, they were kind of ugly, all taped up and battered.

"Is that the image you want to send to the world?" he asked one of our people.

"Absolutely," the Interface person replied. "You see, those boxes get used over and over again. Around here, a box is a box as long as a box can be a box."

The facility manager said that those boxes instantly became the most beautiful boxes he had ever seen.

So how did we go about measuring waste? We broke it down into three distinct categories, then applied those categories to every one of our facilities worldwide:

1. How effective is your use of materials? In a word, resource-efficiency.
2. How much have you reduced your energy use, especially non-renewable energy use?
3. How big a bite have you taken out of nonproductive costs and activities, including administrative costs?

Each category was broken down again, into a number of concerns particular to our business. We make carpet tiles, so, as I said, how we handled the yarn that makes the face of the carpet is right at the top of the list. Using materials effectively meant paying very close attention to the way we cut large carpet rolls into individual tiles. We want to minimize the "windowpane" trimmings that are left over, waste that is analogous to the extra dough you end up with after stamping out a pan of cookies.

We quickly learned that by making very sure the carpet is fed evenly and squarely into the tile cutters, we could substantially reduce those windowpane trimmings—in one notable case, from two inches wide to just under one inch. Now, one inch of carpet may not sound like much; it's only about 2 percent. But when you manufacture millions of square yards of it, I assure you, that 2 percent represents a lot of energy, material, and money. The investment in better devices to guide the carpet into the cutters more precisely was a no-brainer.

Since all nonrenewable energy is considered waste, every facility worldwide is on the lookout to improve their waste numbers by reducing energy use first, and then introducing renewable sources of power. This can happen in several ways.

First, we can actually generate green power on-site, as we do at our Bentley Prince Street facility in Southern California, at our factory in LaGrange, Georgia, and at our Dutch facility at Scherpenzeel. Or we can purchase green power from local utilities when they offer it. Every one of our European plants runs off 100 percent green power, straight off the grid. Third, we can invest in off-site renewables to green our energy mix. We're not hooked up directly to windpower generating stations in North Dakota or New Zealand, but we can buy renewable energy credits (REC) from utilities that are. Whether we generate it ourselves or pay someone else to, the earth wins.

What are renewable energy credits? I'll talk about RECs in the chapter on greening your power, but generally speaking they're tradable certificates that represent a subsidy for a certain amount of renewable electricity (usually one megawatt hour). Using RECs, ordinary grid power takes on certified green benefits that stay with the electrons and the resulting power that is delivered to the user. RECs are not grid power; they represent the environmental attribute of renewable energy that is produced and sold into the grid somewhere else. So a facility buys conventional power from the grid, but "greens" it by buying RECs generated somewhere else from solar, wind, geothermal, low-impact hydroelectric dams, and biomass generators. The price paid for a REC goes a long way toward leveling the playing field when renewable sources compete against coal, oil, gas, and nuclear plants—industries that are largely (and not so covertly) subsidized.

And here's something for folks who remain skeptical about our journey up Mount Sustainability, who think we're buying our way to the top. In our global greenhouse gas (GHG) emissions numbers, we do not count the carbon emissions benefits from the RECs we buy. Why not?

Because the rules for buying and counting RECs are still being ironed out, and there remains a danger of double counting the carbon benefit as well as questions about clear titles to the credits. So we'll wait and see how it gets straightened out. But note that if we did claim credit for the RECs we buy, Interface—with all our petro-intensity—would have reduced GHGs 99 percent, and be essentially climate neutral *today*.

Think about that.

While we're on the subject of energy commonly denominated as British Thermal Units (BTUs), let's take a look at "embodied energy" that goes into producing everything that comes in through our factories' receiving docks. Our basic raw material, nylon 6,6, is made from oil; each pound "contains" (required the use of) about 96,000 BTUs; this is the energy that was used in making and delivering that pound of nylon, from the wellhead to the receiving dock. That is roughly equivalent to the energy in a therm of natural gas, and just a bit less than in a gallon of regular gasoline. So you can see right off that reducing nylon yarn waste frees up a tremendous amount of embodied energy not used upstream by our suppliers. Call it "nega-energy," a term I learned from Amory Lovins. Let me give you one quick example.

In the first two months of 2008, our Bentley Prince Street plant in Southern California saved twenty-eight tons of yarn through an aggressive program of waste control; that yarn was worth about $168,000. But what about all the BTUs that would have gone into making those twenty-eight tons of nylon?

Well, that nega-energy turns out to equal the entire energy bill for the whole Bentley Prince Street factory for a month. We are shooting for an annual waste reduction of about 260 tons, worth $1.5 million, which translates into the equivalent of nearly a full year's worth of Bentley's energy bill that will not be consumed upstream by our suppliers. Who will win? Everyone, especially the earth.

Here's another case study. Our engineering manager, Graham Scott, a member of the original task force, wondered about the effects upstream of reducing the amount of nylon in his factory's entire product line by just one ounce per square yard, about 4 percent. He asked our nylon supplier, Du-Pont, a question it had never been asked before: *How much energy did you use to make and deliver each pound of nylon?* And Graham meant from the wellhead to our receiving dock.

DuPont puzzled out an answer, and to everyone's amazement, that 4 percent reduction freed up enough equivalent energy on an annualized basis (nega-energy) to run our entire factory for half a year.

Today the actual reduction in nylon for that plant's products averages 17 percent, and the nega-energy generated each year (to the earth's great benefit) will run that factory for more than two years, for in the meantime the factory has also reduced its energy usage. Strictly speaking, this is not waste control. This is a very careful redesign effort, and it has its own name: Dematerialization through Conscious Design. Incidentally, we do not count our suppliers' nega-energy in our GHG reductions either.

I began by saying that some folks still think there is no business case for sustainability. But it seems to me that there is no business case to be made for *ignoring* sustainability.

Here's the thing. As you just saw, it is not only imaginable but quite possible that a serious waste-control program will not only pay its own way, but can also offset much—perhaps even all—the energy used at your manufacturing facility. This can have a huge impact on your total greenhouse gas emissions if you are thinking holistically and recognize that your factory doesn't stand alone and isolated. It *is* its entire supply chain.

Done right, a full-court press on waste can help shrink your GHG footprint down to the vanishing point. That's what we've achieved in the manufacture of our Cool Carpet,™ a fossil fuel–intensive product made with net zero greenhouse gas emissions. How did we do this? By eliminating waste (and all the energy that went into it). By substituting less energy-intensive materials, including recycled yarns and backing, and by increasing process efficiency too—even eliminating processes, whenever possible. And by investing in green, renewable energy, both on-site and purchased over the grid.

Finally, when we talk of waste arising from nonproductive costs, I mean things like correcting a pricing error, reshipping a misdirected order, or accounting for the production of any off-quality carpet. Yes, that still happens. And even though an increasing portion of our carpet rejects is recycled, we don't buy that expensive nylon for the pleasure of recycling it. "Eliminating waste" is not just a slogan. It is a philosophy we live by.

Now, I know that every manufacturing operation creates a certain amount of off-quality product. It is standard industry practice to build in allowances for it. We did, too, until 1994. The trouble was, when we took a hard look at our factories across the world, we found that each one had its own ideas about "allowable" waste and off-quality. We couldn't compare one plant with another. There was no common ground. What was our solution?

Remember how a plant—a real plant—operates? With no waste at all. Zero. Everything a plant discards ends up as food for some other organism. Eventually, in a healthy environment, it all ends up right back where it started, in a new generation of plants.

So we asked ourselves this question: What would happen if we zeroed out the whole idea of acceptable waste or allowable off-quality, measuring everybody against one simple standard, perfection. What would our numbers look like?

Well, the numbers that came back at first were pretty eye-opening. In 1994, we had companywide sales of about $700 million. If you looked at all of the imperfect carpets, the clerical errors, the wrong shipments, everything we did or bought that added no value to our customer, it turned out that a full 10 percent of sales, seventy million hard dollars, was going right down the drain as waste—*$70 million!* And remember, we weren't yet counting fossil fuel use as waste. Imagine the outraged cries you would hear if the IRS imposed a 10 percent "value detracted" tax on your business! But nobody was imposing anything on us. We were doing it to ourselves.

And the thing is, like you, I thought we had a pretty good handle on controlling waste. But chances are you're as wrong now as I was then. Looking back on our experiences, I can say with great certainty that when you do decide to shut waste down in a serious manner, you'll find so much low-hanging fruit—savings that are easy, obvious, and cheap—you'll think you're in an orchard.

How do you start? Here are the key steps:

- First, define waste and apply that definition across the board. Reject the temptation to include any allowable waste in your definition.
- Next, set up a procedure to measure that waste accurately and fairly.
- Then, once you've got your baseline established, set annual, year-on-year goals that are both challenging and possible.
- Finally, plot progress and post it for everybody to see.

Naturally, leadership plays a central role. A leader must articulate the vision—zero waste—set the right example, and keep pounding on the drum that waste is everyone's common enemy. A good leader will keep up that drumbeat, consistently and persistently, because some folks are going to figure that if they hide their heads long enough this program will eventually go away. Everyone must have impressed upon them—over and over—that this is real and it is *not* going away. Not tomorrow. Not next month. Not *ever*.

You might not get everyone on board, but neither can you go it alone. What good is a leader without followers? The skills needed to inspire people to change are different from those required to keep track of progress honestly. You need both. And the person closest to the problem—whether they're on the factory floor or the loading dock, or in an office ordering supplies—will be your best source of ideas. This is everyone's fight. Everybody has a role to play. There are no sidelines on which to sit things out.

I have already told you how I came to decide that Interface should be the first truly sustainable corporation in history, and how I challenged our people to make it happen. I was—and remain—committed to staying on message, consistently and persistently, for as long as it takes. But for some of those other critical skills, we were lucky to have Buddy Hay. I'll let him tell you how it looked to him.

"I came to Interface after eight years at Milliken, where I was an engineer with a financial degree," said Hay. "That made me a hybrid. But at Milliken you were one thing or another, so I knew my future there was limited. When a position opened up at Interface, I took it.

"I first met Ray Anderson in the hallway at headquarters. We were walking in opposite directions and he just stopped, put out a hand, and said, 'I don't think we've been introduced.' I told him who I was and that I had just come from Milliken. Ray smiled this big old smile and said, 'Another Christian saved from the lions.'

"You can probably guess that having one foot in engineering and the other in finance was not a problem at Interface. In fact, it equipped me to help start a companywide waste-control program called QUEST: Quality Utilizing Employees' Suggestions and Teamwork. The name was chosen through a companywide contest that was won by Betty Moore from our LaGrange, Georgia, plant.

"Our current CEO, Dan Hendrix, was our chief financial officer back then, and QUEST was his operation. He said that if we could measure real reductions in waste then he could sell them to Wall Street. And so it was my job to find ways to measure it. Ray directed every factory, every office, every Interface facility across the globe to form QUEST teams to get the ball rolling. Then he sent me out to learn about their operations and explain what we hoped to achieve.

"When I showed up, I met a fair amount of opposition. People were already working hard. Their time was already stretched thin. Nobody needed another job. And then there's the question of tradition.

"Understand, making carpets is a business with a long history. When it comes to the environment, it's not a pretty history, either. Anyway, the people in our plants had been doing things their own way for years. Decades, in some cases. And so here I was, aiming to shake everything up. I remember that one manager greeted me this way: 'So you're going to come in here and tell me how to cut waste?' I had about one second to figure out an answer, and luckily, I came up with the right one: 'No, sir. You are.'"

There was a lot of luck involved in sending Buddy Hay out to oversee QUEST. Remember what Dan Hendrix said about selling Wall Street on sustainability? Well, those folks were looking for holes in our business model. I can say without any hesitation that if they thought we had cooked our numbers, or even overstated them the slightest bit, his difficult sell would have been just about impossible. Buddy Hay says it better: "Our metrics are our reputation. If we exaggerate or mislead—even just a little bit—we could undo all the good work that's gone into them. Nothing is more important than getting the numbers right."

Touring our facilities across the globe, Buddy found out pretty quickly that not all of them were created equal. At the best plants, waste was putting a one dollar "waste tax" on every square yard of carpet they produced. But at others it was three, even four times that. You can see why imposing an across-the-board dollar goal—say, eliminating fifty cents of waste per square yard—would be a whole lot easier at an inefficient factory than at a thrifty one. What to do?

Remember those four key steps? We defined waste. Then Buddy established the right way to measure it (per unit of output), and, from those numbers, he created a baseline figure for every facility. Finally, we encouraged every QUEST team to cut that baseline waste number by 10 percent each and every year. Finally, we kept score and made sure everyone knew how they were doing and how they compared with other Interface plants.

In summary:

1. Measure on a macro basis but manage on the micro.
2. Make the waste number relative to output.
3. Index waste costs per unit to a historical baseline.
4. Measure consistently and fairly from one business to the next and share results, but compare each facility only with itself.
5. Post the results for all to see.

The less efficient plants had to stretch to save forty cents worth of waste from each square yard of carpet. The more efficient factories had to make an equivalent stretch to achieve a dime's worth of savings. We deliberately set that 10 percent goal low. We wanted to be realistic and we wanted to succeed. But most of all we wanted to ease folks out of the old habits of doing things the way they had always been done and into a new habit of continuous improvement.

I can hear some of you business people saying, "So what? We invite suggestions from our employees, too." But here's the thing: QUEST wasn't just a fancy name for the company suggestion box. We didn't just encourage good ideas, we rewarded them with hard dollars. Every manager's bonus was tied to how successful she or he was in hitting that 10 percent annual reduction. Initially, every associate at every facility received a portion of their facility's savings in their paycheck, too. But we soon found out this was not the ideal arrangement, and we needed a different approach. Why?

Because no matter how long and loud I might beat the drum about our company's determination to slash waste, not everyone heard—or shared—that goal. They would look at the extra money in their paychecks (a bonus earned by the factory's QUEST efforts for coming up with a good, waste-cutting idea) and wonder, *Now what's this for?* So we shifted the focus to where it should have been all along—to the QUEST team itself—and started directly paying the people who were coming up with all of the good waste-cutting ideas.

Now the incentives were much clearer, and the message that a winning idea to reduce waste could earn you extra money spread through our facilities like wildfire. At first, as Buddy says, volunteers were few and far between. QUEST teams had to be appointed. Now, anyone looking for more money wanted to get involved, the only price of admission was a good idea and the best ideas were rewarded accordingly. Through the years, our QUEST teams have performed magnificently.

Maria Ceballos, a team member at Interface's plant in Southern California, noticed that when yarn was moved around in bins by forklift the heavy cones (spools of yarn) on the bottom of the bins were the ones most likely to be dirtied or damaged. Usually, these would be detected and sent to recycling. But sometimes they sneaked through to the manufacturing process, where they could spoil a lot of carpet. Waste, waste, waste.

Maria wondered, *Why not position those bottom cones to produce the edges of carpets?* The parts that have to be trimmed off anyway? That way, damaged yarn wouldn't get into the product.

Well, each cone of yarn weighs about thirty pounds and costs about $90. Keeping just five of them out of the recycling bin each week (a very reasonable number) saves nearly *four tons* of yarn a year, worth over *$23,000* at today's prices. And don't forget all that nega-energy upstream!

So, thank you, Maria. Your QUEST team associates thank you, too, because your idea helps to meet your annual waste-cutting goal and increases their paychecks as well as yours.

Lina Marshall, one of our yarn preparation associates in my hometown of West Point, wondered out loud why we were buying Cool Fuel (gasoline with an added green tax) to offset the travel of our sales force but not for that of our plant workers? These offsets went to build wind farms, finance a major trucking company's transition from all trucks to intermodal (trucks plus rail) operations, even to pioneer $CO_2$ sequestration in oil fields.

Lina asked a good question, and it set off a chain of events that resulted in our Cool $CO_2$mmute Program. In it we split the cost with our associates to plant trees that offset the $CO_2$ emissions produced by their daily commutes to and from work. The first year 1,500 were planted. By 2008, that number had grown to 11,573!

Some folks hear about this and find it surprising, to say the least, that an idea like Cool $CO_2$mmute might come from the factory floor. Not me. The desire to climb Mount Sustainability is *not* limited to the corner office; it is not just another management thing. It is now part of who we are as a company, and what we stand for. Mission Zero runs deep at Interface. So am I surprised that good ideas flow uphill? Not a bit. In fact, we count on them.

Our European associates have often led the charge when it comes to renewable power, recycling, and waste control. Their factories are some of our very best.

Brian Bennett has been at our Northern Ireland plant for two decades. He took it upon himself to find ways to reduce the width of the backing that provides the structural foundation for our carpet tiles. This backing is made from bitumen, which is another way of saying the bottom of the oil barrel.

By paying attention to the way the machinery guided the backing through the whole carpet tile production process, he was able to use 218 centimeters–wide material instead of 220. Small potatoes? Based on 2007 production figures, Brian's careful work saved us nearly 25,000 square yards of material; enough to carpet a twenty-story high-rise office building.

Bob Mantle has spent even longer—thirty-seven years—at our West Yorkshire plant. As process and materials research manager, he's ideally situated to take action on what my professors at Georgia Tech made sure I learned, that there is always a better way.

At West Yorkshire, we used to mix bitumen and polymers on-site to fabricate the backing for carpets and tiles. This process is very energy-intensive and demands a lot of process heat to come out right. Was there a better way?

There was. Why not use premixed bitumen and polymer? That lowered the factory's requirement for heat, cutting fuel costs, electricity demand, $CO_2$ emissions, and dollars (well, pounds sterling) all at the same time. And more, the premixed bitumen could be obtained locally instead of importing the components from overseas manufacturers. To be sure, some of the energy Bob saved was pushed upstream to our suppliers, but not all of it. The reductions we realized through greater efficiencies and transportation and process savings (not to mention cuts in air and water pollution) were both real and significant.

You might well ask, Why didn't anyone notice these blindingly obvious things before? There are probably a lot of reasons, but one answer suggests itself from my own experience.

Growing up, I was like a lot of boys. I was just oblivious to those dirty clothes on the floor, those wet towels in the bathroom. My mother was always telling me to "open my eyes" and see. I'm not sure I entirely mastered that skill, but I do know that rewarding QUEST teams directly for their good ideas opened a lot of eyes at Interface.

Progress in our war on waste is measured monthly in a scorecard that we distribute worldwide. The QUEST teams that cut the most from their previous year's figures earn special recognition and awards. And the unsolicited competition among the teams is lively.

How are we doing? Let me plot the progress: In the first three and a half years of QUEST, we saved sixty-seven million hard dollars worldwide, far more than enough to pay for the changes to capture the quick and easy savings that we should have noticed long before. There was plenty left over to fund the assault on the harder problems to come.

Three years later we had cut our waste figure in half. By 2004, QUEST's tenth year, eliminating waste had cumulatively saved us $262 million. This tidy sum represented 28 percent of cumulative operating income, and came very close to doubling our net profits, too. The ideas just kept pouring in. Through 2008, the fourteen-year cumulative total of costs we avoided by attacking waste was $405 million.

One of our facilities engineers in our textile fabrics division (which we divested in 2007) proposed to modify the water supply system that fed his fabric dyeing machines. Dyeing fabric is a process that uses a lot of water, and all of it has to be heated (think oil and electricity and smokestacks) and discharged (think pollution) into a nearby waterway. We are talking about tens of millions of gallons a year at just this one facility.

We had already installed a system to recover some of the heat in that water, even a recycling system that would allow us to use the water more than once before sending it to the treatment pond. But all of that required heat exchangers, pumps, and plumbing. Think capital investment.

But remember what I said. The greenest barrel of oil, ton of coal, or kilowatt-hour is the one you don't use. Our engineer's solution fit that philosophy like a glove. How could we reduce the number of gallons we were using in the first place? His solution: a brass nozzle that cost $8.50. The result: two million gallons of water saved per year. That's water we don't have to buy, don't have to heat, and don't need to worry about pumping and treating. Savings? Better than $10,000 a year, at a cost that fit inside a $10 bill. That was one of our better wins—for Interface and for the earth.

Sometimes a new idea leads to far more than just a few percentage points shaved off a waste figure. For example, Billy Ingram, an associate from our West Point, Georgia, facility, wondered why yarn had to be wound onto huge beams—large spools that fed our carpet tufting machines. With so many designs, so many colors, and so many production variables, it was almost impossible to accurately anticipate how much yarn should be wound onto a set of beams for a particular production run. Since we couldn't afford to run out in the middle of production, we erred on the high side, and there was often a lot left over. How much? As much as sixty pounds per beam.

Billy figured out a better way: replace the beams entirely with smaller, portable "creels" that could be set up to match perfectly the amount of yarn required for each run. The result? A patented improvement in his name that cuts yarn overruns by 54 percent, and even facilitates reclamation of the little bit that's left!

It would be wrong to suggest that we embarked on this mission without the help of others. In fact, in 1995, Interface formally created the Eco Dream Team. This team included many of the world's most progressive thinkers on sustainability and represented a wide range of environmental and social interests. The makeup of the team has varied from time to time. Here's a list of those who have participated. You will see that it was one very high-powered group of visionaries:

| | |
|---|---|
| Janine Benyus | L. Hunter Lovins |
| David Brower (now deceased) | Bill McDonough |
| | John Picard |
| Bill Browning | Jonathon Porritt |
| Bernadette Cozart | Daniel Quinn |
| Robert Fox | Dr. Karl-Henrik Robèrt |
| Paul Hawken | Walter Stahel |
| Amory Lovins | John Warner |

We didn't always agree, and the work of being a visionary and the work of running a corporation are often two very different things. But we couldn't have begun our climb and probably can't finish it, without them.

The honor roll of corporations that also have attacked waste seriously is growing every year. They are to be found right across the business spectrum.

Nobody would mistake the Anheuser-Busch facility in Fairfield, California, for a trendy microbrewery. They opened up in 1974, employ about five hundred people, and produce four million barrels of beer a year. And yet, this sizable facility has achieved a 99.1 percent recycling rate on their entire operation; less than 1 percent of its waste products end up in a landfill or an incinerator.

Instead, 94,000 tons of spent grain become cattle feed. Each year they recycle some 700 tons of cardboard boxes, 70 tons of aluminum, 1,200 tons of glass, and 110 tons of scrap metal. And nearly 300,000 gallons of alcohol is recovered to blend into motor fuel. These are substantial numbers, and there are other examples just as significant.

Epson Portland, Inc., a subsidiary of Epson, Inc., hit the mark of zero solid waste sent to landfills back in 2000. Everything that can be recycled is recycled, and everything else is sent to a waste-to-energy plant to generate power. This sole U.S. manufacturing affiliate of the big Japanese Seiko Epson Corporation is not just an idyllic office campus. They make things there, from inkjet printers and cartridges (248 million of the latter between 1999 and 2006) to circuit-board assemblies.

And there is still room for improvement. Waste-to-energy incineration does reduce the consumption of fossil fuels. It is better than throwing all that material into a landfill. But those savings come at the cost of creating new sources of air pollution, and results in the production of energy-intensive virgin materials. So the balance among energy, emissions, and virgin materials, even when carefully weighed, too often is a net loser for the environment. That's why closed-loop recycling is better; it reclaims that embodied energy.

Bayer, Chevron, Cisco Systems, Genentech, Intel, Hewlett-Packard, Kraft Foods, Coca-Cola, Wal-Mart, and Toyota all have moved aggressively in the direction of zero waste, not because it makes them look good in the marketplace, though it does. They're doing it because it would be too costly not to. When they hit that zero waste mark, they will have conquered the first face of Mount Sustainability, an ascent that makes the assault on the other six not only more manageable, but far more profitable.

The objective at Interface has been, from the beginning of QUEST, to generate the savings that would more than pay the costs of moving our entire company up the mountain. So far, this kind of new thinking is working like a charm.

What do the numbers look like at Interface? Here's our own global waste elimination scorecard:

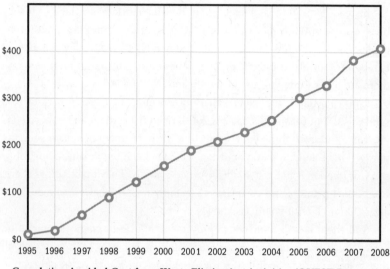

**Cumulative Avoided Cost from Waste Elimination Activities (QUEST Program)**
*($ in millions)*

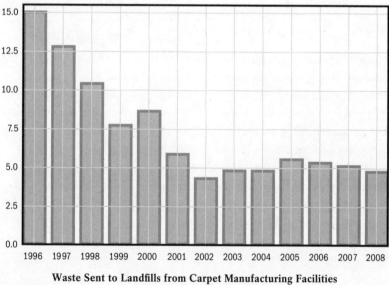

**Waste Sent to Landfills from Carpet Manufacturing Facilities**
*(pounds in millions)*

67% decrease in waste sent to landfills

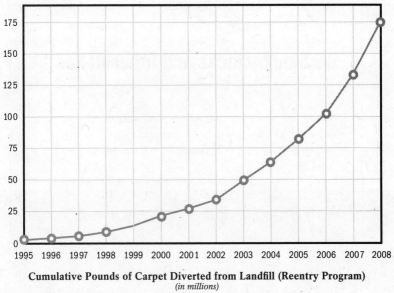

**Cumulative Pounds of Carpet Diverted from Landfill (Reentry Program)**
*(in millions)*

# 6 | Smokestacks and Other Relics

*We stand now where two roads diverge. But unlike the roads in Robert Frost's familiar poem, they are not equally fair. The road we have long been traveling is deceptively easy, but at its end lies disaster. The other fork of the road—the one "less traveled by"— offers our last, our only chance to reach a destination that assures the preservation of our earth.*

RACHEL CARSON, *Silent Spring* (1962)

triking out against waste by opening our eyes to opportunity marks the first climb up Mount Sustainability. Tackling the second face— eliminating (or rendering benign) the emissions that go up our smokestacks and out our effluent pipes—demands considerably more thinking and effort. That's why it is so vital to make sure that your efficiency programs are firing on all cylinders first. We don't want anything weighing us down, because this new climb will be rocky, less familiar, and frankly not very comfortable.

After all, how many CEOs are willing to take a hard, honest look at their company's pollution stream and decide, without being pushed by government regulations or lawsuits, to reduce it, much less to eliminate it? How many would consider a smokestack as anything other than a regulatory problem to be managed? How many legal departments would encourage (or even allow) corporate officers to open this Pandora's box and see what's hiding in the dark corners?

Not nearly enough, and I understand that point of view. Remember, I shared it once. I was busy growing a company, competing in a tough marketplace, finding capital, reassuring Wall Street, doing all the things a CEO has to do just to survive. I already had all I could handle. As long as we stayed within legal limits (that compliance thing again), what was in the river downstream or the air downwind of my plants was someone else's problem. Not mine.

But as an industrialist who did take a hard and honest look at the emissions we were generating, I came to realize that all of this invisible garbage—the chemicals, the trace contaminants, the greenhouse gases—that we discharged from our smokestacks and wastewater pipes far outweighed the solid waste we hauled off to the landfill.

Compare for yourself the 2,563 tons of solid waste we sent to the dumps last year against these figures:

- 113 million gallons of wastewater (470,640 tons)
- 162 tons of regulated air pollution
- 45,000 tons of (wrongly) unregulated greenhouse gases
- 142 tons of smog-generating photochemical pollutants
- 59 tons of acid rain–producing pollutants
- 635 pounds of regulated toxics (and all of them perfectly legal)

And this, after fourteen years of significant reductions!

If the sheer volume of all that fails to impress you, keep in mind something Rachel Carson pointed out nearly half a century ago. Because a lot of this "legal pollution" accumulates and concentrates in the food chain, it can still become very dangerous even if it doesn't start out that way.

So here's the big picture. As my associate, Melissa Vernon, says, "A 'brown' company cannot make a green product." And as you will see, when we get to life cycle assessments, when it comes to being green you are your entire supply chain. If you don't believe that, consider the plight of the New Zealand dairy products distributor Fonterra.

They obtained tainted milk from a Chinese subsidiary; the milk was tainted with melamine—an industrial chemical rich in nitrogen and designed to fool product tests that use nitrogen to determine protein content. Melamine is poisonous, but it's much, much cheaper than protein, and so someone introduced it into the milk supply chain somewhere in China. Thousands of children fell ill, and some died. A worldwide panic over all dairy products made in China, or ones that might have been made there, ensued.

So you see, when it comes to you and your supply chain, no one stands alone.

That's why climbing the second face of Mount Sustainability requires the courage to face what we sometimes can't even see (the pollutants) in order to bring into balance two interrelated global systems: the "technosphere," of which industry is the dominant part; and the "biosphere," which consists of the many natural systems that support all life on earth, including us.

I think another pretty good definition of sustainability might go something like this: the continued, healthy, balanced coexistence of the technosphere and the biosphere for the indefinite future.

Sadly, there is no more of a balance now between these two global systems, no more of a healthy coexistence, than you'd find between a parasite and its victim. To be very blunt, the technosphere (business and industry) uses the biosphere the way a tick uses a dog. Like parasites, corporations, operating by the rules of the old industrial revolution, thrive at the expense of nature. And because this has been the dominant model since the eighteenth century, most natural systems—the forests, the rivers, the air, and the oceans—are in obvious decline.

If we industrialists intend to become sustainable, whether out of a guilty conscience, to respond to our customers' demands, or just to improve our bottom line (or all three), we've got to reestablish the balance between these two realms. There is no way to separate one from the other, and no letting one run rampant over the other, either. They both exist within a spherical shell—the earth's surface, the seas and the air—that, relatively speaking, is tissue paper thin on a basketball-sized earth: That thin, vulnerable shell that is home to all of life, including humankind.

One of the most important ways we can reestablish that balance is to go after the dangerous solids, liquids, and gases we throw into the biosphere, and eliminate the ones that do the most harm. Remember, the earth is not an infinite sink for our wastes.

So what are these pollutants? What if we made a list of them? Each one of us will have different chemicals and substances on that list. But whether you're a microchip maker discharging hydrofluoric acid into a river or a homeowner pouring old paint and garden pesticides into a storm drain, the list, if it's thorough and honest, will not be pleasant to look at.

That was my experience when I opened up Pandora's box and asked for a complete inventory of every chemical we discharged into the air, water, and ground. Most of the substances sounded a lot worse than they were. But a few of them were honest-to-goodness bad actors: benzene, ammonium derivatives, fluorocarbons, heavy metals like lead and mercury and cadmium. Even arsenic and antimony. The list went on and on and on. And every one of them seemed essential to the way we made our products and earned our living.

Now recall how we eliminated the very idea of acceptable waste. Our plan to deal with chemical pollutants followed a similarly bold strategy: to eliminate all harmful releases by the year 2020, and to operate profitable factories that do not even need smokestacks and effluent pipes, that do not generate hazardous waste of any kind. The inventory created the agenda of items for which substitutes had to be found.

Ultimately, we would send out into the world only valuable products (like carpet tiles and broadloom carpets), plus clean air, clean water, and biodegradable materials the earth can use to regenerate itself. You may well ask, is that even remotely possible?

Well, our evolving biosphere did it, though it required billions of years of natural selection. Of course, finding a surviving, healthy piece of the biosphere (like an old-growth forest) is getting mighty difficult these days. And we don't have billions of years, even hundreds, to get this job done, either. When it comes to capping greenhouse gases before irreparable changes occur, we've got perhaps less than a decade. That is a tall, tall challenge.

But ask yourself a question: How far do you think NASA would have gotten if the Apollo program had set its sights on earth's orbit instead of reaching for the moon? I can assure you from personal experience that no football team goes onto the field fired up by the idea of almost winning. BHAGs (big, hairy, audacious goals) that seem impossible can be daunting. But they can also be inspirational, and inspiration can do wonders. It can move people up a mountain they otherwise might never have tried to tackle.

So what kind of gear, what tools are required to begin this second, more challenging climb? The laws of thermodynamics will take you some of the way. The first law (the conservation law) states that matter and energy cannot be created or destroyed. The second (the entropy law) reminds us that matter and energy tend to disperse over time.

When it comes to quantum mechanics things may not be quite that simple. But practically speaking, what do these laws mean for running a business? They mean that when we use something or burn something—gasoline, diesel, coal, electricity, raw materials, even wood in a fireplace—it doesn't go away, even if we can no longer see it. Indeed, even if we can no longer detect it. It just changes form and spreads out into the world. And if we discharge it faster than the earth can reabsorb it into the sunlight driven cycles of nature, it silently accumulates. In the air. In the water. Even in our bodies.

Take carbon dioxide ($CO_2$), the key greenhouse gas driver behind global warming. Every home furnace, every car, every truck, every utility smoke-stack is pumping this stuff into the atmosphere day in and day out. Now, given the recent increase in the price of a barrel of light sweet crude, Economics 101 assures us there will be a resulting spike in oil prospecting. Though efficiencies can produce a lot more energy—faster, cheaper, and with greater social and environmental benefits—that is Economics 201, and most folks haven't signed up for that course yet. So, it naturally follows that oil companies will—if Congress allows—go after those restricted coastal blocs—difficult, expensive deposits found in the deep ocean, the high Arc-tic, or locked up in tar sands and western shales. And this won't happen just in the United States, either.

It reminds me of how a drug addict, having used up all the easy veins in his arm, switches to the ones between his toes to inject his daily fix. It is only a temporary solution for that poor addict. He will either die from his addiction or overcome it. And it is the same for humankind.

If we're foolish enough to burn all that oil, all that natural gas, all that so-called clean coal, we will release thousands of gigatons of $CO_2$. So what? Well, I'll tell you what I am told: The total amount—in absolute tons—of carbon dioxide on earth and on the planet Venus is quite similar. But where you find it makes all the difference in these two worlds.

On the earth, $CO_2$ is (still) mainly locked up in the soil, rocks, forests, and oceans. On Venus, it's stored in its pea soup–like, triple-glazed atmo-sphere. As a result, the average temperature on our world is a pleasant 59 degrees Fahrenheit. On Venus? A runaway greenhouse effect raises average temperatures to above 800 degrees Fahrenheit, hot enough to melt lead. For those who might wish to note that Venus is also a lot closer to the sun, be sure also to take note that the greenhouse gases on Venus keep it hotter than Mercury, which is very close to the sun.

That puts rather a different perspective on the misguided plan to dig up as much coal, oil, and gas as we can find, burn it as fast as possible, and in-ject it all (as $CO_2$) into our atmosphere. Forget oil and gas; there is more than enough coal, all by itself, to kill us all.

But let's keep our focus on business, and what we can do. At Interface, we started this second climb—reducing or eliminating the solids, liquids, and gases that we discharge into the biosphere—by establishing where we were. We surveyed our facilities in North America, Europe, and Asia-Pacific and identified 247 smokestacks that discharged something. Here's what we found coming from them:

- carbon monoxide, generated by the incomplete burning of fossil fuels;
- carbon dioxide, the greenhouse gas that helps make Venus an oven;
- sulfur dioxide, the poisonous precursor to acid rain;
- nitrous oxides, potent greenhouse gases in their own right that react with volatile organic compounds and hydrocarbons on hot, humid days to create ground-level ozone (the bad ozone) and smog, and also contribute to acid rain;
- particulate matter, tiny specks of "ash" ten microns or less in diameter and able to penetrate lung tissue;
- volatile organic compounds, "escape artist" chemicals that are released during the manufacturing process and from the product itself, contributing to indoor air pollution, "sick building" syndrome, and ground level ozone.

That is quite a list. And the survey of our nineteen wastewater effluent pipes was also very revealing. We were legally flushing into the rivers:

- dyes (sulfonated mono-alkyl glyceride and di-azo aromatics, benzene and ammonium derivatives);
- maintenance chemicals (surfactants, butyl cellusolve);
- softeners (sulfonated hydrocarbons, fatty amine ethoxylates);
- buffers (inorganic phosphates);
- pH control agents (ammonium sulfate, ammonia, sodium hydroxide, acetic and citric acids);
- chelating agents (ethylene diamine, tetra acetic acid);
- stain-resistant additives (sulfonated alkyl succinate).

Though not all of our plants put significant quantities of chemicals into their wastewater, and many didn't generate any at all, the second law of thermodynamics reminds us that even a single drop will disperse; and if you put enough drops into the rivers and streams, someone, somewhere, is going to end up drinking them.

I remember being at a water quality conference some years ago and hearing a state official say that he could not guarantee that Atlanta's drinking water did not have aspirin in it. I thought, *Aspirin?* There are many, many drugs out there far worse than just aspirin. How about estrogen, men? How about testosterone, ladies?

So it was no big surprise to read later that an investigative team of researchers, sponsored by the Associated Press, discovered traces of powerful prescription pharmaceuticals in the municipal water systems that serve some forty-one million Americans. These contaminants included antibiotics, heart medicines, steroids, sex hormones, antipsychotic medications. Even chemotherapy drugs. That is the water you and I are drinking. As I said, those "undetectable" drops add up.

Even if the amounts are measured in parts per billion, they can find their way into the food chain. There they can become biologically concentrated. Small, seemingly insignificant quantities of PCBs, heavy metals, or pesticides, when absorbed by a freshwater mollusk, can become dangerous when you or I eat a fish that's made a meal of many such mollusks. The bigger the fish, the greater the concentration. What seems safe at the bottom of the food chain can be harmful, even lethal, at the top.

But if all this pollution is perfectly legal, why should we be concerned? Surely there is good science behind the limits that all businesses, certainly here in the United States, are obliged to observe. Sadly, in too many cases, regulation lags behind good science. Sometimes it catches up, but often taking action is difficult, and the regulators just throw up their hands and say, *Well, so many experts disagree, we might as well do nothing and wait for the dust to settle.* That was true with cigarette smoke. It was true with chronic asbestos exposure. It was true with DDT. It's true now with the so-called controversy over global warming. *Let's just wait,* says the sanguine regulator.

Well, waiting for the last shred of evidence is, in my view, a very foolish thing to do. As I understand the precautionary principle, it says that when the risk of not acting overshadows the cost of acting, it is time to act. When we slow down in our cars before taking a blind curve, that is the precautionary principle in action. It applies to business practices, too; and governments are not exempt either.

If sales fall, if profit margins erode, if customers start going elsewhere, no good business person is going to wait very long to find out what is going on and make changes. It must be the same with the pollution we discharge into the biosphere. No one should wait for disaster to find out what is going on.

With that for a background, here are some key concepts you'll need to understand to meet the challenge of eliminating toxic emissions, five principles that form a scientifically derived template based on the laws of thermodynamics. Please read them all carefully. This is what sustainability demands, absolutely, incontrovertibly. Denial is futile. You cannot negotiate with a sick blood cell and tell it not to worry, that everything will be fine when the regulations finally catch up.

### 1. Substances extracted from the earth's crust must not systematically increase in nature.

This first rule means that the residues from fossil fuels, metals, and minerals—or byproducts created in their use or combustion—must not be sent up the stack, out an exhaust pipe, or into a wastewater stream any faster than they can be safely and naturally absorbed back into the earth's crust through natural processes. Otherwise, they will accumulate, increase, and eventually reach a danger zone. We may not know where all the red lines are, but we can be very sure they exist, and beyond them irreversible damage—to our bodies, to our food supply, to the air we breathe, to our very earth and all of its inhabitants—will occur.

### 2. Substances produced by society (man-made materials) must not systematically increase in nature.

The second rule stipulates that persistent man-made materials and substances must not be produced at a faster pace than they can be broken down and integrated back through natural cycles, or deposited back into the earth's crust and turned back into nature's building blocks. If persistent man-made substances are allowed to accumulate, their concentration will increase and eventually reach dangerous levels. Again, we may not know where all those limits are, but beyond them irreversible damage will occur.

### 3. The productivity and diversity of nature must not be systematically diminished.

We must not overharvest or damage (through the pollutants we release) the very ecosystems that keep the natural cycles (which power the first two principles) going. Ultimately, our health, our prosperity, our businesses, and the economy itself all depend on the capacity of nature to generate new resources. Nature is the infrastructure that undergirds civilization itself. It is the goose that lays all the golden eggs. Rain forests and fisheries, farmlands and aquifers cannot be exploited any faster than they can naturally restore themselves. We must not flood nature with substances that harm its ability to provide us with air to breathe, water to drink, an ultraviolet shield against radiation, climate regulation, and a multitude of other services that keep us warm, clothed, housed, and fed.

### 4. *Fairness and efficiency are linked!*

The fourth rule is the social principle. It mandates fair and efficient use of resources to meet humanity's basic needs. Because there are so many genuine needs, they must be met in the most resource-efficient manner possible. Further, meeting the basic needs of the many takes precedent over providing the "wants," the luxuries, for the few. (The Basic Economic Problem of Economics 101 rears its head again.) Why? Because violating this principle yields a bitter harvest of social and environmental instability. Humanity has already suffered enough from the results of resource wars fought over arable land, freshwater, or oil deposits.

And it doesn't even have to escalate to the point of war for truly global damage to take place. Consider the burning of the Amazon rain forest to open up land for development, or the diversion of rivers in central Asia to grow cotton in the desert.

If people living near an old-growth forest have no economic alternative to cutting down irreplaceable trees for firewood, all humanity suffers the loss of habitat, the loss of biodiversity, a vital carbon sink, and a source of life-giving oxygen. We all pay the price of increased erosion, flooding, desertification, and global climate disruption.

So does that mean running your business sustainably has to bring down the living standards of those at the top in order to lift up those at the bottom? No, it does not! The fifth principle addresses this false choice.

### 5. *Resource-efficiency is the rising tide that will float* all *the boats higher.*

The final principle of sustainability contrasts old technology, whose primary aims were based on labor efficiency, with the new technologies and the new industrial revolution, whose primary aims are gained through resource-efficiency. Old technologies allowed fewer and fewer people to produce more and more, and made sense in an age when people were scarce and nature seemed infinitely bountiful—in the eighteenth century.

But new technologies, based on resource-efficiency, will put people to work in gainful employment (the aptly named green-collar jobs) in ways that conserve precious resources through cyclical, renewable processes. And in an age when populations are exploding and nature is in hard retreat, those new technologies cannot arrive too soon.

The first four of these principles form the theoretical basis of Karl-Henrik Robèrt's framework for pursuing sustainability, *The Natural Step*. Robèrt, a Swedish research oncologist, developed his framework back in 1989, and it has stood up well because, unlike others, it's scientifically based, thoroughly peer-reviewed, and readily understandable. Robèrt's work perfectly complemented Paul Hawken's thesis in *The Ecology of Commerce*, the book that changed my own life so dramatically. The fifth principle has been espoused by many others, and it follows so naturally that I include it as a practical and necessary addition to Robèrt's ideas.

As we apply Robèrt's *Natural Step* rules (Robèrt calls them *system conditions*) to business operations, we see at once that we must systematically reduce our economic dependence on virgin raw materials and fossil fuels. We must systematically reduce our economic dependence on the production of persistent, unnatural, man-made substances. We must systematically reduce our economic dependence on the wasteful use of natural resources.

The social equity principle demands that we move toward the fair and efficient use of resources to meet all human needs, and put people to work to raise—not lower!—their standards of living. We must lift the poorest among us out of grinding poverty while repairing our damaged earth. This is, without much doubt, the greatest technical, moral, and ethical challenge humanity now faces.

How did we begin to put these principles to work at Interface? First came the realization that these principles defined the top of Mount Sustainability. They became our magnet, drawing us always toward the summit.

So in 1996, immediately after publicly subscribing to those four (now five) principles of sustainability during a visit by Robèrt to Atlanta, we formed a companywide Toxic Chemical Elimination Team. Their mission was to work with our upstream suppliers to eliminate all ecologically damaging chemicals from our facilities. No one stands alone.

Their initial target list included every one of the chemicals that trigger mandatory reporting to the federal Environmental Protection Agency—the infamous SARA 313 chemicals, so named because they appear in Section 313 of the EPA's Superfund Amendment and Reauthorization Act (SARA).

Specifically, the team was charged with:

- reducing the use of ozone-depleting chlorofluorocarbons and hydrofluorocarbons in Interface facilities. Most of these chemicals were refrigerants used in chillers, air conditioners, watercoolers, and refrigerators. They were inventoried and are gradually being replaced with legally compliant equipment as the old equipment is retired.
- eliminating volatile chlorinated chemicals like methylene chloride and 1,1,1 trichloroethane. This goal was accomplished.
- reducing the use of SARA 313 chemicals. Many chemicals were eliminated, and incoming raw materials are screened to identify any SARA 313 components.

The objective? To make sure that every Interface facility, no matter where it's located, no matter how lax the local environmental laws might be, complies with the strictest rules on air and water pollution in effect at any of our facilities anywhere in the world; that is, the strictest rules anywhere apply everywhere at Interface. We just do not believe a brown company can make a green product.

What about water filters? What about stack scrubbers? Don't they keep those bad actors out of the air and water? Sorry. They're Band-Aids at best. They only concentrate the problem. We can't throw used filters away and comply with the first two rules of sustainability. Remember? There is no "away." All contaminants disperse. We would just be moving it off-site and handing our problem to someone else, creating the kind of externality we criticize in others.

"End-of-pipe" solutions, like filtration and scrubbing, are unsustainable. They are just necessary and temporary bridges to better, longer-term solutions. As architect and sustainability pioneer Bill McDonough has written in *Cradle to Cradle*: "We need to move those filters from the ends of our pipes and smokestacks and put them into our brains, to redesign our products and our processes intelligently."

Once our toxic chemicals teams knew what we were discharging, they went to work. After some initial disappointments, they eventually decided that we had to drastically reduce the number of suppliers we use. Why? To eliminate toxic emissions we had to work upstream with our suppliers to keep bad actors from entering our factories in the first place. Consolidating our suppliers made that an attainable goal. Let me explain.

Commercial raw materials are full of substances and chemicals that violate the first and second laws of sustainability. Screening them out is a perpetual job. They will sneak back in through any crack or crevice you leave unguarded. The sheer effort of patrolling the corporation's borders to keep them out can seem overwhelming. Just put together a list of your suppliers and everything they send you—not by trade name, but by chemical composition—and you'll see what I mean. Keeping the entry points, the border crossings, to a minimum was necessary. What we soon discovered was that it was also very smart.

After our SARA 313 team compiled a suppliers list, they discovered a winning formula that not only made it very difficult for those bad actors to get through our factory doors, but has also saved us—not cost us—quite a lot of money. But it didn't come easily.

Our first stab at trying to understand how we used dangerous chemicals started (and stopped) with the lists developed by various U.S. state and federal regulatory agencies. For every chemical that appeared on those lists, we developed a policy of use curtailment or elimination. Sounds good. But it just didn't work. Why?

First, because many of those lists are notoriously out of date. They lag behind scientific research by years; moreover, their rigor depends on a sort of political resolve we seldom see. If a chemical wreaks havoc with our immune systems today, it may take two decades for the cancers to show up. Politicians just don't think in terms of decades. It is so unimaginably distant that it might as well be someone else's problem. In other words, it becomes an externality.

Second, our program to eliminate toxics depended on our suppliers telling us what was really in the materials they were selling us. While a few of them had a good handle on the chemistry behind their products, most of them knew very little (and perhaps did not want to know). Some of them were depending on their suppliers, who as often as not were depending on still someone else.

By the time we received assurances that a particular vendor's products were safe, it was pretty much meaningless. Nobody really knew.

So we abandoned simple "trust," for "trust, but verify." It took our team a couple of years and the work of third-party researchers to develop a chemical screening protocol of our own. However, then we could evaluate all the stuff we received from our vendors through a standardized screening process based on the most recent science, not an outdated and flimsy regulatory list. But despite a sizable investment of money and time, this approach did not quite render our borders totally safe from toxic interlopers either.

It turned out that our vendors still were not completely forthcoming about the chemicals they used in their products. Some of them worried about revealing proprietary formulas. Others (maybe most) just didn't want to open up their own Pandora's box too far. It took us a while, but ultimately we abandoned the effort to make them do so.

Then, in early 2001, we assembled an interdisciplinary team to think long and hard about what we termed "benign by design" might really mean, and how we as a company might create a truly watertight screening process. As a result, we decided to continue our previous screening protocol while adding solid reassurances to our vendors that their confidential information would stay protected. It was then that the final piece of the puzzle—cutting that long suppliers list—fell into place.

You see, back then we had twenty-eight suppliers for chemicals in just one division alone. Division management told them we were going to cut the number down to three. Fewer vendors meant less paperwork and much larger contracts for the winners. They had to comply with our chemical screening, but the rewards were substantial. Carrot plus stick. The result?

Today, an extremely effective shield is in place against vendors sending us things we do not want. We have used this approach to screen out lead, mercury, perfluoronated alkyl surfactants, and other persistent bioaccumulating toxic substances and chemicals. What has all this cost us?

Nothing. Annual savings run about three hundred thousand dollars. By consolidating our supplier base, the fewer but larger contracts allow us to enjoy discounts we had not seen before. And even more important, our protocol has given our suppliers a very good reason (and a tool they can borrow) to take a hard look at *their* suppliers, setting up a ripple effect that has spread, as more companies are motivated by enlightened self-interest to invest in benign, even green, chemistry. The process by which an individual product or chemical—and its environmental impacts—gets tracked back to its origins in the earth is accounted for in a life cycle assessment (LCA).

Ideally, such LCAs will illuminate the environmental impact of a product from its birth as a raw material to its end-of-life disposal or recycling. It's the right way to identify environmental problems in your supply chain or product design, as well as to help you choose between seemingly equal alternatives. Very often, what seems equal turns out to be anything but.

Where do we use the most energy? The most water? What step in the process (from birth to death to rebirth) generates the most waste? The most greenhouse gas emissions? The most harmful chemicals? A rigorous LCA will have answers to all of these questions. Here's just one quick example.

Consider greenhouse gas emissions that come from running an automobile factory. You would first slice the pie into three portions: emissions that happened up your supply chain (the mines, the steel mills, the glass manufacturers, plastics, computer component companies, etc.); inside your plant (as you assemble the vehicle); and, finally, those generated downstream (by those who buy, drive, and junk your cars). Here's a small test: Where would your gut instinct place the greatest portion of GHGs?

Answer: If you're building inefficient trucks (like the now-infamous SUV), the biggest slice of that GHG pie is generated from driving your product around for its anticipated street life, not from your suppliers and not from your own manufacturing processes!

For a service business like an accounting firm, the answer would, naturally, be very different: The largest source of GHGs comes from heating, cooling, and powering the building that houses your offices. A bottler of fancy designer waters would find that the manufacturing portion of his GHG spectrum is quite small but for the production of its package, the plastic bottle. But delivering all that heavy water to market (and in some cases, as you will see, that means shipping it over entire oceans) dominates the entire GHG footprint.

No LCA number should be taken as gospel. The exact, absolute figures are probably not terribly meaningful at this stage (unless you are buying offsets to balance them out). What is critical is their relative scale, their trend over time, and the red flags that a good LCA will generate, highlighting specific products, processes, chemicals, and designs that merit a much closer look. It is knowledge, and as the old saw goes, knowledge really is power. It's the closest we've come yet to God's currency.

So, using LCA tools and strict screening processes, how far up this tough, steep slope have we scrambled? At the start we owned and operated 192 smokestacks. With acquisitions, that number grew to 247. Divestitures shrank that figure to 160. Today, we are down to 107.

We started off with 19 wastewater effluent pipes. They, too, grew in number through acquisitions, then went down to 7 with divestitures, and today we operate only 2.

Since we began in 1996, with a carefully determined baseline, our net greenhouse gas emissions are down 71 percent in absolute tonnage (and please remember how some folks claimed the 7 percent reduction called for by the Kyoto Protocol was just not possible). And 40 percent of this reduction has come from eliminating waste, improving operating efficiency, and substituting renewable forms of energy for fossil fuels. The remaining 60 percent has come from verifiable offsets, not counting renewable energy credits. As I said earlier, if we also took credit for the RECs we purchase, Interface would be essentially climate neutral. Furthermore:

- We've cut our wastewater stream by 72 percent when measured against units of production (a square yard of carpet). What comes in will go out, so this is also our reduction in freshwater usage.
- We've eliminated a third of our smokestacks, which were made obsolete and closed down by smart changes in our production processes.
- We've shut down 71 percent of our effluent pipes.
- During the same time, our sales increased by 60 percent. That translated into an 82 percent reduction in net GHG intensity (measured against sales).
- Our EBIT (earnings before interest and taxes) doubled.

Let me give you some very practical examples of what we did.

Our InterfaceFLOR division in Canada totally eliminated the use of all nine of Canada's listed hazardous compounds. They also eliminated every gallon of process (nonsanitary) water by ending wet printing of carpet tiles (more on this later). They went on to cut their total air emissions by 30 percent, as measured against their 1995 baseline. And note that this was not accomplished by reducing factory output. Just the opposite; they increased their production during the same period by 242 percent!

The dye-house manager at one of our fabric facilities in Maine felt that he was using too many antistatic chemicals to dissipate static electricity from the fabric. He saw a triple-play potential: eliminating unnecessary materials (waste); cutting chemical pollutants (in the effluent pipes); and slashing operating costs. Win, win, and win again. He worked closely with his suppliers, and switched to a different, more benign antistatic agent—and eliminated the use of acetic acid entirely.

Our Bentley Prince Street plant replaced an enormous industrial drying oven with a low nitrous oxide, high-efficiency model, cutting nitrogen oxide emissions by 50 percent.

Another of our Maine facilities installed computerized controls on its waste wood–fired boiler. Burning waste that would ordinarily go to a landfill is a good idea. Computer controls that boost the combustion efficiency of that waste-eating boiler, reducing particulate emissions (soot and ash) and carbon monoxide in the stack gas is a great idea.

At our Rockland React-Rite facility, a water-cooled jacket, condenser, and refrigerated chamber were installed on a smokestack. The result: Airborne hexane emissions were cut by 75 percent.

Two of our European plants eliminated all latex from their effluent water streams. Our factory in Southern California reduced total chemical use by 40 percent and water consumption (a very big issue in dry, sunny California) by 800,000 gallons a month by reusing the water from their dye-bath operations. This is where white, semifinished carpet receives its color on the way to being transformed into finished carpets and carpet tiles.

What about toxics?

Well, keep in mind that a shut-down smokestack and a bone-dry water discharge pipe can't put anything into the environment. But beyond that, here's some of what we've been able to accomplish.

- Our Bentley Prince Street backing facility eliminated all four of their hazardous-waste sources by substituting green cleansing chemicals.
- Interface Europe has completely eliminated all dyes containing heavy metals of any kind.

- InterfaceFLOR no longer uses antimony to flameproof carpet tiles, or lead as a polymer stabilizer.
- Interface Architectural Resources (since divested) eliminated all toxics from the adhesive system on panel assembly-and-finish lines. This cut corporate VOC (volatile organic compound) emissions by fifteen tons per year.
- Our Pandel division (also, since divested) stopped using lead, cadmium, and barium stabilizers in foam products.
- Interface Flooring Systems Canada reformulated the chemicals used to make carpet-tile backing, significantly reducing the use of plasticizers, resins, and fire retardants.
- Companywide, solution-dyed yarns, which do not require energy- and chemical-intensive wet processing, have gone from zero to two thirds of all the yarn we use each year. Therefore, upstream, in our suppliers' plants, water, chemical dyes, and energy usage have been reduced enormously. Benign by design.

And remember, Interface is climbing this face of Mount Sustainability on our own initiative, with the help of our suppliers, our employees, and our customers. Not because the government has prodded us into action.

And we're not climbing it alone.

Last year Wal-Mart announced an impressive array of energy and efficiency initiatives that came from their companywide sustainability plan, which is somewhat similar to our own Mission Zero. And it is not greenwash; they've already exceeded their goal of selling one hundred million compact fluorescent lightbulbs. Moreover, they convened a "summit" with their suppliers to make very sure all of them understood that Wal-Mart would be measuring energy use and emissions right up the supply chain. Scores were going to be kept and purchasing decisions made on that basis.

When a corporation that big changes direction, even small improvements have sizable results. Just cutting back on the unnecessary packaging used by their suppliers will save Wal-Mart's supply chain more than half a million tons of $CO_2$ emissions by the year 2013, the rough equivalent of taking one hundred thousand automobiles off the road permanently. Best of all, Wal-Mart's sixty thousand or more suppliers are having to reassess how they make things, too!

Dell, the computer maker, is another example of what can be accomplished when a company decides that just compliance isn't enough. The $55 billion manufacturer employs close to sixty thousand people across the globe. Dell purchases something close to $100 million of materials every day of the year. I can only begin to imagine the scope of the challenge they faced when, in 1996, they decided to go after the toxic chemicals used by the company and its chain of suppliers.

Like us, they assembled a list of those bad actor chemicals and substances. They identified asbestos, cadmium, lead, mercury, halogenated flame retardants, and chlorinated paraffins, among others. They had an additional problem to face, too. While carpet tile may burn in a building fire and might be incinerated at a municipal site, virtually all computers end up being melted down to recapture the precious metals inside them. While most of this recycling happens in reasonably controlled situations, sometimes it takes place in informal backyard burner sites that release plumes of toxic pollutants, most especially brominated compounds that can release persistent, bioaccumulative, toxic chemicals with the smoke.

Their response was a companywide chemicals policy that first identified substances and chemicals to avoid, then created new standards that banned them. And not just at Dell plants in countries with stringent environmental laws. Everywhere. And not only at Dell facilities, either, but at every factory that hopes to do business with them—some four hundred companies around the world.

As Mark Newton, Dell's senior manager for sustainability, said, "Our success in this green movement or, for that matter, in any aspect of quality, depends on our suppliers."

And those suppliers are likely to pay very close attention. Like Wal-Mart, Dell's enormous purchasing clout and commanding market share mean that any solution they find to the problem of hazardous chemicals quickly becomes affordable and available to the global computer hardware market. And so their environmental vision has become, de facto, the new industry standard.

Being big, however, is no guarantee of success. The Coca-Cola Company invested $40 million in research aimed at ridding the world of conventional vending machines. It's a worthwhile target, too. There are about ten million of them scattered around the globe. They run around-the-clock, rely on inefficient compressors, and, worst of all, use hydrofluorocarbon (HFC) refrigerants. HFCs not only attack the ozone ultraviolet radiation shield, they are also a very potent greenhouse gas that is considerably worse than $CO_2$. Coca-Cola's goal: to develop a machine 40 to 50 percent more efficient and HFC-free.

But for all its hard work and well spent money, even Coca-Cola had trouble convincing manufacturers to make better machines, and bottlers (which are owned independently) to buy them. Neville Isdell, the company's chairman and then CEO, said, "We have the technology and we know that it works. The problem is, the economic logic doesn't hang together."

Which might prompt one to recall the question about the value of a forest. We'll talk more about economic logic, both old and new, in a later chapter. But suffice it to say that any economic evaluation that concludes that it is cheaper and more cost-efficient to cause serious harm to the only world we have is not particularly logical. You can be sure that externalities of some kind are disguising the true economics.

Coca-Cola has had more success on the water front. Some folks in the West African country of Mali accused the company of polluting a stream that ran by its local bottling plant. The plant, like those vending machines, was independently owned. It met all local environmental standards, and its owner wasn't interested in spending any money on a new water treatment plant.

"As a business," said Isdell, "you're faced with two choices. You can go on making defensive arguments or you can take a totally new approach."

Coca-Cola chose wisely. They gave that bottler money to finance modern pollution-control equipment. Now their discharge is good enough to use as irrigation water; and, with a grant from the U.S. Agency for International Development (USAID) to improve the municipal water supply, some twenty-two thousand people have access to safe drinking water. The river is better. Life is better. And yes, local sales of Coca-Cola have benefited from it, too.

From the other side of the aisle, Pepsi's Frito-Lay division has embarked on a bold strategy at its Casa Grande chip factory. Frito-Lay built a factory in that middle of the New Mexico desert town to transform more than half a million pounds of potatoes each and every day into bags of chips. The factory devours vast amounts of water and energy, and creates equally vast amounts of potato peelings and waste.

And what is the strategy? To make an environmentally benign potato chip by taking the plant off the power grid, running it on renewable sources of energy (including potato peelings), and using recycled water, not precious freshwater.

"This might not make a hell of a lot of sense initially," said David Haft, Frito-Lay's group vice president for sustainability and productivity, "but long-term this is where we have to be."

And perhaps the long term is not very long at all. "Our evaluations were not made with hundred-dollar-a-barrel oil in mind," said Rich Beck, senior vice president for operations. "If the price of energy and water continues to rise, we will be very happy we made these investments today."

The SC Johnson Company, so well known for its Johnson Wax, is a global giant in consumer products, with sales of over $7 billion in more than one hundred countries. To raise the gates against those bad actor chemicals, and to reformulate their existing products to be more chemically benign, they created a classification scheme they call their Greenlist.™

Developed in 2001, this companywide list classifies the raw materials used in all of their products according to their impact on the environment and human health. The company then uses the list to select the best available raw materials for new products and to phase out certain ingredients in favor of those considered to be more environmentally preferred.

Today, their Greenlist provides ratings for more than 95 percent of the raw materials SC Johnson uses, including dyes, fragrances, insecticides, packaging, preservatives, solvents, and more. Each material is rated from 3 to 0. An ingredient with a 3 rating is considered best, 2 is better, 1 is acceptable, and 0-rated materials are only used on a rigorously justified, limited basis. They also use their Greenlist to look up the supply chain and assess whether their suppliers can demonstrate high environmental performance, such as receiving a ISO 14001 certification—an international, third-party environmental management standard, designed to help organizations minimize the effect of their operations on the environment.

The motivations behind all of these significant changes may differ. For me it was that spear in the chest moment when I first read Paul Hawken's book, which had been prompted by our customer's question, "What is Interface doing for the environment?" For others it might come from the desire to improve the quality of a product or the health of their employees, to differentiate themselves from their competitors, or because of a directive from a board of directors.

Any way you choose to look at it, you can fight change and watch the world pass you by, or wait until you are dragged into expensive, mandated programs that may or may not be cost-effective. Or you can become a leader and, with new thinking, find your own best way forward, and enjoy the benefits—financial, environmental, and social—of true early-mover leadership.

I am always keen to know what our customers expect of us. I keep on listening to them, hard. What about you?

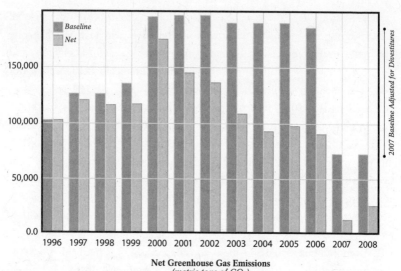

**Net Greenhouse Gas Emissions**
*(metric tons of CO₂)*
71% net change in GHG emissions
*½ from improved efficiencies and renewable energy; ½ from development of offset projects*

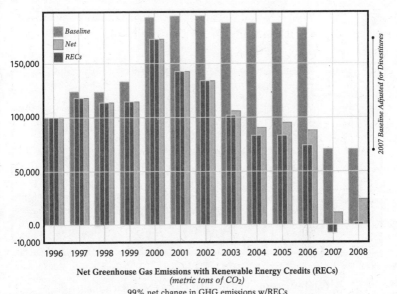

**Net Greenhouse Gas Emissions with Renewable Energy Credits (RECs)**
*(metric tons of CO₂)*

99% net change in GHG emissions w/RECs
*37% from development of offset projects; 35% from improved efficiencies and renewable energy; 27% from RECs*

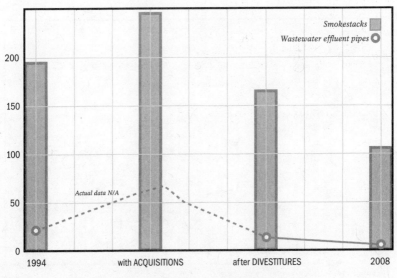

**Smokestacks and Wastewater Effluent Pipes**

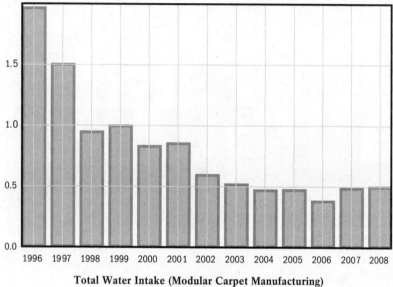

**Total Water Intake (Modular Carpet Manufacturing)**
*(gallons per square yard)*
74% decrease in water intake per unit of production

**Total Water Intake (Broadloom Carpet Manufacturing)**
*(gallons per square yard)*
38% decrease in water intake per unit of production

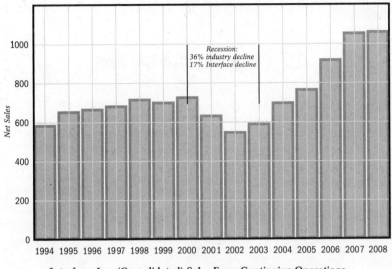

**Interface, Inc. (Consolidated) Sales From Continuing Operations**
*($ in millions)*

# 7 | Plugging into the Sun

*We've embarked on the beginning of the last days of the age of oil.*
*The market share for carbon-rich fuels will diminish as the demand*
*for other forms of energy grows. Energy companies have a choice: to*
*embrace the future . . . or ignore reality, and slowly—but surely—be*
*left behind.*

MIKE BOWLIN, former chairman and CEO, ARCO,
and chairman, American Petroleum Institute

Embracing the future certainly sounds good. Who could be against some-thing like that? And yet, many have resisted the invitation for one very good reason: Clean-tech energy sources from solar, wind, and biomass just have been too expensive. Pull out the rug of government subsidies and they'd collapse overnight, wouldn't they?

There is more than a kernel of truth to that, though I'm pretty sure that if all the perverse subsidies for oil, coal, gas, and nuclear energy sources were removed and the externalities incorporated into prices, we might see much the same thing happen to them. Does this mean that climbing the third face of Mount Sustainability—greening your energy mix with renewables—is im-possibly steep? That without a strong and steady market signal sent by govern-ment to encourage renewables (tax incentives, R&D credits, and bulk purchases), there is no market for them?

It does not. It does mean that you've got to watch your step and choose your way carefully. And it does mean that new thinking—new ways of as-sessing costs and benefits—is called for. Most assuredly, it means increas-ing efficiencies and reducing energy usage to an irreducible minimum, for only then can any of us afford to harness renewable sources at a meaning-ful scale.

Part of the trouble is, once again, inertia. We have been dependent on fossil fuels for so long that this seems not only the normal way to conduct our lives and run our businesses, but the only way. From the onset of the first industrial revolution nearly three hundred years ago (with Thomas Newcomen's invention of the steam-driven pump in 1712), substituting fossil fuels for labor has been synonymous with progress, and we're all for that, are we not?

But it is not normal; continued dependence on fossil fuels can no longer sustain progress. (Indeed, take a look at your own energy costs and you'll see that it is already holding us back.) Turning away from the frantic and thoughtless consumption of oil, coal, and natural gas will not spell the end of the world; it's the beginning of a new world of efficiency and clean technologies—and new fortunes.

That is not to say that the postpetroleum era won't look different. I think the age of steam looked pretty different to those who witnessed its birth, too. But I have no doubt that the new era will bring a world of immense opportunity, spurred on by dramatic technological change that reaches everywhere energy is consumed. Try to think of a place where energy is not consumed, and you'll realize the vast scale of these opportunities.

As I write these words, the price of a barrel of crude oil has hit a succession of all-time highs, before retreating, as high prices discouraged demand. There are many sound reasons to think that high prices are structural, and will be with us permanently. There are also some who would argue that we're in the grips of a speculative bubble, that energy prices will soon ease, even collapse. Isn't that what happened the last time?

Yes it is, and I suppose if all you are looking at is what energy prices may do next week, next month, even next year, you can safely predict fluctuations both up and down. And there is a powerful feedback mechanism built into the price of oil: As costs rise, all economic activity drops and demand levels off, even falls, sending prices back down again.

But here's the thing. The last time we faced prices like these, OPEC had turned off the taps for purely political reasons. There was plenty of oil in the ground relative to the global demand for it. It was the delivery of that oil to market that was being constrained artificially. The result?

In 1972, crude oil traded at $3 a barrel. By the end of 1974, it quadrupled, to $12. This precipitated the recession in whose grips we found ourselves during Interface's start-up. We called it an oil shock, and it was. But there were other shocks to follow. The one-two punch of the Iranian revolution and their war with Iraq pushed oil up from $14 a barrel in 1978 to $35 a barrel in 1981. Saudi Arabia's oil minister, Ahmed Yamani, warned his fellow OPEC members that those sky-high prices could lead to a fall in demand. His fellow oil ministers didn't pay attention.

Fortunately, many Americans *were* listening. They responded to spiking energy costs by installing better insulation in their homes, achieving greater efficiency in industrial processes, and buying automobiles that went a lot farther on a gallon of gasoline. Burning oil to generate electricity died a long overdue death. These factors along with a global recession caused crude oil prices to collapse below $10 a barrel in 1986.

But today's oil shock is very different. No one is throttling the pipelines or holding back the tankers. The wells are pumping for all they are worth, and then some. Why?

Because most oil-exporting countries (and the companies that own, refine, and distribute petroleum products) are amassing profits at a rate more commonly found in the illegal drug trade. Oil prospecting is under way in ever more remote regions of the world. The drilling ships that operate in the deepest waters are fully booked for the next four years.

Consider that fact when you hear someone say that opening up more American offshore waters to drilling will quickly cut your fuel costs. Meanwhile, existing fields are subject to ever more costly recovery schemes to squeeze that last drop of oil from the ground.

And yet, all of this feverish activity is still not enough to put a meaningful brake on rising prices. Why is that? Because all that pumping, surveying, and drilling has not materially closed the gap between a surging global demand and a peaking, static (if not diminishing) supply. New oil coming onto the market is snapped up by willing, even anxious, consumers. There is no slack in the system. New oil discoveries lag usage by millions of barrels each year.

When oil futures take a nervous jump because a single pipeline in Nigeria gets blown up, you know the system is stretched mighty thin. And for the first time, India and China (where the price of oil is subsidized and fourteen thousand new cars hit the road each and every day) have joined the United States and Europe in doing the lion's share of the stretching.

And so, any way you look at it, energy prices—whether we're talking about natural gas, unleaded regular, a kilowatt-hour of electricity, or the cost of petroleum-derived raw materials—are once more on everyone's mind. Folks are starting to wonder once again if they can keep their houses warm (or cool), or if they can afford to fill their cars and drive to work. While fewer miles are being driven, the Automobile Association of America reported record numbers of motorists running out of gas on the nation's highways in 2008, as people tried to squeeze just one more mile out of an empty tank.

At Interface, we have a different set of challenges. Can we buy that oil-based raw material we need to produce our product? Can we operate the machinery that makes the carpet tiles that directly provide four thousand families (some sixteen thousand people) with good livelihoods? What is it going to cost to ship our goods to our customers? How much will it cost us to recover and transport all of those millions of pounds of old carpet we'd like to recycle into new carpet?

When hit with a spike in cost, most of us respond by cutting back somewhere: setting the thermostat down in winter; or up in summer; driving less; buying less. Maybe we even trade in an inefficient vehicle and buy something that doesn't guzzle gasoline (though right now you can hardly give away an SUV, or find a hybrid to buy).

And of course, in the back of our minds, most of us are also aware that burning fossil fuels is the driving force behind global climate disruption. Some of us are even getting nervous about losing complete access to affordable chemical feedstocks. Dow Chemical, a supplier of the precursors of some of the materials we use in our carpets, was forced recently to raise prices 25 percent across the board just to keep even with its own purchases of oil.

When you consider all the vital things we make from petroleum, you quickly come to the conclusion that burning it up in a V8 is like kindling your barbecue with hundred-dollar bills. Yes, it does work. No, it does not make the slightest bit of sense. So, even though all the incentives to cut back energy usage may be in place, as an industrialist and the founder and chairman of a company that makes things, I know there must be a limit to how much efficiency we can realize.

Efficiency measures really do reduce our demand for energy and raw materials. But there must be a limit to how little energy we can use and remain in business. And though we don't yet know how far we can go, this we do know: The cheapest, most secure barrel of oil is the barrel not used through efficiency, or nega energy.

Measured against our 1996 baseline, Interface has already cut our non-renewable, fossil-derived energy by 60 percent (calculated by how much of it is required to produce a square yard of carpet). Total energy usage is down

44 percent. And we did it in an era of relatively cheap oil, and not only maintained our quality, but improved it. It has put us on a very favorable competitive footing now that oil and oil-derived raw materials are no longer cheap. And that competitive edge will only grow with time and rising prices for fossil-fuel derived energy and virgin petro-materials.

But there is a law of diminishing returns in most everything, probably efficiency, too. Go too far down that path and you might discover that, like a marathon runner on too strict a diet, being too lean may make you unable to run the race. After all, we could save a bundle of energy costs by shutting down a factory, but we can't do that and still make carpet tiles.

So we must begin to shift the discussion away from how much energy we can save profitably and begin to look at how much—and what kinds—of renewable energy we can buy, produce, and use profitably and sustainably. How else do we sever that fossil fuel umbilical cord to the earth? How do we cure an addiction to oil? Certainly not by drilling for and using even more of the stuff.

Inevitably, the biggest, cleanest, and most secure source of energy takes center stage—the sun. The opportunities appear almost overwhelmingly encouraging. As we know from research by David Ginley, Martin A. Green, and Reuben Collins, reported in "Solar Energy Conversion Toward 1 Terawatt" (*MRS Bulletin*, April 2009), the sun floods the earth with 173,000 terawatts each day. (One terawatt equals 1,000 gigawatts, and just 1 single gigawatt is roughly the generating capacity of one modern coal-fired power station.)

Compare that 173,000 terawatts to the 15 terawatts all of humanity uses each day to satisfy its energy needs, and you will get a sense of just how immense this resource is, clean and abundant from that marvelous fusion reactor that is just eight minutes away (at the speed of light).

But sheer quantity doesn't tell the entire story. If it did, we'd be irrigating our deserts from another inexhaustible source, the world's oceans. We don't because we intuitively understand that all of that superabundant saltwater would have to be desalinated, treated, pumped, and delivered, and all of that is very, very costly.

Similarly, all of that superabundant solar energy has to be collected, transformed into electricity, conditioned to meet utility and machine standards, and distributed. And there are costs and losses at every step along that way, too.

There are some business people who will tell you that solar technologies won't really take off until their high capital costs fall to a point where they are on a par with traditional, grid-supplied energy, something they call "grid parity." Once grid parity is achieved, they say, consumers will surely choose equivalent cost energy from the sun instead of from pollution-belching power plants. Well, sure. It is a little bit like saying you'll get to the top of the mountain just as soon as the helicopter arrives.

The trouble is, waiting has costs, risks, and penalties for your business, your country, and the earth, costs that might seem harder to assess but are no less real and, in fact, are getting starker and more critical with each and every year. And there are unmistakable competitive benefits that come from *not* waiting, too. Because of the hard work that went into our efficiency and waste control and renewable energy mix, Interface enjoys those advantages today, while our competitors do not. You see the point, I'm sure. When paradigms shift, early movers win.

We are not alone in this, and the advance of what I like to call the "solar revolution" is quickening. According to Paula Mints, an analyst at Navigant Consulting, in her paper "Where Are We Going and How Will We Get There—PV Production Capacities and the PV Value Chain," presented at EPIA, the second International Conference on PV Investments, global placement of solar photovoltaics was 3,073 megawatts in 2007, compared with 1,985 megawatts in 2006, a 55 percent annual growth rate that followed a 41 percent growth rate in 2006 and a 34 percent one in 2005. Those are growth rates that will get anyone's attention. So what exactly is it that all those folks are buying?

The image that comes to most people's minds when they hear the words "solar electricity" is a glass-covered panel of individual cells made from silicon—the same basic stuff that computer chips are made from, and for the same reasons. Both technologies require the properties of a semiconductor.

In a solar cell, whether it is polycrystalline (lower efficiency but with a much lower cost) or made from a single crystal (higher efficiency, higher cost), the photons in sunlight "knock" negatively charged electrons out of position, creating gaps, or "holes," in the atomic lattice that neighboring electrons seek to fill. When they do, other electrons move into *their* holes, and so on, until a small current begins to flow. The current is harvested by a capillary network of conductive wires, collected, and routed into larger wires as direct-current (DC) electricity. Gang up enough cells, and useful amounts of power are on tap for as long as the sun shines.

But that is not the only way to convert sunlight into electricity. Wind power is just solar energy one step removed. The heat of the sun creates pressure differentials that create wind, and harnessing it to generate electricity can take advantage of vast areas of the earth—on land and sea, in city and country alike—and turn whole continents into "solar-powered" (wind-driven) generators.

Another technology, concentrating solar arrays, uses sunlight that is directly focused by a parabolic mirror, to boil a working fluid—sometimes water, sometimes molten salt—to generate steam that drives a conventional turbine. Some of these designs even allow for all-night storage of that superheated, molten salt, so the station can deliver power to the grid throughout the night.

While every rooftop can be a power plant with photovoltaic cells, solar concentrators require dedicated fields of computer-controlled tracking mirrors and are, by necessity, centralized. All three—wind, distributed solar, and centralized solar—will have their place in the post-petroleum energy mix of the twenty-first century.

But traditionally, low conversion efficiency (a lot of collector surface is required to make a useful amount of electricity) and steep costs (the price per square foot of those panels) have been prohibitively high hurdles. And while there are some very bright people working to push conversion efficiencies up (some of the best are at my school, Georgia Tech), the financial sector came up with the most dramatic solution to making solar electric energy competitive and available today: the power purchasing agreement, or PPA. More on that later.

But the world of simple costs and benefits is changing, and fast, especially as the price of fossil fuels keeps rising while the price of solar technologies drops. Isn't it interesting that the price of oil shoots up as demand for it grows, while the prices of solar technologies fall as the demand for them grows?

A farmer planting a quarter-acre of corn might see a return of about three hundred dollars a year if all of that corn is sold to make ethanol. Plant a wind turbine instead and he stands to harvest ten thousand dollars a year in electricity sales, and he can still grow his corn. That, too, is a payoff that will gain the attention of any businessperson.

In 1995, a kilowatt-hour of photovoltaic electricity cost about fifty cents. By 2005, that number had fallen to twenty cents, and it is still dropping. And keep in mind, as legislation focuses on ways of reducing $CO_2$ greenhouse gas emissions by placing a price on carbon dioxide generation, there will be no "carbon tax," or greenhouse gas surcharge applied to renewable electricity. As investment costs come down with innovation and ever larger volumes of production, the primary renewable energy costs (the amortization of the investment, spread across the units of energy produced) will drop even more. The risk factor is very different, too. Unlike oil, coal, gas, or nuclear power, we know the cost of the fuel, sunlight and wind, is and will always be, exactly zero.

As a direct result, the market for solar electric projects is booming. T. Boone Pickens, nobody's fool when it comes to energy investments, is teaming with General Electric to build a 1-gigawatt wind farm—the world's largest—at a cost of $2 billion. Is some of this just froth? A new, green bubble to succeed the ones that have inflated and burst before?

Perhaps. But the fundamental mismatch between static or diminishing oil supplies and surging global demand for energy has not changed. Long term, it will not change. People need energy. Developing countries need energy even more. The gap between supply and demand for fossil fuels is bound to grow. The threat of global climate disruption looms dangerously. And while the chance of government intervention in the form of "cap and trade" legislation (to limit greenhouse gas emissions) or a carbon tax on traditional power sources (to put a price on carbon) is, I believe, all but certain, I'm equally sure that subsidies will be extended and expanded for low- or no-carbon technologies. You can take a look at your own energy bills and determine what that will mean.

This is why I believe we are not in a solar bubble, but in the early stages of a solar revolution, a sea change, a paradigm shift away from petroleum (especially imported petroleum) and coal, and toward the opportunities inherent in energy sources that are large, dependable, and more under our control.

Business has begun to respond to these opportunities. Here are some of the deals announced in just the first quarter of 2008:

- Norway's Renewable Energy Corporation, ASA, is investing close to $2.5 billion in an integrated solar manufacturing complex in Singapore.
- Germany's Q-Cells AG, one of the world's largest solar manufacturers, is projecting up to a $3.5 billion plant investment in Baja California, Mexico, close to the U.S. border.

- Evergreen Solar has signed $1 billion worth of long-term sales contracts.
- Intel, the microprocessor giant, announced a spinoff, SpectraWatt, to develop solar cells for companies that make solar panels.
- HP signed a deal with Xtreme Energetics, a company that produces concentrating photovoltaic panels, whereby HP will provide transistor technology to better focus sunlight on Xtreme's solar cells.

Clearly, this isn't just for home hobbyists anymore. Soon, solar photovoltaic systems will not look like rows of strange windows where windows ought not to be. They will have a new and different name. They will simply be called, "the roof."

At Interface, the big, hairy audacious goal embodied in our Mission Zero has been, from the beginning, to make the switch to 100 percent renewable energy by the year 2020. We'll hit that aggressive mark, and then our dependence on the trust fund of fossil fuels (nature's stored natural capital) will be behind us for good. All of our manufacturing, sales, and office facilities around the globe will be heated, cooled, lit, and powered by current income energy sources: solar, wind, geothermal, biomass, and low-impact hydroelectricity.

We started up this third face back in the days of sixteen-dollar oil! How far have we climbed? In 2008, a full 28 percent of our total energy usage came from renewables, including 89 percent of our global electricity (we use a lot of energy other than electricity). And eight of our ten plants have already achieved the 100 percent renewable electricity mark today, with more than ten years still left to go to 2020.

They are:

- Bentley Prince Street, City of Industry, California, where renewable energy supplies 100 percent of the plant's electricity requirements from an on-site solar photovoltaic array and renewable energy credits (RECs), which help make wind, solar, and biomass viable alternatives;
- InterfaceFLOR Commercial, LaGrange, Georgia (two locations), with 100 percent of the electricity used in manufacturing coming from Green-e–certified renewable energy credits, biomass, and on-site solar photovoltaics;

- InterfaceFLOR Commercial, West Point, Georgia, gets 100 percent of the electricity for its manufacturing processes from wind, biomass, and Green-e–certified RECs;
- InterfaceFLOR Commercial, Belleville, Ontario, 100 percent renewably powered through wind energy RECs;
- InterfaceFLOR in West Yorkshire, UK, with 100 percent of the plant's entire heat and power needs supplied by wind and biodigester gas;
- InterfaceFLOR, Craigavon, Northern Ireland, receives 100 percent of its electricity from wind power;
- InterfaceFLOR, Scherpenzeel, The Netherlands, derives 100 percent of its electricity from wind and an on-site solar photovoltaic array.

How did we achieve so much so soon when we all know that, while renewable energy might be getting closer to "grid parity," it is still not there yet? In truth, this wasn't easy. And there were some surprises along the way.

Initially, with a lot of new thinking, we did have to revisit traditional business standards for assessing investments and demonstrate better priorities than the traditional ones. We had to digest the possibility (or if you believed the accountants, the certainty) that the conventional payback period for an on-site solar electric system might be somewhere between way too long and never, in conventional terms. In fact, the first numbers I saw for photovoltaic panels were actually negative; the system would last seventeen years and payback would take thirty-five. What kind of an investment is that?

A very good one, as it turned out. You see, the folks in the green eyeshades had calculated, but miscalculated. They had not considered (and used) all the pertinent numbers. But they weren't thinking "in the round," as I like to say (another phrase for interdisciplinary), because they'd never had to do that before. I can't fault them, either. At most corporations, if they'd tried to extend the boundaries of their financial assessments into product design and marketing, I expect they would have been told to stick to their numbers.

You see, no one was sure in 1994 what making carpet with sunlight would mean for our bottom line. No one realized that a sizable piece of our market was looking for products that created smaller footprints back then;

and no one knew that that potential market segment would materialize, much less grow exponentially. Not even I could have anticipated how something with a seemingly dismal thirty-five-year payback could end up being a terrific investment. But it was. You'll see what I mean when I tell you the story.

Remember how that environmental task force we convened in 1994 struggled to find some way to turn a vision for Interface—that it should become the first truly sustainable business in history—into a reality? Well, they took that struggle to heart and mind, and by 1996 the entire company was energized and searching for ways to become more efficient, use fewer resources, discharge fewer and less harmful substances into the biosphere, and find renewable sources of energy.

You already know about our antiwaste program QUEST, and how we raised the screens to keep bad actor chemicals out of our facilities, smokestacks, and discharge pipes. Well, our first application of photovoltaic power was at our Intek textile factory in Aberdeen, North Carolina. It was a small 9-kilowatt unit (at peak sunlight) that operated a single 10-horsepower motor. The Intek installation was tiny, just a token effort to learn and begin to move in the right direction. The installation was successful; the 10-horsepower motor drove a series of mirrors that tracked the sun and reflected daylight into the plant through translucent openings in the ceiling. But bigger and more important things were in the wings.

Mike Bennett, the plant engineer at our Bentley Prince Street factory in Southern California, drew up a list of possible projects that would demonstrate a commitment to sustainability. BPS makes commercial broadloom and modular carpets, so they had a number of processes going on that were both energy- and water-intensive. QUEST already had Mike on the lookout to hunt down waste, and remember, we'd defined all fossil fuel use as waste.

Now Southern California is a very dry place, so saving water was a top priority, and remains one to this day. But it is also a very sunny place; on average, it has about two hundred clear days a year.

Coincidentally, Mike had a letter from the California Energy Commission sitting on his desk. It turned out that they were looking for energy partners interested in doing large, innovative projects. Grants were available for good proposals. And the U.S. Department of Energy's TEAM-UP program (Technology Experience to Accelerate Markets in Utility Photovoltaics) indicated it might be willing to kick in some funds to help reduce the cost per kilowatt-hour closer to grid parity with conventional electric power.

To Mike, the fit—abundant sunshine, clear marching orders from headquarters, state and federal agencies willing to commit hard dollars to a worthwhile project—seemed just about perfect. And so, with a good deal of wind at his back, he worked up a proposal to put a stake in the ground, to build a place where Interface could conduct real research on the potential for solar electricity to power its industrial operations worldwide. And how was he going to do that? With another small, inexpensive demo project?

No. He came back with a plan to install an on-site system that would cover nearly half an acre of ground; 450 state-of-the-art photovoltaic panels. At the time, it was designed to be the largest industrial solar array in America.

The sheer size of the installation and its estimated cost (about $1.2 million) meant that the proposal had to go through an approval process at the corporate level. Did the investment really make sense? Were there other projects that offered more bang for the buck? Could we even afford to take a leadership position in industrial photovoltaics?

Dr. Michael Bertolucci, head of Interface Research, had to pass on the merits of the proposal. How much power would be generated? Where would that power go? What would those solar-kilowatt hours be worth to us, and to the local utility?

"I came from a deep background in physical chemistry. Making molecules dance for industrial purposes is hard science," said Dr. Bertolucci, who spent years managing various Research and Development departments for General Electric's Plastic Businesses. "I was very aware of the technical limits constraining photovoltaic arrays. We'd made a lot of progress on the first two faces of Mount Sustainability, waste control and rendering our water and air emissions benign. But we hadn't made as much progress on face three, renewables. The costs were just too high.

"But I knew what Ray meant when he was talking about transforming Interface. I grew up in the wine region of Napa Valley, where I could stand in my backyard and see the entire grape-growing ecosystem at a glance. It was all contained by mountains to the east and the west. Everything—every grape, every vine, every vineyard, every case of wine, every dollar—had to come from the fertile ground between those mountains. And not just once, but again and again, year after year. It was sustainability in action—not that we called it that—and I had lived it.

"But was a million-dollar solar electric array the best way to demonstrate our commitment? Looking at the power the array could generate—about 127 kilowatts—the classical, scientific answer was, No. Why go to all that expense, all that effort, that many precious capital dollars, just to satisfy six percent of one factory's electrical demand?

"I was taught to solve problems in industrial chemistry. But when I stepped back and looked at the photovoltaic array proposal again, what it would *mean* as opposed to how it would *perform*, I realized that much of what I'd been taught was flawed. In fact, my classical approach to problem solving turned out to be the problem. What is the payback period for being a global leader? What is the return on investment for making a public commitment to a better world? How will our main market—interior designers and architects— respond? Classical scientific analysis is not equipped to answer any of those questions."

And as I said, neither was classical accounting. But I knew that Dr. Mike was really onto something when he started asking different questions. He was looking beyond the simple numbers of kilowatt-hours, costs, investments, profits, and losses to see the problem from brand-new angles. He was starting to think in the round. As Dr. Mike will tell you, sustainability is like entering a familiar room through a different door. Everything looks different.

But no CEO can ignore his own accountants when they are flashing red lights. That's what you are paying them for, after all. With its costs perfectly clear and its benefits financially uncertain, the solar project might have died then and there despite Dr. Bertolucci's enthusiasm or my directives. It did not, because someone else started asking good questions, too.

Mike Bennett, the BPS plant engineer, knew the 127-kilowatt array could power thirty houses. But he didn't have thirty houses to run. He had a carpet factory. He wondered, *What could that big array power if it were hooked-up directly to the energy-hungry, carpet-making machinery at Bentley Prince Street?*

A quick survey revealed that the largest industrial photovoltaic array in the United States, if channeled to run the carpet tufting machines of Bentley Prince Street, could produce one million square yards of carpet each year—a million square yards of solar-made carpet. Bentley Prince Street's sales and marketing people were brought in. Could they sell a product like that: Solar-Made™ carpet, something the world had never seen before? And their answer was, *Bring it on!*

Here at last was a green light that was every bit as clear and bright as the red ones we'd seen from accounting. And so we took that bold step. The array went up in 1996. At peak sunlight, it generated 127 peak kilowatts of photovoltaic voltage, connected directly to the California electric grid. In effect, this ran the plant's electricity meter backward. (To get an appreciation for how far industry has come since then, consider the system Google installed at their corporate headquarters in Mountain View, California, in 2007: not 450 solar panels, but *9,000!*)

And Solar-Made™ carpet was born, a brand-new product that generated incremental sales those accountants had overlooked in their preoccupation with investment and simple cost comparisons, sales that made the payback of those expensive PV panels a slam dunk. And the return on our investment continues. I think Judy Pike, our director for sustainability and supply management at Bentley Prince Street, told that story best.

"We were in competition with two other carpet manufacturers to win a big contract with the University of California system," said Judy. "There was a lot at stake, twenty million dollars' worth of carpet orders in the next three years. The university sent us a two-hundred-page questionnaire that dealt with every environmental aspect of our manufacturing process. Of our entire company, really. They sent the same questionnaire to our competitors, and then they came to our factory to see exactly what we were doing, and how we were doing it.

"It was a brilliant, sunny day, and the UC people stood beneath our photovoltaic array. Something just clicked, and one of them turned to me and said, 'This is real.' It turned out our competitors all looked great on paper, too. But when it came to actually doing something tangible that demonstrated an on-the-ground commitment to sustainability, we were head and shoulders above our competition. And we won that contract."

All the talking, all the advertising and marketing in the world, could not have bought that recognition without the actual *doing.* When I say the goodwill of the marketplace has just been astonishing, that's what I mean.

So that is how what seemed like a terrible investment came out golden. And it is why I am convinced that making decisions in the round, including marketing, sales, and the customer, always yields more accurate assessments, as well as better decisions. I'll give you another example of new thinking, separate from Interface.

Jim Rogers is the CEO of Duke Energy, the big utility and energy company based in Charlotte, North Carolina. Like just about every electric utility (especially those who burn a lot of coal), they are a *very* large source of both air pollution and $CO_2$. Take a look at the figures reported out by the biggest corporations in the world, and you'll find that of the top ten corporate emitters of carbon dioxide, seven are electric utilities. It's worth mentioning here that the number one emitter is not a corporation at all, but the U.S. federal government! More on *that* problem later.

So it is no surprise that, just like those accountants who poured cold water over our proposed PV array in Southern California, Duke's system planners were sure that solar energy was just too expensive to make economic sense. That the cost the typical homeowner would have to pay to install a system would be orders of magnitude higher than the benefits they would see in a reduced electric bill.

But then Jim Rogers stepped outside classical analysis and asked a different kind of question: *"What if Duke bought solar panels in bulk, drove the price down, and teamed up with our ratepayers to install them?"*

Well, he might be the boss, but you can imagine what some of his own people would think about that (actually, I have a keen appreciation of delivering visions that go "around the bend"). Why on earth should an electric utility company buy expensive solar panels that reduce our customers' electricity consumption? Are you serious? We'd be losing revenue *and* adding costs!

Remember, Duke is an electric utility—one of the biggest—and it has to operate with all the technical, regulatory, and political restrictions firmly in mind. Change comes hard. Looked at through that narrow lens of conventional, linear thinking, Jim Rogers was suggesting something completely unprecedented. But he was starting to "think in the round," taking that extra step to look at a problem from a new vantage point.

"If we had 500,000 solar units on the roofs of our customers," he said, "we could install them. We could maintain them. And we could dispatch the energy they generate. In effect, they would constitute a distributed 1,000-megawatt *power plant* that would allow us to mothball one of our costly, inefficient plants."

How would that help the company? Duke Energy's whole-system efficiency would improve, and they could save enough in fuel *not burned* to make that big, expensive solar program a surprisingly attractive investment. Add in the potential effects of a national carbon tax, and that attractive investment becomes something of a no-brainer. But there are even more downstream benefits to reap.

What if that distributed solar power plant allowed Duke Energy the option of not building a new nuclear generating station that might take a decade to permit and build? Or a coal-fired station that left the company vulnerable to future $CO_2$ costs or political restrictions—things no one can quantify today? Well, it seems to me the payback on Duke's solar program might be just about instantaneous.

Perhaps that is why in May of 2008, Duke announced it would purchase the entire output of one of the nation's largest photovoltaic solar farms, planned for Davidson County, North Carolina. And as I write this, Duke has just applied for regulatory approval to install solar panels at homes, schools, stores, factories, and other locations in that state.

What's more, Jim has said for the record that he would rather invest in his customers' efficiency projects than in new generating capacity. And he's right on target. Why *not* build "nega-watts" in the form of high-efficiency appliances, air conditioners, and lighting, instead of buying new coal or nuclear megawatts?

That is a new paradigm, though it's based on a concept that Amory Lovins has pushed for decades.

I guess some things just take a while.

As I've said, it's not just rising oil prices or advances in the laboratory that are driving these deals. Some very serious invention has also been going on in the financial community to make solar electricity more affordable. Instead of forcing businesses to jump that high capital-cost hurdle, they have charted a way around it. Their innovation?

The power purchase agreement (PPA) is a contract that allows you to buy green power without having to buy the solar panels. For homeowners and corporations alike, it has the potential to become a real game changer. A solar PPA, in essence, turns you into a power-producing solar utility. You enter into a long-term agreement with a company that will:

1. build a turnkey solar electric array on your site with their money, not yours;

2. buy all the power you can generate;
3. maintain your array to keep it running for the life of the agreement;
4. allow you to run your business as usual, with none of the potential problems of owning and operating a power plant;
5. deliver green energy to you, and the surplus to the grid, at a dependable, predictable cost you can plan on, with no hidden fuel surcharges (or maybe, carbon taxes) to surprise you or your CFO. The cost to you depends on the details of the agreement, but in general it will be equal to or less than what you are paying now for electricity; and
6. allow you to renew the agreement at the end of the contract period, or to buy the system at a depreciated price.

Sound like a good thing? It can be. That's why companies like Staples, Whole Foods, Wal-Mart, and Kohls have jumped on it. Greentech Media forecasts that PPAs will capture 75 percent of all residential and commercial solar installations in the next two years.

Local governments are also getting into the act, perhaps because they've grown tired of waiting for the federal government. Even as the cry goes out to Washington—*do something, do anything*—some local governments are offering their own power-purchase agreements to put more green power on the grid.

In Northern California, the city of Berkeley approved a loan program to pay the upfront costs of solar projects for business and residential property owners who would pay back the loan over twenty years as part of their property taxes. Other cities, as well as the state of California, are considering similar measures to help finance renewable energy projects.

When it comes to finding renewable sources of energy, some towns have moved beyond considering and straight to action. One of them, LaGrange, Georgia, is right in my neighborhood. It is the home of InterfaceFLOR's American carpet tile facility.

LaGrange is very definitely not just another sleepy small town in western Georgia. A strong, entrepreneurial spirit runs through its municipal government, which not only provides the usual services—police, fire, schools, and a library—but also sells electricity and natural gas. And while its fee structures are cheaper than those offered by private utilities, it still makes enough money on these business ventures to completely eliminate property taxes, so it keeps the utility money in the community.

Not bad.

One of the other services LaGrange provides is trash pickup and disposal. While some cities use one of the giant national waste-hauling contractors (and pay much higher fees), LaGrange has always found it better, faster, cheaper, and more profitable to do it themselves. But those national contractors do have something LaGrange did not: access to spare landfills.

There was a problem: LaGrange's own municipal landfill was filling up. Space was going to run out in just a few years, and when it did the city would have to either find a new site or throw in the towel and hire someone to come in and haul their trash away (though we know, of course, there is no away), and pay more for the privilege.

Finding a new landfill site was not their only problem, either. Methane gas was seeping out of the town's existing landfill into the air, and into the groundwater, too. Methane is also called "swamp gas," and is just as malodorous as it sounds. A permanent squadron of buzzards circled the LaGrange landfill site, and the smell was a constant environmental assault on the people who lived nearby (where the value of their land suffered just as much as their sense of smell).

This was not a problem unique to LaGrange. Landfill gas is one of the largest sources of methane emissions into the atmosphere, and it is a very potent greenhouse gas. In fact, its global-warming potential is twenty-one times greater than that of carbon dioxide (really sixty times, but it remains in the atmosphere a shorter length of time than $CO_2$). It is also quite dangerous; methane is highly flammable. It can collect in buildings and explode.

One way or the other, whether they moved to another site or not, LaGrange's landfill gas problem had to be dealt with to prevent both its emission into the atmosphere and its offense to surrounding property. But building a water-treatment plant to remove it from the groundwater would cost millions. Finding a new site to accommodate more trash was going to cost LaGrange another $10 million to $20 million. That is, if they could find one, and if they could still afford to truck their garbage to it, in an era of pricey diesel fuel.

All these costs were going to turn LaGrange's smoothly functioning, entrepreneurial municipal budget upside down. Surely there was another answer, one that would stop that methane from escaping into the air and water and extend the life of the existing landfill. But if there was a solution, Patrick Bowie, LaGrange's director of utilities, couldn't see it.

"We were getting closer and closer to the point of no return," he said. "Even if we raised our costs and outsourced our garbage collection to a contractor, we still had the methane gas problem. You know, I came to LaGrange convinced that a municipal utility couldn't possibly operate as efficiently as an investor-owned utility. But I was proven wrong.

"When a customer has a problem here, they don't have to call some automated number a thousand miles away and hope for the best. They just call me, and it gets solved quickly and efficiently. And contrary to what some folks think about government, we could do it cheaper. That was what we were all about. But our landfill problems were putting our promise to provide good, competitive services to the folks of LaGrange in serious jeopardy."

Dave Gustashaw, Interface's former vice president of engineering in LaGrange, is as hard core an engineer as they come. He ran an alternative energy laboratory at Georgia Tech—a kind of toy shop for aspiring engineers interested in finding their own better way—when he was not solving impossible problems for us at Interface. And like all good engineers, he didn't recognize obstacles. He just saw problems in need of a solution. And he thought he might have one.

What if all that escaping methane was collected and piped to the local Interface plant, where it could be burned for process heat in place of natural gas?

"I went to the EPA, the Department of Energy, everyone in Washington connected to the issue to see if anyone had done something like this before. They told me sure, capturing methane and burning it is a great idea. But not at a small, municipal landfill. A 'real' landfill gas project required a minimum of a million tons of garbage in place to produce three hundred cubic feet per minute of methane. That took a giant landfill, a giant collection, compression, and treatment plant, and giant up-front costs. Well, that was just a steaming pile of assertions as far as I could tell. Where were the numbers to back them up? They didn't exist. So Patrick and I sketched it all out on a clean sheet of paper."

What emerged from those informal design sessions was new thinking and a landfill gas project that broke all the rules. It was too small. Not enough methane would be generated. The distance between the landfill and our factory (nine miles) was too far. It would never work, and what's more, if by some remote chance there *was* enough methane, Interface couldn't use it all anyway.

Dave Gustashaw attacked each of those issues and found a sound engineering solution for every one. He and Patrick Bowie presented their findings to the mayor and the city council. Three walls of the meeting room were plastered in dense diagrams and calculations.

"It was as impressive a presentation as I have ever seen," said LaGrange's mayor, Jeff Lukken. "We all knew what was at stake. We all knew we were facing very major costs if we did nothing. And Interface was behind us all the way. That helped immensely. So after Dave and Patrick wrapped up their presentation, we all looked at one another and nodded. The vote was unanimous and I said, 'Let's do it.'"

The result: a public-private partnership between Interface and the city of LaGrange. The city committed $3 million in capital costs to capture and pipe the methane to our factory (running the pipes was the most expensive part). Interface committed $50,000 to modify two of our boilers to run on landfill methane instead of natural gas, cutting our total fossil fuel use by about 6 percent. And we also bought that landfill gas at a 30 percent discount to the cost of natural gas (per unit of energy). And, oh, by the way, we found another customer for the gas we couldn't burn, my old friends at Milliken!

The city has realized an income stream of about $300,000 a year in gas sales. This will go on for the whole forty-year life span of the project, transforming an otherwise useless, indeed harmful, pollutant into dollars. And since the value of LaGrange's landfill gas tracks the market price of natural gas, as fossil fuels grow more expensive, the income stream from the landfill will also increase. In the summer of 2008, LaGrange sold a record $117,000 worth of landfill gas in just *two months*. The payoff grows!

And pumping the gas out of their landfill has stopped it from infiltrating the groundwater, so there is no longer a need for a multimillion-dollar wastewater treatment plant. And that awful smell? Eliminated. But I have saved the best part for last.

Remove the methane and the entire landfill deflates; the volume goes down, increasing its capacity and extending its life. That means the city won't have to hunt for a new site for an estimated fifteen years. This is win-win-win at its very best.

- The city of LaGrange reaps a huge financial return on a modest investment, converting a polluting waste stream into a lucrative revenue stream; avoiding enormous capital costs associated with unregulated methane emissions; and postponing the need for a new landfill for fifteen years.
- A stinking public nuisance is eliminated and an environmental injustice corrected.
- Our factory reduces its fossil fuel energy use, and our costs, too!
- The earth is spared greenhouse gas emissions that contribute twenty-one times as much as plain old carbon dioxide.
- Interface receives the benefit of a greenhouse gas offset of twenty-one times six percent of our fossil fuel use at LaGrange, an amount equal to 126 percent of our plant's total energy use.
- Because of this, we can now declare our LaGrange operations completely climate neutral.
- For a further modest investment in offsets, we can neutralize the greenhouse gas emissions for our entire supply chain and declare our products to be climate neutral for their full life, wellhead to end-of-life reclamation.
- Furthermore, our climate neutral carpet, dubbed Cool Carpet™ by our marketing people, is a marketplace coup, producing a surge of incremental sales.

So you see, decisions made in the round are right and smart. In the new thinking of sustainability, "extraneous" factors like market presence, reputation, and leadership are every bit as real and positive as the hidden subsidies to fossil fuels are real and negative.

Whether that means a photovoltaic array on your roof, investing in someone else's wind farm (the renewable energy credit route), buying green power from your local utility, or solving your town's landfill problems, there is no reason to stand by and wait for grid parity anymore than you would exclude Treasuries from your investment portfolios because their yield is not as good as those from junk bonds. In uncertain times, certainty, whether in energy supplies or your investments, can offer tremendous value. And nothing is more valuable than market share.

As fossil fuels grow more expensive and less predictable, blending renewables into your energy mix is not just prudent diversification, it is sound financial practice. Especially when they can be bought with PPAs on fixed-price contracts, with no capital costs or price risk to you. Are you confident of what oil, gas, coal, and electricity will cost next year? In five years? No?

Well, neither am I. But nobody hikes the price of sun and wind, and some renewables are clearly competitive on price alone today.

I did a back-of-the-envelope calculation one day that showed the United States could have met its Kyoto commitment, a 7 percent reduction in greenhouse gases, on landfill gas alone, at a profit to everyone. However, in its dubious wisdom the Senate eschewed Kyoto in a 95–0 vote before the treaty was ever presented to them for ratification.

It is true that the third face of Mount Sustainability—ramping up on renewables—once seemed impossibly steep to us, a place for daredevils and fools. Yet, the challenge has been transformed by technological, financial, and operational innovation, and by the inexorable effects of supply and demand, into a field of enormous opportunity, a field that is not yet crowded, but neither is it empty. The solar revolution has begun.

Those who act to claim their place in it will reap the kind of early competitive advantages that people wise enough to buy land along railroad routes once enjoyed. So you see, as I said at the beginning of this chapter, we have a very simple choice to make: Embrace the future, or be left behind.

Take a look at the following charts and you can track both our steady, upward progress on face three, and our profitability. They are not connected by coincidence. They are connected by our commitment to Mission Zero; and the benefits we have so far enjoyed—new energy sources, new products, new profits, new markets, motivated associates, marketplace goodwill, and risk reductions—will continue for as long as the sun will shine. This doesn't assure constant, upward trends for a cyclical business, but it certainly mitigates the "downs" in the business cycle.

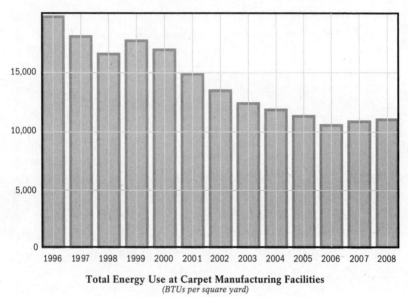

**Total Energy Use at Carpet Manufacturing Facilities**
*(BTUs per square yard)*
44% decrease in energy use per unit of production

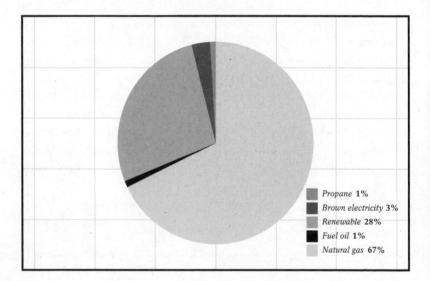

Propane **1%**
Brown electricity **3%**
Renewable **28%**
Fuel oil **1%**
Natural gas **67%**

**Energy Consumption Profile**
*(2008)*

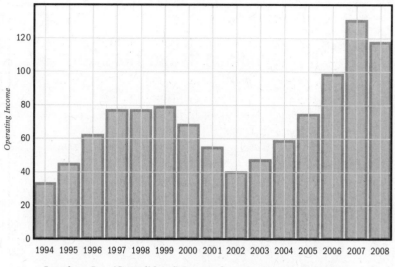

**Interface, Inc. (Consolidated) Income from Continuing Operations**
*($ in millions)*

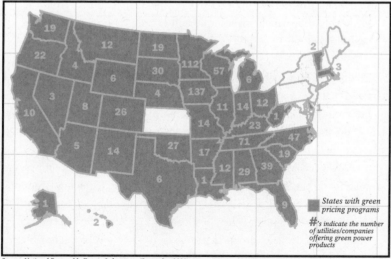

Source: National Renewable Energy Laboratory (September 2008)

**Utility Green Pricing Activities**

# 8 | Round and Round They Go

*The separator started up, it swallowed an entire load of carpet tiles and cleanly separated them. All three of us just stood there and watched it work. Without saying a word, we all knew this machine was going to be the key to recycling carpet.*

ERIC NELSON, vice president,
Interface Americas Re-Entry 2.0

Remember Interface's definition of sustainability?

To operate this petroleum-intensive business so as to take from the earth only that which is naturally and rapidly renewable—not one fresh drop of new oil—and to do no harm to the biosphere.

And recall the very cogent comment one of my associates made after I delivered that first speech on sustainability in 1994: "Isn't it strange how we call our factories 'plants'? They don't look like plants and they don't work like plants. A plant runs off solar power, rain, and soil. What if our plants worked more like that? Isn't that what you're really talking about?"

It surely was. And just as introducing renewable energy into our plants can take us up the third face of Mount Sustainability, replacing virgin raw materials with recycled or renewable materials will allow us to climb face four, as Jim Hartzfeld points out:

"A plant's waste (e.g., dropped leaves) is 100 percent biodegradable. In fact, some other plant probably uses its waste as food and turns it right back into soil, and more plants. Nature functions cyclically and with essentially zero waste. One organism's waste is another's food. I used to say that nature was the model. I realize now that nature is the real thing, and our poorly designed industrial system is a deeply flawed artifice. Nature is also the teacher. As we study her lessons, we've got to learn to run our homes, our institutions, our cities, and our businesses the same way she does, not only on sunlight, but also cyclically and waste-free.

"Nature is self-organized to make the environment more agreeable to the plants and animals that depend on it, not less. So must industry. Plugging into renewable sources of energy reduces, and ultimately eliminates, our dependency on fossil fuels and our contribution to climate disruption. Using ever greater amounts of recycled materials reduces, and ultimately eliminates, our dependency on virgin raw materials. Those virgin materials that took eons to create, decades to mine, will be gone—used up—within a few generations, and also require more energy to produce than their recycled counterparts.

"But we have learned that there is no one right way to make use of recycled materials, just as there was no one form of renewable energy appropriate for every application. Consider the nine most energy-intensive industries—aluminum, metal casting, chemicals, oil refining, glass, cement, mining, paper, and steel—and you will see what I mean.

"It is not too difficult to picture an aluminum manufacturer ramping up the recycled content of their cans, and the same is true for paper, steel, and glass. But for chemicals? Refining? For cement? While batches of newsprint can be made with varying amounts of recycled content, you would be severely challenged to do that with chemicals, and you surely have your work cut out to do it with carpets. Carpets have been around for thousands of years, but that does not mean they are simple.

"Think about what you see when you look at a floor carpeted with Interface carpet tiles. There's a lot more than meets the eye, a lot more than just patterns of color and texture. A well-chosen carpet can turn a noisy, chaotic office landscape into a safe, inviting, and serene environment. But beneath that pretty surface is a carefully designed and constructed layer cake of materials, each one selected to deliver maximum performance, each one vital to the way the carpet looks, feels, works, and lasts.

"The uppermost face yarn—the part that you see and touch and walk on—can be made from nylon (of several varieties), wool, polypropylene, polyester, or a blend of materials. Typically, it represents about one fifth the weight of a new carpet tile. The face yarn is tufted into a primary backing layer, usually made of polyester, which is then coated with latex on its underside to hold the nylon yarn in place.

"Next comes a film of vinyl plastisol. This is a viscous mixture of polyvinyl chloride (PVC) resin, plasticizer, and naturally abundant materials such as calcium carbonate and ash. The film is fused with heat into a pliable solid layer. To this is bonded a sheet of fiberglass, and beneath that is a second coating of vinyl plastisol, also fused with heat into a continuous film. Depending on the way the carpet is installed on the floor, there could be a final layer of glue. (Getting rid of that glue is another story.)

"All these components come together smoothly, quickly, and efficiently, and are built to last when we make a square of carpet tile. So, carpet for recycling doesn't come back to us as an easily-peeled-apart sandwich. In fact, it returns in heavy, dirty stacks and rolls, even bales, that may have been tossed into a truck with other carpets from other installations, and it may be made from any number of different fibers. Some constituents are valuable, others not, and some (like dirt and sand) must be positively excluded to make recycling work at all.

"Put all these factors together," Jim concludes, "and you can begin to see why finding a way to sort, then disassemble the old carpet into pure, reusable parts has always been a very tough proposition."

It is not for want of raw material. Some eight hundred million square yards—that's *five billion pounds*—of old carpet (most of it with nylon face yarn) get pulled up and thrown out each year in the United States alone. Each pound of nylon carpet contains the embodied energy equivalent of more than a gallon of regular unleaded gasoline. Just imagine throwing away five billion gallons of gasoline every year! Who in their right mind would do such a thing?

Well, strange as it seems, we *Homo sapiens* (self-named "wise men") do. Though many of the economic facts of life have changed, our old, linear, take-make-waste, industrial system has not—yet.

For the most part it still operates as though it is easier and cheaper to buy new, virgin materials than to reuse old ones. Why not, when the industries that drill for the oil that spawns those virgin materials are heavily subsidized? Why not, when throwing all those billions of pounds of carpet away (though there is no such place as away) conveniently turns it into someone else's problem? Why not, when the true cost, including the economic penalties inherent in fossil fuel consumption—the externalities—are paid for by society as a whole, while the profits earned from its destructive effects are retained by the oil producers?

And so, in a totally perverse way, it made perfect sense for the carpet industry in general, and Interface in particular, not to consider recycled raw materials, right up to the fateful point when our customers began to ask that critical question, "What's Interface doing for the environment?"

Since then, the costs—competitive disadvantage, environmental, and moral—have become too high for our industry to ignore. What happened at Interface in 1994 is, I expect, happening now in a great many other companies, extending way beyond those making carpets.

From the moment my eyes were opened by Paul Hawken's book, I knew that someday, somehow, we would have to close the loop and use 100 percent recycled or renewable content to become sustainable. Reduce, repurpose, reuse, recycle, redesign were not original ideas, but we felt daunted by the significant costs and uncertain quality of materials available for recycling and, not the least, by the complete lack of technology.

The technologies just did not exist. Taking old carpets apart—when they had been built to last—and turning them into new carpets required new machines, new chemical processes, and new business relationships, and called for the development of new technologies and products that no one had yet invented.

So we took it upon ourselves to get it done. Let me tell you the story. It begins with how a carpet tile is made.

Interface carpet tile has been manufactured for decades with a backing that includes those two layers of vinyl, a dual fiberglass backbone, and is produced by an energy-intensive process that uses a lot of virgin, oil-derived PVC plastisol.

On the market now for more than thirty-five years, this GlasBac® backing provides Interface carpet tiles with superior dimensional stability (it keeps the tile square and flat), weight, and floor-hugging suppleness. No other material is even close in providing these qualities. The tiles require little or no glue for installation. This is an important feature, since glues and adhesives are not only messy and costly, and work against flexibility, but their fumes contribute to sick building syndrome. Just think about how glue smells and you'll understand why a room full of glued-down carpet can be nauseating.

Still, even with the best carpet tile backing in the world, we knew we had to get moving on the recycling front. Using less material, producing less waste, and running more efficiently with less energy were good starts, and we wanted to squeeze those resources dry. Employing renewable energy whenever and wherever possible was also absolutely necessary. We are doing more of that every year. But so long as our basic raw materials—nylon and vinyl plastisol—still came from oil wells, we could never cut our connection to those wells without first bending our traditional, linear, manufacturing processes into a closed loop.

There wasn't much we could do about the nylon in the beginning. But the technology for stripping off the vinyl layers did not seem completely beyond our reach. There was a fly in the ointment, though. Recovering vinyl might be the low-hanging fruit in carpet recycling, but it has become an environmental hot button, and not entirely without reason.

Many architects, interior designers, and building owners and operators are honestly concerned about the effects on human health of products that contain PVC, products like water pipes, shower curtains, bottles, all kinds of containers, toys, and, yes, carpet tiles. And their concerns are justified if the production of PVC is not properly managed, if it is used incorrectly or disposed of improperly.

Yet, with proper management—that is, wise choices at each of several critical points or stages—PVC does not pose a risk for human health for workers, building occupants, or the general public. It does pose a risk when it is hauled off to the regional landfill, though. If it catches fire in a low oxygen environment (like under a landfill), PVC can generate some very undesirable toxins.

And there is a lot of PVC out there—billions (maybe trillions) of pounds are already locked up in existing products. And 33.5 million metric tons of new PVC are produced every year, adding to an already sizable disposal problem.

What should we as a society do with all this petroleum-derived material? Should we burn it? No, who wants those toxins in the air? Bury it? Who knows what it will contribute to the groundwater over the centuries? Besides, it is too valuable a resource to just throw away, and it becomes more valuable with every uptick in the price of crude oil. What's more, finding landfills with room is getting expensive, too; and remember, sometimes landfills catch fire.

Or should we find some way to reuse those precious, energy-intensive organic molecules? We conducted a very detailed, science-driven life cycle assessment (see Appendix A for comparison), and it clearly identified that recycled PVC is the environmentally sound way to go.

Having produced our share of PVC-containing products in the form of fusion-bonded carpet and carpet tile backing, Interface launched our closed-loop recycling efforts by focusing on the PVC backing, not just from our own products, but from those made by our competitors and from noncarpet sources, too. If waste equals food, we wanted our recycling machinery to have plenty to eat. But how should we go about salvaging this superior material to give it life after life? And were we sure it would be worth the effort in view of possible alternative materials?

It took an all hands on deck R&D program, but by 1996 we were able to start integrating reclaimed vinyl into one of our carpet tile backing layers. We called it GlasBac® RE, and it was a significant and noticeable improvement, a good first step. However, it was not enough by itself to eliminate our need for millions of pounds of virgin vinyl. And it did nothing at all to address the problem of recycling the nylon yarn in the carpet's face. You might think of it as a partial answer to half the problem.

Then, in 1997, our Interface-Americas division was able to produce the first fusion-bonded carpet made from 100 percent postindustrial, recycled yarn. We called it Déjà vu. It was another pioneering step in the right direction.

While we were able to build on these early incremental efforts and, by 1999, offer carpet tile products that used both some postindustrial recycled nylon and some postconsumer recycled vinyl backing, it took more years of research and development to come up with the next quantum leap: a new, proprietary thermoplastic process we called Cool Blue.™

We'd attempted to transform old carpet tile backing into new through the tried and not-so-true means of melting and extrusion; the material would be heated to over 400 degrees (because it had to flow like a liquid), and then be poured into the tile assembly process. But there were some real disadvantages with this approach.

First, the process took an awful lot of heat, and to generate all that heat we needed an awful lot of fossil-derived energy. Second, the hot, melted backing material lost too many of the needed physical qualities that were inherent in the original polymer. Finally, when you heat any plastic to temperatures that high, it is going to give off gases, those same volatile organic chemical emissions we were working so hard to totally eliminate from our operation.

Cool Blue™ changed all of that. The recycling line is installed at our carpet backing plant in LaGrange, Georgia, seventy miles southwest of Atlanta.

A three-hundred-foot assembly line snakes through the factory floor, beginning with large bins labeled Cool Blue Food. We feed those bins with carpet backing scraps and other plastics that had been ground into fine particles. The particles are fed into what resembles a giant pasta machine, which spits out the plastic crumbs onto a conveyor belt. No super hot extrusion is required.

The conveyor belt then passes through a huge oven, where direct heat is applied only to the crumbs. Then a giant roller applies just the right amount of pressure to "squash" the warm, soft crumbs into a continuous sheet of carpet tile backing.

Cool Blue™ is a big-time (and expensive) innovation; it uses much lower process temperatures to soften the plastic, which offers some significant advantages. The low temperature keeps the polymer intact, allowing us to use 100 percent recycled PVC (no more virgin material needed to "sweeten" the mix). And we can run the entire line off the heat generated by the landfill methane gas I described in the last chapter. As John Bradford, our vice president for research and development, put it: "Alternative, renewable energy; renewable, recyclable materials; and a high performance backing made from recycled materials—it's like the trifecta for sustainability."

Remember Judy Pike's customer's comment? This isn't blue sky. This is real!

Cool Blue™ increased our capacity to recycle waste into new carpet backing from approximately five million pounds a year to fifteen million pounds a year. That is a big step up, and it also allowed us to keep old PVC material from ending up in incinerators or landfills, where it could remain for centuries and run the risk of burning.

That's why, after a long, hard look at PVC in a vigorous life cycle assessment, we came to a conclusion that has been, to say the least, a bit controversial. After all, Interface is the industry leader when it comes to operating with the earth in mind. How could we use something like PVC in our products, a material that in some well-meaning people's minds is *bad*?

Well, there is a great deal of science behind our decision, and it says that PVC is *not* bad if managed properly. There's a decision maze to work through, but in the end it comes down to this: We *know* that PVC is safe in our carpet tiles, and it beats all other contenders both in performance and in environmental footprint by a mile. Managed and used properly, PVC poses no more danger in our carpets than a carpet made from lamb's wool. Moreover, it offers the capacity to sequester millions of pounds of existing (not new) vinyl in a safe, usable form. It is a bit like injecting atmospheric $CO_2$ into underground caverns, except the vinyl we recycle is put back to work again and again, obviating virgin material every time, while $CO_2$ must be isolated once and for all—forever.

Cool Blue™ helped to put real distance between us and the oil wells. While that was the environmentally right thing to do when oil was eighteen dollars a barrel, it is a very smart business thing to do now that oil is far more expensive. Was it worth the trouble? You bet!

And yet, as good as these steps were, there was still no good way to clearly separate all that valuable nylon face fiber from the backing, and if you could not separate it cleanly and efficiently, neither could you recycle it in a closed loop (back into itself). Even if you found some way to separate the two, the three available technologies for turning recycled nylon "fluff" from old carpets into the raw material for new ones—remelting, dissolution, and chemical breakdown—were considered hard, really hard, and just about impossible. Either the end product was too contaminated to use, the recycling chemicals were too toxic, or the whole endeavor was just too expensive to justify.

That is where an Italian inventor and a German American engineer come into my story.

Sergio Dell'Orco owns Dell'Orco & Villani, a small company near Florence, Italy, where he and his family manufacture machines that recycle textile waste back into usable fiber. In 2006, Dell'Orco teamed up with Frank Levy, a textile engineer who had immigrated to the United States from Germany in 1946, to see if there might be some way to use Dell'Orco's machines to do something similar with old carpets.

As I have indicated, the technical challenges were tall, and Dell'Orco had the same problems with recycling carpets that we had. Physics and chemistry are the same everywhere. But he had years of experience designing all kinds of machinery for turning old clothing, mill waste, and fabric scraps into new blankets, automobile door panels, hood liners, and dashboards—even the waterproof fabric that lines water treatment ponds.

His machine shop was small by comparison with what you might find at a big corporation, but it contained a lot of creativity. And he was his own boss. There was no one to tell him what he couldn't do.

And so it was there, in a Florentine machine shop, that Dell'Orco invented a machine that could cleanly separate old carpets into their constituent components. And, as I said, there are a lot of old carpets—those five billion pounds a year, just in the United States.

"Placed in one spot," said Levy, "this used carpet would need a hole one mile by one mile by one hundred feet deep every year for the United States alone. If incinerated, the carpets might release toxic chemicals. If buried, they might never totally disintegrate, posing terrible problems for future generations." After years of tinkering with separators of all descriptions, Dell'Orco was able to modify one of his separators and quickly come up with a design that could take on carpets. At last we had a solution to the most perplexing technical challenge of Mount Sustainability.

"Our equipment takes apart the components that make up the carpet," said Dell'Orco. "By reusing the components in closed-loop recycling, business people can be both profitable and socially responsible." Levy had spotted the need, Dell'Orco created the solution, and Interface was ready for it.

We first learned about their work at the Carpet America Recovery Effort (CARE) annual conference held in 2006 at the Southern Pine Conference Center at Callaway Gardens in Pine Mountain, Georgia. CARE is a joint industry-government organization that was founded in 2002 and is dedicated to increasing the recycling and reuse of old carpets and reducing the amount of waste carpet going to landfills. Interface is a sustainable leader sponsor of the organization, and our vice president for research, Stuart Jones, was there, attending that conference for us.

"I was in a conference room listening to a presentation when a gentleman came by and dropped a plastic bag filled with white fiber on the table," said Jones. "The bag's label said the fiber was postconsumer, recycled nylon, but it looked like brand-new, virgin material. I turned to ask him what it really was, but he'd already gone. Fortunately, he'd stapled his business card to the bag. On it read 'Frank Levy, President, Stellamcor Corporation' and included his cell phone number.

"So I called him up to ask what was really in that bag. He said it was pure, recycled nylon from old carpets, and that he and his associates in Italy had perfected a machine that could cleanly separate the face fiber from the backing. No harsh chemicals, no contamination. Well, I've heard a lot of blue sky before, so I was skeptical. He said, 'Come to New York and see for yourself.' Not long after, I was on a plane to visit Frank's shop out on Long Island.

"He sat me down and showed me a videotape of a machine that took in old carpet in one end and cleanly separated it; the face was turned into fluff and the backing came out looking like something we'd be happy to use to feed our Cool Blue machine. It looked perfect, but you can make anything look good in a promotional video. So I said, 'Nice movie. But will it work in a real industrial setting?' And he answered, 'Come to Italy and see for yourself.'"

Stuart called two of his colleagues in Georgia, Eric Nelson, our point man for recycling, and John Bradford, our vice president for research and development.

"I was convinced that they really had something," Stuart recalled. "It was a real *Eureka!* moment. I called Eric and John at eleven o'clock that same night and I told them that I'd found the next Cool Blue."

That got them all on a plane to Italy. Two pallets of old carpet tiles also made the trip.

"Frank met us at the airport," said Eric Nelson. "Along with Sergio Dell'Orco and a third partner, Giulio Tandera. These three guys had formed a company that owned the carpet recycling technology. They showed us the scaled-up version of the demo model Stuart had seen in the video. We unpacked our pallets of old tile and loaded Dell'Orco's machine.

"The separator started up; it swallowed the entire load of carpet tiles and cleanly separated them into their raw material constituents. All three of us just stood there and watched it work. Without saying a word, we all knew this machine was going to be the key to recycling carpet," Stuart said. Here, at last, was the foothold we needed to take some giant steps in our ascent of face four of Mount Sustainability. And so in December 2006, Frank Levy and Sergio Dell'Orco came to the United States to meet with Interface's CEO, Dan Hendrix. Four days later they emerged with an agreement. Interface would have an exclusive partnership with Dell'Orco, Tandera, and Levy, and worldwide rights to their carpet recycling technology.

Our next move was to place a $4 million order to install a production-scale recycling line at our plant in LaGrange, Georgia. To our GlasBac® RE and our Cool Blue recycling programs, we could now add something new and very significant, something that could begin to break the stranglehold that oil-based chemicals have traditionally had on our industry. We called it, ReEntry 2.0.

As I write this, we are ten months into ReEntry 2.0 and we're still climb-ing the learning curve. Some of the key challenges have been installing and testing all of that new equipment, running various materials through it, staff-ing the recycling line, finding ways to rapidly identify all the different materi-als an old carpet is actually made from, developing outlets for waste streams of each different material, and, finally, finding the best ways to recycle the nylon fluff at the end of the process. We've made some amazing progress.

- The amount of carpet tile and broadloom carpet that we divert from landfills around the country is growing every month, now approaching one million pounds per week.
- We're on pace to divert and process more than 40 million pounds of carpet in our first year.
- We introduced the world's first-ever nylon 6,6 yarn with postcon-sumer recycled content in finished carpet tile products this year—something no one else, anywhere, has done.

ReEntry 2.0 has not just been a good thing to do to lessen our dependence on oil. Like our big photovoltaic array in Southern California, it has drawn new customers to our company, customers who are as excited as we are about our ability to take back their old carpets and recycle them into new ones. Like Judy Pike's customer's comment again, "This is real!" Some early examples:

- the Georgia legislature: thirteen thousand yards of new carpets;
- a University of Georgia dormitory: nine thousand yards of new carpets;
- the Mecklenburg County (North Carolina) office building: twelve thousand yards of new carpets.

And ReEntry 2.0 has opened a door to some large corporate clients (some of whom had given their business to our competitors in the past), in-cluding the Disney Corporation. And there are other sizable companies right in line behind them.

Some challenges remain. The sheer logistical problem (and cost!) of mov-ing all those millions of pounds of old carpets from around the nation to LaGrange is daunting. Our response: look into opening regional recycling centers, each with its own ReEntry 2.0 line. Our goal is to locate them close to where the carpets are to confine transportation costs to the nylon and vinyl we want back, and to drive the cost to be in line with, or below, the costs of sending the entire carpet to a landfill.

Right now, only one yarn supplier can accept our reclaimed fluff and turn it back into yarn. To break the back of that tidal wave, those five billion pounds of old carpets that swamp American landfills each year, we will need other companies that can bring larger productive capacities to bear. And we are meeting with the biggest suppliers of nylon yarn to enlist them in doing exactly that. Remember, they are paying steep market prices for the oil-based precursors of nylon yarn they have to buy. ReEntry 2.0 can be, in a sense, an all but bottomless oil well, and one that is located right here in the United States.

What else is going on with face four?

- Interface Europe manufactures needle-punch products with 40 percent to 75 percent recycled material in the ground layer. In needle-punch carpet, two layers of loose fiber are tightly entangled by the repeated penetration of barbed needles. The ground (bottom) layer offers the easier potential for recycled material, since it will not detract from the aesthetics of the carpet.
- Adding and blending recycled polymers to our European-made Graphlex backing system saves our facility in Craigavon, Northern Ireland, fifteen thousand kilograms (thirty-three thousand pounds) of virgin raw materials *per week*.
- Using Cool Blue™ technology, Interface Flooring Systems in the United States and Canada transform all their scrap into crumbs for recycling into new vinyl carpet components. So long, landfill!
- ReEntry 2.0 has become a distinct business center and potentially a very profitable one. Our recycling lines are running two shifts, and the recovered material is being sold at a premium (remember what has happened to the price of virgin nylon!) to make not only new yarn, but engineered plastic automobile parts, too!

Here are the key concepts:

- Recycling *decreases* the quantity of virgin raw material that must be purchased.

- Recycling *decreases* our dependence on petro-based raw materials from the earth's crust.
- Recycling *reduces* the amount of nonrecyclable product waste, keeping old carpets and its scrap out of landfills.
- Recycling *reduces* the amount and cost of petro-derived energy needed to manufacture products, salvaging the embodied energy and moving us toward climate neutral!
- As it becomes profitable, recycling *increases* the amount of capital available to invest in other sustainable technologies.
- Recycling creates cost savings for our customers, allowing us to serve them better, and hedges against skyrocketing petroleum costs.
- Recycling and climate neutral contribute to LEED certification in a green building. Both help earn innovation points.
- And recycling creates goodwill, attracts new customers, and generates new, incremental sales.

The technologies for all these advances did not exist when we started. One by one, they have fallen into place. Today old carpets can become new carpets in nature-emulating closed loops: fiber into fiber, backing into backing. No old carpet need ever again go to a landfill. We're even happy to take in our competitors' products, too.

The most direct path up face four of Mount Sustainability is found by minimizing, and ultimately eliminating, our reliance on nonrenewable, petroleum-based products and processes. So what will be our next step beyond recycling? After all, if nylon production were to stop tomorrow, we would eventually have to look someplace else for a suitable raw material. What do we think that material might be?

We think the development of products made from renewable resources is the answer. Biopolymers such as corn-based polylactic acid (PLA) hold great promise. This is the dawn of a carbohydrate economy that will complement—someday, perhaps replace—the hydrocarbon economy. It evolves right alongside solar energy, leading to the solar-carbohydrate economy of the future, as we get ready for the end of oil.

PLA fibers are derived from starch-based agricultural products: today, corn; perhaps tomorrow, rice, sugar beets, or sugarcane. The starch portion of these crops is converted into sugar and fermented to produce lactic acid, which is processed and polymerized to form PLA. PLA polymers are then extruded into fibers, which can be used to make polyesterlike yarn. What are the benefits?

- PLA production uses 20 to 50 percent less fossil fuel resources than traditional oil-based polymers, so there are fewer greenhouse gas emissions associated with PLA production.
- PLA fibers are completely biodegradable; they turn back into lactic acid at the end of their service lives. No complex separation or processing is needed. Waste becomes food quickly and efficiently, "dust to dust" with a biotech wrinkle.

In short, we are moving closer and closer to running our factories as "plants," and even growing our own raw materials—not like plants, but as plants—and running all of it on sunlight. Furthermore, the corn we use to make PLA will not cut into the supply of food for people; it can all be #2, nonfood grade. (#2 corn has more moisture, more damaged kernels, and more foreign matter in it than food-grade corn.)

How far have we taken this concept? Interface introduced its first commercial modular carpet products blending PLA fibers with nylon during the 2004 NeoCon Trade Fair in Chicago. These fiber blends are now being tufted into over twenty Interface modular styles, giving our customers another environmentally friendly choice. We continue to work with our suppliers to increase the toughness of the fiber, so it can be blended in ever greater proportions.

Now I've said a great deal about the challenges and opportunities that recycling presents to industry. But I've skipped over the one place where recycling has the deepest, oldest roots—in the home. I'm not entirely sure when it began, but I do know it goes way back, before the first Earth Day. After all, in 1690, William Rittenhouse, the owner of a paper mill in Philadelphia, Pennsylvania, began collecting discarded rags and cotton to turn into paper!

By the dawn of the twenty-first century about ten thousand cities and towns here in the United States had some kind of curbside recycling program under way. And yet, until recently, recovering plastics, glass, metal, and paper was not a financially winning strategy. There are stories, some even true, about how municipal recycling is just another government boondoggle, a "feel good" program that costs more than just hauling everything off and dumping it somewhere else.

Well, as I've said over and over, there is no somewhere else (another name for away), and the financial facts of life are changing. Landfills are filling up. The costs of operating those big diesel trucks have increased. Raw materials (especially those tied to oil) are becoming more and more expensive; and in their used state, more valuable. So industries are getting smarter about adding recycled materials to their supply chain.

Despite all that, many homeowners still find separating their various recyclables into neat bins more than they really want to be bothered with. Cities are looking at heavy investments in automated sorting machinery at a time when budgets are already stretched thin. Programs that work modestly well in the rich suburbs have failed in poorer communities.

Until now. Because here's the story about a young man who looked at how trash was being recycled and saw an opportunity to do very well both for himself and for the earth, too. He started asking new questions; he started thinking in the round, and he went to work to find that better way. His name is Ron Gonen, and he is cofounder and CEO of a company called RecycleBank in Philadelphia.

Ron Gonen's experience with recycling goes pretty far back. "I went to Germantown Academy, thanks to a great financial package based on my skills as an athlete," he says. "It's a beautiful private school in the suburbs of Philadelphia, and I was on the swim team. I knew I was lucky to be there, and I was always looking for ways to give something back. I was one of the founders of a conference for high school students focused on hunger and homelessness, and convinced the school to convert the cafeteria's utensils from plastic that was thrown away every night to silverware."

Years after he graduated from prep school, Ron was in his first year at Columbia University Business School when he got a call from an old high school friend and fellow Philadelphian, Patrick Fitzgerald. Would Ron join him for dinner?

The two had that dinner, and Ron's old friend mentioned how the city-wide recycling effort in New York seemed to be faltering. Why? Because folks just couldn't be bothered to separate their trash into neat little piles of paper, glass, metals, and all. Everyone was too busy. Expensive ad campaigns by the city hadn't had much effect.

But what would happen, Ron's friend wondered, if instead of spending money on ads to encourage people to recycle, someone rewarded them for it directly?

Ron thought there might be a pretty good business in that idea. He took the entrepreneurial plunge—a step I can certainly understand—and together with Fitzgerald founded RecycleBank in 2004 back in their hometown of Philadelphia. Not just to beautify a campus, but to make some money while doing his bit to help to save the planet.

"Everybody talks about global warming and climate change," said Gonen. "But what do those phrases really mean to the way most people live? The answer is, not much. I wanted to find a way to attack those big, difficult problems, not from the top down, but from the bottom up. You don't experience firsthand species going extinct every day, but everybody deals with garbage, trash, taxes, and the high prices they encounter in stores. I knew a big part of those high prices came from companies using virgin materials: new gas, new oil, new metals, and glass.

"What if we could recapture most of those valuable materials—things we've been paying to get rid of—and use them to create products again and again? What if there were a business model that turned the stuff we throw away into serious money? And I thought, *Yes!*

"Using my own savings and some very important seed capital from Columbia University, Patrick and I went to work. We discovered that in the Philadelphia area, each family generates on average about 1.2 tons of recyclable materials each year. The city was paying about seventy dollars a ton to have it hauled off to a landfill, where all the oil, energy, trees, glass, and metals are basically lost forever.

"And because nobody wants to live near a landfill, you've got to put them far away, so there's a lot of transportation costs involved, too. Plus, as landfills are filled, new sites have to be found and purchased. It gets expensive very, very fast. What if we could save the city money on every ton they *didn't* have to truck off to a landfill, and capture a piece of that for ourselves?"

At Interface, we call electricity saved through smart conservation by Amory Lovins's term, nega-watts. What Gonen was talking about was "nega-tons." But there was still the problem of getting enough people to recycle.

"We couldn't earn a decent profit unless we boosted the number of households that recycle *way* up," said Gonen.

His solution was deceptively simple: use a high-tech bin to measure how much recycling a family contributes and reward them by giving them RecycleBank Dollars that they can turn around and spend at local stores.

"We've got a simple recycling bin, but with a high-tech radio frequency chip embedded in it. The collection trucks were modified to scan those chips, weigh the material, and credit the household accordingly. The more they recycle, the more RecycleBank points appear in their account," said Ron. "The points translate into real money that can be spent at national chains like CVS, Dunkin' Donuts, Whole Foods, and Starbucks, as well as local stores like the Chestnut Hill Cheese Shop, or the Reading Terminal Market, stores that are looking for ways to build customer traffic. Today there are over 1,200 businesses that accept RecycleBank points, 80 percent of which are local neighborhood businesses."

And so, what did rewarding folks for doing the right thing mean for recycle rates?

"It sent it through the roof," said Gonen. "Places where rates used to bounce around below 20 percent are up now close to 90 percent."

Who wins? "Everyone," says Gonen. "We guarantee our customer cities that they'll save a lot of money on waste that no longer has to be hauled off to a landfill. We charge them a percentage of that savings.

"Though the price for recycled materials began to drop when the recession of 2008 hit," said Gonen, "the value of recycled materials has consistently risen, especially aluminum and paper. So those who sort and sell—and those who use—the material win. Households turn trash into money they can really spend, and the stores they visit see more customers coming in to redeem their Recycle Dollars. We've turned an expensive problem into several major income streams. We're growing our company by changing how people think about what they consume and waste."

Now *that* is thinking in the round, new thinking, and sustainability at its best—doing well by doing good.

Right now RecycleBank serves over 300,000 households in fifteen states and is in the process of offering service to over a million more homes. *Fortune* magazine has named it one of the Top Eleven Green Businesses, and the World Economic Forum recently recognized RecycleBank with a Technology Pioneer Award.

"We've taken the straight line of buying things, using them, and throwing them away, and bent it around into an environmentally and economically efficient circle," said Gonen. "Like Ray Anderson says, in nature

there's no such thing as waste. Everything is used. We're just following nature's lead when new products are made with glass, metal, and paper that's
been captured from old ones. The fluctuations in the value of recycled
metal, plastic, and paper don't change the fact that as more people want
more goods and services from a finite earth, those same values must rise. In
an era of expensive oil, gas, and electricity, our approach to recycling saves
cities and companies money, and drastically cuts their greenhouse gas emissions. We win, the cities win, the merchants and the manufacturers win,
and the people win. We're making healthy profits and growing, doing the
right thing for the planet every step of the way."

And I'd say that all sounds pretty familiar, too.

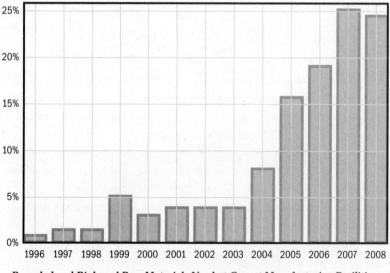

**Recycled and Biobased Raw Materials Used at Carpet Manufacturing Facilities**
*(% of total material used)*

# 9 | Getting Out of the Breakdown Lane

*When you take out the carbon, you take out the costs.*

Tim Riordan, vice president
for supply chain, Interface, Inc.

I began this book by describing myself as a "radical industrialist." Well, I might also be described as a "cold-eyed, entrepreneurial environmentalist." Now, there are very few environmentalists of any description who use military metaphors in their writings or speeches. I guess they are so sick of our being at war with the earth for so long, and to such a harmful extent, that they just naturally shy away from that language.

But in discussing what must be done to climb face five of Mount Sustainability—making our transportation systems resource-efficient—let me deviate from the norm and borrow something from former vice president Al Gore. He observed that wars are usually broken down by historians into three general categories:

- Local battles
- Regional or theater wars
- Global, strategic conflagrations, or world wars

He noted that most environmental challenges fall into these same three categories. The pollution from a smokestack is a local problem. Acid rain, deforestation, or dead zones in the ocean are regional issues. And there is no battle more global and strategic than the one to arrest humanity's assault on our one and only atmosphere with fossil fuel–generated carbon dioxide.

Our efforts to turn Interface into the world's first truly sustainable corporation can be seen in much the same way. Our QUEST for zero waste is made up of hundreds of local initiatives. Ridding Interface of harmful chemicals and substances is a struggle that involves our suppliers, and is conducted on a wider stage. The same might be said about integrating renewable technologies and energy sources into our operations.

But fixing the problems that arise from a transportation system designed around cheap oil defies easy categorization. Yes, there are things we can do locally to lessen the impact of skyrocketing oil prices. And we can begin to act on a broader stage by purchasing carbon offsets for company travel, making wiser, more deliberate choices about how we ship our goods, and even rethinking the wisdom of large central factories serving widely distributed customers.

In retrospect, though initially we didn't plan it consciously, we can see that it makes a lot of sense for our production facilities to be close to their markets in North America, Latin America, Europe, Southeast Asia, northern Asia, and Australasia. And this also has the beneficial effect of creating good jobs for the people who live in the areas we serve. Consequently, this rule now drives our production strategies.

But we can't go out and build distributed manufacturing, much less recycling centers, overnight. And, though supply chains are shorter this way, we still don't own, much less design and build, the vehicles that move our products. Fixing our transportation systems, as a company, as a country, as a world, is complex, and it demands actions at all three levels: local, regional, and global. And on the political level, too. Borrowing again from Al Gore, who said in a speech at the TED 2006 conference: "Oil and politics stand at the crossroads of three deepening crises: a climate crisis, a security crisis, and an economic crisis."

These three crises have us all tied up in knots, wondering which string to pull first. How can we import less oil from the Middle East? By a national policy of "drill, baby, drill"? But does drilling more, to give an addict more of what he's addicted to, make sense? Should we raise mileage standards? Impose a carbon tax? Politically, can we do *anything* that will raise prices when folks are already having a hard time making ends meet? If we did raise gas prices with taxes to discourage driving, how should the tax revenues be used?

We humans have woven such a tangled web that we can't see our way clear to untangle any one knot without making the others worse. That is why ending our addiction to oil is the key. It is the sharp sword we must use, not to untangle those knots, but to slice them clean apart.

To do that, we need to think locally, regionally, globally, and politically. We need to make smarter personal decisions about oil, about what we drive and where we drive. And we need smarter regional solutions for moving people and goods from city to city and place to place. We need to reengineer a global transportation infrastructure that was designed with the nineteenth and twentieth centuries, not the twenty-first century and beyond, in mind. And we need political leadership worthy of the name, smart and courageous enough to tell us the truth, and not just what they think we want to hear.

But right now we're stuck in the breakdown lane, still hooked on cheap fossil fuels, even though they aren't cheap anymore. Business and industry, like the suburban homeowner who lives far from work, like the florist who fills her shop with exotic blooms from other continents, like just about *everyone*, has grown up with the basic assumption that energy was, is, and always will be dirt cheap. The "sunk costs" in this assumption and the investments in oil-driven mobility are truly enormous.

But most of us know from our own experience that no investment, no matter how golden it seemed at first, continues to perform forever. There comes a time when we must take a hard look at an underperforming investment and decide to either write it down or ride it down. That is where we are today with humanity's investment in the age of oil. We're either going to write it down—burn the bridges and invest in something that really works— or we will remain stuck, ride it down, watch our investment dwindle, and suffer the consequences.

Our passionate affair with fossil fuels began in about 1712, with the beginning of the first industrial revolution, a revolution of coal and steam and iron founded on substituting machines and energy for labor. And it worked for a good long while. Through the wholesale burning of oil, coal, and gas, humans became hundreds of times more productive.

Back in the early eighteenth century that meant using steam-driven pumps to permit Cornish miners to work deep deposits of coal that would have remained underwater. Today it means buying midwinter fruits raised in another hemisphere, irrigated, fertilized, harvested, and transported clear across the globe to our supermarkets, all accomplished through a stupendous expenditure of energy.

As Amory Lovins noted in his address to the 1989 Green Energy Conference in Montreal, the United States has the mightiest and most mobile society in the history of the world, but it is a mobility that runs almost entirely, some 96 percent, on oil. And oil's importance goes far beyond just moving people and things around.

Oil allowed us to build and operate the vast fleets, armies, and air forces that defeated our enemies in World War II. Oil drove the economic boom times that followed that war, that golden era I experienced when I graduated from Georgia Tech. It kept a dangerous foe at bay during the cold war.

Oil has given us thousands of synthetic products, including the nylon and polymeric backing that Interface uses to make our carpets. It allowed American industry to ship much of its energy-intensive (and most polluting) industries to distant lands, and to still buy their finished products cheaper than if we'd made them here. Indeed, without cheap oil, globalization—like just-in-time manufacturing—would be a nonstarter.

You can make an excellent argument that globe-spanning supply chains that sent American chickens to be processed in China, then shipped back to America as frozen breasts and thighs, never made sense. Or how about this one: Brazilian iron ore that gets turned into steel in a Chinese mill, then is used to manufacture appliances that are shipped to California, and then are trucked to a retail store in New York.

I am sure there were perceived financial reasons behind this cat's cradle supply chain, even if it does defy the laws of sustainability and common sense. But I am equally sure that *whatever* sense it seemed to make in an era of cheap oil, it makes a whole lot less sense now, and will make less and less in the future.

You can think of all that mobility and wealth and power and productivity as adding to the profit side of the ledger. But there is always another side of the books to consider.

Right now, *today*, the total costs—direct and indirect—generated by the wholesale burning of fossil fuels are shooting up, while any return on investment from them is either stagnating or in decline. That is true on every level—personal, regional, national, and global. The very same oil that once created so much wealth and power has become a source of profound weakness. High oil costs are driving inflation up and the value of the dollar down, which (since oil is sold in dollars) boosts oil prices even more. That's a feedback loop of the worst kind, in which we seem to be inextricably caught.

High prices are eroding the very prosperity oil initially created. They threaten to sweep away a number of key U.S. industries: steel, automobiles, airlines, construction, chemical manufacture, and long-haul trucking, just to name a few. Some have already failed. More will follow.

But I do keep wondering, how smart did you have to be to realize cheap oil was not going to last forever? That rising demand and shrinking supplies might actually mean something in the marketplace? Smarter than some well-paid CEOs were, apparently.

And it is not just the big dogs who are feeling the pain. A lot of logging goes on here in Georgia, and logging runs on diesel. Even a small family operation can easily burn through hundreds of gallons of fuel a day. Their costs have soared, but their ability to charge more has not. "You can't get any work if you raise your prices," said one logger, who was filling up the tank for his bulldozer at a gas station not far from our plant in LaGrange. "People are only going to pay so much to get their land cleared."

He's caught in a bind, just like the automobile companies that can't sell enough gas guzzlers (because nobody wants them) to cover the R&D costs of coming up with more efficient vehicles. Many corporations are similarly caught short, and we are all paying for our dependency on fossil fuels.

We pay for it with every breath of polluted air. We pay for it when we are stuck in a traffic jam. We pay for it when there are no fast, clean trains to take us where we want to go because all the state's money went to build more roads. And we will all pay—for generations—as the planet continues to warm, with all the accompanying consequences.

Our taxes pay for direct federal subsidies to the oil industry, too, even though our dependency on their oil makes us vulnerable to political blackmail. The emissions that come from burning oil and coal not only destabilize the climate, but also ratchet up regional tensions over dwindling resources. To oil, add arable land and clean, freshwater, and what do you have? Peak oil, peak water, and peak soil—all at the same time.

Staying with oil, the quest to find and produce ever greater quantities of fossil fuels skews our moral compasses, too. We're encouraged to destroy pristine wilderness because it *might* contain a few weeks' worth of petroleum (or not) that *may* (or may not) come on line sometime in the next decade or so. We pay a very steep price when we tolerate (or worse, install) tyrants who, by accidents of nature, control recoverable reserves of the stuff.

And we're also on the hook to cover the many, and growing, costs associated with protecting oil at its source and keeping it flowing from dangerous parts of the world.

You will have noticed, I suspect, that all these costs are rising.

World oil production has essentially stagnated since 2005 at about eighty-six million barrels per day. This despite soaring demand. Production in the United States, Canada, Iran, Indonesia, Russia, Britain, Norway, and Mexico has already peaked. Venezuela and Nigeria are flat or beginning to decline. China and Saudi Arabia are not quite there yet. And, of course, there's Iraq, where the problem is less about the geology and more about the politics. But the basic business point here is that oil is very valuable stuff, and more people are chasing after fewer barrels. The cost implications of that situation are clear enough.

Americans alone import 10 million barrels of oil a day (about 3.6 billion barrels of oil a year). As recently as 2003, the national oil bill was "only" about $70 billion. At today's oil price, it is pushing $500 billion (as T. Boone Pickens has been telling us), and half of that is going to OPEC, hardly our friends.

So, maybe it is only natural to look at the size and complexity of all these challenges and say, *I can make my office more efficient, and I can start blending green energy into our mix, but what can I do about the price of oil?* And the simple answer is, *Not much.* Crude oil is fungible; if, say, we don't buy it from a particular supplier, Saudi Arabia or Mexico, the world price doesn't change. However, it does change as China puts some fourteen thousand new cars on the road each day. *Each day.* And they are, all of them, hungry for oil. There really is not much we can do as individuals about that, either. (I'll return to what can be done in a later chapter that's about what government should and should not be doing.)

But that doesn't mean we should sit with our hands folded and do nothing. Because there is one place we do have real leverage, and that is in how much fuel we use.

During the last oil crisis, in the midseventies, Americans cut oil use by 17 percent, while gross domestic product (a misleading metric, but a common one) increased by 23 percent. Oil imports fell 50 percent, and especially from the Persian Gulf, by 87 percent. As a direct result, OPEC lost control of oil pricing for nearly a decade, until world oil consumption caught up with supply again. In other words, for a time our ability to adapt and innovate exceeded OPEC's ability to throttle supply and fix prices.

There is an important lesson in that. We can do it again and, with leadership at every level, we will. Whether that means retooling Detroit (or Silicon Valley) to build plug-in hybrids, or strong, lightweight vehicles that run on natural gas, we can master the technologies. But the plain truth is, reengineering transportation systems to become resource-efficient is not going to be easy, fast, or cheap. However, with leadership, it can be easier, faster, and less expensive than sitting on our collective status quos. Take a look at how Interface uses oil and you'll see what I mean.

My company uses oil when our people drive to work, and when we meet with customers or ship our samples. We use oil to obtain raw materials (which themselves are made from oil) and to collect old carpets and bring them back for recycling—to keep from using so much new oil.

We use oil to move our products around our factories, from factory to factory, and to our customers around the world. Just looking at our North American operations, we spent about $25 million in 2007 to move products, excluding package freight (which are mainly carpet samples going out to designers and potential customers). Our 2007 transportation picture looked like this:

- 83 percent of our product moved by over-the-road trucking (both partial loads and full);
- 13 percent moved by rail;
- 4 percent moved by ship;
- 1 percent went by air (but only in emergencies).

Truck, rail, ship, and aircraft. Oil, oil, oil, and oil.

You can see why—compared with boosting efficiency, ridding your business of undesirable chemicals and substances, even when compared with greening your power mix with renewable energy—making transportation more resource efficient is a very hard nut to crack.

You can enter into a power purchasing agreement today and be generating green power in short order, and with zero capital cost. But can you buy a hybrid freight truck? Can you utilize less impactful railroads, when so much of the national rail infrastructure has fallen into disrepair? Can you get your products to your customers on time and on budget, and still be sustainable?

Not overnight. But we can get ourselves moving in the right direction to find solutions to these big and complicated problems, solutions that make not just environmental sense, but solid business sense, too. I am talking about the kind of solutions that return more than just a feel good PR benefit. We actually can satisfy our transportation needs more efficiently and more sustainably, while generating savings at every step. In other words, we can treat bad transport—moving people and goods around in ways that consume a lot of oil—like waste, and go after it accordingly.

Our strategic approach looks something like this:

- Our goal is a net zero transportation impact to the environment— net zero carbon.
- Our approach is to minimize emissions and offset the remaining emissions.
- Our ultimate objective is to maintain a net zero impact while relying on offsets for no more than half the reduction by 2020.

Let's drill down a bit deeper and look at some of the tactics. They are similar to the ones we took when we launched our waste elimination program, QUEST:

- quantify the problem, one continent at a time (what works in Europe or Asia may not work in the United States or Canada);
- identify areas of opportunity;
- develop solutions; and
- implement them.

Let's talk about quantities of energy and emissions. How much energy does go into moving a shipment of carpet tile? The answer is, it all depends. Are we using long-haul heavy trucks? Partial-load vans? Rail? A jet? When we send a package and check that Overnight Delivery box, do we know how much energy we are consuming, or the amount of greenhouse gases we're agreeing to generate? We do now, though once we didn't.

Common sense told us that sending products out by truck had to use less energy than sending them by air. But when we ran the numbers we were surprised at just how big the difference was.

Relative to loading a tractor trailer with boxes of carpet tiles and rolling them over the road to our customer (the base case), switching to rail reduced the BTUs per ton mile (and greenhouse gas emissions) by 75 percent! This comparison is strictly mile for mile; it's not complete enough to accommodate the fact that a smaller truck still must pick up the cargo for final delivery. But the 75 percent difference is so incontrovertibly large that the overall point remains valid. What did it do for cost?

In the United States, using rail to cover the greatest distance between the factory and the customer saves Interface's customers, on average, about half the cost of sending that same shipment out by truck. That really adds up! And keep in mind that the opportunities for using rail are quite limited here in comparison with Europe.

The federal Bureau of Transportation Statistics conducted a careful analysis of energy and transportation, and their results show that we are very definitely on the right track. It takes about 31,000 BTUs of energy to move a ton of freight by air. Move that same ton by truck and the energy intensity falls to about 2,300 BTUs. What about going by rail? It drops to an astonishingly low 370 BTUs per ton mile!

What about greenhouse gas emissions? The pattern is the same.

Here's another important metric: Shipping products by sea reduces the amount of energy required (again, by comparison with a truck) by 86 percent! Though shipping by sea is not something we can avail ourselves of in the United States, there are very big opportunities for Interface to make use of oceangoing ships in our Asian operations.

As you saw from those Bureau of Transportation Statistics numbers, the real gorilla in the greenhouse is shipping anything by air. So clearly, when the option exists to move things by rail or ship, we can reduce our energy footprint substantially by choosing wisely. Checking off the box to guarantee next day delivery by air increases the energy (and carbon) by 800 percent! When the option exists to use UPS Ground instead of UPS Air for parcel freight, we can save energy, greenhouse gas emissions, and dollars. As our vice president for supply chain management, Tim Riordan, has said, "When you take out the carbon, you take out the costs."

(Incidentally, as we'll see later, our chief product designer, David Oakey, says exactly the same thing about product development.)

That is exactly what our European factories discovered. Though our plant in the Netherlands once sent about 650 metric tons of carpet tiles to Italy each year in thirty trucks, using rail has shrunk their energy and $CO_2$ footprint by 40 percent, and it reduced their shipping costs by 25 percent!

By substituting river barges for trucks, they can move 1.7 million square meters of carpet per year from the factory in Scherpenzeel to the port city of Rotterdam, and realize a 50 percent reduction in energy and $CO_2$ footprint, while cutting 10 percent off the cost.

As fuel prices rise, the savings will grow, making the more sustainable choice also the most financially sound and competitive choice. That is the way this big, complicated problem is going to be solved, one smart, self-interested decision at a time.

But sometimes self-interest points us in the other direction. Controlling our carbon footprint, even when it seems to save money, is not always the best strategy. Remember what I said about the next order at Interface, that it's just like that next heartbeat: If you don't get it you're dead? Well, I like to think that just about every person in Interface understands that. Our sales force is really tuned into the message, and they believe that getting samples of carpet to potential customers fast gives them a competitive edge. Not next week. Not in a few days. Tomorrow. But speed (think air) and reducing carbon footprints are opposite goals. What did we do?

We let our sales force keep checking off that "next-day delivery" box, but they had to make a few other changes in the way they conduct their business, changes that were tough to implement but have offset all the effects of all of those overnight deliveries, and then some. I'll let Tim Riordan tell you that story at the end of this chapter.

So, what about moving products? For example, what about shipments that exceed the carriers' size limits for overnight delivery, or not time-critical enough to warrant overnight delivery, but not big enough to fill an entire trailer?

We found tools such as UPS's $CO_2$ Calculator to be extremely helpful. Using its EPA SmartWay Transport program, it quantifies the carbon impact for our parcel freight shipments in the United States and across the world. Using the UPS calculator and other metrics developed in-house, we are working to establish and understand our transportation footprint, including:

- setting a baseline year;
- developing metrics to monitor our performance;
- collecting and sharing best practices between business units.

For example, from our baseline year of 2005 to our most recent assessment in 2008, the greenhouse gas impact of our parcel freight shipments declined by 23 percent. And driving down the $CO_2$ drives down the costs as well. We averaged close to fourteen dollars per package in 2005. That number has fallen to just over twelve dollars today.

We accomplished this through several conscious strategies. Naturally, we strive to select the most efficient means of shipping for every occasion. While samples and small packages sent by air sometimes can be justified, nobody is shipping thousands of yards of carpet that way, except in the most extreme customer service emergency. We use rail whenever possible. Our Southern California operation is even reactivating an old abandoned siding, so they can use rail day in and day out.

And since transportation costs and energy are both dependent on the weight of the goods being shipped, all efforts to reduce the weight of carpet tiles to save materials and energy, while maintaining—or improving—their performance, pay off in lower transportation costs, too. Dematerialization by conscious design works to reduce transportation impacts as well as upstream energy usage.

Our principal designer, David Oakey, has spearheaded this effort. "I was a design consultant for a decade before coming to Interface," said Oakey. "And while most designers concentrate on the look and feel of their creations, I was just as interested in combining the aesthetics with finding ways to make my clients more profitable. And what I discovered was this: The surest way to that goal was by making the best-looking product while using the least amount of raw material. That was and remains the fundamental key."

Oakey worked for years in the world of European carpet design, where the weight of the face fiber—that energy-intensive nylon—was as low as eighteen ounces per square yard. But back then, Interface carpet tiles contained over twenty-four ounces, and often much more. (For years, twenty-eight ounces was an industry standard, promoted by sales volume–conscious fiber producers.)

And so, to add to the one and one half gallons of regular gasoline that represents the energy required to make that square yard of nylon (one and one half pounds), we can add the cost, both in BTUs and dollars, of shipping that tile to our customers.

An earlier story bears repeating, as David tells it: "Ray's vision of sustainability and our push to reduce the amount of stuff that goes into a carpet tile converged. And when we did the numbers, we were very surprised to learn that by reducing the face weight of our American carpet tile by just one ounce per square yard—about 4 percent—we would save half the amount of energy needed to operate the entire American carpet tile factory. One ounce!

"We did better than cut that one ounce. Since 1994 our carpet tiles have shed more than four ounces, a 17 percent reduction in the amount of nylon required. And that was without giving up anything in the way of performance, comfort, or durability. That reduction in nylon created energy savings upstream equivalent to more than two years of the Interface factory's usage." The transportation savings (energy and costs) are icing on the cake. Win, win, and win.

While David worked hard to add lightness to the face of our carpet tiles, we've been hard at work reducing the weight elsewhere, too. The results? In 1995, one square yard of our typical carpet tile weighed 9.55 pounds. Today, it weighs 8.19 pounds. And the savings have been realized without compromising quality. In fact, by any measure, our quality has never been better. That is a real achievement.

Regardless of lighter tiles, there is still no getting away from trucks, and that's why Interface is a charter partner in the U.S. Environmental Protection Agency's SmartWay Transport program.

SmartWay was introduced by the EPA and a select group of fifteen shipping and business leaders, including Interface, in 2004. It is a market-based partnership to reduce fuel use, greenhouse gas emissions, and air pollutants from the freight sector. Big trucks are a very big part of those three problems.

According to the EPA, trucking accounts for about 27 percent of all greenhouse gas emissions here in the United States. If every truck on the road improved its miles per gallon by just 1 percent, savings would be 245 million gallons of diesel a year! One percent does seem to be an easy mark to hit.

That's where SmartWay comes in. They help freight haulers reduce their numbers without going broke in the process. They work with transportation companies to find ways to improve the bottom line by improving their operating efficiency and reducing fuel consumption. They also help to find financing to pay for investments in efficiency measures, connect freight operators with the right technologies to fit their needs, and get recognition (read, publicity) for their good efforts. What are the big saves in the world of long-haul trucking? Here's what the people at SmartWay have found:

- Four to eight percent can be saved by going with single-wide or wide-base tires optimized for efficiency.
- Aerodynamic tune-ups: Having side skirts, gap fairings, base flaps, and nose cones on the trailers saves 4 to 10 percent.
- Hybrid chilling systems that run off ground power when it's available, allowing the truck's engine to be shut down, cuts a full 10 percent!
- Similarly, a small auxiliary power unit provides electricity cheaply, allowing the truck's engine to be switched off. Idling is the enemy! This yields another 8 percent saved.

So, multiply that incremental 245 million gallons saved for each 1 percent by twenty more from this list and, to paraphrase something the late Senator Everett Dirksen once said, a million gallons here, a million gallons there, and pretty soon you're talking about real money. Not to mention emissions.

But those are just calculations. What has SmartWay actually accomplished? In just two years, SmartWay partner companies were able to reduce both their diesel consumption and their GHG emissions substantially. More than four hundred freight companies are on track to save over $1.2 billion on fuel and remove more than 4 million tons of $CO_2$ emissions from the air. By 2012, the SmartWay program could (with full industry participation) cut nationwide annual fuel consumption by 3.3 to 6.6 billion gallons of diesel fuel, eliminating 66 million metric tons of $CO_2$ emissions and up to 200,000 tons of nitrogen oxide ($NO_2$) emissions.

Teamed up with low-cost loans from the Small Business Administration, operators of big, long-haul trucks have seen fast positive cash flows on Smart-Way investments such as:

- truck-stop electrification to power onboard refrigeration or heating (meaning you don't have to let a truck idle overnight);
- auxiliary power units; again, to prevent excessive idling by using a

small motor—or even an advanced battery pack—to keep from having to run a big diesel engine to do a little bit of work;

- low rolling-resistance tires (single wide-base and duals);
- truck and trailer aerodynamics (reducing drag by smoothing the airflow around a moving vehicle);
- exhaust pollution-control devices. These won't save any oil but they will reduce particulate emissions—the black soot you see coming from a big diesel's exhaust stack—by 40 to 90 percent;
- SmartWay biodiesel and E85 ethanol fuels programs. These do save oil, though any corn-based fuels program has to be analyzed very carefully for its net energy balance (Does it produce more than it uses?), as well as its effect on food prices.

And don't forget, you'll stand a better chance of winning a shipping contract from Interface, and a growing list of others, if you are a SmartWay partner, for there are many more businesses—small, medium, large, and huge—that feel exactly the same way.

One of them is Procter & Gamble. This company, with close to $80 billion in annual sales, decided to wring transportation costs out of the steady stream of trucks that connect their factories with their distribution points. Trucks were leaving only partly loaded, even though the teams responsible for the work swore there wasn't any more room.

And so they employed Auto VLB™—an automated "load-building" computer software system that optimized the loading of each and every truck and categorized shipments as "must go" and "can go." This system allows better planning and truck selection; big shipments went out on big trucks, and smaller shipments could go out on smaller, more economical trucks. It sounds pretty basic, but they met with some opposition.

There were plenty of people in P&G's logistics arm, comfortable with the status quo, who thought they were already doing everything reasonable. They sure didn't need another system to tell them how to do their jobs. But Procter & Gamble was persistent. They got the computerized load-building system working and found that no, trucks were not going out full. And no, existing systems did not optimize the load; and yes, with diesel costs heading skyward, P&G really did need a new way of doing things. The result?

Automating the movement of goods saved Procter & Gamble 7 percent of its transportation costs the first year it was used. While the GHG reduction will grow with Procter & Gamble's business, those saved dollars will also grow with every uptick at the fuel pump.

One of the poster children for outsized transportation footprints has got to be Fiji Water. These are the folks who bottle and ship and sell spring water they collect on an island way out in the middle of a very big ocean. When they did an audit to see where they stood, they found that a full 40 percent of their company's total carbon footprint came from ocean freight and distribution (like carpet tiles, water is heavy).

Stung by public criticism over marketing such a clean and healthy product in such a carbon-intensive, unsustainable way, Fiji Water set themselves the goal of cutting their 2010 GHG emissions by 25 percent, which is a significant step in the right direction. More promisingly, through optimizing loads and making changes in distribution, they have already reduced their trucking miles by 26 percent and cut the fuel used by their trucks on Fiji by half.

Their industry-leading competitor, Nestlé Waters, has taken an across-the-board approach to reducing their transportation footprint. The leader in bottled water has $3.5 billion in annual sales, 20 factories, and 750,000 truckload shipments each year. They spend $500 million just for third-party carriers to move their product, above and beyond their internal transport costs.

Using lightweight trailers that maximize the amount of product carried while reducing the weight of the truck has allowed Nestlé to increase their average payload per truck while reducing the total weight transported, the number of trips made, the miles driven, and the diesel fuel burned. And, as we discovered, adding lightness to their new half-liter bottles has made a difference, too. The new bottle uses 13 percent less plastic, 30 percent less paper in the labeling, and a whopping 25 percent less energy to manufacture, yet it delivers everything the old-style bottle could offer.

Staples is an $18 billion distributor of office products and supplies, and their bright red, white, and lime-green delivery trucks are a familiar sight all across the United States. Staples discovered that a minor change in their truck's electronic control modules—adjustments to limit maximum speed to sixty miles an hour—instantly boosted their average mile per gallon from around 8.5 to 10.5 mpg. The cost per truck? Under seven dollars! Adding simple aerodynamic fixes like a "nose bubble" on the leading edge of the cargo box reduced fuel burn even more, for a total of 30 percent fuel reduction on each truck.

Multiply that savings by all those trucks and you can see why there is no reason to wait around for a silver bullet to start reducing fuel usage and greenhouse gas emissions. Not if all that can be accomplished while increasing profits today.

No discussion of transportation fixes would be complete without Wal-Mart. There have been many things about this megacorporation to criticize, such as the disastrous effect they can have on local businesses and communities. If our collective passion for too much stuff is at the root of the problem in achieving true sustainability, Wal-Mart is likely where much of that stuff comes from.

And they are big! If Wal-Mart were a country, its $312 billion in 2007 revenue would rank the company just behind the Netherlands' economy. So when it decides to make a change, the results can also be very large. And Wal-Mart has set its sights on doubling its fuel economy right across its fleet of seven thousand trucks by 2015. That's a big goal, but the company aims to hit it and stands a very good chance. Wal-Mart reached the 15 percent savings mark the first year, and it's on track to slim down its transportation fuel consumption by an additional 25 percent by the end of 2008, almost halfway to its goal in just the second year. That's better than sixty million gallons of diesel fuel per year Wal-Mart won't be buying and 670,000 tons of $CO_2$ it won't be spewing into the air. That's like taking 67,744 cars off the road forever. Wal-Mart paints with a big brush!

They accomplished all this by adopting many of the measures the SmartWay program suggests: reduced idling, speed controls, auxiliary power units, high-efficiency tires, and lighter trailers. And yes, Wal-Mart, like Interface, is a longtime SmartWay partner, and it is one of only two member corporations that are both a SmartWay carrier and a SmartWay shipper. Its very size has made it a force the truck manufacturers must reckon with. When Wal-Mart says it wants an efficient vehicle or none at all, change happens.

"They are pushing beyond what the trucking industry has already decided to do. Because of their size, I think they will create economies of scale for still more efficient trucks," said Daniel Becker, director of the Sierra Club's global warming program.

Great Dane Trailers, which is developing a more aerodynamic trailer for Wal-Mart, says the retailer is more involved than any other carrier in developing fuel-efficient trucks. "Wal-Mart is doing more than any other fleet I know of," said Charles Fetz, vice president of research and development at Great Dane.

Tim Yatsko, Wal-Mart's senior vice president of transportation, says the biggest piece of the solution will come from another supplier sector, with future deployment of hybrid diesel-electric engines. Wal-Mart is pitching in $2 million a year for research and development by two teams of national truck tractor manufacturers, International Truck and Peterbilt, and Wal-Mart will buy and use the prototypes. These hybrid engines will deliver a 50 percent increase in efficiency on top of the 25 percent Wal-Mart expects it will rack up by 2008.

To put these changes in perspective, they will put a big, new eighteen-wheeler's gas mileage ahead of nearly all the SUVs Detroit is still trying to sell.

"All of this work has to pay for itself," Yatsko said. "Changes and additions to the fleet have to provide a return on investment or they cannot be sustained."

Amen to that. But now just try to imagine what would happen if all vehicles in the United States were required to double their efficiency. Why, the automakers might have to actually design and build them. And then what? I think Amory Lovins said it best in his important book, *Winning the Oil Endgame* (Rocky Mountain Institute, 2007): "It would be like finding a new Saudi Arabia under Detroit."

Coming back to our sales force, here's Tim Riordan's account:

"When we first took a look at Interface's transportation needs we concentrated on what we thought were the big numbers: the energy required to move products by truck, by rail, by air, and by sea.

"As it turned out, the cars we were all driving was a big number, too. We went after car commutes with Cool Fuel and Cool $CO_2$mmute programs, which basically offset all the daily comings and goings of employees.

"But each of our sales associates logs many, many thousands of miles a year, and some of them were driving very inefficient, company-owned vehicles. There were a lot of luxury cars and SUVs in that fleet, too. This was a problem on a number of fronts. They were expensive to operate, but even more than that, they were giving customers a very mixed message. Why would a company like Interface send its people around in gas-guzzling SUVs?

"We spoke with a number of automobile manufacturers, looking for the cleanest, greenest vehicle they could offer to replace those carbon-hogging trucks and luxury cars. The problem was, the cleanest, greenest vehicle tended to be a car equipped with high-efficiency, pollution-control devices designed to meet California's very stringent standards. And at first, the carmakers refused to sell us any for delivery outside of California. Clean California cars were built to be sold in California, not Georgia. But then one of them, Subaru of America, came through.

"In the end, they were the only manufacturer that would sell us so-called PZEV (partial zero emission vehicles) for delivery in *any* state. PZEV is the industry's way of saying low emissions. Subaru looked even better after we visited their factory in Lafayette, Indiana. We learned that it was the first auto assembly plant in America to achieve zero landfill status. Nothing from its manufacturing operations goes into any landfill. Ninety-nine percent of their waste materials are either recycled or reused, with the remaining one percent sent to a waste-to-energy plant. It is a big automobile plant that puts out less waste than the typical American family. Well, that's just very impressive."

And the clincher?

"Subaru offered to sponsor the planting of thousands of trees through American Forests' Global ReLeaf program. "It equated to the sequestration of 21.6 metric tons of carbon per vehicle. That made our new fleet of cars climate neutral for the first sixty-thousand miles. We know American Forests well. They are a world leader in tree planting for environmental restoration. When we reached the end of that program, Subaru signed up with a firm called Native Energy to continue offsetting our carbon emissions from fuel use. Native Energy offered credible and verifiable offsets derived from third-party verified projects.

And as it turned out, the other automakers' unwillingness to sell us clean vehicles was not all their fault. The lack of environmental leadership in Washington had spawned a crazy quilt of environmental regulations at the state level. There were relatively clean California cars, Canadian cars, Vermont cars, and New York cars, but there are dirtier versions of those same cars everywhere else. This forced carmakers to design and build two versions of the same vehicle. We cannot imagine having to tailor how we made our carpet tile state by state. How silly can it get?

Since it costs extra money to make a car that pollutes less, the manufacturers decided they didn't want to boost prices everywhere and potentially lose customers. So they just bit the bullet and limited the PZEV's availability only to where they had to sell them. But it gets worse: Under terms of the federal Clean Air Act (that's right: the Clean Air Act!), anyone (dealer, consumer, automaker) involved in an out-of-bounds PZEV sale could be subject to civil fines of up to $27,500!"

Now, I doubt the automobile manufacturers were truly worried that the federal government might fine them for selling cars that were too clean. More likely, they just didn't want to add costs that might lose them a few sales here and there. But by going the extra mile, by certifying their cars to both the highest California standard as well as the lower federal one, Subaru won our business. The other carmakers lost out. Call it another cost for tolerating a rudderless ship of state.

Tim mentioned our Cool Fuel and our Cool $CO_2$mmute programs.

In our Cool Fuel program, BP provides a corporate rebate to Interface based on the gallons of fuel we purchase from it. Interface then uses this rebate to purchase emission offsets that, in effect, zero out the impact. Though, if the offset is a tree, there's a time lag while the tree grows. Right now, the costs for these offsets are no more than what is recovered through the rebate program. So the Cool Fuel program is not only climate neutral; it is also cost neutral.

Since August 2002, Interface associates with company cars have purchased and consumed more than 1,440,000 gallons of fuel using the Interface Cool Fuel Card. For each gallon of fuel burned, twenty-five pounds of $CO_2$ is emitted into the atmosphere, requiring Interface to offset more than 16,000 metric tons of $CO_2$. Maybe it's a bit complicated, but we offset tons of $CO_2$ as we burn gallons of gas.

Using the rebate from fuel purchases, Interface buys $CO_2$ credits from a variety of sources to offset these emissions. The credits come from a blended portfolio of social and environmental projects, including projects for renewable energy, carbon sequestration, intermodal transport, and climate-neutral product manufacturing in other industries.

Cool $CO_2$mmute was designed as a way for every associate, no matter where they work, to "walk the talk" on our journey up Mount Sustainability and to show others the way. Launched in 2002, Cool $CO_2$mmute opened up the same possibilities of offsetting car travel for all Interface associates. It is a voluntary program that's up and running at several facilities to offset the $CO_2$ emissions generated by employees driving their own cars to and from work. The Cool $CO_2$mmute program allows every participating associate to purchase trees, planted by American Forests, to offset their greenhouse gas emissions.

In Cool $CO_2$mmute, Interface shares half the cost of planting those trees with our associates, bringing their average cost down to less than twelve dollars per year. That is such a good deal that some employees have even elected to offset mileage for their spouses and other family members. So far, more than 32,000 trees have been planted through the Cool $CO_2$mmute program.

Trees for Travel™ is another $CO_2$ offset program. Since 1997 we've sponsored the planting of more than ninety-eight thousand trees to offset 190 million airline passenger miles of business travel by associates. We've partnered with American Forests to reforest areas of California's Mohave Desert, where the native trees have been under assault by years of drought, wildfires, and beetle infestation. But we've got a long way to go to put things right; the number of trees that eventually will be needed to restore the forest has been estimated to be over 650,000.

There's one more success story to relate about cars and personal travel, and it comes from Interface's UK subsidiary locations in Northern Ireland, Yorkshire, and Hertfordshire. At the time, Andy Wales was our UK point man for sustainability.

"We make carpet tiles," he said, "which, from the standpoint of sustainability, is not the best place to start. Our raw material is petro-based, and we have to transport our products around the world. We're already the largest buyer of green tariff electricity in the UK, and we actively encourage video-conferencing rather than air travel. But the highly emotive area of company cars needed to be incorporated into our sustainability drive, too.

"After several months' development, we produced a company car program based on whole life-cycle costs. It took into account the car's total lease costs, including servicing, fuel costs, and company insurance premium, which is then divided by the contracted mileage—usually three years and seventy-five thousand miles—to arrive at a cost per mile rating. The key element, though, is harnessing the life-cycle cost in a manner that rewards drivers wishing to choose a car with lower life-cycle $CO_2$ emissions."

Andy explained how the scheme works. "Staff are graded into bands according to rank. You can choose a car for your band or select one for a lower band, including the eco-band. If the car chosen in the lower band has an emissions level below the highest emissions level for that band, the driver will receive a financial allowance as a reward for choosing the less polluting vehicle. I know it sounds slightly complicated, but it works easily enough in practice.

"We publish the company car list so everyone can clearly compare the emissions ratings of any car. This has gently moved the company car discussion away from a car's prestige and toward its pollution rating."

The system rewards with cash any Interface employee who chooses a less polluting vehicle. The reward can amount to thousands of pounds per year. And while it may seem at first glance that we are allowing senior management to get away with driving more polluting cars, in practice nothing could be further from the truth. We lead by example at Interface, and everyone—from the factory floor right to the top—knows that.

"We see our car policy only as the first step," said Andy. "In the future, we'll be looking at hybrid and alternative fuel cars, and beyond that to cars powered by hydrogen fuel cells. We want to be involved in pushing the agenda for greener cars."

Does all this seem like an odd goal for someone in the business of making carpet tiles? Not at Interface.

When you take carbon out, profits go up. Efficiency equals profits, profits equal good jobs, and good jobs mean a strong economy. And that is why digging for barrels saved (what Amory Lovins calls nega-barrels) here at home makes so much more business sense than drilling new fields or looking for ways to squeeze the last drops of petroleum from dying fields.

"Our energy future is choice, not fate," Lovins says in *Winning the Oil Endgame*. "Oil dependence is a problem we need no longer have—and it's cheaper not to. American business can lead the nation and the world into the post-petroleum era, a vibrant economy, and lasting security—if we just realize that we are the people we have been waiting for."

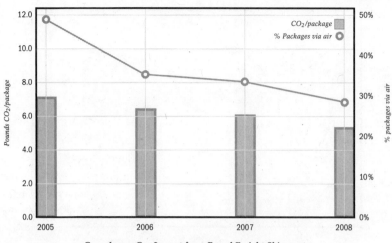

**Greenhouse Gas Impact from Parcel Freight Shipments**
*(North America only)*

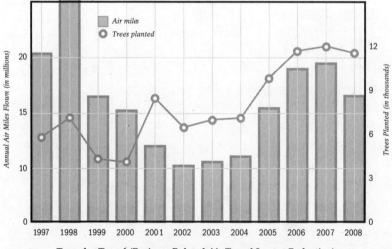

**Trees for Travel (Business-Related Air Travel Impact Reduction)**

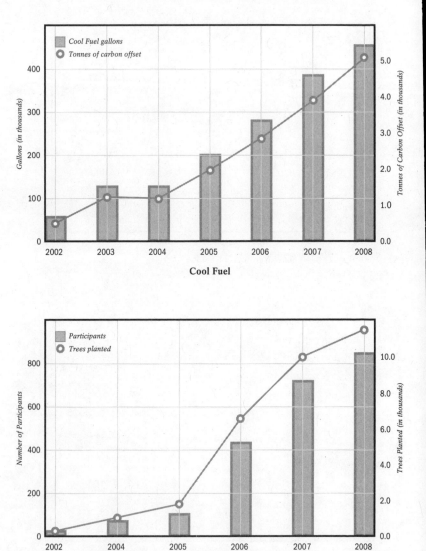

**Cool Fuel**

**Cool CO₂mmute**

# 10 | The Circle of Influence, or Love on the Factory Floor

*Visiting Interface and seeing the creativity applied to establish more sustainable practices made it undeniable that the rest of us can do the same. We don't have to spend time wondering if we can do something. Instead, we can move on to figure out how.*

DOUG McMILLON, CEO of
Wal-Mart's Sam's Club

Henry Ford once said, "I am looking for a lot of men who have an infinite capacity to not know what can't be done." To that wise quote, though it splits an infinitive, I would add, men and women, because this chapter is about all of us. Men and women. People.

To conquer Mount Sustainability's sixth front—what we call "sensitizing stakeholders"—you can set aside all the new chemistry, the new engineering, and the new ways of financing sustainability measures. Because without people—from our own associates to our suppliers and installers to our customers—we'd still be wondering how to answer that first question, "What is Interface doing for the environment?" Without the engagement of all stakeholders, the answer would be nothing.

I know "stakeholder" is a familiar enough term in the business world, but what does it really mean when we say it? Just this: To us, a stakeholder is anyone with an interest (or a stake) in what Interface does. Our stakeholders include our employees and customers, our investors, our suppliers, the design community, and the folks who live in towns where we have offices or factories; any place we have an effect on the local economy or environment. And that is a lot of people, because for an industrial company that really acts as if there is no away, everyone lives downstream.

So what does it mean when we say we want to sensitize them all? It means we want to draw a wide circle of influence around our industrial processes, our people, and our capital and energize everyone inside with new and better values, values that honor the earth and offer a chance—perhaps the last one—for a healthy planet for our children's children. And we seek to widen that circle and the community it embraces with every step we take up Mount Sustainability.

I've already written at length about changing our manufacturing processes. What Mr. Ford was getting at, and what this chapter is all about, is the power of men and women to change themselves, their corporations, and their communities, and through their example and leadership, the world. This is the Power of One.

As you might expect, this wide circle covers a lot of territory, but it all begins with the *Natural Step*'s fourth rule:

### 4. *Fairness and efficiency are linked.*

The fourth rule is the social equity principle. It mandates fair and efficient use of resources to meet all of humanity's basic needs. Because there are so many genuine needs, they must be met in the most resource-efficient manner possible.

Let me say it again: Fairness and efficiency are linked. And by "fairness" I mean not just to our own associates (because fairness must begin at home), but fairness to everyone we deal with or have an effect on—those stakeholders again. And fairness is also linked to respect—for the associates who make our carpet tiles; the people who install them; the customers who specify, pay for, and enjoy them; those who take them back for recycling into new carpets and products; and, ultimately, for the earth itself.

To be honest, back in 1994 I had an intellectual appreciation of the importance of fairness in our company and in the world at large, but I confess that I did not have the same "spear in the chest" epiphany for that issue as I felt about the environment. But that changed in 1997, when the link between fairness and efficiency—indeed, between fairness and survival—was driven home with a point that was every bit as sharp as that spear in the chest. It's not a story I often tell, and many people, even inside Interface, have never heard it. But here goes.

The 1990s, after the 1990–92 recession, were boom times for Interface. After we had turned the steering wheel in the direction of sustainability, we were moving from one success to the next. Sales grew from $625 million in

1993 to $1.28 billion in 1998. That's the kind of performance that will make anyone proud, and, as you will see, a bit arrogant, too.

I'd recruited a new top management team to take over the reins and allow me to concentrate on our march up the slopes of Mount Sustainability. Everything was running like clockwork: Our flagship Interface Flooring Systems was healthy again, after the recessionary downturn of the early 1990s. And then a bomb dropped.

One of our major competitors, Shaw Industries, decided to establish its own exclusive carpet installation network throughout the country. We thought contractors in that network might be obliged to use Shaw products and no others. That was serious enough, but the next bomb that went off was a whole lot bigger. Our biggest supplier of fibers and yarn, DuPont, decided that they, too, would create a network of installers; maybe they would be loyal only to DuPont.

Unchallenged, it would be like a game of musical chairs. When the music stopped, Shaw and DuPont would be safe in their seats and we'd still be standing. Their two networks could either effectively block our routes to markets or create an unhealthy monopoly for DuPont. To do nothing did not seem to be a tenable strategy. We felt we had to respond. But how?

Our management team, brimming with confidence, decided the best defense was a big offense, and opted to build a third network of contractors, loyal only to Interface. So, with our board's approval and $100 million in acquisition money (eventually $150 million), we launched ourselves into what would shortly become an epic three-way battle—a fight that turned our biggest supplier (DuPont) into our biggest rival and our biggest customer. You see, at the time we were still selling carpets to the contractors in the DuPont network. And so, through twenty-nine acquisitions in rapid-fire order, we built our rival distribution channel. We called it Re:Source® Americas.

This was surely a strange new world, and tensions ran high, both at Interface and among our new installer associates. They were used to living—and thriving—by their wits with accountability only to themselves. Their relationships with their customers were one on one and very personal. Our corporate culture seemed foreign to them. Much of their record keeping was manual. And not one of them had a computer system able to talk to our systems at Interface. It was like a cottage industry.

Then, as DuPont and Shaw built up their exclusive networks, our sales reps began to see large portions of their dealer customer base disappear. Our "captive" contractors lost some of their freedom to source products from our competitors, and saw their (now our) supplier and customer bases shrink. Some of these businesses saw a 50 percent drop in year-on-year sales.

As a direct result, our Bentley Prince Street unit saw its contractor base shrink from around two thousand to about two hundred. As sales shrank, so did the earnings of our sales force. Tensions grew even more, because nothing generates tension like taking money out of someone's pocket. Not surprisingly, people started to bail out.

How did our confident management team deal with all of this?

Not well. Perhaps they were blinded by past success. After all, nothing fails like success because success doesn't prepare one for adversity. Perhaps they were overwhelmed by frustration that a strategy that had seemed so necessary and so promising could sink into a quagmire so fast. They continued to hang tough, and told Interface's worried associates in so many words, *It's my way or the highway*. Well, many of our top-performing salespeople chose the highway. By golly, it's true. Respect and effectiveness are linked? You don't say!

Let's face it. In the clarity of hindsight, Interface had shot itself in the foot through insensitive and autocratic management, plain and simple. We failed to value people properly, respect their needs, and treat them fairly. In times of intense stress, rather than patiently involving people in the decisions that would materially affect their lives, our managers resorted to old-fashioned edicts. When that carefully recruited and assembled management team decided that the only way out of the mess was to sell Interface lock, stock, and barrel, I stepped back in and took over.

Soon, half the once so confident management team was gone. But the half that remained was much wiser, more humble, and rededicated not only to finding a better way to run our global corporation, but to saving it. Their new, collaborative management style encouraged real teamwork, instead of just talking about it. It empowered people with the authority to make real change, and respected and recognized their individual needs and differences.

The sales force was rebuilt. Business systems were put in place. Relationships were restored. Frustration gave way to real enthusiasm for our company and its mission. And a lesson had been learned the hard way. We must never again forget that fairness and respect—like charity—begin at home with our own people.

Our stock price took a hit, and many external observers no doubt thought that here at last (finally!) was proof positive that there was no business case for sustainability. But the truth is, those waste-cutting measures we had adopted helped us survive a very tough patch. The energy and commitment our associates gave to climbing Mount Sustainability pulled us out of the hole and back into the light. It had been a test in a crucible our people won't forget.

Perhaps the damage to Re:Source was irreparable, for despite our best efforts with new management, when another recession struck our industry in 2000, we found Re:Source by and large unable to cope. One by one over the next five years we divested all Re:Source locations, typically to local management. A sad chapter closed; lessons, indelibly learned.

Many say that sustainability is a goal without a goalpost, and we need constant effort and reinforcement to stay on track. I see it a bit differently. The top of the mountain is our goal, rather well defined as zero environmental footprint; but having gotten there, we know we will have to work just as diligently to stay there. By sensitizing people to our mission, we keep the culture shift that is happening within Interface moving in high gear. The shift is infectious, sparking parallel shifts among our suppliers, customers, and communities (including the financial community).

So, you can divide our efforts into two parts: what happens inside the circle, and what we can do to bring more people into it from the outside. Let's talk about what happens inside, first.

Our own culture shift in the direction of sustainability has many components. It begins with constant emphasis on safety in the workplace. It extends to organizing women's networks within the company, to counterbalance any good old boy networks still in place. And it includes diversity efforts, both inside the company and outside in our marketplace. It includes our Fairworks™ program, which purchases carpeting from traditional weavers in poor, rural Indian villages. These beautiful, handwoven products are adapted into modular flooring designs that find a natural home in some of the most elegant buildings in the world's greatest cities.

All of these examples are inside the circle of sustainability's sixth front. What about outside?

It is here that we witness the power of influence. By that I mean sustainability initiatives started at other corporations, including some of our competitors! Some of them happened with our help; others responded to our example, our leadership, or to a good old competitive challenge. This is how

Interface can become more than just sustainable, and actually be restorative, not just by the progress we make, but also by the initiatives we influence others to take. By showing others the way and giving them the courage to begin their own climbs, we intend to make this world better with every square yard of carpet we sell.

That's the right thing to do. At first, in 1994, I thought it even meant helping a competitor, though many members of our Eco Dream Team of advisers thought that unwise. In time, they persuaded me of the critical importance of the success of Interface's sustainability initiative. They meant success in every sense, especially financial success. I quickly got it. We would succeed and prove nature's way is the better business model, at the expense of the inefficient adapter, the competitor who didn't get it.

Moving a small industry such as carpet manufacturing would have a negligible effect on the global scene, but proving a better business model (read, competitive advantage), inevitably at the expense of our competitors, would influence much larger companies in much larger industries. That's the path we chose, and daily we see that there is no natural limit to the power of influence.

Interface is a very small pebble in the world's economy, something like 1/60,000 of global commerce in 2008. But our consulting arm, Interface-RAISE, has worked with some of the world's largest corporations to help them adopt sounder, more competitive business practices.

Here's what Doug McMillon, the CEO of Wal-Mart's Sam's Club, said: "Visiting Interface and seeing the creativity applied to establish more sustainable practices made it undeniable that the rest of us can do the same. We don't have to spend time wondering if we can do something. Instead, we can move on to figure out how."

Now add the considerable heft of Wal-Mart, the world's largest retailer and a company with more than $300 billion in revenues, to our small mass. You can toss a pebble into a pond and not much is going to happen. But toss in a boulder like that one and see if there's any place those spreading ripples *don't* reach.

From the conversations I have had with other business people and the audiences I meet at my speeches, from the letters I receive (and read) and the popularity of green venture capital funds, I'd say the ripples we helped start back in 1994 are spreading fast and growing.

I began this book by describing how some folks viewed my spear in the chest epiphany as good ethics but bad business. Well, there may still be some who argue that sustainability is not economically feasible, that business will never find a profit outside the old, take-make-waste paradigm, but there are far fewer of them around today. More and more business leaders recognize that good ethics *is* good business.

That is not to say that you have to run your enterprise with a foot on the brakes, missing out on opportunities in the name of sustainability. Just the opposite: Financial success is the key to achieving sustainability. A bankrupt company is clearly not sustainable. But sustainability is also a big key to achieving financial success. We have proved that earning a bigger and a better, more legitimate profit is possible.

We've slashed waste, improved efficiencies, eliminated harmful chemicals and substances, ramped up our use of renewable energy, invented ways to use recycled material, and are on the hunt to make transportation resource-efficient. New thinking produces mind-blowing innovation that cuts across all the faces of the mountain. We are still hard at work on all five of those fronts, and likely will be as long as there is an Interface, for the finish line for sustainability is just a way station to being a restorative company. But as I said at the very beginning of this chapter, without motivated people none of it would ever have happened.

Who are these people, anyway? They are:

- the people we work with;
- the people who invest money in our company;
- the people who supply us with the raw materials and other goods and services we need;
- the people who specify our products;
- the people who deliver our products to the market, and install and maintain them;
- the people who buy our finished goods—our end-use customers, the sources of all our heartbeats;
- the people who return old carpets to us to recycle and transform into new carpets;
- the people who are engaged with municipal governments, schools, churches, libraries, volunteer organizations, in every town where we have an office or a plant;
- the people who live in those communities.

So how can we get such a large and diverse group all moving in the right direction? The short answer is, not easily. Some of you may be old enough to remember that *Pogo* comic strip where one of the characters says, "We have met the enemy, and he is us." That is surely the case when we consider what humanity has been doing to our planet for a long time now.

But in the years since I issued the challenge to that environmental task force, I have seen firsthand that people *can* choose to be something more than nature's unthinking enemy. We can choose to be its thoughtful guardian, its wise partner; we can model our practices on the tried and true mechanisms that nature evolved, and make money every step of the way. We just have to rid ourselves of some old, unworkable ideas that seemed right, and start using new and better ones that are right.

That is exactly what sensitizing stakeholders is all about. Some have called this front "social sustainability," to distinguish it from environmental or financial sustainability. But truly, these are three legs of the same stool; or better, three stages of the same rocket whose payload is profits. We need them all if we hope for our kind to be around for a while.

That said, there is no silver bullet; no one person who can get this job done. John F. Kennedy's call to land an American on the moon within ten years could not have been carried out by words alone. It took a motivated organization, money, family sacrifices, real national leadership, and, yes, cold war competition to put Neil Armstrong's boots on Tranquility Base. Sparking a new industrial revolution is not going to be any easier, and likely it will be considerably more difficult.

There are many, many small steps that need to be taken by many, many people to reach that Mission Zero summit. Recall that when I issued that challenge in 1994 I had no idea how to turn my vision into reality. Yes, I had conviction, but a real plan did not materialize for at least a year. For that I needed the help of that Eco Dream Team that I told you about earlier, as well as of every one of my colleagues in that task force's meeting room. And when they returned to their individual business units around the globe, they needed the help of every one of their colleagues to turn the challenge into action.

At some companies, when the CEO issues a bold directive the machinery cranks up to educate and motivate the various, far-flung business units. Step-by-step instructions are issued, a medialike making/training/testing bureaucracy is created, and results are measured every which way from Sunday. Fall below some mandated norm, and it's my way or the highway time.

But Interface was born with a different spirit, one that was, and is once again, fiercely independent and entrepreneurial. I once left a good job because of its stultifying top-down management. I had a better idea of how things should be run. So when I returned to day-to-day management of Interface in July 1999, I made sure our people got all the authority, all the independence, they could handle. I knew that issuing edicts from Atlanta to become sustainable was not going to cut it, anymore than telling contractors they could sell only our carpets, or else.

We quickly rediscovered that the best way to solve local problems was to use local smarts. We had already learned that in our waste-trimming QUEST program, and it worked exactly the same way when it came to energizing people about sustainability. How did we begin?

We organized Play to Win™ team-building exercises—rope courses and all—to reestablish and reinforce the idea that all of us were in this together, that we could handle things we once thought impossible. Our business was global. Our workforce was global, too, with all the differences in cultures and customs you can imagine. But unless everyone learned to freely—even aggressively—question the status quo, to anticipate and embrace change, to identify opportunities, to be flexible and react quickly there was no hope of becoming the kind of organization that might one day be the first sustainable corporation in history.

Wayne Gretzky, one of the greatest hockey players of all time, calls this, Skating to where the puck is going to be. But that requires staying nimble and ready to move away from where you are and where you feel comfortable—the status quo—into an uncomfortable, opportunity-filled anticipation of the future.

Managers had always been the traditional source of such ideas, but we needed to go way outside tradition to find our way up the mountain to sustainability. Many of the waste-saving suggestions in QUEST came from the folks who were closest to the problem. That was no accident. Our first waste-hunting QUEST teams came straight out of those Play-to-Win™ exercises. In the exercises people were urged to always seek out that better way, the one my professors at Georgia Tech promised was out there, and to view our question-everything approach to problem solving as a worthy challenge, not as a threat. It also encouraged people to move outside their comfort zones and let go of their old, established patterns of behavior. People were even given permission to fail, but to learn from failure and try again.

In January 2000, after the Y2K buildup had already put our marketplace into decline and, though we didn't know it, the dot-com collapse was imminent, I called together our top 125 managers from around the world to see how we were all doing. Once again, everything was on the table and no holds were barred. The company's mission, its vision, and the strategies we'd adopted to achieve it were up for grabs.

Out of that meeting came a focus on what we called the Five Ps: people, product, process, place, and profit. Something else emerged; you might say this became a watershed event. There was 100 percent agreement among the 125 managers there that sustainability was firmly rooted in Interface's DNA. I took enormous pride and pleasure in that declaration.

Back to the Five Ps. We'd certainly made changes in our products and our processes. They were evolving to meet the challenges of our hard climb up Mount Sustainability. Check. But people have to evolve, too. The Play to Win™ program had helped to break down the fears (of failure, of standing out, of saying something that might compromise a career) and given our associates new skills. Check again.

Interface had also sponsored Why? conferences for customers, combining the concepts of Play to Win™ and sustainability in an understandable, interactive format that built valuable friendships and lasting relationships. Meanwhile, companies hoping to do business as suppliers to Interface had been put on notice that we would be paying close attention to their own practices. Remember? No one stands alone. In fact, we would be rating them the same way that we rated our own operations.

You've read earlier that a brown company can't make a green product. To that I would add that a green company can't use brown suppliers, either. Each of our companies, yours and mine, is its supply chain.

But a company is also its people, not just its suppliers and customers, and if our associates (like most of society) didn't understand the basic principles of natural systems, or how individual and collective human actions affect them, then we couldn't hope to be a truly green company, no matter how many kilowatts of solar power we generated.

We learned a lesson from our scary experience in the late 1990s. We never again tried to educate our people through rote, one-size-fits-all methods. Rather, we left it up to the individual business units to find their own better ways to get the job done. And that, for us, has proven to be a winning formula. I'll let Karin Laljani, our senior vice president for market strategy and sustainability at InterfaceFLOR in Europe, tell you how she does it:

"I find that when someone wants to work for Interface, one of the main reasons is our position on sustainability. So they are already aware of who we are and what we stand for. But we put them through a course of study to make sure they really know what it means.

"We have a four-level program for our associates. We call it Fastforward to 2020—the year Mission Zero sets as our corporate sustainability goal. When associates join Interface Europe, they attend a level 1 induction course that covers our sustainability ethos, our Mission Zero plan, and our corporate strategy for reaching it. We administer a multiple-choice test at the end to make sure the core concepts are understood.

"Level II is tailored to address where our new associate fits into the organization, and what he or she is doing here. This level goes into great detail about how Mission Zero relates not only to a person's job, but their life outside work, too. We hold competitions among participants, and the winners receive awards for their commitment and their progress at an annual meeting.

"Level III, critical analysis, is a strategic two-day course for senior managers/directors/VPs to discuss sustainability at a detailed and more technical level. The participants are given four to six weeks to complete an assignment that includes their making proposals on how we reach Mission Zero faster. Level IV is for about ten to fifteen selected spokespeople, who go through a full day of media training to become more effective 'sustainability ambassadors' for Interface. We run all four levels several times a year, including refresher courses. They really are popular, because they are fun and interactive, and they've been terrific at generating new ideas.

"Through our sustainability ambassadors program and our PR efforts, we reached out to more than two hundred million people last year. And there are special initiatives with suppliers of raw materials, marketing agencies, and transportation partners, too.

"I often speak at conferences. And my greatest satisfaction is when I get the audience to understand that their organization can change like ours did. By copying our model, they find out how to cut their own Mission Zero journey by three to five years. The message that touches most participants is this: Whether we created the mess we are in today or not, do we not have the duty to do something to reverse it, if we can?"

Karin, with Interface Europe CEO Lindsey Parnell, has been the driving force behind our new Fairworks concept. "It's the most ambitious outreach effort we have done, and it is at the heart of our social sustainability program," she said.

Almost three billion people around the world live on less than the equivalent of two dollars per day, while many traditional-craft skills, and the cultures surrounding them, are being lost. What's more, modern production methods—especially those used to mass produce goods—can be hugely detrimental to the environment.

The Fairworks vision is simple: Harness the skills of local artisans around the world and work with them to develop beautiful flooring products in the fairest way possible, and in as environmentally and socially responsible a way as possible. To do this, Interface:

- **Sources locally available materials**
  Wherever possible, we use natural or recycled raw materials that are found as near as possible to where the products are made.

- **Innovates traditional handicraft skills**
  We draw on the skills of the local artisans, fusing traditional techniques with contemporary practices.

- **Increases earning opportunities for local communities**
  To achieve this, we work closely with local organizations and nongovernmental organizations (NGOs).

The first commercial product to come from this pioneering collaboration between Interface and talented local artisans is just now, in 2008, coming to market: We call it Just™ carpet.

"Just is a high-end, crafted product," said Karin. "But it's not purely decorative. You can stand on it, walk on it. It meets light- to medium-use contract standards, and it is simply gorgeous. There is nothing else like it in the world of commercial flooring. So what is clearly a good thing to do for the traditional weavers who make it for us is also a good business move for us at Interface."

Across the globe Interface business units use methods that are designed to work best with their own local cultures. But there were some general rules we set from Atlanta.

We like to rely on self-organized teams to assess how things are going locally on all seven Mission Zero fronts. We make sure quarterly "sustainability meetings" are held to ask the big, tough questions. How did we do last year? What did we learn from our mistakes? Our successes? How are we doing so far this year? How do we stand in comparison to other parts of the Interface organization? Have we improved? Held our ground? Or slipped? And, most important, what can we do better in the next few months to become more sustainable—really, less *un*sustainable—on any of Mount Sustainability's seven faces?

And we bring those metrics back to the corporate level and analyze them closely. Are they rigorous? Do they make sense? Do they accurately reflect what is really happening out there? Once we are positive the numbers are solid (because our metrics are our reputation), we publish them so all of our associates can see how their performance stacks up against other Interface businesses.

While our preference is always for the local level to take the initiative, not every solution can be found there. Just as we had to make global decisions about which chemicals to bar from our factories, some programs are better run from the corporate level. Our Diversity Connect™ program is one example that could have gone either way, but ended up being managed locally, with our board of directors' direct support.

Diversity Connect™ brings women- and minority-owned and operated flooring services into our circle of influence to manage large contracts for Fortune 1000 corporate clients, educational institutions, retail stores, hospitals, hotels, and a wide range of federal, state, and local government entities. Through it we offer real opportunities to suppliers that are small, minority-, women-, disabled-, or veteran-owned, businesses run by people from historically underrepresented communities.

Sales through the Diversity Connect channel increased by 85 percent between 2005 and 2007, with purchases increasing by more than $7.5 million, and we intend to stay on that growth curve and continue affording these businesses the opportunity to grow with us as valued suppliers of goods and services. The directors' support comes through the direct involvement of Dianne Dillon-Ridgley, an African American member of the Interface board.

Bringing our whole supply chain—both upstream and down—into our circle has other benefits, too, for them, for us, and for the earth. When we apply the tools and skills we've developed at Interface to their businesses, we usually find we can reduce their environmental footprint to one degree or another. But there are large benefits to Interface, even if the savings seem small. Why?

When you examine the total carbon footprint of one square yard of our carpet, you quickly discover that Interface is directly responsible for only 10 to 20 percent of it; everyone else, from the user, the installer, the distributor, all the way back to the wells and mines, contributes the overwhelming 80 to 90 percent. So any change we can help them make in their operations has an outsized positive effect. It not only promotes and encourages the concept of sustainability and widens our circle of influence, it shrinks our own environmental footprint.

And by the way, if you don't think that reducing your carbon footprint is terribly important now, you may want to reconsider when you start being taxed on its size. Is that coming? Yes, I believe it is.

What else have we done inside Interface to push the sensitivity front?

- We've adopted streams to clean and maintain.
- We've sponsored a television program to expose the plight of the nearby, polluted Chattahoochee River.
- We're planting flower and vegetable gardens on our factory grounds, and creating bird sanctuaries, too.
- We send our associates to go out into local schools and civic organizations to be mentors and ambassadors of sustainability.
- We sponsor school science fairs and help kids explore and experiment with renewable energy, recycling, and benign chemistry.
- We influence college involvement by offering internships to top students, as well as give those top performers a career path that allows them to practice what they've learned.
- On the local educational front, we urge our people around the world to seek out and identify local schoolteachers who want to carry out an environmental education exercise with their students but don't have the funds. Each year we identify up to thirty such projects and fund them. Thus far, we have touched some forty thousand children through this program. Funds come from the Interface Environmental Foundation, whose funds come from prizes we have been awarded and speaking fees I and others generate. Recycling at its best—money, in this case.
- At the other end of the education spectrum, we have endowed a

chair at my old university, Georgia Tech, in the School of Industrial and Systems Engineering. It is the chair for Natural Systems, and the person who holds it is charged with learning from nature how to redesign the industrial system.

From elementary school children building a wind turbine, to an inventor creating a machine to recycle carpets, to a company team cleaning up a river, to a small business owner seeing her dream of a thriving, growing enterprise come true, they are all part of the social sustainability front.

But how on earth can we measure social equity progress? We aren't dealing with BTUs, or pounds of scrap carpet, or kilowatt-hours coming from the sun. We're in the realm of ideas, the ones that spur people on to want to save those BTUs, to reduce waste, to pump up power from renewable sources. Every business person has heard the old adage "What gets measured gets managed." So how do you manage something that might not be measurable?

We use something we call Sociometrics to report progress on this front. It is the people counterpart to the Ecometrics reporting that helps us keep close tabs on such things as greenhouse gas emissions, energy used, and waste sent to landfills.

At Interface, our Sustainable Strategies Group focuses on measuring our progress by keeping tabs on the social impacts of sustainability. What do they actually measure? Each quarter, they assess each business unit's progress in solving problems in:

- safety;
- health;
- environmental issues;
- diversity;
- community outreach and involvement.

They record the contributions each business unit makes—hours, dollars, or in-kind—to community organizations and NGOs working to make the world a better place, such as Habitat for Humanity or Riverkeeper, a nonprofit organization established in 1990 to protect and preserve the integrity and natural environment of America's rivers, including the Chattahoochee right here in Georgia; and local conservancies, too.

In LaGrange, where we helped to solve their landfill problem, we also helped fund the rehabilitation of some historic but run-down housing right in the center of a blue-collar community, at the same time supporting the entrepreneur who renovated them and made them once again habitable.

We also track how many talks associates give on doing business with the earth in mind, to whom, and to what effect. I give about 150 speeches a year, including interviews for books, radio, TV, and movies, and with several other headquarters associates, we altogether reach about three hundred audiences a year—large and small!

We also like to find out how many voluntary community outreach hours were logged, either by doing restorative work (like cleaning up a stream) or volunteering to help raise money for a local school or library. We also track how each business unit is doing to make sure women have a fair shot at any management position they are capable of filling.

Early in our mountain climb we embraced our environmental initiatives under the label EcoSense. We developed Ecometrics for measuring progress and later, Sociometrics. Essentially, those together formed a road map to sustainability and a report card to show how far we have come on our journey. To build EcoSense into our compensation system, we award EcoSense Points for the successful completion of nonfinancial activities—social and environmental—that fall under the following categories:

- environmental management systems;
- quality management systems;
- sustainability training;
- sensitizing stakeholders;
- employee safety and education;
- resource-efficient transportation;
- ecometrics;
- purchasing.

I'll give some examples. Associates who participate as mentors in a school are awarded points for sensitizing stakeholders. Interface facilities that receive ISO 14001 certification are awarded points for high-quality environmental management systems. And by the way, I am glad to report that Interface has more of its divisions registered under the International Organization for Standardization's ISO 14001 Environmental Management System Standard than any other company in the commercial interiors industry.

The EcoSense points are pooled with the more objective measures of progress generated by associates from each business unit, and not only is an award given at the end of the year for the facility that comes out on top, but people's paychecks reflect their individual contributions, too.

Every corporation does exhaustive financial reporting, and environmental reporting is becoming more and more common. The processes are familiar and fairly simple. But social responsibility and sustainability reporting is still in its infancy, and corporations like ours are trying to help pave the way. One way we can help do this is through our consulting arm: InterfaceRAISE.

We chose to call it "RAISE" because its job is to find ways to help other companies:

- reshape corporate cultures and *raise* awareness;
- measure progress toward sustainability and *raise* standards;
- uncover new opportunities and *raise* expectations;
- inspire process and product innovation to *raise* profits.

I'll give you an example of how it works. In an October 2005 internal speech, Lee Scott—CEO of retail giant Wal-Mart—issued a challenge to his company and its business partners that has had far-reaching implications for how their business will be conducted. Believe me, it will impact customers, communities, and the environment.

Specifically, Scott detailed Wal-Mart's simple, straightforward environmental goals.

1. To be supplied by 100 percent renewable energy.
2. To create zero waste.
3. To sell products that sustain our resources and environment.

What prompted such an ambitious set of goals? Are such goals possible, especially for a company with some two million employees and more than six thousand individual facilities worldwide?

Scott, like other forward-thinking business leaders, put his faith in the concept of sustainability.

His October 2005 declaration made Wal-Mart's journey toward

sustainability a corporate mandate, a public promise, and a notice to all they do business with: Sustainability is a critical part of our business. How did InterfaceRAISE help Wal-Mart get there?

It began with a small group of executives at a retreat in the fall of 2004, in Bentonville, Arkansas; a kind of sustainability summit. I was there at Wal-Mart's invitation, and made brief remarks about Interface's sustainability initiatives. Perhaps I helped a bit that day, but it was clear to me that our greatest assistance to Wal-Mart would be in their supply chain, by helping some sixty thousand companies reinvent themselves to meet the Wal-Mart standards that were sure to come.

At the retreat, Wal-Mart executives became enthusiastic and energized about sustainability. Subsequently, as part of the learning process, InterfaceRAISE staff hosted two groups of Wal-Mart executives in LaGrange, Georgia, for a cultural immersion at this, our flagship manufacturing facility (now known as "the living lab" in InterfaceRAISE training sessions).

The cultural immersion is now a core product of InterfaceRAISE. It includes minilectures and abundant time for the client to have one-on-one discussions with the Interface management team and experts. A key outcome of Wal-Mart's cultural immersion experience was the realization that this journey is as much about people as it is about recycling and energy use.

Andy Ruben, Wal-Mart's vice president for corporate sustainability, had this to say about their visit: "People and companies need to look at their ability to make change in the world. Interface has value for being a living model that continues to evolve its sustainability practice. Their influence is their journey, and the length of their journey, and at what depth the company integrated sustainability and change. That has influence."

It sure has. At the most recent Wal-Mart Sustainability Summit, which was held in 2008, some four hundred chief executives from the giant retailer's supplier chain were in attendance. Why were they in Bentonville?

Wal-Mart discovered that being a greener business can be an engine for innovation in products and packaging, even in delivery systems. And it is pushing hard to help its tens of thousands of suppliers move in that direction, too. Wal-Mart will be judging all of its suppliers on their packaging, using metrics that governing the quantity and environmental friendliness as one buying criterion. It plans to measure their energy use and emissions, with the goal of using climate impact as a buying criterion, too. And the company has integrated sustainability into the performance evaluations of their buyers and managers, which in turn help determine their raises and promotions.

However, the effect at Wal-Mart radiates inwardly, too. A Wal-Mart executive told me that they had never before launched any initiative that energized their employees to the extent that the sustainability initiative had.

Could I have imagined, even in my wildest dreams, that a decade after I issued that challenge to my colleagues, to turn Interface toward sustainability, that a company like Wal-Mart would be right there beside us? That our example, our trailblazing, could help bring it about?

But Jim Hartzfeld, the managing director of InterfaceRAISE (and one of the sixteen disciples present at that first sustainability meeting), has seen it happen. He put it this way: "Interface has been on this path for over a decade, exploring the theory and applying it in a competitive industrial context. We created InterfaceRAISE to use our firsthand experience to help other companies move more quickly up the learning curve by showing them our scars and medals, like a sherpa in a climbing expedition. We can help other companies climb the learning curve better, faster, and more cost-effectively than if they go it alone."

And Wal-Mart has done just that. Here are just a few of their recent metrics.

- In 2007, they opened three high-efficiency stores, called HE.1, that use 20 percent less energy than a typical supercenter.
- In January 2008, they opened the first of four next-generation high-efficiency stores (HE.2). This store is 25 percent more energy efficient than the 2005 baseline, and it has reduced refrigerant use by 90 percent.
- In May 2008, Wal-Mart achieved its goal to sell only concentrated liquid laundry detergent in all of its United States and Canadian stores. In three years Wal-Mart expects to sell more than eight hundred million bottles of concentrated detergent. As a result, they anticipate saving (for their customers!) 400 million gallons of water, 95 million pounds of plastic resin, and 125 million pounds of cardboard. And they have avoided shipping enormous quantities of water.
- As the owner of one of the largest private trucking fleets in the world, as we have already discussed, the company is partnering

with truck manufacturers to radically improve its efficiency, as well as retrofitting its existing fleet with diesel-saving technologies.

- Last year they sold 137 million compact fluorescent lamps (CFL), surpassing their goal to sell 100 million bulbs. This will save users $4 billion in energy costs and prevent almost one billion incandescent bulbs from reaching landfills. Moreover, it prevents twenty-five million tons of carbon dioxide from being released. That's the equivalent of taking one million cars off the road.

So you can see that sensitizing stakeholders is all about who we are, what can we offer our colleagues, our customers, other corporations, and our communities. And by community I don't mean just where we go to work in the morning. I mean our homes, our children's schools, our churches, our chambers of commerce, our YMCAs. The entire earth is our "community of interest."

As InterfaceRAISE works with its clients to reshape corporate cultures and raise expectations, the question often arises, Is the Interface experience transferable?

Let me answer that with a quick story.

A representative from a very large American multinational food corporation, an early InterfaceRAISE client, was visiting us, along with some of her colleagues, to learn how we actually make money by shouldering our environmental responsibilities. To say that she was skeptical about what they could learn in a carpet factory is a huge understatement.

When the group took a short break from the meeting, she went out onto the factory floor to see just how deep this whole Mission Zero thing really went. She stopped a forklift driver who was transporting a big roll of carpet and asked, "What do you do here?"

"Ma'am," the truck driver, James Wisener, said, "I come to work every day to help save the earth."

Stunned by his answer, she started probing that forklift driver with more questions. Finally, James said, "Ma'am, I don't want to be rude, but if I don't get this roll of carpet to the next process right now, our waste and emissions numbers are going to way up. I've gotta go."

She returned to our conference room a changed person. Recounting the story to her associates, she said that she had never before seen such a deep alignment of vision in an organization. From the top to the bottom. The only word she could think of to describe it was "love." Love on the factory floor? Well, yes, maybe that is one way to describe it. The way I see it, it's where that higher purpose I wrote about earlier meets deep, personal commitment. And that is how an organization changes. Mine, and yours.

Though sustainability may be a destination (as I see it), there is no finish line, neither are there borders. Every time a customer decides to go for platinum LEED certification, or a supplier cuts its transportation costs by 25 percent, or an investor wants her money to grow green, or another company looks to our example and asks, "Why can't we do that?" our circle grows just a little bit wider.

You can see now that what began in that conference room some fourteen years ago with just a charged-up CEO and a few stunned colleagues has become a whole lot bigger as its influence has spread. I think fifteen years from now we'll be able to say the same thing once again: "Where will it take us?"

Almost anywhere on earth. Every creature, large and small, has a stake in this. Whether that stake flourishes and grows or withers and dies is not up to the government. It is, remarkably, providentially, up to you—and me.

Here are some charts that measure our progress on the social sustainability front. They are far from complete. But then, so is our journey.

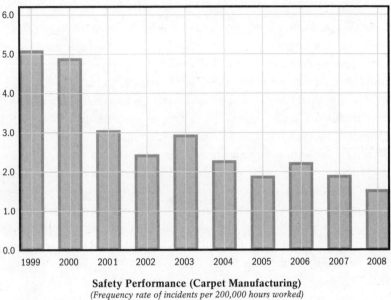

**Safety Performance (Carpet Manufacturing)**
*(Frequency rate of incidents per 200,000 hours worked)*
68% decrease in accident frequency rate

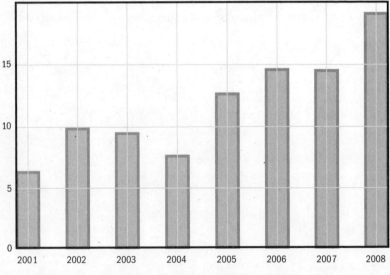

**Average Hours of Training per Employee**

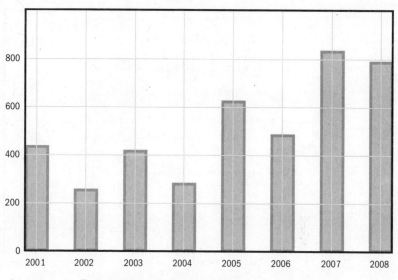

**Company Contributions to External Organizations**
*($ in thousands)*

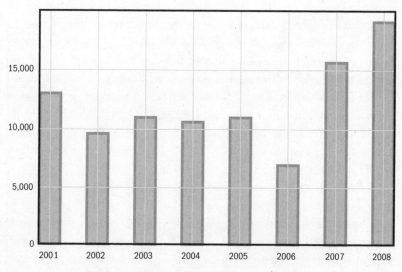

**Employee Volunteer Hours in Community Service**

# 11 | The Final Ascent

*Man and nature have come apart, and I think the closer we can start
to connect with nature and be a "system," the better off we will be.
There's a lot we can learn.*

DAVID OAKEY, Interface design consultant

Redesigning commerce" is the seventh and final face to climb in our ascent of Mount Sustainability. Actually, I think it's not so much a separate face but, like the famous Hillary Step just below the summit of Everest, it's that last steep push where everything has to come together to reach the top. And yes, it does sound like something no one corporation—not even an entire industry—could possibly achieve on its own. Change the way our whole market-driven economy conducts business? That's a stretch!

But if you narrow the field of view down to how your company conducts its business, opportunities to make productive and profitable changes will appear. In particular, as David Oakey said, using nature as a design tool, a model, and an inspiration, availing yourself of her millions of years of evolutionary fine-tuning, can be especially fruitful.

But there is a real limit to how much any one of us can do alone on this last, steep climb. I know, because we at Interface have tried very hard to make real progress on this front, and while we have seen some spectacular successes in letting nature guide us in our product design, we've come up short on retooling commerce with sustainability in mind (though not for lack of trying!). Let me tell you about it.

First, it's important to realize that nobody planned the industrial revolution. It evolved as opportunities to substitute fossil fuels and machinery for human and animal power multiplied. Architect Bill McDonough was one of my original dream team of advisers. He really helped us get our climbing map right. If I may borrow from his book, *Cradle to Cradle* (North Point Press), the industrial system this ad hoc evolution created:

- puts billions of pounds of toxic materials into the air, water, and soil each year;
- produces some materials that are so dangerous they will require constant vigilance by future generations;
- results in gigantic amounts of waste;
- puts valuable materials in holes all over the planet, where they are difficult if not impossible to retrieve and recycle;
- requires thousands of complex rules and regulations—not to keep people safe, but to keep them from being poisoned too quickly;
- measures productivity by how few people are working;
- creates prosperity by digging up or cutting down natural resources and then burying or burning them;
- erodes the diversity of species and cultural practices.

Just imagine a creature living in a natural world with even some of those characteristics. Do you suppose it would survive for very long?

Yet, our present-day business practices evolved right along with this first industrial revolution. As Albert Einstein's observation haunts us: "Problems cannot be solved by the same kind of thinking that created them." And this observation surely applies to redesigning commerce. If the old business practices are what got you into a fix, they probably won't be much help in getting you out of it. Which business practices am I talking about?

The ones that focus on producing, delivering, and discarding ever greater quantities of goods as a measure of our prosperity. You can see that something is just not right in the numbers when you realize that both Hurricane Katrina and the *Exxon Valdez* oil spill added to our gross domestic product. When a child falls so ill she must be taken to the emergency room (because she has no health insurance and no doctor), she's increasing our GDP, too. How can any of that possibly make sense?

If you bother to look, you will notice that the whole game of modern commerce is riddled with economic distortions that make it hard—even impossible—for markets to see, and respond to, the true costs of all that frantic producing and delivering and discarding. Some of these distortions manifest themselves in perverse incentives, financial rewards that actually encourage us to do the wrong things.

Some distortions take the form of direct payments, government interventions to set market prices, preferential tax policies, government-guaranteed loans and liability protections, and building infrastructure to benefit a particular technology or industry. You can probably think of dozens of examples. Here are a few that come to mind:

- subsidies to oil companies to support more production of that to which we are already addicted. You just don't do that to an addict;
- a federal highway system that guaranteed our slavery to the automobile;
- subsidies to purchasers of SUVs under the guise of helping the small-business person who needs a truck in her or his business;
- governments that happily hand out money to some farmers to keep agricultural land fallow . . .
- . . . while handing out money to encourage other farmers to overload other croplands to the point of erosion, compaction, and chemical poisoning;
- subsidies for ethanol production that ultimately drive the cost of food up by supporting plant-based "refineries" that use almost as much energy as they yield;
- in Germany, the coal industry is so heavily subsidized by the state that it would be far cheaper, according to one economist, to shut the mines down and send all the miners home at full salary for the rest of their lives than to continue to operate them;
- India spends a full 14 percent of its gross domestic product—about $40 billion a year—for agricultural and industrial subsidies;
- in the United States, the Price-Anderson Act legislates away our nuclear industry's liability problem by placing artificially low limits on what people can collect from a nuclear utility in the event of a catastrophic accident. It's an insurance policy our government (that's you and I) provides at no cost to the nuclear industry—not a penny in liability premiums is collected. Take the subsidy away and no right-thinking board would ever approve a nuclear investment.

Think about that when you hear someone mention grid parity, or say, "Renewables can't compete with nuclear energy on price."

You know, when Mahatma Gandhi was asked what he thought of Western civilization, he wryly answered, "It would be a very good idea." The same might be said about our "free" market. It, too, would be a very good idea. But a strange and perverse hybrid that is called "free" and is anything but is the one we've got. Call it Market 1.0.

What about Market 2.0? What do we mean when we say we want to "redesign" commerce? For one, Market 2.0 focuses on delivering services and value in a closed-loop, waste-equals-food fashion that emulates nature rather than endlessly making, delivering, and discarding new products made from irreplaceable, nonrenewable raw materials.

But as our long hunt at Interface for processes and machinery to properly recycle carpets showed, this is not just a conceptual challenge; it is a huge technological one, too. We had to work long and hard to begin to solve the recycling problem. But the conceptual part of that equation seemed to fall into place quite easily back in 1995. We called it the Evergreen Service Agreement.

Paul Hawken already had spoken to the issue of selling services rather than things in 1993 in *The Ecology of Commerce*. He called it and wrote, "What we want is transportation from our car, cold beer from the refrigerator, and news or entertainment from our television."

So, using Hawken as a springboard, we asked ourselves, what do people want from carpets? Who wakes up thinking, I need to own twenty thousand pounds of nylon today? Do people really need to buy carpets? And we came up with a surprising answer—especially for a business that manufactures them: No. What people do need is:

- beautiful interior spaces;
- comfort underfoot;
- noise control;
- cleanliness;
- ambiance;
- durability;
- functionality;
- flexibility;

- confidence in the quality and safety of the product in use; as well as
- confidence in the company that made it.

What if Interface could provide all of those things while retaining ownership of the carpet, the responsibility for its upkeep, and its ultimate recycling? Could we sell a "floor covering service" by *leasing* carpets to our customers instead of selling them? Would there be economic advantages in such a redesign of our commercial model? How about environmental advantages?

Turned out that the answer to all those questions was a resounding Yes!

This model of "delivering the service of products rather than the products themselves" was proposed in the mid-1980s by Swiss industrial analyst Walter Stahel, who became an early addition to our Eco Dream Team. (Later on, the concept was analyzed in a Harvard Business School case study of our Evergreen Lease.) Stahel proposed that manufacturers find new and more sustainable goals that placed a high value on results, performance, and customer satisfaction, rather than selling as many widgets as they possibly could.

Leasing falls nicely into this model, and it certainly is a familiar option in nearly all corners of the business world. It happens all the time, and for a variety of reasons, not the least of which is that it allows a company (or an individual) to avoid a sizable capital expense, replacing it with smaller and more immediately tax-deductible monthly operating expenses. Think of leasing a car rather than financing one to own it. The arguments for (and against) such an arrangement are familiar and quite similar.

By leasing the services of our carpets to our customers, Interface would see a monthly cash flow that would even out the natural ups and downs in an order-driven transactional business. By maintaining those leased carpets, we would stay in close contact with our customers, and make our carpets last longer. Those are all good things. The closer I am to my customer—that next heartbeat—the happier I am.

The customer would get a beautiful floor at zero capital cost. We would keep that floor looking good for the life of the contract, and, when it was over we would recycle the old carpet into new (when the technology materialized). There would be powerful economic advantages all around. What about the environmental question?

That's where the advantages were the greatest. Most carpets are removed from a building long before they need to be. The numbers are different for every installation, but in general, 80 percent of the wear happens to just 20 percent of the carpet. Carpets get replaced because of a change in interior design or fashion, or because some high-traffic areas (such as corridors and cafeterias) start to look tired after years on the job. Facility managers often say that a carpet "uglies out" before it wears out.

But if we owned the carpets and maintained them ourselves, we could offer our customers the flexibility to change their floors to suit their needs. Carpet tiles lend themselves especially well to this concept. If a single tile were damaged or stained, we could replace just that one tile, keeping the entire job looking new and fresh almost indefinitely. And the relatively small areas—the 20 percent that experiences the greatest amount of wear—could continue to look new for the life of the lease with periodic face-lifts. Where does the environmental benefit kick in in this equation?

Instead of the old "install and tear out" approach, through a constant program of selective refreshing and replacement we would prolong the life of 80 percent of the material, saving the embodied energy and the greenhouse gases, and reducing the carbon footprint.

Recall that when we reduced the nylon content of our carpets by just 4 percent we saved enough energy, enough oil, enough greenhouse gas emissions to reduce our GHG upstream by half every year. So an 80 percent reduction, even a deferral, is a serious environmental benefit.

And if we owned and maintained the carpets, we would be sure to be there when the time came to recycle them, yielding even more environmental benefits (though, as you've already read, we had no idea how to recycle a whole carpet tile back in 1995; we've learned that only recently).

So we were cantilevered a bit, but we got busy and figured out what such an arrangement might look like in detail. As a result, the initial Evergreen lease was structured to allow Interface to retain ownership of the carpet, from manufacturing through installation, maintenance, and beyond to reclamation, when the old carpet was removed and remade. We would install the carpet, maintain the carpet, replace the carpet as it aged, and, at the end, reclaim it, all for a fixed monthly fee that would show up in our customer's operating, not capital, budget—satisfaction guaranteed.

More, we guaranteed the function and appearance of the carpet for the life of the contract, which, from our perspective, might be a very long time—ideally the life of the building itself. Like a slate roof, our carpet tiles could be renewed one tile at a time, always looking new. Our customers would see the benefits of a single-source supplier, a comprehensive floor-covering service paid for by a single monthly fee, cash-flow efficiency, financial reporting advantages, and the chance to participate in a groundbreaking sustainability program with powerful environmental advantages.

What could be wrong with all of that?

Our Evergreen launch customer was the Southern California Gas Company: twenty-five hundred square yards of our carpet tiles were installed in its Energy Resource Center (ERC) in Downey, California, the company's first green demonstration building. This is where we had met the environmental consultant, John Picard, who had said, "Interface just doesn't get it," and was to become the first member of our Dream Team. Well, here we were, a sea change later, thanks in part to Picard's comment, structuring the first ever carpet lease. Already we were in the details, being sure it would qualify as an operating—not a capital—lease under the definitions set down in the Financial Accounting Standards Board Rule 13 (FASB 13). Why was that so important?

Because an operating lease brings additional financial benefits to our customer. Operating leases are not reflected on a balance sheet, so our customers would see an improvement in their return-on-assets figure and their debt-to-equity ratio. But to qualify, four specific requirements had to be met:

1. Interface could not transfer ownership of the carpet to the customer.
2. Interface could not offer the customer a "bargain purchase" option to pick up ownership of the carpet at the end of the term.
3. The term of the lease could not exceed 75 percent of the life of the product.
4. The "present value" of the total lease payments could not exceed 90 percent of the fair market salvage value of the carpet at the end of the lease (otherwise, the customer is actually buying the carpet on time which, under the rules, is not considered an operating lease at all).

We could accommodate the first three of those rules without breaking a sweat. But the fourth was a problem. Why? Because back in 1995, used carpets could not be recycled, certainly not economically. Oil was very cheap, virgin materials were relatively cheap, and nobody knew how to separate the various components of a carpet tile into recyclable components cleanly. And so the salvage value of old carpet was zero to a financial intermediary (e.g., a bank), even if we went out on a limb (cantilevered again) and guaranteed the salvage value, assuming the risk of whether the technology would materialize.

The IRS required that the risk attached to salvage value be borne by the owner, in our case, the financial intermediary. To the IRS, that meant the Evergreen lease was a capital, not an operating, lease, and that wiped out many of the financial benefits we wanted to offer to our customers.

We knew it was going to be a complicated sell, but we thought we had an answer to even that thorny problem. By discounting the carpets and charging more for the monthly maintenance and using our own money instead of the intermediary, we could comply with that difficult FASB rule. And so Jim Hartzfeld, Dan Hendrix, and I went out and lobbied hard for Evergreen, making personal presentations to customers we felt were financially sophisticated and possessed an environmental ethic.

We spoke to companies like Procter & Gamble, the University of Texas, British Petroleum, Ford, General Motors, Ernst & Young, the Environmental Protection Agency, the Tennessee Valley Authority, and in Canada, the government owned Crown corporation, British Columbia Building Corporation (BCBC).

While nearly all of them were interested in hearing about the Evergreen lease, and we had plenty of nibbles, almost without exception, they didn't bite. They bought Interface carpets, which was great, but not the lease.

Score one for the old business practices, zero for the new.

We regrouped and simplified the contract, slimming it down and minimizing legalese so that it is readily understandable (see Appendix B). We extended our warranty and began offering our own financing to jump-start what we were sure was the right approach: selling services rather than carpets. But at the end of the day, we wrote a grand total of six Evergreen lease agreements. This Market 2.0 approach, with all of its many financial advantages and environmental benefits, failed to gain an appreciable market foothold. Why? I think there are at least ten key reasons:

1. Obtaining the "services" of a carpeted floor through our Evergreen lease was more complicated than just buying and owning the carpet outright.
2. Our customers recognized the benefits—financial and environmental—of the Evergreen lease, but faced internal "turf" obstacles when they tried to move funds out of capital and into operating expenses.
3. Capital costs seemed almost free to our customers, as they "disappeared" into a depreciation account. Once spent, they're gone. But operating costs appear every month.
4. Some of our customers thought the seven-and-a-half-year lease (calculated to comply with the accounting rules) was too long. They did not wish to be locked into a long-term contract to maintain their carpets. They wanted to be free to choose any product or service provider they might desire, and to maintain control over who had access to their buildings.
5. Other customers thought the lease period was too short. The carpet would look good and last for twenty years. Why should they pay for it as though it would only last for seven and a half?
6. And how much did it really cost them to use their own staff to maintain their own carpets, anyway? Internal budgets often were imprecise and did not cover the many added steps Interface would perform (special cleaning, replacing tiles, etc.), and this made the lease costs seem high by comparison . . .
7. . . . and the number one budgetary rule of all facilities managers is this: Thou Shalt Not Spend More Next Year than the Rate of Inflation Dictates!
8. While our own sales force received the same commissions for a job whether it was a lease or a purchase, many of them felt that selling Evergreen was a lot harder, slower, and more technically involved . . .
9. . . . and they were right. The Evergreen lease had to appeal to more constituencies than a simple purchase. The needs of facility managers, the financial people, the executive leadership, the purchasing department, the architects and interior designers, the consultants, and the real estate divisions all had to be identified and met. Often those constituencies had different interests—

purchase price, tax implications, facility maintenance, sustainability, and so on. Every "sweet spot" had to be found and addressed, and that took time and really was a lot harder.

10. Sticker shock. The combined price of a floor-covering service,
its maintenance, cleaning, replacement, and recycling seemed too
high, even when it was actually less than the customer's total
combined costs when they owned that same carpet. As one potential customer told us, "I'm as green as anyone, but if your lease
costs me one penny more than an outright purchase, I'm not going for it."

In a word, the Evergreen lease was ahead of its time—far ahead. But its
time could yet come.

In the years since we have solved much of the recycling part of the equation, and virgin nylon, like the oil from which it is derived, is no longer
cheap. But the Evergreen lease still faces obstacles to success. It may be an
impossible sell without a change in the rules and a revision of the tax laws to
accommodate the delivery of services rather than products. Removal of oil
subsidies and the imposition of a cost on carbon would help, too, and I am
convinced they are coming.

The University of Texas at Houston is a longtime loyal customer, and as
anxious as any to embrace the lease. When it wouldn't work for them, that
was the nail in the coffin—it wouldn't work for anybody. The lease did fail
with UT Houston in 1999, but the university and Interface are both committed to environmental responsibility, so the will is there for both to keep
trying.

They too realize the current leasing regulations are like some of those
other perverse incentives that do not give a manufacturer any reason to reuse or lengthen the life of a product. In a rational and resource-constrained
world these must become a top priority. What can be done?

One, the recycling loop needs to be completely closed, and at Interface,
our Cool Blue and ReEntry 2.0 lines are beginning to do exactly that at
commercial scale and competitive cost. Second, the salvage-value dilemma
must be resolved. In order to do this successfully, the FASB and IRS regulations need to be reevaluated to allow products heading for recycling at the
end of their useful life to be included in operating leases.

Recycling old products into new is a good thing, and it must be encouraged through targeted incentives, rather than discouraged by perverse provisions that encourage consumption and waste. In nature, the incentive is obvious—survival. It's the same for us, though we humans seem to have a hard time seeing it.

As those reindeer on St. Matthew Island found out, resource depletion does not end well.

In the southwestern desert, monsoon rains in the summer often create temporary pools of water that, out in the middle of sun-scorched desolation, can teem with brine shrimp. Soon, even though that pool might be a thousand miles from the nearest ocean, seagulls appear to feed on them. All this activity takes place as the relentless summer sun evaporates their environment day by day, inch by inch.

The resource that supports all that life—water—is literally vanishing out from underneath and around them, evaporating into the air. So the creatures who call those desert pools home are in a big hurry to complete their life cycle—to grow, reproduce, and lay eggs—before the inevitable day comes when the water is gone.

Industrial civilization has been following that example. A process that took eons, and won't happen again, has bestowed on us a vast wealth of fossil fuels. And we are frantically taking, making, and wasting our way through that resource—literally sending it up in smoke. The difference is, the water those brine shrimp depend upon will return in a year or two with the new monsoon rains. Fossil fuels will not. The shrimp eggs can wait for years in the hot, parched sands. We cannot. Our responsibility, our charge, is to find ways to work with what we've been given by nature, and to emulate nature's highly effective ways: to eliminate the very concept of waste; to make what we need from available, renewable resources; to close the loop; and to feed our production lines to make our products with renewable or recycled raw materials. We must do this because, in the long term (and perhaps much sooner than that) there is no other way.

David Oakey, the design consultant you've already met, put it well when he said, "Man and nature have come apart, and I think the closer we can start to connect with nature again and be a 'system,' the better off we will be. There's a lot we can learn from nature. Sustainable design, or as I call it, 'respect for the environment,' leads my thinking process."

So what does nature have to say about the way we conduct our commerce and design our products? Quite a bit, as it turns out.

As I mentioned before, I speak to about 150 audiences every year through many kinds of media. I describe the personal path that I have chosen, and the surprisingly profitable one it has become for Interface to follow, in this drive to achieve sustainability by the year 2020. One of the most effective exercises I use in those speeches goes something like this:

First, I have everyone close their eyes and picture in their mind's eye their ideal comfort zone, that place of peace and repose, tranquillity and creativity, the place that makes them feel the happiest—their perfect comfort zone. Then, with their eyes still closed, I ask those who are picturing a place that is outdoors to raise their hands. Finally, I ask folks to open their eyes and look around. What do they see?

A room full of raised hands and a lot of surprised expressions. It seems nearly everyone thought that their perfect place—a forest, a meadow, a sparkling river—was something only they were imagining. Instead, it was all but universal. In hundreds of cases, with audiences all over the world, it has never been otherwise.

And so it was only natural that we started to ask ourselves a related question. How does nature design its own carpets and floors? To find out the answer, let me have David Oakey tell the story.

"Five years ago my design team held a workshop with Janine Benyus. She introduced the concept of biomimicry—using nature as a design mentor and a source of inspiration—and she challenged us to integrate nature's principles into design concepts for carpet tile.

"The science of biomimicry provides us with a framework that we can use in the design process, a road map to sustainability that is complementary to the seven fronts of Mission Zero. In Janine's book, *Biomimicry: Innovation Inspired by Nature*, she talks about a set of natural design rules:

- "Nature runs on sunlight.
- "Nature uses only the energy it needs.
- "Nature fits form to function.
- "Nature recycles everything.
- "Nature rewards cooperation.
- "Nature banks on diversity.
- "Nature demands local expertise.
- "Nature curbs excesses from within.
- "Nature taps the power of limits.

"So we sent our designers out into the forest to see what they could learn about how nature would go about designing a carpet. They were befuddled at first. They thought they were being sent out to copy flowers and leaves, but they discovered something far more interesting than flowers or leaves.

"What they came back with was 'organized chaos'; no two square yards of forest floor were the same, yet they all blended perfectly together in a harmonious whole. They realized that there is no perfect flower and there is no solid color; it's just a diverse system. This chaos was characterized best by the word 'entropy.'

"The goal then turned to designing a modular carpet the same way. In nature, each 'module' is slightly different in pattern and color, and that was the whole challenge. It was a challenge for the designers to let go of the aesthetics of 'perfection' and sameness, and we needed to get our engineers' assistance. How could you make it so that in one production run, the color and design of every single tile would come out slightly different?

"Suddenly you were bringing designers and engineers together to make it happen, something that had not been done before. The problem was solved, and thus began a new product line named in honor of that afternoon stroll through the Georgia forest—Entropy.™

"Designing carpet the way nature would had many advantages. We found out by accident that we could actually lay it randomly instead of in a monolithic fashion. We found out that it was easy to make repairs, because the tile didn't (couldn't, if we tried) match exactly in relation to the other tiles, so it didn't make any difference if it looked slightly different. It was *better* if it did!

"Off-quality practically vanished; inspectors could not find defects among the deliberate 'imperfection' of no two tiles alike. And it practically eliminated installation waste. Now, every tile could find a place in a symphony of color and pattern, all different, all harmonious and pleasing, with none having to be discarded as 'wrong.' Dye lots now merged indistinguishably, obviating the need for extra tiles of the original dye lot—inventory waiting to be used. And the user could now rotate tiles to equalize wear the way we rotate tires on our car to extend their useful life."

And so how has this product been received by the market? In a word, *spectacularly!* Entropy™ became the biggest-selling product in the shortest period of time in Interface's entire history. And it's not only because of the many technical advantages that emulating nature has given this product. It has everything to do with that perfect place I ask my audience to imagine.

"Nature's designs are organic," said Oakey. "Natural shapes depend upon their functions. They are not linear. They are not based on lines and are therefore not limited by them. Entropy™ looks beautiful on a floor for the same reasons that a carpet of leaves, twigs, earth, and rocks looks beautiful on the floor of a forest."

In other words, it reproduces that perfect place we all imagine when we close our eyes and subliminally brings outdoors indoors. It's no wonder a product like that sold so well! As David said, we discovered—after the fact—many other advantages in applying the principles of biomimicry to carpet design.

Repairing traditional carpet requires calling in specially trained repair professionals. The randomness of Entropy™ allows for much more flexibility. For instance, if a tile in a hotel room is damaged, the housekeeping staff can replace it—not worrying about which way to lay it—and in a matter of minutes the room is ready again. It's really that simple.

Here's another example of biomimicry-assisted design. Have you ever wondered how a gecko lizard can cling upside down to the ceiling? It can even hang from a glass surface, using just a single toe. That is one powerful adhesive! Could we use something similar to hold our carpet tiles in place? After all, carpet adhesives can be nasty chemicals that contribute to indoor air pollution, and we have vowed to rid our product line of them.

Is there something we can learn from a lizard?

These questions were posed at an out-of-the-box brainstorming session at InterfaceFLOR in 2006. It turned out that a gecko makes use of a powerful adhering mode known as van der Waals forces, a kind of intermolecular bonding that happens between microscopic hairs on the gecko's feet and the molecular layer of water that's present on nearly everything. But simply asking the question, How does nature do it? inspired our people to come up with something completely revolutionary: TacTiles, a patent-pending, 2$^1/2$-by-2$^1/2$-inch adhesive tape made from polyethylene terephthalate (PET) plastic—the same material that is used to make soda bottles.

These tape squares are attached to the underside of the backing of adjoining InterfaceFLOR carpet tiles, sticky side up, bonding the tiles laterally to each other—not to the floor—to create a "floating" carpet that gravity keeps in place. Because TacTiles contain no liquid components, their use virtually eliminates the issue of volatile organic compounds (VOC), so they can be used to install tile almost anywhere at any time, even in an occupied space. The glue they replace could react in devilish ways with the floor, especially with uncured concrete, to produce VOCs; but no more with TacTiles.

TacTiles allow installers to lay our carpet tiles directly on top of most hard surfaces without attaching the carpet to the floor. They offer a far lower environmental impact, and save installers a tremendous amount of time.

"TacTiles reflect the company's Mission Zero promise by providing 'total performance with zero glue,'" said John Bradford, our vice president of research and development, whom you have met before. "The use of TacTiles versus traditional glue showed a ninety percent lower environmental impact, according to life cycle assessment. TacTiles also reduce waste from the installation process. Instead of bringing rollers, fans, spray equipment, and ten-pound buckets of glue to the site, installers using TacTiles bring only two-pound boxes of TacTiles and a handy, four-pound dispenser."

When you build your design around a natural model, good things happen and people become excited. I'm sure you've heard your mother say, "It's nature's way," referring to the right way of doing something. I'm sure you've also heard her say, "It's only human." That's usually when she's saying you've made a mistake. That is one key difference between how nature does things and how we humans perform. Nature learns from mistakes and evolves a better answer—or else. We humans can find it hard to break free of the status quo, even though it may be leading us to bankruptcy. Even killing us. How long would an organism that refused to learn survive under nature's rules?

We've taken a look at some of the things that Interface has done to move away from the old practices of the first industrial revolution and toward the new, sustainable practices of the next. Other companies, different from ours, will pursue their own, different strategies and technologies. As this new industrial revolution gathers speed, the winners will be the most resource-efficient. At whose expense will they win?

At the expense of the resource-*in*efficient. Technology, at its best, will emulate nature and eliminate those corporations that can't—or won't—adapt to the changing environment of resource scarcity.

But wait, some of you might say, isn't technology the problem here? Didn't you say that we can't solve our problems using the thinking that got us into them? How can technology help us when all you have to do is look around to see that technology is nature's sworn enemy?

The argument between technophiles and the technophobes—one saying that technology will save us, the other that technology will doom us—has been going on for a long time without a resolution. I think the time has come to reconcile these opposing points of view.

The key is in recognizing—and incorporating—the major differences between the first industrial revolution and the next. Done right (and the seven-face climb up Mount Sustainability is a good road map to *right*), we can reconcile those seemingly opposite points of view. I'll show you what I mean.

There is a well-known environmental impact equation popularized by Paul and Anne Ehrlich that declares $I = P \times A \times T$. I is environmental impact (the bigger, the worse), P is population, A is affluence, and T is technology. Some aspects of the equation are subjective and therefore not quantifiable. But the equation is still useful in a directional sense to help us understand what is going on in the industrial system. Increase any of these factors and you make things worse, from an environmental point of view. Increase them all and you've got a pretty good description of what's been going on for the last three hundred years.

Population is part of the problem. Affluence is part of the problem. And technology is part of the problem. In other words, impact comes from people, what they consume, and how it's made. This seems to reinforce the technophobe's point of view. You can see from the equation that just better or worse, or more, technology will never lead us out of our environmental mess, no matter how vigorously the technophiles assert that it will. Is a laptop computer "better technology" than an old IBM PC? Sure it is. But the extractive, abusive, take-make-waste processes that went into its construction are not only the same, they are likely worse. A lot of stuff has been mined, extracted, and distilled to produce that laptop.

How would the technophiles respond? By recognizing that the technologies that have dominated the industrial system—call them $T_1$—share some attributes. They are extractive, linear (take-make-waste), driven by fossil fuel-derived energy, wasteful, abusive, and focused on increasing labor productivity (more things per man-hour).

The equation looks like this: $I = P \times A \times T_1$.

But what if the characteristics of T were improved, not just here and there, but with its very basis fundamentally changed to incorporate the technologies of the next industrial revolution? Renewable instead of extractive? Cyclical rather than linear take-make-waste? Focused on resource efficiency rather than labor productivity? Benign in their effects on the biosphere, rather than abusive? And what if they emulated natural processes, in which there are no wastes? Mightn't it be possible to restate the environmental impact equation as $I = \dfrac{P \times A}{T_2}$?

Move T from the numerator to the denominator and we can change the world. The mathematically minded will see this immediately. Now, the more technology of the right kind, the better. By harnessing technology to reduce environmental impacts, the technophiles and the technophobes, the environmentalists and the industrialists could be aligned and allied in their efforts to redesign and reinvent commerce (and save civilization).

Such a transformation will not happen overnight. There must surely be a transitional equation: $I = \dfrac{P \times A \times T_1}{T_2}$.

But in time as the new industrial revolution takes hold, $T_2$ must supplant $T_1$ altogether in the way we make things.

Furthermore, $T_2$ begins to put millions of unemployed people to work, increasing resource-productivity by using an abundant resource—labor—to conserve the natural resources that are in decline. Technology becomes the friend of labor, not its enemy. Technology becomes part of the solution, not a prime mover behind the problem.

You can see that tinkering with technology won't do the job. A better, different T must move to the denominator. But how will it get there? Will simple market forces do the job of phasing out $T_1$ and replacing it with $T_2$?

I don't think so. In their book, *Natural Capitalism: Creating the Next Industrial Revolution*, Paul Hawken, Amory Lovins, and L. Hunter Lovins put it this way: "For all their power and vitality, markets are only tools. They make a good servant but a bad master and a worse religion. They can be used to accomplish many important tasks, but they can't do everything, and it's a dangerous delusion to begin to believe that they can—especially when they threaten to replace ethics or politics."

You see, it is all well and good to drive a hybrid car, install solar panels, eliminate waste, and change your lightbulbs to more energy-efficient types. All of that can and will happen, one mind at a time. But to redesign commerce, we have to do more than change the bulbs.

We have to change the laws.

# 12 | On Leadership, Programs, and Policies

*We choose to go to the moon in this decade, not because it is easy,
but because it is hard; because the goal will serve to organize and
measure the best of our energies and skills; because the challenge is
one we are willing to accept, one we are unwilling to postpone, and
one which we intend to win.*

PRESIDENT JOHN F. KENNEDY, September 1962

With those words, the thirty-fifth president of the United States, standing under the hot sun on a football field at Rice University, issued a generational challenge. He dared America not only to dream the impossible, but to achieve it. The Russians had launched their *Sputnik* into orbit first, sent a man into space first. So when President Kennedy committed our nation to landing a man on the moon and bringing him back safely in ten years, many people doubted we could accomplish it. But less than seven years later Neil Armstrong and Buzz Aldrin stepped out onto Tranquility Base.

From the moment the forty-fourth president of the United States takes office in 2009, America—and the rest of the world—will be watching to see if this new leader can also "organize and measure the best of our energies and skills." Not to put an American on the moon, but to meet another generational challenge: steering a course through the triple storms of a climate crisis, a security crisis, and an economic crisis, all striking at the same time.

As I write this, no one knows the name of that president yet. While there are substantial (some would say enormous) differences that separate the candidates, what I have to say in this chapter—about what government can do to help plot that safe and prosperous course—is applicable across the political spectrum. We don't have a Republican problem or a Democratic problem. We have a global problem that needs the very best from all of us.

Will a new president step back from leadership and place blind trust in what he perceives to be an all-seeing, all-knowing market? Will he succumb to temptation and issue more regulations, unfunded mandates, and edicts? Or is there a better way here, too? The kind of future our children and grandchildren will live to see depends on getting this thing right. What should he do?

Well, I expect you already know my thoughts about placing too much faith in that mythical invisible hand of the market. Trusting in its ultimate wisdom (just like mistrusting anything government comes up with) may be bred into the bones of most business people. But as long as the market is steered by invisible subsidies and perverse incentives, as long as it remains blind to the real costs—economic, social, and environmental—it cannot steer a safe course through the storm any better than a blind helmsman can keep a ship off a reef.

If the market is blind to the externalities and prices are dishonest, what kind of allocator of resources can it be, stumbling along in its blindness?

Looking to government for all the answers is not a solution either. I hope by now you realize that everything we have accomplished at Interface in the name of sustainability has been done with good old capitalist self-interest firmly in mind. Cost savings, returns on investment, product innovation, customer service, and market share—not just sustainability—were the stars we were steering by. And that is why we are succeeding. Sustainability has been our transit and our compass. And governmental edict has had nothing to do with it.

There were no incentives, no tax breaks, no subsidies, mandates, or government agencies forcing us to do a thing. In fact, from our experience with the landfill gas project (the one the Environmental Protection Agency said was way too small to work), I'd say we were leading them.

That's not the same thing as saying government has no role to play in retooling our industrial society. Our regulatory system of laws and limits, goaded into action by people like Rachel Carson, has slowed the rate of abuse that we inflict upon the world. Her *Silent Spring* created a shock wave that led to virtually all of the legislation of the 1960s and 1970s that was aimed at protecting the environment, including the creation of the Environmental Protection Agency.

And there are victories to celebrate as a result. The air over Pittsburgh is clearer. The Cuyahoga River doesn't catch fire anymore. Fish may be found far up the once toxic Thames in London. Regulation has also internalized some of the externalities—by imposing clean-up costs on industries and municipalities—but nowhere near all of them.

Still, the overall global trends are nearly all moving in the wrong direction. Populations of many species are crashing. Biodiversity is plummeting. Rain forests and aquifers are vanishing, and deserts are growing, as are oceanic dead zones caused by polluted runoff in our rivers. The human footprint is also growing, while the planet's carrying capacity (remember St. Matthew Island?) is declining.

That the government doesn't get it was proven to us when our Evergreen lease bumped up against IRS rules that made it too difficult to lease our carpets to our customers. And there was that truly remarkable and perverse Clean Air Act prohibition that left some automakers unable or unwilling to sell us a fleet of clean California cars in Georgia.

Add to these examples all the other perverse incentives written into law—sometimes in the open, usually not—that favor one industry or one technology over all the rest, and you'll see that without intelligent government action that dares us to achieve the impossible, that sets smarter goals and writes wiser laws to encourage rather than block innovation, our entire society will never make it to the top of Mount Sustainability.

Let me offer a bit of historical perspective on the topic of that avowed enemy of commerce, government. After all, quite a few folks in the world of business view the government as nothing but an obstacle to a profit. And sometimes it is.

For a long time now commerce and government have been locked in a struggle for control. Sometimes one of them gets ahead of the other, and nobody likes the result. The truth is, the government can't run a business any better than a business can run a government. Someone once said that there should be "no empires without umpires," and I think he was onto something. But I prefer to say that you can't have a football game without players (business) anymore than you can have one without referees (government).

Where did this all begin? If we go back in time (and not very far), some people who called themselves "noble" had life and death powers over the common folk, who were literally chattel (property), and any nobleman could treat them as he pleased. He could work them to death, even kill them for sport, if he so desired. In response, the field of ethics emerged. Ethics is about doing the right thing, and today we know that one person holding the power of life and death over another is manifestly wrong.

But what if a "nobleman" of more recent times—say, a wealthy property owner—covets a specific tract of land to develop for his own personal profit or enjoyment? Let's give that land a name, the northwestern corner of Wyoming—an amazing natural wonderland of mountains and geysers. Should he be able to build a fence around it to keep everyone else out? Should he be able to pave it over with buildings and theme park amusement rides, and charge admission?

To head off just such a possibility in 1872, the United States Congress, under President Ulysses S. Grant, set aside Yellowstone National Park for all Americans to see and enjoy. Later, President Theodore Roosevelt, urged by that explorer, writer, mountaineer, and naturalist John Muir, raised the public's awareness of the natural wonders of America. Still later, Woodrow Wilson created the National Park Service, along with the Grand Canyon, Yosemite, and Grand Teton National parks.

So the notion evolved that ethics should extend to the land, and become part of our system of laws. The ethical thing to do, the right thing to do, was to protect these cathedrals of natural beauty for all people and for all time.

Then, in 1933, Aldo Leopold pushed the definition of "land ethics" when he observed that what happened to the plants native to even the most common, unscenic places of the world determined something he called "habitat." That's Latin for "it inhabits" and refers to a natural area where specific organisms can live.

Habitat, in turn, supports animal life, dictating what species are able to live there and prosper. From this, the field we know today as "ecology" developed; the science of studying the interconnected relationships among flora, fauna, fungi, and even the microbial world that form the entire web of life.

From that new perspective, some smart folks began to ask new questions, such as, "If the brown bear stops breeding above elevations of five thousand feet (as it has), what does it mean for us Homo sapiens? How are humans affecting the web of life, the biosphere that we are clearly a part of?"

Then that brave and brilliant woman, Rachel Carson, came up with one answer to that question in her landmark book, *Silent Spring*, which was published in 1962. In it, she asserted (and proved) that the chemicals that industries were discharging into the environment were causing hidden but growing harm to the entire web of life, from the insects to the birds to the fish, right on up to us—people. Suddenly, she showed us we were all connected. What happened to one creature—a bird dying in a too-fragile egg—could spell a big problem for us all.

The chemical industry, an integral part of the modern industrial system, fought her tooth and nail (and lost), and her book launched what we think of today as the modern American environmental movement. But really, what she did was to extend the field of ethics beyond people and land to include all creatures great and small. And, as I said, from this stunning realization, this extension of what it meant to do the right thing, came the laws aimed at protecting the environment.

That included the rules and regulations Interface was complying with (and thinking that was all we needed to do) back in 1994. But I know—and now you know—that that doesn't take us even one step up the slopes of Mount Sustainability.

Am I suggesting that government needs to tell us all how to become sustainable? Not on your life. Winston Churchill once said that you can count on government to come up with the right solution once it has tried all the others. But sometimes, *sometimes*, governments do hit that sweet spot between the blind market that's leading us off a cliff and the dead hand of overregulation that stifles innovation and commerce.

We saw it happen back in the 1970s, when the Arab members of OPEC announced that they would no longer ship oil to any country that supported Israel. That meant the United States, its allies in Western Europe, and Japan. Oil prices skyrocketed, and our economy experienced an enormous drag that pulled it down into recession.

The U.S. government, under two Republican presidents, responded with a blend of commands—lowering the maximum speed on federal highways to 55 mph, creating the Strategic Petroleum Reserve—and strategies aimed at lowering energy consumption.

The most effective strategy—bar none—was when Congress issued corporate average fuel economy (CAFE) standards to U.S. automakers in 1975. This law mandated a 27.5 average mpg for the entire U.S. fleet, an improvement of about 7.5 mpg over the status quo. How companies would hit this new mark was left up to them and the market. The result?

We have already discussed the dramatic result. Between 1975 and 1985, the United States cut its oil use 17 percent while its GDP grew 27 percent (a 35 percent reduction in petro-intensity). Oil imports fell 50 percent, and imports from the Persian Gulf were slashed by a full 87 percent. We showed the world that we could innovate our way out of a problem from the demand side faster than OPEC could squeeze off the supply. And as I have said, OPEC's ability to set world oil prices was shattered for a decade.

There is a powerful lesson to be learned from that.

Sadly, when our success sent crude prices tumbling in 1985–86, U.S. automakers turned their considerable talents to making cars bigger, heavier, and more powerful, but not more efficient. While some engines could squeeze out more horsepower per gallon than before, the lumbering vehicles to which they were bolted grew so obese that the improvements were largely negated. According to one auto industry analysis, the average new U.S. light vehicle in 2003 had 24 percent more weight and 93 percent more horsepower, but traveled only 1 percent more miles per gallon. Meanwhile, U.S. oil imports from the Middle East tripled.

There is a powerful lesson in that, too. The status quo is an opiate.

We all have heard about those Department of Defense specifications for hotdogs that run to hundreds of pages. But note that Presidents Nixon and Ford didn't tell GM how to boost the efficiency of its cars anymore than President Kennedy told NASA how to design its rockets. They set bold national goals, energized people to achieve them, and created targeted incentives that nudged folks in the right direction. They put money into solving the really big problems but let individuals and private industry figure out the best ways forward.

There are other examples of big national problems being solved on a big national level. Back in 1919, a young Army officer named Eisenhower traveled across America and experienced up close and firsthand how hard it was to drive from one city, one state, one coast to the next. Roads started and stopped willy-nilly. Routes were circuitous, and the surfaces were a patchwork of paving, gravel, and double-tracked dirt. It was, in nearly every way, a nineteenth-century (or worse) transportation system, not up to the demands of a growing, twentieth-century nation.

Then, in the 1940s, Eisenhower saw the German autobahn. Even damaged by war it was an engineering marvel. It must have stuck with him, because when Ike became president in 1953 the creation of an interconnected network of good, high-speed roads was high on his agenda: the interstate highway system. Though the system had been planned for decades, Eisenhower put the weight and authority of the United States (with some—maybe too much—help from Detroit) behind the project, and work began in earnest. We are all familiar with the results, both good and bad.

Today we have a very similar situation with our national electric transmission system. I call it a system, but it really is more like a balkanized hodgepodge of two hundred thousand miles of power lines, owned and operated by five hundred or more different entities.

Now consider the boom in wind-generated electricity we explored in chapter 7. The vast majority of that power is found in windy, rural areas far from where the vast majority of electricity is consumed. A rough calculation suggests that North and South Dakota alone could generate half of the country's total electrical needs, but the country would have to move to the Dakotas to use it. Why?

Because there is no national "highway system" of modern, high-voltage, direct-current, low-loss transmission lines to move that infinitely renewable power from where it can be created to where it is needed. And making piecemeal changes in our existing grid means dealing with multiple companies, state and local governments, individual property owners, and more permits than I have time or space to list. Laws that govern utility investments work against multistate projects, giving local utilities no easy way to recover their investments. It's a mess.

It is very much like that nonsystem of roads Ike found on his drive out west in 1919. It's in such terrible shape that when T. Boone Pickens broke ground for the world's largest wind farm on the plains of Texas, he had to buy a corridor of land to string his own transmission lines to move that power to the nearest city.

It is a pathetic state of affairs that we've got a twentieth-century power grid that can't serve our twenty-first-century needs so that a nation that's addicted to foreign oil and filthy coal can shed its addiction, a nation that has enormous reserves of renewable energy can tap them efficiently. The blind market, giving carbon a free ride, can't see its way to the right solution. Without a president who is willing to throw the weight and authority of the United States behind a new, national, high-voltage, direct-current transmission system, it won't happen. The parallel with the highways and Ike is obvious.

So here's the thing. Government doesn't know enough about your business or mine to tell us how to run it sustainably. But there is a clear place for leadership and a place for enlightened public policies that support—not distort—the market for sustainable business practices.

Someone has to identify and strip away those perverse incentives. Someone has to set smart goals and level the playing field to create an honest market; that is, to get the prices right, so that industry is free to innovate in the direction of sustainability and survival. That's why I believe there is a place for the federal government to think deep, look long, and enable everyone who competes in the market to choose rightly.

I can hear some gnashing teeth. *Maybe that would work in Europe, where people don't mind being told what to do. But not here in America!* What evidence is there that such an approach might work here?

Well, how about Alaska?

In a misguided effort to keep a fishery from being depleted, before 1995 the annual catch season for Alaskan halibut lasted all of three days. That's right, three days. And thanks to the government, those days were on the calendar. There was no concern for weather. If you were a halibut fisher, you were out on the ocean come hell or high water on only those days, and you pulled in as many fish as you could.

Naturally, when you landed them, you found the market was glutted with everyone else's halibut, and so despite all the terrible risks you'd taken, prices were low. There had to be a better way, and there was.

A public-private partnership between the government and those salty, independent fisherman decided to privatize the halibut fishery by dividing the annual quota into "catch shares" that were owned by the fishermen themselves. The result?

Today the halibut season lasts eight months, not three days, and fishermen can decide to land their catch when the price is right. Where once the incentive was to catch as many fish as possible in the shortest amount of time, now the fishermen sometimes prefer to catch even fewer fish than their quota allows. Why? Because conservation and care for the fishery drives up the price of halibut! Who wins? The fishermen *and* the fish.

Market mechanisms plus smart government intervention can work wonders. Unfortunately, that which is clear in the business world can get pretty fogged up in Washington. I know. I experienced that change in perspective up close and firsthand.

In November 1996, just two years after my spear in the chest epiphany, I was nominated to be on the President's Council on Sustainable Development (PCSD). President Bill Clinton had created the PCSD in 1993 to be a high-level body that would represent business, the environmental community, labor, women's advocates, universities, government at all levels— national, state, city—and Native Americans. The job was to find consensus among widely divergent views about achieving sustainability on a national scale and to bring that consensus to the president for action.

Well, I was still trying to figure out what sustainability meant for Interface. I had a business to run and plenty of challenges of my own to meet, so I was reluctant to sign up for a new job of any description.

But then my friend Huey Johnson from San Francisco reminded me that when the president calls, you do not say no, and that "one policy is worth ten thousand programs." You might say Huey was onto that leadership principle I mentioned earlier—that there is a natural limit to what any one of us can do, but no natural limit to the positive power of leadership. That is the true power of one. So I reluctantly agreed.

The culmination of PCSD's work during Clinton's first term was a report entitled "Sustainable America, A New Consensus." It advocated noble goals. Here they are, as they were delivered to the president just before I showed up.

### Goal 1: *Health and the Environment*
Ensure that every person enjoys the benefits of clean air, clean water, and a healthy environment at home, at work, and at play.

### Goal 2: *Economic Prosperity*
Sustain a healthy U.S. economy that grows sufficiently to create meaningful jobs, reduce poverty, and provide the opportunity for a high quality of life for all in an increasingly competitive world.

### Goal 3: *Equity*
Ensure that all Americans are afforded justice and have the opportunity to achieve economic, environmental, and social well-being.

### Goal 4: *Conservation of Nature*
Use, conserve, protect, and restore natural resources—land, air, water, and biodiversity—in ways that help ensure long-term social, economic, and environmental benefits for ourselves and future generations.

### Goal 5: *Stewardship*

Create a widely held ethic of stewardship that strongly encourages individuals, institutions, and corporations to take full responsibility for the economic, environmental, and social consequences of their actions.

### Goal 6: *Sustainable Communities*

Encourage people to work together to create healthy communities in which natural and historic resources are preserved, jobs are available, sprawl is contained, neighborhoods are secure, education is lifelong, transportation and health care are accessible, and all citizens have opportunities to improve the quality of their lives.

### Goal 7: *Civic Engagement*

Create full opportunity for citizens, businesses, and communities to participate in and influence the natural resource, environmental, and economic decisions that affect them.

### Goal 8: *Population*

Move toward stabilization of U.S. population.

### Goal 9: *International Responsibility*

Take a leadership role in the development and implementation of global sustainable development policies, standards of conduct, and trade and foreign policies that further the achievement of sustainability.

### Goal 10: *Education*

Ensure that all Americans have equal access to education and lifelong learning opportunities that will prepare them for meaningful work, a high quality of life, and an understanding of the concepts involved in sustainable development.

All those goals sounded fine to me (how could you argue otherwise?), and many of the folks on that council believed in them, heart and soul. Their report offered a truly inspirational vision of a sustainable society, and one that would be difficult to fault from nearly any point of view. Indeed, we would be living in a better country today—cleaner, richer, safer, and more widely respected—if we had accomplished half of what was in that report.

But as time went on I came to realize that not everyone on the council was there for the same reasons. In the harsh clarity of hindsight, a skeptical observer would note the presence of Enron's Ken Lay on the council and come to the appropriate conclusion. At the time, Enron was the country's seventh-largest corporation, and Ken surely had his hands in the energy market; though, like a lot of folks, I was (and remain) unclear about what those hands were doing. Thinking back, I'm really not sure why he was there. But who am I to judge?

However, I had to learn for myself what a swamp full of alligators Washington could be. The message was hammered home when another council member took Jim Hartzfeld (my liaison to the council) aside to ask, "Why is Ray really here? What does Interface stand to gain? What's your angle?"

Were we hoping to sell more carpets to Congress? To the military? Push through a tariff on imported carpets? *What was my angle?* I was surprised and more than a little bit shocked when Jim relayed the questions. Though I'd competed in the world of business for decades, I was still innocent about politics.

After President Clinton was reelected, Vice President Al Gore (to whom we reported) charged the renewed PCSD with implementing the "vision statement" of "Sustainable America" and, in particular, to take on the issue of global climate change. (He was on that case even then.) In his charge to the council, he challenged us to "look long, think big, and be creative."

It was around that time that I found myself nominated to be a cochair of the whole council. I admit to being every bit as reluctant to take on this larger job as I had been to join the council in the first place, if not more so. But in for a penny, in for a pound, and believe me when I say it was a further education in the limits of government. I'll explain.

In spite of some cynicism here and there, we all honestly thought we were doing something useful by helping the administration prepare for the lead up to the negotiations that would produce the Kyoto Protocol, the international treaty designed to reduce greenhouse gas emissions. While Al Gore did sign the protocol, the effort to ratify it in the U.S. Senate (a necessary step to actually doing something) broke down and went nowhere.

It all came to a head on July 25, 1997, when the U.S. Senate unanimously passed by a 95–0 vote the Byrd-Hagel Resolution. It stated that the sense of the Senate was that the United States should not be a signatory to

Kyoto. Senators were terrified that reducing greenhouse gas emissions by 7 percent over the next fifteen years would just cripple American industry. And that sounded truly dire. Who could be in favor of something like that?

For a little context, it is worthwhile restating that as Congress gave up and ran for cover, Interface was cutting its net greenhouse gas emissions not by 7 percent, but by 71 percent (in absolute tons) within twelve years, while our sales were increasing by two thirds and our earnings were doubling. Interface wasn't crippled by reducing our greenhouse gas emissions; we profited from it. So that congressional terror was pretty much stuffed with hot air, lobbyist cash, and so much dead straw.

As a result, the world left the United States behind. The resulting accord—signed by 182 other countries—was never brought to the U.S. Senate for a vote, and it was held up for ridicule by a new president who was hostile to science in general and the science of climate change in particular.

Not surprisingly, with no leader in sight, with science all but banned from the White House, with efforts to accurately assess the scope and severity of the problem thwarted (indeed, with a great deal of active countermeasures in full cry, trying to fuzz up the science and the urgency), U.S. greenhouse gas emissions rose 16 percent between the year the President's Council on Sustainable Development was chartered and midway through President George W. Bush's second term. Today the United States remains the only developed country in the world that has not ratified the treaty. And, lest we forget, we remain, with China, the two most significant greenhouse gas emitters.

This calls to mind philosopher Edmund Burke, who said that all it takes for evil to succeed is for good men to do nothing. Now, global warming has no conscience, no soul. It cannot be evil. But sitting idly by and doing nothing to stop an impending catastrophe that will cause harm to many millions of people around the globe (not to mention millions of other species) *is* evil. Deliberately choosing ignorance over knowledge *is* evil. And sowing deliberate misinformation to keep people from acting in their own self-interest, that's evil, too.

For all that we failed to accomplish, the council did manage to start something important, even if it was by accident. It granted something very important in leadership: permission. There were many dedicated government workers who were assigned to help the council. They came from throughout the executive branch, from the General Services Administration, the Department of Energy, the Environmental Protection Agency, the Food and Drug Administration, the Department of the Interior, the Department of Commerce, the National Oceanic and Atmospheric Administration (NOAA), and even the State Department. For some of the people it might have been just another job, like drawing up specs for hotdogs.

But I know that more than a few, having taken advantage of the permission granted them, left with their minds opened to new ways of thinking, new ways of protecting the environment, new determination to do so, and new ideas for running the biggest organization in the world, the United States government. I know, because today, almost a decade later, some of them have taken up where PCSD left off.

One PCSD veteran influenced the chief architect for the government's General Services Administration. Against substantial headwinds from a disinterested administration, he pushed through a regulation that required every new federal building to be LEED certified. Why is that important?

The Leadership in Energy and Environmental Design Green Building Rating System, developed by the U.S. Green Building Council, provides standards for environmentally sustainable construction. There are sixty-nine possible points that can be awarded for green features, and buildings can qualify for four levels of certification:

- **Certified**: 26 to 32 points
- **Silver**: 33 to 38 points
- **Gold**: 39 to 51 points
- **Platinum**: 52 to 69 points

Since buildings collectively are the largest source of greenhouse gases here in the United States, and the government builds and owns a lot of them, GSA's policy was a big step in the right direction.

Another PCSD alumnus, Bill Becker, began as a Department of Energy liaison to the council and rose through the DOE to run its Central Region operations, before leaving to join the University of Colorado's School of Public Affairs in Denver. In 2006, Bill called me with an unusual proposal. How would I like to reconvene PCSD?

*Why?* I asked.

*To assess the country's progress in implementing the PCSD's recommendations.*

Well, my first reaction was, *No way*. We already knew the answer; there wasn't much progress to assess. But, as we talked, Bill convinced me that it could be worthwhile; then he and I persuaded Jonathan Lash, president of the World Resources Institute and the other PCSD cochair, to join in issuing the invitation. The Johnson Foundation graciously offered their exceptionally fine conference facility, Wingspread, in Racine, Wisconsin. And invitations were issued to some forty people, including a representative cross section of former PCSD members.

At the first meeting, one participant, environmentalist and deep thinker David Orr of Oberlin College, observed that the last thing the country needed was another report that no one would ever read. Instead he came up with an idea that completely superseded the original intent.

He proposed that our job should be to write a one-hundred-day action plan for the next president of the United States. The goal: to lay out the steps a new president could take—with or without congressional approval—to jump-start the United States on mitigation of its greenhouse gas emissions. This became our new mission. Soon we adopted a name, too: the Presidential Climate Action Project (PCAP).

A nonpartisan blue ribbon steering panel was recruited and brought on board. It included business people and climate experts, policy experts, politicians, and a former NASA administrator. And by the way, would I cochair this larger effort with former senator Gary Hart?

In considering whether to accept the cochair, I thought, one way or the other, any presidential candidate is going to have to face up to the climate crisis. Al Gore saw to that soon after PCAP convened, when he published and filmed *An Inconvenient Truth*. I believed that that, coupled with Hurricane Katrina, created a propitious moment and another one of those supersaturated solutions that had precipitated this time into a vast shift of public attitudes.

When the people lead, the leaders follow.

At the same time, the cause-and-effect connections that join wasteful energy use, the economy, national security, dependence on imported oil, and global warming was being driven home further as oil prices started to spike. Folks were starting to look at their SUVs with very different eyes as they pumped one-hundred-dollar bills into the tank.

It was clear that one way or the other any candidate would have to face up to the economic crises, too. Commodity prices had soared. Long commutes had become unaffordable. The housing market was slumping. The stock market was sliding, threatening some of the biggest, oldest names on Wall Street. Businesses were shutting their doors. People felt pinched from every direction. And those high energy prices meant our dollars (which were worth less by the week) would be filling up the bank accounts of some of our avowed enemies. Trillions of dollars, largely borrowed from China, were ending up in some very bad places.

Clearly, it was all part of one tangled mare's nest of interconnected problems. Maybe we could help the next president cut through all the knots that make solving each of these challenges dependent on solving the others, and by doing so inform both campaigns. So I agreed with Bill and David, and together we said, *Let's do it.*

In June 2007, we all convened for the first of four planned National Leadership Summits—the one that quickly morphed into David's concept to design an action plan, PCAP—at Wingspread.

Wingspread, designed by Frank Lloyd Wright, was built as a fourteen-thousand-square-foot home in 1938. In 1959 the Johnson Foundation took it over and turned it into an international educational conference facility. It sits on beautiful rolling farmland near Wind Point, a peninsula on the western shore of Lake Michigan. The name Wingspread itself has amazing convening power, and the response was all we could have hoped for.

I think that every one of us there at Wingspread realized that this was way more than just a rehash of the old, Clinton-era PCSD. We weren't seeking consensus. We were planning a step-by-step campaign to achieve nothing less than a 90 percent reduction in U.S. greenhouse gases by 2050, with an interim 30 percent reduction by 2020 (the year Interface expects to be at zero emissions).

There were other significant differences. PCAP was to be like a rifle aimed at a very specific target: climate mitigation. It was a big enough subject, for sure, but the members were largely of one mind. Their differences were mostly rooted in their various areas of expertise.

The old PCSD had been more of a shotgun aimed at reaching consensus on the broad spectrum of environment, social equity, and economic development issues, a monumental undertaking considering the diverse backgrounds and viewpoints of the council members.

The venues for meetings were dramatically different, too. The PCSD typically found itself buried in some basement ballroom of a Washington,

D.C., hotel with no windows and the only light coming from incandescent chandeliers. (What's wrong with this picture for an environmental organization?)

For PCAP, the idyllic setting of Wingspread—light, airy, relaxed—together with the hospitality of the Johnson Foundation was wonderfully conducive to collegial discussion among the forty or so invited attendees at each of the five meetings (a fifth was added when we realized we needed it).

Ultimately, the value of each organization's effort will lie in results. The PCSD's work was largely ignored by both the Clinton and Bush administrations. The PCAP results will lie somewhere between zero and spectacular, depending strictly on some very early decisions made by the next president of the United States.

The June 2007 summit at Wingspread, its objective altered by David Orr's suggestion, began to develop the detailed battle plan for the next president's first one hundred days, a plan that focuses on what we can and must do to push that greenhouse gas needle back out of the red zone and in the direction of safety and stability.

Every step we recommended had profound implications for reducing this country's dependence on dirty, imported energy, and increasing our competitive standing in the industrial world, as well as mitigating climate disruption, and increasing national security, and economic opportunity. Or, as the recommendation was eventually entitled: "Security, Opportunity, and Stewardship" (SOS, pun intended).

It amazes me how the United States can lead the world in patents, technical innovation, and basic science and yet fail so miserably when it comes to transforming that edge into good American jobs. A nineteenth-century American inventor, Charles F. Brush, designed the first wind turbine to generate electricity. His company, Brush Electric in Cleveland, Ohio, grew up to become part of General Electric. And Charles Fritts was the American inventor who created the first working solar cell in 1884. Yet today American industry takes a backseat to German, Japanese, Chinese, even Danish, clean-tech companies.

Why have we allowed it? Could all the perverse incentives that make nineteenth-century energy and technology appear cheaper have something to do with our failure to grasp the greatest business opportunity of the twenty-first?

This must change, and putting all our faith in the blind-as-a-bat market won't get it done. It can't. Despite their different focus, on one thing the PCSD and PCAP agreed completely: *We've got to get the prices right, and only then can a sighted, informed, and honest market play its proper role.*

Further, it is going to take a president standing up in front of the nation and daring us to achieve the impossible again—to get off carbon, stop bankrolling our enemies, and generate American energy and good American jobs, not to mention new fortunes for the entrepreneurs who make it happen. As our work progressed, I felt more and more that PCAP might be just the thing to put that ball in motion.

What did we recommend? There are some 180 very specific actions, and you can read them all at www.climateactionproject.com. But here are the top ten:

*Mister President: In your first 100 days, you must . . .*

1. . . . . make a bold and immediate commitment to climate leadership in your inaugural address. Use it to rally the entire nation with an Apollo-like challenge to build a new and prosperous twenty-first-century economy of security, opportunity, and stewardship, powered by clean and renewable energy.
2. . . . announce that you intend to put America on the path to reduce its greenhouse gas emissions 30 percent below current levels by 2020, and 90 percent below current levels by 2050. You must set aggressive national goals to cut petroleum use in half, achieve an average vehicle efficiency of 50 miles per gallon, and obtain at least 20 percent of our electricity from renewable sources by the year 2020.
3. . . . take the lead by announcing that the largest single consumer of energy and generator of greenhouse gases, the United States government, will become climate neutral—zero net carbon emissions—by 2030. (The government's own Mission Zero!)
4. . . . . leverage that declaration to jump-start the market for clean technologies via the government's enormous and wide-reaching procurement policies. Establish a ten-year horizon (rather than two) for tax incentives for all renewable energy technologies.
5. . . . mobilize the market by putting a price on carbon with upstream cap-and-auction; end public subsidies of fossil fuels; and

offer a billion-dollar "platinum carrot" award, over five years, for transformative technologies that help America reduce its greenhouse gas emissions. Allocate a billion dollars yearly to states and localities that adopt policies that help the nation meet its carbon reduction and energy security goals.

6. . . . set off an economic boom by creating millions of new green jobs economywide. Establish a program of voluntary training and service for disadvantaged young people. Begin a rural renaissance in which farms and rural communities become the nation's chief suppliers of energy.

7. . . . prevent "carbon lock-in" by banning the construction of new coal-fired power plants that are not able to capture and store their greenhouse gas emissions; and do not provide public subsidies to new carbon-intensive fuels, such as liquid fuels from coal.

8. . . . rapidly increase CAFE standards for all U.S. vehicles, starting now.

9. . . . rebuild the federal capacity to lead by appointing (or reappointing) bona fide climate experts to climate-critical positions within the federal government, and rescind the Bush administration's executive order that permits political oversight of (and interference with) scientific reports.

10. . . . assert your executive authority to move the nation forward when rapid action is required for the public interest.

That last point is especially important. In PCAP's interim publication we noted that for too long the federal government's system of checks and balances has been more like checks and checkmate. The blame for this must be shared by both the executive and legislative branches. Clear, even compelling, ideas and strategies tend to get lost in the swamps when they arrive in Washington.

But this country has already experienced a disturbing extension of executive powers. Nobody at PCAP wanted a Guantánamo approach to solving our greenhouse gas, economic, and security problems. Running away from the rule of law is not a model we wished to follow.

In times of crisis some of our past presidents have entered that gray area between executive and legislative authorities. Teddy Roosevelt bypassed Congress and took his agenda straight to the people to win support. He believed he could use the presidency as a bully pulpit to move the nation in the right direction.

With a war to win and domestic prices spiraling out of control, President Franklin Roosevelt submitted two key pieces of legislation to Congress to stabilize prices. When they didn't act, he issued this challenge to them on Labor Day 1942.

> I regret to have to call to your attention the fact that neither of these two essential pieces of legislation has as yet been enacted into law. That delay has now reached the point of danger to our whole economy. In the event that the Congress should fail to act, and act adequately, I shall accept the responsibility, and I will act.

Congress got the message. FDR was never forced to carry out his threat. Instead, he was given wide discretionary powers to lead the nation through the generational challenge of the Second World War.

Today we face another generational challenge. Years of disinterest and delay have led us to another point of danger for our economy. America spends more than a billion dollars each day on imported oil, an unhealthy fraction going to the Middle East. When it is burned, it is gone forever, except for its legacy of destruction. At the moment we're spending $10 billion a month to fight wars in Iraq and Afghanistan, places we feel compelled to defend because of oil.

Meanwhile, jobs vanish, health care costs skyrocket, our schools can't afford to buy books, our roads crumble, and politicians argue over whether oil companies should be allowed to conduct exploratory drilling off our coasts. This is an unconscionable push, considering that they haven't drilled in 80 percent of the properties they already have under contract, and can't build and schedule rigs fast enough to put a new drill bit in the mud for the next four to five years.

And then there's global warming. It is a far more insidious emergency than the one that burst into flames with the attack on Pearl Harbor. It makes itself felt in scattered, incremental ways that are easy to ignore and seem, even to honest observers, unrelated. After all, what difference is there between three hundred parts per million of atmospheric carbon dioxide, and 400 ppm? What *is* a part per million anyway? And does it really matter if sea levels rise a few inches? A foot? Two feet? A meter? More?

As trite as the story has become from telling and retelling, the human reaction to global warming is a lot like that old saw about the frog that gets dropped into a pot of hot water. Naturally, he jumps out. He's no fool. But what happens when that frog is dropped into a pot of cold water? Not much. It feels pretty good. Then the burner is lit, the cold water becomes a bit warmer. Is the frog concerned? No. The water keeps getting warmer and warmer, degree by degree, until that frog is parboiled dead.

Until quite recently when energy prices became too high to ignore, far too many of us were like that frog, doing the backstroke while the waters grew warmer and warmer, degree by degree, all around us. That is why today— right now—we need to see some leadership from our government—our Congress and our next president.

From my own experience with the President's Council on Sustainable Development I know that it's not going to be easy. Not everyone is going to be pulling in the same direction. Some will try their damnedest to derail anything that seems to give government an edge in its eternal battle with commerce. And sometimes they will be right to do so.

But there's no getting away from the fact that we have not accomplished very much without genuine leadership in the past, and are unlikely to in the future. The next president of the United States is the one person with the potential to challenge, to inspire, to lead. He can take comfort in the many governors, mayors, civic leaders, federal agencies, and corporate executives who are pointing out a safe course through these concurrent crises— economic, environmental, and security. But he will need to act, and quickly, more quickly I believe, than relying on Congress will allow.

To get something done in a timely manner, the forty-fourth president is going to have to use (or, like FDR, threaten to use) executive authority to implement policies and programs that do not, by law, require legislation. That is why every PCAP recommendation was thoroughly vetted. Those things a president can do on his own and pass the test of constitutional legality have been identified in that first one-hundred-day action plan.

Congress may be consulted. Congress can even participate. But Congress must not get in the way.

Actually, if the president succeeds in using the bully pulpit to mobilize a nation to rise to this new generational challenge, I'm willing to bet Congress will not want to be left out of the parade. Indeed, soon enough you will think they were leading it by themselves all along the way.

A recent example of just this kind of leadership was shown by former vice president Gore on July 17, 2008. Speaking in Washington, he invoked JFK's call to land a man on the moon and said, in part:

> I'm proposing today a strategic initiative designed to free us from the crises that are holding us down and to regain control of our own destiny. It's not the only thing we need to do. But this strategic challenge is the linchpin of a bold new strategy needed to repower America. Today I challenge our nation to commit to producing 100 percent of our electricity from renewable energy and truly clean, carbon-free sources within ten years. This goal is achievable, affordable, and transformative. It represents a challenge to all Americans—in every walk of life—to our political leaders, entrepreneurs, innovators, engineers, and to every citizen. Our entire civilization depends upon us now embarking on a new journey of exploration and discovery. Our success depends on our willingness as a people to undertake this journey and to complete it within ten years. Once again, we have an opportunity to take a giant leap for humankind.

Amen. And I do not think he overstates the case in the least. But like JFK, Gore was ridiculed by experts who had all kinds of reasons why it couldn't be done. I heard a lot of the same talk when I steered Interface onto our Mission Zero course. It would be too expensive. The technology wasn't there yet. We'd surely fail. It was just not possible.

Yet, again, as Amory Lovins has often said, *If it exists, it must be possible.* So I would invite all of these experts to come to Georgia and see just what a quest for sustainability has meant for us. It exists—in our factories, our products, and our people. It is possible.

But there is a limit to what even a president, a Congress, or an entire country can do. There's an entire world out there, and much of it—even most of it—is still headed in the wrong direction, Kyoto Protocol or no.

One of the wisest things President Clinton ever said was that the one thing that really scared him was the prospect of China developing in the same way we did. And they surely seem to be, with new coal-fired power plants going up every few weeks, and thousands (something like fourteen thousand) new cars hitting the roads every day.

China's spectacular growth has been fueled almost entirely by coal and, now, gasoline. But as some climate scientists like to say, there isn't enough oil left to burn to make a decisive difference, but there's more than enough coal to kill us all. What can we do to change any of that?

Plenty. Remember this axiom: *There's a natural limit to what any one of us can accomplish, but no limit to what leadership can do.* Especially with the right followers. For, in my experience, it is the followers who make the leader—whether it's the people of Interface or America.

And, just as Interface has done well by doing good, this country—so long an environmental outlaw—with a little nerve, a lot of leadership, a committed populace, and the kind of innovation we own, can prosper by showing the world how it's done. Retooling the world's industrial base, transforming it from a dead end, eighteenth-century model into a new, sustainable model suitable for the twenty-first, may well be the greatest business opportunity that industry and entrepreneurs have ever seen.

Consider:

- One quarter of the world's population—1.6 billion people—lack access to electric power.
- Wood, dung, and agricultural residues still provide fuel for cooking and heating for 2.4 billion people.
- A total investment on the order of $4.2 trillion will be needed for new power generation worldwide between 2000 and 2030. Will that be invested wisely in renewables or foolishly in more fossil fuels?
- The global population is projected to increase from 6.7 billion in 2008 to 9 billion by 2050. Most of this growth will take place in cities. That means building the equivalent of a new city of more than a million people each week for the next forty-two years.

Two thirds of the growth in global energy demand during the next twenty-five years will take place in developing countries. If we have any hope of avoiding disastrous climate change, that growth has to be based on clean, renewable energy. And who should create the technologies that will supply that clean, renewable energy? When climate-friendly, sustainable technologies become the engine of growth in the global economy, American companies can drive that engine.

Unless somebody leads, nobody will. Why not us?

Great nations rise to great challenges, and no challenge today is greater than the one we face in shedding those old, unworkable wings and crafting new ones that will allow this civilization to fly—sustainably. This challenge reaches right down to the core of our relationship with the earth, and tests our capacity to make smart changes, tests that go way beyond showing what we can do as individuals. And they go way beyond what even a country as big and rich and smart as ours can do alone.

The key is leadership (and followership): in our families, where we can work to reduce each home's consumption of energy and resources; on the community level, where we can grasp this once-in-a-lifetime opportunity and turn a crisis into new businesses, new jobs, and new wealth.

In schools we can ditch obsolete curricula that mindlessly, unwittingly lock in the status quo and teach (even encourage) destruction in favor of a sustainable, thinking in the round, interdisciplinary systems approach to environmental problem solving.

In corporations beginning their own Mission Zero climbs up Mount Sustainability, profiting from the technology and know-how they create, saving on their bottom lines through efficiency, and selling better products to supportive customers everywhere to add to their top lines.

And on the national level, with one bold stroke and in one hundred days, the United States can become a major and committed leader and, once again, an inspiration to the world.

We really have no good alternatives. Bill Clinton said, "Creating a low-carbon economy will lead to the greatest economic boom in the United States since we mobilized for World War II." But only if we bring the rest of the world along with us. Unless we act, unless we lead, the world will hide behind the skirts of the United States, and do nothing.

We can talk about survival until we're all blue in the face, but too often denial prevails. The truth is, unless you happen to live in the Arctic, or in a low-lying river delta, or rely on a vanishing glacier for your water (or for your job at a ski resort), sustainability and global climate change are both too slow, too incremental, too much someone else's problem for most people to feel anything like a sense of urgency. And we humans are particularly adept at not responding to things—even big, critical, potentially fatal things—that we feel we can afford to put off, or even ignore.

Yet if we leave this threat ignored, we will cross that red line, we will exceed earth's carrying capacity and pump so much man-made carbon into the atmosphere that we will leave our children, and theirs, trapped in a bleak zone of immense and unrecoverable harm.

Mitigating the destruction of the earth is where our greatest opportunities, as well as our biggest challenges, are to be found. Most of us feel the urgency of the economic crisis in our everyday affairs. And our crisis of national security is made plain every time we go to the airport, every time we listen to the news, every time we read about an enormous budget deficit or see a photograph of a fallen soldier.

But perhaps you are still wondering, how can I be so sure that this emerging crisis—man-made, global climate change—is even real?

# 13 | Science and Skeptics

*Carbon dioxide is being added to the Earth's atmosphere by the burning of coal, oil, and natural gas. This will modify the heat balance of the atmosphere to the extent that marked changes in climate, not controllable through local or even national efforts, could occur.*

President's Science Advisory Panel, November 1965

No discourse on sustainable business, no book that calls attention to what we humans are doing to the environment, can omit some meaningful comment on global climate disruption. Note that I do not call it "global warming," which, if you happen to be a Canadian, a Finn, even a Russian, might sound pretty good. Who would be against milder winters? Longer growing seasons? Less snow to shovel?

No one knows exactly how hot summers might become in Spain, or how many increasingly violent hurricanes might churn through the Gulf of Mexico, or how little snow might fall in the mountains of California (the snow that becomes drinking water to slake the thirst of a very big, very populous, and very dry state). All of those things are weather, and weather is, by definition, tough to predict from one year to the next.

Not so climate. Climate is stepping back from weather and seeing the bigger picture. A downpour might strike a desert one afternoon. That's weather. But the desert remains a desert because of climate. And climate change is anything but good.

With climate there are not only good theories, but solid forecasts. What do these global forecasts say will happen if we continue to consume fossil fuels and pump gigatons of man-made $CO_2$ into the atmosphere we all share?

- **Average global temperatures will rise.**

  Nine of the ten hottest years on record have occurred since 1995, with 2005 the hottest ever. The 2003 heat wave that struck Europe killed more than twenty-six thousand people, and fully half the summers could be that hot by 2040.

- **Sea levels will rise as glaciers and polar ice melt, and they are melting right now.**

  The American Rockies have experienced a 16 percent loss in snowpack. Mount Kilimanjaro has lost 80 percent of its ice. Our children may know the snowy Alps (source of the Rhine, Rhone, and Po rivers) only from pictures on candy bar wrappers. "Let's put it this way," said Bruno Abegg, professor of economic geography at the University of Zurich. "I wouldn't invest in a ski resort in Kitz-bühel." Greenland and West Antarctica, each one alone, could raise sea levels 20 feet if they lose their ice cover. Large areas of low-lying coastal countries will be flooded permanently. These areas include many of the world's great cities.

- **Increased storm intensities.**

  Warm sea surface temperatures are hurricane fuel. Adding more fuel (more heat) will cause them to intensify, with implications for all coastal interests—and the insurance companies that cover them. The higher atmospheric temperatures of today will be reflected in higher ocean temperatures thirty years from now. Because the oceans are so much more massive than the atmosphere, the heat transfer from air to ocean is slow, but inexorable.

- **Decreased access to fresh water.**

  "Water is the oil of the twenty-first century," said Andrew Liveris, CEO of Dow Chemical. When glaciers disappear or snowpacks thin, rivers run dry. The water supplies that our great cities (and most of the world's businesses) rely upon may vanish—literally—into thin air. And it is worth noting that many of the world's nuclear reactors rely on river water for cooling, too.

- **Disrupted ecosystems.**

  Forests will be ravaged by fires caused by long-term drought, and scoured by pests normally killed off by cold winters, as cold winters become scarce. Fertile croplands (especially the American

Midwest) will become, perhaps dramatically, less productive, while the southeastern forests of America become savannahs.

- **Displaced people.**
  The Katrina effect will expand to include entire countries and whole regions—hundreds of millions of climate refugees.
- **Species extinction.**
  Many plant and animal species are unlikely to survive climate change. New analyses suggest that 15 to 37 percent of a sample of 1,103 land plants and animals would become extinct eventually as a result of climate changes expected by 2050. For some of these species there will no longer be anywhere suitable to live. The synergistic link between certain flora and fauna will be broken, as one migrates northward faster than the other, its symbiotic partner, can migrate. The result: species extinction. This is the death of birth.

Talking about Katrina reminds me of a vacation trip my wife, Pat, and I took the week following Hurricane Katrina's collision with the Gulf Coast. We were on Cape Breton Island in Nova Scotia, about as far from New Orleans's Ninth Ward as you can get and still be in North America. We'd been glued to the television the whole week, watching CNN, keeping up with the unfolding catastrophe, astonished at the unrelenting cascade of government failures, more astonished that something like that could actually happen in America. I had to get away, so one morning I drove our rental car to a trailhead and took a walk up a forested mountain trail.

I was alone on that trail, and as I neared the top, huffing and puffing along, my eyes on the path in front of me, I heard a noise, stopped, and looked up.

There on the trail, not sixty feet away (about the distance between home plate and the pitcher's mound), stood a bull moose. He was standing crossways to the path, blocking it completely, enormous, at least seven, maybe eight feet tall from hooves to antlers—and he was looking at me.

I actually considered (for just an instant) clapping my hands to shoo him away. But then I caught myself and thought, *Don't be stupid! This is his trail. I'm the intruder here. If he charges me, I'm dead.*

So I backed off, turned, and retreated down the mountain, keeping a watchful eye on the trail behind me. My heart was pounding. It was an amazing experience. I had come face-to-face with a force of nature.

Well, when I got back to where we were staying, the news from New Orleans had only gotten worse. And after meeting that moose, I could not miss the metaphor: *That trail was the moose's territory. I was the intruder. How human of me to want to shoo him away and claim that trail for myself, and how very foolish. Had I challenged him it would have been at my own peril. If he had charged me, I'd be mincemeat.*

Do you see the metaphor? The atmosphere is nature's trail, as are the meandering Louisiana rivers, the wetlands, the deltas, and the barrier islands. We challenge nature on her trail with our greenhouse gases, our man-made river channels, and our chopped-up wetlands at our own peril.

On August 29, 2005, nature charged out of the Gulf of Mexico, and Louisiana and Mississippi—an area roughly the size of all of England—were mincemeat.

Now, I doubt if there are many scientists who would say that Katrina (or Rita, Wilma, or more recently, Ike) were caused by global climate change. But I think there are also very few who would say they were not exacerbated and fueled by abnormally high sea surface temperatures. Katrina blew up from a category 1 hurricane to a category 5 in just a few days. Wilma did it in just one day. So, why was the Gulf of Mexico abnormally warm? The precautionary principle says we must not assume it was an accident. We must ask, *What is going on?*

There are very few scientists who would not agree that hurricanes and floods, storms and droughts, will become more frequent and more fierce, the weather more erratic (the bane of every farmer!) as the atmosphere and oceans, with that thirty-year lag, grow warmer still in the years ahead.

Nevertheless, if you read the writings (or, more commonly, listened to the rants) of climate skeptics you would come away thinking that no one really knows enough about these issues to justify changing the way we live our lives, do business, or write laws. People in the media, in their attempts to appear balanced, have given the folks on the far fringes of anti-climate science a soapbox on which to stand, right up there with (and seemingly equal to) scientists who have studied climate all of their lives.

Sadly, the uncertainty they peddle has been cultivated (and quite often financed) by corporations who are stubbornly—and, frankly speaking, stupidly—clinging to a fatally flawed business model. It makes you wonder, what part of *unsustainable* do they not understand?

The UN Intergovernmental Panel on Climate Change (IPCC) recently issued a report that lays the blame for global climate disruption at our feet with a more than 90 percent certainty.

They said, "Greenhouse gas forcing has very likely (>90 percent) caused most of the observed global warming over the last 50 years. This conclusion takes into account . . . the possibility that the response to solar forcing could be underestimated by climate models.

Many climate doubters and global warming deniers have raised some serious questions about how the IPCC came up with that 90 percent figure—indeed, about how they decided on anything at all. And the thing is, perversely, I find I am in agreement with them, but for very different reasons.

Here's an amazing revelation from studying the IPCC's methods. Government representatives were allowed to vote on and revise the IPCC summaries, no matter what the data said. As a direct result, China (think coal) and Saudi Arabia (oil) got to veto anything they didn't like. The United States (think do nothing) also had line-by-line veto power. You can imagine what happened in a swamp like that.

The deniers call this "politicized science" and say that the IPCC summaries were just one big exaggeration, when in fact the reverse is true. They are almost surely understated.

It would be like giving a convicted thief a say over the wording of the laws that govern theft. You can bet the final text would go light on thievery. So goes the politicized UN Intergovernmental Panel on Climate Change.

The doubters also believe the IPCC report seriously overstates the impact of human emissions on the climate. But the actual observed climate data clearly show the report dramatically understates it. Here's just one example, and there are many.

Last April (2008), in an article titled "Conservative Climate," *Scientific American* noted that objections by Saudi Arabia and China forced the IPCC to remove a sentence stating that the impact of human greenhouse gas emissions on the earth's recent warming is five times greater than that of the sun. In fact, the lead author, Piers Forster of the University of Leeds in England, said, "The difference is really a factor of ten."

While politicized science (an oxymoron if there ever was one) is watered down and conveniently misleading, the real science of global climate change is well understood, and its acceptance in the rigorous world of peer-reviewed science is all but universal. It goes like this:

Certain gases—carbon dioxide ($CO_2$), nitrogen oxide ($N_2O$), methane ($CH_4$), and chlorofluorocarbons (CFC) of all kinds—act like blankets thrown across the globe. They trap heat near the earth's surface. As atmospheric concentrations of these gases increase, the blanket thickens and global temperatures increase. There is practically no dissent among scientists about this.

The most prevalent of these gases, carbon dioxide, represents about 77 percent of the total (though it constitutes only 0.0387 percent of the total atmosphere), and is fairly easy to monitor and even trace back in time in ice cores, so it serves as a useful proxy for all greenhouse gases. That's one reason you hear about $CO_2$ so often.

There are also cooling effects: particulate matter from volcanic eruptions and sulfate particles from coal-fired generators that reflect incoming sunlight. Coincidentally, these cooling effects are essentially canceled out by the warming effects of the non-$CO_2$ gases (though the acid rain from sulfates remains a separate problem). This leaves $CO_2$ as the net contributor to warming. This is the other reason you hear about $CO_2$ most often. Scientists use arcane measures called "forcings" to describe warming and cooling effects.

Where do humans enter the picture?

Business, industry, and you and I and everyone else emit about nine billion tons of carbon into the air each year, including the effects of deforestation. (That translates into thirty-four billion tons of $CO_2$.) We do it when we start our cars. We do it when we turn on our lights or burn coal to run a generating station. We really do it when we hop on a jet. We also contribute to it when we eat margarine made from soybeans that were grown where rain forests used to be.

The earth and all of its natural systems (the forests, grasslands, croplands, and oceans) after participating in the natural flows, can capture and "sequester" about 3.7 billion tons of anthropogenic (that's from us) carbon per year. That is the earth's capacity for the uptake of man-made atmospheric carbon.

The difference between what we emit and what the earth can absorb is: $9.0 - 3.7 = 5.3$ billion tons of excess carbon per year. That 5.3 billion tons goes into the atmosphere and stays there (some of it for many centuries!), increasing atmospheric concentrations of $CO_2$ by 2 to 3 parts per million each year. If it's 387 ppm this year, next year it will be 389, then 392, then 395, and so on, year after year after year.

Unchecked, that $CO_2$ will rise and pass that red line that our best scientists believe is out there in the vicinity of 450 ppm, which will induce a global average temperature change of 2 degrees Centigrade (3.8 Fahrenheit). IPCC scientists believe the red line is the threshold of catastrophic change in our climate. It may come later. It may come sooner, but $+3.8$ degrees F is a very important limit.

And while a simple calculation suggests we have around twenty years to go before we hit that red line, it is worth remembering that the earth's ability to absorb excess carbon may diminish, and we—and by "we" I mean all of humanity—will have lost ground. Here, from a special report published by *Scientific American*, is what some of the very best science has to say:

- **Carbon intensity is increasing.**
  The amount of carbon dioxide per car built, burger served, or widget sold had been consistently declining until the turn of the century. But since 2000, $CO_2$ emissions have grown by more than 3 percent annually. This is largely due to the economic booms in China and India, which rely on polluting coal for power production. But emissions in the developed world have started to rise as well, increasing by 2.6 percent since 2000, according to reports made by those countries to the United Nations Framework Convention on Climate Change. Researchers at the Massachusetts Institute of Technology also recently argued that U.S. emissions may continue to increase as a result of growing energy demand.

- **Carbon sinks are slowing.**
  The world's oceans and forests are absorbing less of the $CO_2$ released by human activity, adding to the faster rise in atmospheric levels of greenhouse gases. Deforestation is a two-edged sword, as sinks shrink and $CO_2$ releases from them increase. The ability of the ocean to take up carbon declines with warming and acidification; and $CO_2$ in water yields carbonic acid, which also threatens any creature that makes a shell. Not incidentally, the food chain starts with such creatures.

- **Impacts are accelerating.**
  Warming temperatures have prompted earlier springs in the far north and have caused plant species to spread farther into formerly icy terrain. Meanwhile, summer sea ice in the Arctic reached

a record low this year, covering just 1.59 million square miles, thus shattering the previous 2005 minimum of 2.05 million square miles. Though melting sea ice does not raise sea levels, larger expanses of blue ocean reduce the earth's albedo (its reflectivity), resulting in greater heat absorption.

"The observed rate of loss is faster than anything predicted," said senior research scientist Mark Serreze of the U.S. National Snow and Ice Data Center in Boulder, Colorado. "We've got so much open water in the Arctic now that has absorbed so much energy over the summer that the ocean has warmed further. The ice that grows back this autumn will be thin."

So, as oceans grow warmer they are less able to sequester carbon, for the same reason a warm soft drink loses its $CO_2$ fizz. As forests die and croplands succumb to encroaching deserts, they too are taken off the board as carbon absorbers. As vast regions of tundra and permafrost warm and melt (as they are doing already), they release enormous amounts of methane, a greenhouse gas many times more potent than simple carbon dioxide. What does this mean? These feedback mechanisms that reinforce themselves will almost certainly shorten the time we have to act, and may goad nature to charge that much sooner.

Here's the takeaway message: Atmospheric concentrations will continue to increase until the gases we send into the air and the earth's ability to absorb those gases come into balance, that is, the difference between them is driven to zero. We can get there by reducing our greenhouse gas emissions or by helping the earth to increase its carbon uptake (by restoring the forests, for example), or by a combination of the two.

Though every bit of added sequestration counts, we are emitting nearly three times as much greenhouse gases as the earth is able to absorb. It should be obvious from those numbers that we cannot avoid crossing those red lines by planting more trees, because there simply is not enough land. We must reduce our fossil fuel use to reduce the billions of excess tons of carbon we belch into our air.

To do that our emissions (not just those of America, but of the world) must be cut by 80 percent. If we can do that (and I believe there's every reason to think that we can), then by 2050 we will limit atmospheric $CO_2$ to "just" 450 ppm—reach that red line, but not go beyond it. So when you read or hear of a plan to cut GHG emissions by 80 percent, this is where that number comes from. It was not pulled out of a hat.

In time, we may even drive concentrations below the present level, to a safer level. NASA scientist James Hansen is calling for a return to the 350 ppm level. Though highly ambitious, that goal seems to me to be not quite ambitious enough, for temperatures were rising in the last century when, concentrations were still below 350 ppm. That says to me that eventually humankind will have to find ways to return concentrations to near preindustrial levels, below 300 ppm.

Here's another frightening possibility. If earth's sequestration capacity falls far enough, a 90 percent reduction, even total elimination of greenhouse gases, may become necessary *for survival*. A world without fossil fuels? You think Kyoto's 7 percent was difficult!

So this crisis—climate change—is very real, and will soon be coming to a town, a shoreline, a mountain, a business near you. It cannot be solved by any one nation acting alone. Indeed, that is a sure recipe for outright failure.

That is why we in the developed nations need to get our act together on this, to show some real leadership, and to seize what Amory Lovins likes to call an "insurmountable opportunity." But before we can preach the gospel to the world (or try to sell it to them), we need to put our own house in order.

Global climate change should not be a partisan issue. Republicans, Democrats, independents, and apolitical citizens alike all have a stake in our continued physical and economic well-being. Public policy (and the leadership that must precede it) must be informed by sound, peer-reviewed science. We must turn a deaf ear to the voices assuring us, *Everything will be fine, don't worry! It's all under control!* That's the sort of fatal message that kept cardplayers at their tilting tables in the grand salon of the *Titanic*. Denial is deadly.

It is time for a national awakening to the perils—as well as the prospects—inherent in this crisis. For as long as we continue to intrude on nature's trail and challenge her in her domain, thinking we can shoo her away and claim it all—every last bit—for ourselves, we do so at our own great peril. We can expect her to charge again and again. Her trail is simply not ours to do with as we please. We must shake off the complacency of the status quo and start acting in our own enlightened self-interest.

The fate of the earth rests on that kind of global awakening. Literally billions of individuals must decide to stop doing things that seem harmless, and seem to cause no noticeable change. But decide they must. The bad news is that, until quite recently, the call to action was muffled and distant.

The good news is, the awakening is already happening.

# 14 | Awakening the Mind and Spirit

*I used to think we could solve the environmental crisis by throwing
enough good science at the problem. I was wrong. The primary
threat isn't pollution, climate change, biodiversity loss, or habitat
destruction. It's selfishness, greed, and apathy. We need a spiritual
and cultural transformation to deal with that.*

Gus Speth, dean,
Yale School of Forestry and Environmental Studies

In chapter 2, I explained how Paul Hawken's book, *The Ecology of Commerce*, indicted me as a plunderer of the earth. I was a captain of industry, a success by anybody's measure. And by my very success I was also an instrument of global destruction, an unwitting participant in driving humanity straight off a cliff. I say unwitting because even though the evidence was all around me, and had been since Rachel Carson published *Silent Spring*, I just hadn't seen it.

Hawken's book opened my eyes to a world I had never imagined. And that final, sad picture of St. Matthew Island—windswept, deserted, strewn with bones—has stayed with me. But Hawken also offered a ray of hope. Business and industry was the only institution large enough, wealthy enough, pervasive and powerful enough to lead humankind out of the mess we were making: not government, not religious institutions, not colleges and universities.

And yet, we saw in the last two chapters that government does have an important role to play. It must set the goals and write the rules. It must energize people, play referee, and occasionally intervene to keep the game (and market) clean and honest. If there is a limit to what any one of us can do, but no limit at all to the good effects of leadership, then our leaders, once they move from the back of the parade to the front, can begin to make a difference. So then what about our universities? Our religious institutions? Do they also have some responsibilities (and opportunities) here? Can they also make a difference?

You bet they can.

Hawken and others have highlighted the many ways in which the biosphere is under assault. The trend lines are nearly all downhill, and the end, if we do nothing, is certain. Every person, every nation, every corporation on earth depends on nature's uninterrupted services for its survival. If nature does not make it through the transition from the first industrial revolution to the next, none of us will. That's the bad news.

But we have some good news to consider, too. The trends in ethical awareness, and the development of the concepts of sustainability and corporate social responsibility, are rising. Small-scale local businesses and giant multinational corporations alike are discovering that applying an ethical sustainability filter to everything they do can add to their top and bottom lines, because the marketplace is rewarding good behavior.

What it comes down to is this. You and I happen to be alive at a critical juncture of those two opposite trends. We have the power to destroy this living earth, and that destruction is ongoing, even accelerating. But more of us are realizing that change is necessary and within our grasp if we just decide to reach for it. How will it all come out?

We'll know soon enough, for I believe that where these two trends— accelerating destruction and a growing awareness—intersect is where the fate of humankind will be decided. And there are other tributary trends feeding into this fateful confluence.

One is the revolution in technology that is beginning to produce a spectrum of new, clean technologies—renewable, cyclical, benign and resource-efficient. Through their research, colleges and universities clearly are playing a significant role in this revolution. Another good trend is the ascendancy of women in business, the professions, education, and government. Women can be extremely effective problem solvers when they bring their right-brain skills to industries and institutions long dominated by left-brained men.

After all, it was those left-brained, pragmatic preoccupations with simple bottom lines, immediate returns, and other "practical" issues that got us into this mess. Surely another kind of thinking is needed to get us out.

Colleges and universities, where new technologies are born and where women are not held back by longstanding (and often hidden) traditions, stand at the headwaters for both these tributary trends.

So are the voices being raised by religious people of all denominations. They look at the state of the earth and see not just a business and industry problem, not just some flawed rules that we inherited from the first industrial revolution, but a direct assault on divine creation itself.

The historical roots of their awakening to creation care go back at least to the realization that the biblical command to establish dominion over the earth was a call to be a shepherd—a steward—and not a license to kill. It has become the duty of many religious people to take on that shepherding role, not to subdue and dominate the earth (which is, as we have seen, a very short-term proposition), but to respect, cherish, and protect it. We'll examine what some of them are doing and saying a bit later in this chapter.

When it comes to how we educate our young people about their one and only planetary home, the problems go back a very long way. Our universities, our top schools (even my own alma mater, Georgia Tech) have been very good for years at turning out professionals equipped with skills appropriate to the first industrial revolution, but not to the new one.

While there has been a tremendous surge of interest in sustainability, and some universities now have a sustainability officer leading the charge to look for green solutions, some areas of academia have been slow to catch on. The courses that many teach offer no sustainable solutions for the world their graduates will find. They are still part of the problem.

Aspiring mechanical engineers still learn everything about internal combustion engines and not enough about fuel cells. Budding electrical engineers are still taught all about coal-fired central power plants, and not enough about distributed generating capacity from clean, renewable resources like the wind and the sun (or the local, methane-rich garbage dump!).

Ceramics engineers still learn the traditional, abusive, heat-beat-treat methods that, quite literally, go back a thousand years or more. Meanwhile, they overlook the abalone's natural nanostructural methods that use self-organized proteins and minerals dissolved in cold seawater to produce a ceramic product—mother-of-pearl nacre—that is superior to any man-made ceramic.

There are colleges, universities, and institutes where textile engineers still learn to make Kevlar®—the tough fiber used in bulletproof vests—from petrochemicals (oil) and boiling sulfuric acid. Yet they know little, or nothing, about how a common spider manages to create a superior fiber—five times stronger, lighter, and more resilient—at room temperature, and out of nothing but bugs. That's biology. Why should any right-thinking engineer get involved with all of that messy biotech stuff?

And yet, it seems to me that any right-thinking engineer should look not only at what has worked in the past, but especially at how it can be improved in the future. Isn't a few billion years of accumulated engineering wisdom—low temperature chemistry in water, naturally powered, infinitely recyclable—worth paying some attention to? And it's not just the technology side of education that needs to be retooled with sustainability in mind.

Sadly, some of our economics students continue to be taught that prosperity can be measured by how much stuff we make, use, and throw away. That the gross domestic product figure is a good measure of progress, when we know that it measures just about everything except the things that make life truly worthwhile. What use is a number that assigns a monetary value of zero to the time parents invest in raising their children? In assuring our own future? I'm sure you see the problem there; it goes beyond financial metrics.

Will economics students continue to be taught that externalities (the costs that industry shifts to society and the environment) don't count in our economic system? Or will they learn true, full-cost accounting methods that would incorporate into oil's price the cost of wars in the Middle East and the crippling costs we shift to future generations through global climate change? If we did, the price of a barrel of oil would double, perhaps triple. Which school has the nerve to suggest something like that?

Moreover, will our entire system of economics still cling to and worship at the shrine of the Basic Economic Problem: all economic progress is driven by the gap between what we have and what we want (want, not need)?

Some ag students continue to learn petroleum-intensive, industrial methods for how to cultivate annual food crops. Shouldn't they study benign, cyclical methods that run on abundant energy from the sun, and find ways to cultivate self-rotating, pesticide-free, perennial food crops that are truly sustainable? They do exist, you know, at Wes Jackson's Land Institute in Salina, Kansas.

Some designers continue to be taught that good design is when there's nothing else to add (Microsoft, are you listening?). But when every step, every component, every link in the supply chain serves to broaden, deepen, and darken your environmental footprint, wouldn't it be smarter to define good design as when there's nothing else to remove? Just as Michelangelo revealed *David*'s perfect hand by removing the marble that imprisoned it.

Our law students are still taught that simple regulatory compliance (which we know is years out of date) and defending their clients' bad behavior are their highest callings. Shouldn't they be urged to go beyond compliance, embrace ethical behavior, and insist that their clients come along with them?

Will our business students continue to be taught, explicitly or not, that the earth is theirs to exploit? Or will they learn the value of high environmental ethics, as well as high humane ethics?

Teachers in all these areas have a special responsibility to challenge the status quo, a responsibility that goes well beyond what even a captain of industry must bear. Corporations might resist change, but relative to a university, they can turn on a dime.

But a university somehow cannot. Change comes slowly in academia, and so the harmful effects of obsolete curricula tend to persist. Here's the decision that you leaders in academia are going to have to make consciously. You can either pass on and perpetuate an old, outmoded, and destructive body of knowledge, ensuring that it will remain (and cause more harm) for another generation or two, or three; or you can wake up to the responsibility—and the satisfaction—of challenging the obsolete status quo in your curricula. To break with that potent opiate, *We've always done it this way.*

To those of you who might say, *Hang on. I've got all I can handle already,* let me make a few observations. We, all of us (especially those of us in the United States), have both a generational mission and a historic choice to make. If we don't choose wisely, we will, at best, be handing over the field to others (and forgoing the financial returns that come with leadership). At worst we'll continue to serve as the world's negative role model—a country that consumes too much, throws away too much, generates a size 20 greenhouse gas footprint, and doesn't seem to get it. That would give the rest of the world, particularly the developing world, ample reason to follow our dubious lead toward assured destruction.

I am convinced that business and industry must lead us out of the hole we've dug or, to put it bluntly, if business and industry don't come aboard, it's over for Homo sapiens. Yet, those entrusted with educating the next generation have a unique responsibility, one replete with enormous opportunity as well as peril.

You don't need to teach a college course in American history to know that there have been other, similarly challenged generations that come to mind: the one that brought democracy to the world; the one that fought to end slavery;

and the generations that gave women the right to vote, defeated evil in World War II, and landed a human being on the surface of the moon.

They, too, were burdened by what fate had handed them. But I believe our challenge is not so much a burden as an honor. We have the chance not only to solve a three-headed crisis—a simultaneous environmental, financial, and security crisis—but to take the right steps to ensure our whole civilization's prosperity into the indefinite future. That's our children's children's children's world, and beyond, that I'm writing about. Think about it for a moment. How often does a chance like that come along?

Today's fifth-graders will be graduating college seniors in 2020, the year Interface's Mission Zero has set as a goal for reaching the summit of Mount Sustainability. Will we make it to the top? Be able to stay there? Not without their help.

What must those graduates learn today, next year, five years from now if they hope to work for us, or for companies aiming to stand up there on the summit of Mount Sustainability with us? What must they learn now if they hope to be part of a prosperous, fulfilling society then? Certainly not about internal combustion engines, coal-fired power plants, and the rest of that first industrial revolution thinking.

I am very pleased to say that my own alma mater has chosen wisely. Not that it was always so. While my industrial engineering professors were the first to teach me to be on the lookout for that better way, the school I attended was not turning out engineers who challenged basic industrial principles. Civil engineers learned how to make a bridge stronger, lighter, more resistant to wind and weather. But they were not taught to ask whether the bridge ought to be built at all. That came a bit later.

I've loved Georgia Tech for as long as I can remember. Thirty-two years after I graduated with my degree in industrial engineering, and well into my career as CEO at Interface, I found myself on the Georgia Tech Advisory Board (GTAB), a sounding board for Georgia Tech's president on strategic issues. Six years later, I became the chairman of that board, and it came at a most propitious time. It was 1995, the first year of President Wayne Clough's tenure.

Dr. Clough set out to establish his own agenda for the institution, part of which was to engage the entire faculty and administration in a collegial effort to rethink and rewrite Georgia Tech's vision and mission statement. In due course a first draft materialized, and I received a copy.

To my dismay, the notion of sustainability was missing from the document. Nor did the words "environment" or "ecology" appear, even though Tech had established a center for sustainable technology only the year before.

I began to agitate and, well, suffice to say, the final version of that mission and vision statement, in its lead paragraph, committed Tech to work for a sustainable society, and had other references to sustainability and the environment throughout. Sustainable technology, along with biotechnology and telecommunications technology, were identified as the three major strategic areas of study to move the university into the twenty-first century. How have they done in the years since?

The Institute for Sustainable Technology and Development (ISTD) has evolved into a universitywide advocate for sustainability. Like our own Mission Zero, it is guided by a long-range (in their case, twenty-year) plan to achieve sustainability at Georgia Tech.

Instead of carpet factories run by the sun and the wind, turning out beautiful, fully recyclable products, the ISTD is looking for an institutional transformation in education, curricula, research, and campus management practices. And, like Interface, they've come a whole lot further than anyone might have guessed possible since they set that high goal. In fact, Tech made Princeton Review's "2008 Green Rating Honor Roll," coming in fifth in the nation, ahead of every other technical institute.

That makes me proud, and it feels good.

Starting from that famous beginning, Georgia Tech is now among the world's best in the areas of green policy, green practices, and integrated academic curricula. It has:

- twenty-one endowed chairs (including our own, the Anderson-Interface Chair of Natural Systems) and twenty-three research centers that include significant sustainability components;
- a goal that every student takes at least one of more than one hundred courses with a sustainability emphasis;
- institutional environmental sustainability programs that embrace green cleaning, solid-waste recycling, drought-tolerant vegetation, and storm water capture and reuse;
- a sustainable food project that encourages environmentally responsible dining habits, and a green portal that serves as a central

resource to promote green behaviors, activities, initiatives and events right across the entire Georgia Tech community;

- a commitment that every building will meet LEED certification standards;
- a center for biologically inspired design learning from Janine Benyus and biomimicry that nature is a spectacular source of innovative ideas.

But long before Tech could stand beside (or lead) the very best universities, the faculty had to be won over. President Clough did this by investing in research programs that advance sustainable technology and development. I expect there is a no more effective way to get faculty to pay attention to something new than investing real money.

At the same time, Tech also had to build credibility and trust with real, on-the-ground institutional practices. In business we call this walking the talk. For Tech it meant a serious recycling program; institutionwide green purchasing; new, LEED-standard green buildings; and truly sophisticated concepts for managing waste, electricity use, and storm water runoff on campus.

As it closes in on the final stretch of that twenty-year agenda, Tech is moving sustainability right into its academic program. Its ultimate goal is to incorporate concepts of sustainable technology and development into every discipline, no matter how distant or unrelated it might seem. Remember, biology seemed pretty distant and unrelated to ceramic engineering until they took a close look at an abalone.

Like Interface, Georgia Tech stresses the point that sustainability is everyone's responsibility, and that each discipline, interdisciplinary field, and profession has a particular contribution to make, even if it isn't obvious at first. Interdisciplinary research initiatives are going on in:

- **Energy:**
  fuel cells; advanced batteries; organic photovoltaic materials (natural solar cells); electrical testing and evaluation; long-term strategic energy paths; and a program to double, perhaps even triple, the efficiency of conventional PV cells using three-dimensional collectors rather than flat plates.

- **Sustainable business and industry:**
  using biological solutions, including biomimicry, to find efficient, practical, and sustainable answers to design and engineering problems; advancing the economic competitiveness of U.S. businesses through the application of new technology; developing sustainable, closed-loop systems that employ product reuse, recycling, and remanufacturing; environmentally conscious design and manufacturing; and an institute for leadership and entrepreneurship to help students find their own ways across the chasm I jumped when I founded Interface.

There are many more examples I could (and probably should) cite. For one, Tech is shining a very bright light on the link between sustainability and profitability. Technological Innovation: Generating Economic Results (TI:GER) is an interdisciplinary program that prepares students to commercialize new technologies and deliver innovative products to the marketplace.

TI:GER is a collaboration among various Georgia Tech colleges and the Emory University School of Law across town that brings together law, economics, management, science, and engineering graduate students in a classroom and research environment. It combines classroom instruction, team-based activities, and internship opportunities into a total educational experience.

And every year there's a business plan competition that pits the very best budding entrepreneurs against one another. An award is given (along with a tidy sum of seed money) to the winner; sustainability is now on the list of criteria by which the business plans are judged.

Finally, with a grant from a wealthy alumnus, Tech has created the Institute of Sustainable Systems (ISS) to be the umbrella organization for all sustainable initiatives. ISS's coordinating role will help Tech avoid needless duplication while encouraging even greater interdisciplinary cooperation.

I do not wish to leave you with the idea that Georgia Tech is out there all alone. Quite the opposite. The Association for the Advancement of Sustainability in Higher Education (AASHE) has, at last count, 660 two- and four-year colleges and universities on their membership rolls. Businesses, NGOs, government agencies (even grade schools!) can participate as partner members. What's driving this rush?

In a Princeton Review survey of 10,300 college applicants, 63 percent said that a college's commitment to the environment could affect their decision to go there. You can bet that that will get the attention of a lot of admission directors. When the people lead, the leaders follow, in this realm, too.

Campuses across the country are setting dates in the not too distant future for achieving carbon neutrality (the College of the Atlantic in Maine already claims that distinction). They are hiring sustainability coordinators and competing with one another in buying green power.

In a *New York Times* interview, Cheryl Miller, vice president of a company that helps campuses compare their environmental practices, said, "I don't think we've seen activism this strong since apartheid."

One high-profile effort, and likely the most debated, is the American College & University Presidents Climate Commitment. This pact was signed over the last two years by more than 550 institutions, representing about 30 percent of American students.

In it, participating colleges and universities promise that within a year they will inventory their greenhouse gas emissions. Within two years they will formulate a plan to arrive at carbon neutrality—that is, zero net $CO_2$ emissions—"as soon as possible." And since there is a definite spirit of competition among them, the race is on to win that zero footprint seal of approval.

They also have to agree to at least two of seven measures, including such measures as buying 15 percent of their energy from renewable sources and having all new buildings designed to LEED certification standards.

Some schools find that the easiest way to achieve a zero footprint is to buy offsets. Those offsets allow a university to burn the same fossil fuels, operate the same inefficient buildings, and waste as much material as ever, but pay for someone else to plant trees, perhaps in another country, or develop a wind farm in Texas. I can understand why they might find this approach attractive. Compared with the costs of reducing their own footprint, buying an offset can look very cost effective. And, very often, these offsets are both real and meaningful. Though there is no central clearinghouse to certify their legitimacy, they can still be examined and certified by independent third parties. When the offsets meet a set standard—and that standard requires independent verification, record keeping, and auditing measures—colleges and universities can have some faith in them. Are there abuses? Probably. But it is surely better than nothing. Yet it's quite possible that there are more than a few offsets out there that have accomplished very little in the way of sustainability, no matter who bought what and for how much. Trees planted this year in a developing country can disappear very quickly next year due to the actions of farmers intent on expanding food production.

One vendor of offsets offers this interesting deal. For a contribution of $22,570, a college can offset 2,488 tons of its emissions. And for just $35.70 a year, any student can claim to be the proud owner of a "carbon neutral" dorm room. But are these worth the price? Maybe, but does anybody really know?

The question of offsets is not limited to colleges and universities. Interface could—right now—buy our way to carbon neutrality. That's right. Every last cubic inch of our net greenhouse gas footprint could vanish tomorrow if we decided to use offsets rather than take real action. We could continue to buy virgin nylon (oil); we could ship our products by the least efficient means (oil, again). We could change just about nothing at all, even regress, write a check, and claim to be 100 percent climate neutral. It might look good in a sales presentation or an advertisement, but would it be the right thing to do?

Doubts about offsets were one big reason why Dartmouth College declined to sign on to the presidential pact. "How will Dartmouth be different if we're carbon neutral?" asked Mary Gorman, an associate provost at Dartmouth. "We decided we'd rather invest here and actually get real reductions." So, while Dartmouth does not have a hard timetable for becoming carbon neutral—no Mission Zero—it did complete an energy audit of the entire campus, and is spending $12.5 million to make buildings more efficient. That's commitment! Meanwhile, there are different ways to "skin that cat." Emory University, here in Atlanta, asked itself a very similar question, but commissioned a report to answer the question, appointed an expert advisory panel, of which Interface was a member, and came up with a range of solutions that they are systematically implementing as budgets allow.

Don't get me wrong. Interface uses offsets, and the Kyoto Protocol sanctions them, in principle, as a good way for governments and private companies to earn carbon credits that can even be traded on a carbon market. Kyoto established the Clean Development Mechanism (CDM), which validates and measures projects, no matter where they are located, to ensure that they produce authentic benefits that would not otherwise have been realized.

So when carbon cap-and-trade comes into force, offsets will definitely play a big role. The trouble is, there are a lot of folks out there certifying offsets as real, and they don't always agree. Different methodologies are used for measuring and verifying emissions reductions, depending on the project type, size, and location. For example, the Chicago Climate Exchange uses one set of protocols and the CDM another. In the fledgling voluntary carbon market, a variety of industry standards exists.

My best guess is that this muddled situation will settle out when carbon carries a price and we start paying for the privilege of discharging greenhouse gases into the atmosphere. Personally, I will welcome the day when we pay taxes on bad things like pollution and waste and carbon emissions rather than on good things like income and profitability. Once a dollar figure is attached to anything the game gets a lot more serious, and a tax shift like that could change the world as we have known it, by placing a price on carbon and other pollutants.

If your business were paying a carbon tax, you would want to know, for certain, that your competitors were paying the same kind of tax, based on the same metrics, using the same transparent calculations. And if buying offsets allowed you or your business to avoid those carbon taxes, you can also bet that the legitimacy of those offsets would be scrutinized very closely. A single, common certification standard will emerge and be applied across the board. And that will be a good thing.

Here's another good thing. There is considerable movement afoot among business schools to train people with the right skills. My personal favorite remains the early mover, tiny Bainbridge Institute in Washington State. There a husband and wife team, Gifford and Libba Pinchot, life-long environmental champions, took their own entrepreneurial plunge to beat all the big schools into the field.

Case Western Reserve, Northwestern, Stanford, the University of Michigan, and George Washington University now have concentrations in sustainable enterprise. The Yale School of Management offers a joint degree—an M.B.A. and Master's of Environmental Management. For a person seeking a green M.B.A., the problem is not so much finding a program that offers what you're looking for, but picking the best one.

To help with the search, the Aspen Institute publishes a biennial survey called *Beyond Grey Pinstripes*. Its Center for Business Education publishes this ranking of business schools to spotlight M.B.A. programs that integrate social and environmental stewardship into their curricula and research.

The survey measures course work, faculty research, and something they call "institutional support," a wide spectrum of activities that includes social and environmental impact management, seminars and conferences, internships, student competitions, and career development services. *Beyond Grey Pinstripes* places a "sustainability rank" next to every business school's name. In 2008, their top ten green M.B.A. list looked like this:

1. Stanford University
2. University of Michigan
3. University of California, Berkeley
4. University of Notre Dame
5. Columbia University
6. Cornell University
7. Duquesne University
8. Yale University
9. New York University
10. University of North Carolina at Chapel Hill

The pace of this good trend is both positive and accelerating. A survey of ninety-one business schools released in October 2008 by the World Resources Institute and the Aspen Institute found that 54 percent require a course in ethics, corporate social responsibility, sustainability, or business and society. That's up from just 34 percent in 2001. The Wharton School at the University of Pennsylvania has created its Institute for Global Environmental Leadership, and Interface holds a position on its Advisory Board.

A lot of people, both inside the academic world and out in business and industry, are paying close attention to this trend. Anita Roper, the sustainability director for Alcoa, said, "Whether it's called sustainability education or not, there is definitely a demand for the skills you get from courses based on sustainability concepts."

Stuart Hart, who holds the SC Johnson Chair for Sustainable Global Enterprise at Cornell (number six on that top ten list), said, "Prospective M.B.A. students from all over the world can focus on those business schools that are most responsive to their needs and aspirations when it comes to fusing societal contribution with business competitiveness. It turns out that these prospective students also happen to be the highest possible caliber applicants on the market." To me, this clear trend in education—from the institutional side and the student side of the equation, despite the sometimes slow response from the institutional side—justifies a high degree of optimism about our future.

While optimism is the fuel that drives every entrepreneur, some folks might look around and ask why anyone has any right to be optimistic. How dare we be optimistic as summer sea ice in the Arctic vanishes? How dare we be optimistic as the developing world (and, most especially, China) builds more coal-fired power plants and puts thousands of new cars on the road every week? How dare we fool ourselves into thinking we can turn this enormous ship away from the rocks and onto a safer, sustainable course?

But optimism is not just about facts, trends, and likely outcomes. It is also about faith and hope. I know that from my own experiences.

When I wrestled with the decision to leave a good, dependable job and start Interface, you can believe I assembled all the facts and figures that I could muster. But in the end, they were inconclusive. Would breaking with the past and taking that leap into something new be a great success or a dismal failure? There was just no way to know. And there was only one way to find out. Armed with liberal amounts of faith, belief in myself, and hope—and scared to death—I took that leap.

So must we. Faith, belief, and hope—with a healthy measure of fear—can build a bridge to something new, something better, where the simple facts fall short, or maybe become clear much later. And the same might be said about religion. It's called "faith" for a reason.

What role does religion play in making what seems like a purely technological transition from the first industrial revolution (and the obsolete thinking that continues to support it) to the next?

At first you might not think there is such a role. After all, science and religion have been at odds almost as long as government and commerce. You only have to think back to Copernicus's and Galileo's experiences with the church. Things really came to a head in 1859, when Darwin's *Origin of the Species* was published.

God stood on one side, science on the other. It seemed like a collision was imminent, and would leave just one of them standing. Either the Bible was correct as written, or not. Either science was the path to enlightenment, or not. If everything we see, hear, touch, and taste on earth is the product of divine design (and if it always has been), then that spells a fate that is leading us to a dead end, a St. Matthew Island collapse. Enlarged to encompass the collapse of the entire world, then isn't that, too, part of a divine plan?

After all, Genesis 1:28 says, "And God blessed them, and God said unto them, Be fruitful, and multiply, and replenish the earth, and subdue it; and have dominion over the fish of the sea, and over the fowl of the air, and over every living thing that moveth upon the earth."

Given such dogmatism, can the enormous gap that stands between science (especially the environmental and biological sciences) and religion ever hope to be resolved?

One answer to that has risen to the surface. It's called "creation care." And it, too, has deep roots. After all, not long after that first "dominion" passage, Adam is told in Genesis 2:15 that it is his job to "serve the Garden," not to subdue it, and certainly not to destroy it. (Another translation says "tend the garden.") Surely that means that if Creation is to serve us, we must also serve Creation. And that dominion must incorporate elements of wise and sustainable stewardship.

Seen in those terms, the Bible is an environmental handbook that commands us to conservatorship, and by doing so brings those two old archenemies—science and religion—together constructively. Why?

Because an ignorant gardener cannot truly tend a garden. A shepherd who knows nothing about sheep cannot tend to his flock. He has to know what conditions they require, what they need to eat, where their food grows most plentifully and reliably, and how to keep that whole situation going—to care for everything from the insects, to the grasses that grow, to the wool off lambs' backs—from now into the indefinite future. You might say, he's got to become an ecologist.

Though wary of mainstream environmental groups, a growing number of Christians view stewardship of the environment as a responsibility mandated by God. That was the driving force when, on February 8, 2006, eighty-six evangelical leaders and Christian organizations issued a call to reduce carbon emissions to combat global climate change. That was a big day!

This Evangelical Climate Initiative was signed by pastors from all across the nation, by the presidents of thirty-nine evangelical colleges, and even by the head of the Salvation Army. Here are its main points, and while they come at the climate problem from a perspective that's different from a scientist's, I believe their call to action will sound very, very familiar.

Claim 1. *Human-induced climate change is real.*

Claim 2. *The consequences of climate change will be significant, and will hit the poor the hardest.*

Claim 3. *Christian moral convictions demand our response to the climate change problem.*

Claim 4. *The need to act now is urgent.*

Conclusion. *We the undersigned pledge to act on the basis of the claims made in this document. We will not only teach the truths communicated here but also seek ways to implement the actions that follow from them. In the name of Jesus Christ our Lord, we urge all who read this declaration to join us in this effort.*

You can read the details that support each of those individual claims at www.christiansandclimate.org/learn/.

The thirty-million-member National Association of Evangelicals adopted this "Evangelical Call to Civic Responsibility" that emphasizes every Christian's duty to care for the planet and the role of government in safeguarding a sustainable environment. This statement has been distributed to fifty thousand member churches. It says:

> We affirm that God-given dominion is a sacred responsibility to steward the earth and not a license to abuse the creation of which we are a part. Because clean air, pure water, and adequate resources are crucial to public health and civic order, government has an obligation to protect its citizens from the effects of environmental degradation.

*Christianity Today*, an influential evangelical magazine, has weighed in on global warming, saying that "Christians should make it clear to governments and businesses that we are willing to adapt our lifestyles and support steps towards changes that protect *our* environment." (Emphasis added. I find the use of the word "our" to be slightly off target here, as it implies possession by humankind, perhaps an unconscious carryover of a dogmatic religious mind-set.)

This broadly based call to action has not been accepted uniformly. Indeed, it has split the evangelical community into highly antagonistic camps. One side believes it is their duty to become that wise shepherd, to protect the earth and all its creatures. The other is deeply suspicious of adopting anything that smacks of "environmentalism," an "ism" they consider to be associated more with liberal politics than biblical values.

According to Jim Ball of the Evangelical Environmental Network, most evangelicals "don't know many environmentalists, but they have the idea that they are pretty weird—with strange liberal, pantheist views." John C. Green, director of the Ray C. Bliss Institute of Applied Politics at the University of Akron, put it this way: "While evangelicals are open to being good stewards of God's creation, they believe people should only worship God, not creation."

Why should Christians care about the environment? I believe the signatories of that Evangelical Climate Initiative would say creation care has nothing at all to do with politics and everything to do with the fundamental responsibilities of faith:

- because we should care for the world as God does;
- because God has commanded us to be good stewards of the earth;
- because it is a way of showing love for our neighbors, even if, from a climate perspective, our neighbors live in flood-prone lowlands or parched deserts thousands of miles away.

I know of nothing in Jewish or Islamic religions that contradicts this view.

The last reason cited above seems particularly important to me. If we continue to live lives that contribute, no matter how locally, no matter how incrementally, to global climate disruption, then are we prepared to take responsibility for deadly droughts in sub-Sahara Africa and Australia? For rising sea levels that inundate Bangladesh? For the next Katrina? For the decimation of western forests in the United States? If we don't care for people, if we don't care for the earth, how can we say that we are obeying God's commandments? In my church, we sing,

> *This is my Father's world,*
> *And to my listening ears*
> *All nature sings and 'round me rings*
> *The music of the spheres.*

So here are two important trends.

Colleges and universities are raising awareness and sensitivity in their students, changing their own operations to become increasingly sustainable, helping to draw the map to sustainability for all disciplines, and providing the critical research necessary to get the facts—all of them—absolutely straight. And they are preparing change agents, ready to change the world.

And our churches are waking up to the very inconvenient truth that if we behave as though the earth were ours to conquer and rule, sure enough, it will end up at our feet, bloody, broken, and conquered, as Daniel Quinn has pointed out in *Ishmael*.

These two good trends represent two good reasons to be optimistic, to be hopeful, despite all the evidence to the contrary that is accumulating. Good people with awakened hearts and minds are now, today, making a difference.

Karen Armstrong, a former Catholic nun and the author of numerous works on comparative religion, once asserted, "All the great traditions are saying the same thing in much the same way, despite their surface differences. They have in common," she says, "an emphasis on the overriding importance of compassion, as expressed by the Golden Rule: *Do not do to others what you would not have done to you*." She also has observed that religion is not just about belief, but also about behavior: "Faith without works is dead."

It seems to me that if we "do unto" this world as we would have it do unto us, then the path ahead is as plain as day. If what we say, what we write, and what we believe are less important than what we do, then our next steps should be equally clear. Do something! Anything! Then do something else, and something else. We learned early on at Interface that this is the way to start to climb.

We have climbed up the shoulder of Mount Sustainability, attacking its high summit from not one direction, but seven. We've soared up some, struggled up others. We can see the top from where we stand. But what will it take to make that final push to reach it?

As I write this, Interface has only twelve more years to go before the Mission Zero goal of 100 percent sustainability by the year 2020 should be achieved. Many of our first steps were painfully obvious. Many of them were easy to measure, easy to fine-tune, and easy to explain to our employees, our customers, and our investors.

But now, in this high, thin air, the way up seems in some ways more difficult. Perhaps it will be harder to measure, harder to explain. Perhaps to some the final push to the top is not even possible. They wonder if Mission

Zero is a real goal, or is it just an inspirational one? A place we will actually get to one day, or just aspire to?

To find out, we asked InterfaceRAISE—our own consulting arm, which works with other corporations seeking to find their way up Mount Sustainability—to design a summit meeting that would engage and inspire Interface people from all around the world to imagine the next leg up the mountain.

So, the date and place were set: May 6, 2008, in the forested mountains of northern Georgia, near the small town of Young Harris. We undertook to share our best ideas about what was needed to move Interface from now to Mission Zero, from here to the top of the mountain.

The name given to the summit meeting? The Next Ascent.

# 15 | The Next Ascent

*We've got to be willing to explore the unknown, challenge our own assumptions, shake up our expectations, and find new ways forward.*

DAN HENDRIX, CEO, Interface, Inc.

**D**ear reader—or, if I may be so bold, fellow plunderer—it is true that the first industrial revolution generated enormous wealth, prosperity, and economic growth. At least, in our part of the world. It used to be hard to look at that record and see any reason why we should not want more of the same.

But, in our new enlightenment, we've come to see that a lot of damage to the earth was done in the process of generating all of that wealth. As I said in the short chapter on the science of climate change, it's likely we've done more harm than we know (or more harm than is politically correct to admit).

I have been much taken with Jared Diamond's book *Collapse*, in which he makes the point that a society can be thriving culturally yet dying biologically. In other words, life seems to go on as usual, as societies consume natural resources—water, arable land, energy—at an unsustainable rate. It's hard to look around us today and not see exactly those forces at work.

Yes, there's a lot of doom and gloom out there. And yet, as we have seen in the last two chapters, there are good trends to consider as well. Folks are demanding a change in government, not just in political parties. They actually seem to want some leadership from the leaders. Educational institutions are competing with one another to go green. And people of faith are waking up to the fact that establishing dominion over the earth is a command to be a wise shepherd, not to behave like a vandal.

Development and deployment of clean technologies of all kinds are ramping up, moving more of that troublesome T—from the numerator to the denominator. Women are climbing higher in corporations, institutions, and government. They bring a different way of thinking and a different way of doing business, and that is exactly what we need, because the old ways of thinking are what got us where we are today.

But are all these positive trends enough? Like many entrepreneurs, I am an optimist, but still deeply concerned. I think there is reason to think that we are moving—belatedly and often unwillingly—in the right direction, because more of us realize that the kind of thinking that worked just fine in the age of steam has led us into a trap. And more of us realize that doing what we've always done—only more so—will not get us out of it.

As in any crisis, there is both opportunity and danger. That is exactly what these simultaneously unfolding environmental, financial, and security crises offer us today.

Three crises at once are a lot to deal with, perhaps unprecedented, but either we adopt newer, better, more profitable and more sustainable practices, or our children and grandchildren will wonder why we played Russian roulette with our nation, the world, and their lives. Will our children celebrate our wisdom? Or will they curse us for having the knowledge and the tools to solve all three of these crises, but for still having done nothing?

While I remain hopeful, time is growing short. In the United States, the curtain rose on the age of oil with Edwin Drake's drilling of a sixty-nine-foot oil well in 1859, on Oil Creek near Titusville, Pennsylvania. Now, just 150 years later—just two lifetimes—that curtain is closing. Recall David Brower's six-day biblical analogy of the age of the earth which he so often used in his speeches? If the industrial revolution began at the very end of that week, "one-fortieth of a second" ago, how much briefer is the age of oil?

Our supply of coal—a resource so abundant that burning it all could generate enough greenhouse gases all by itself to render the earth uninhabitable—is also showing signs of a tightening. China will hit peak production first, likely in just a few decades. The United States, a global superpower when it comes to coal reserves, will not be far behind.

So it's clear: We do not have the luxury of time. Whether economically recoverable supplies of oil and coal can no longer keep up with demand 50 years from now or in 650, whether we're living through the last 0.5 percent of an era or the final 6 percent, doesn't really much matter. We are living at the end of an epoch. As Arab oil minister Yamani often says publicly, the Stone Age didn't end because they ran out of stones.

Similarly, the age of whale oil didn't end because our forebears ran out of whales (though they came close). It ended when people started filling up their lanterns and stoves with rock oil made from coal, and then from petroleum, available at far lower prices. You might say that the whales were saved by technical innovation, powered by good old capitalist self-interest. Imagine that!

Similarly, the age of fossil fuels will not end because there's no more oil, coal, or gas to dig up and burn. It will end because the finite supply cannot meet the exploding demand for them at a price—a climate price, a financial price, and a security price—that we are willing (or even able) to bear. It will end because better, smarter, and more profitable alternatives have become available. It will end because enough of us will realize that paying the price for a systemic shift away from fossil fuels is a whole lot cheaper than footing the bill for the status quo, including growing dependence on the Middle East. And like the age of whale oil, the fossil fuel epoch will be retired, very likely, by technical innovations powered by good old capitalist self-interest.

In 1994, a simple question, *What is Interface doing for the environment?* became the driving force that compelled us to discover a new business strategy, and to design it to succeed in the face of tightening resources—a strategy that connected profitability and the environment with a notion called doing well by doing good. And though we started off with no compass, no map, and no path to follow, we have come amazingly far. I think it might be worth restating just exactly how far.

- Since 1996, our baseline year, Interface has cut its net greenhouse gas emissions by 71 percent (in absolute tons).
- During the same span, our sales have increased by 60 percent. Carbon intensity, relative to sales, declined 82 percent, and profits doubled. As profit margins expanded, our shares went from two dollars in 2003 to twenty dollars in 2007, before yielding to the worldwide market sell-off of 2008.
- Our global use of renewable energy went from 0 to 28 percent. Renewable energy provides electricity to power 8 of our 10 factories or 89 percent of total electricity.

- Our consumption of fossil fuels per square yard of carpet declined 60 percent.
- The energy content of our carpets—the total number of BTUs required to make one square yard—fell by 44 percent.
- Our companywide waste elimination measures saved us a cumulative $405 million in avoided costs, paying for the transformation of our company. Sustainability has been self-funding.
- Water intake per production unit was reduced 75 percent in modular carpet facilities, 47 percent in broadloom facilities, 72 percent overall, thanks to conservation efforts and process changes.
- We've kept 175 million pounds of old carpet out of the landfills, and reduced our generation of scrap for the landfills by 78 percent.
- The percentage of recycled and biobased materials used to manufacture our products worldwide has increased from 0.5 percent in 1996 to 24 percent in 2008, and it is increasing rapidly with new technologies and the development of reverse logistics.
- Since 2003, we've manufactured and sold over 83 million square yards of Cool Carpet with no net global warming effect—zero—to the earth.

In the early 1950s at Georgia Tech, I was taught in Economics 101 that all wealth ultimately comes from the earth: the forests, the fields, the mines, the oil wells, and the oceans. If so, it must follow that wealth creation at the cumulative expense of a finite earth is, by definition, not infinitely sustainable. Humanity cannot keep trying to live off a bank account we did not open and cannot add a penny to. Though it might take a while, because that account (the earth's fossil fuels) started off big and full (like Daniel Quinn's high cliffs), there will come a day when our checks come back stamped "Insufficient Funds" and Quinn's craft crashes.

What should we do about that? Should we keep the music playing for as long as we can, and squander our children's inheritance? Or should we find ways to create wealth sustainably through the efficient use of resources, renewable energy, and closed-loop manufacturing processes that use recycled waste as raw materials?

Will we bankrupt our future, or assure it? With all the hope and optimism in the world, the jury is still out. There could be a lot of pain for Homo sapiens before we shed our hubris and figure out the sustainable way forward.

I bet Economics 101 was wrong in many ways other than its definition of the Basic Economic Problem, and we can develop a new economy, solar-driven, cyclical, and resource efficient. In that new economy, wealth will come from meeting needs, not wants, with more brain power and less stuff.

You know that I began this journey unwillingly. If you'd asked me what sustainability was in 1993, I'd have said that it's earning a big enough profit this year to stay in business the next. I was a businessman, an industrialist, and a cold-eyed capitalist entrepreneur. And I still am.

But at age sixty, I was beginning to picture the day when I would be looking back at the company I'd created, this third child of mine. What would it be when it grew up? What could I do to make sure it continued to thrive, to go from being a child prodigy to a world-beating virtuoso? And what kind of world would it live to see? What would my grandchildren's children see?

These were strategically important questions to me personally, as well as for Interface, in the highest sense of the word "strategic." I'm talking about ultimate purpose now, and there's no more strategic issue than that. And as you've read, I found answers to those questions (and even more) in some very unlikely places:

- in the way a gecko can climb a wall and hang upside down from a ceiling;
- in the way nature designs a forest floor;
- in the way an environmental problem like landfill gas could be turned into an environmental success story, as well as an income stream;
- in just how much waste there is in the industrial system and in my company;
- and in an Italian inventor's machine shop.

But it all started with Paul Hawken's book, *The Ecology of Commerce.* I read it, and in the course of a single night all thoughts of retirement, of travel, of chasing a little white ball vanished. The institution of business and industry was thoughtlessly destroying this world, yet business and industry was the only institution that could lead a movement to save it. If business and industry had to lead, who would lead business and industry? Unless somebody did, nobody would. Why not us?

Mind you, I didn't know how we would get from where we stood in 1994 to the top of that high, high mountain. But thanks to the work of a lot of really great folks at Interface, and with the help of our dream team, we have figured out which way to climb. With one eye on the clock and the calendar, I've been climbing ever since; and the people of Interface are right there with me.

It has been a good job well started, but for all the progress we've made, we're not standing at the top of Mount Sustainability yet. And the clock is still running. How do we get from where we are now—today—to where we want to be when the year 2020 rolls around? With zero environmental footprint? Doing no harm and taking nothing from the earth not quickly and easily renewed by the earth?

That brings me back to the Next Ascent. To find out how we'd get from here to there, sixty of our top management and sustainability leaders traveled from all across the globe to the mountains of north Georgia. There, on a forested hilltop overlooking the little town of Young Harris, in a retreat called Brasstown Valley, they were given this challenge: Find a way to take Interface up that final climb, to the Mission Zero summit.

Here's what happened.

Like 1994, 2007 was a banner year at Interface. We not only enjoyed great financial success, but we made equally great progress in finding solutions to some big technical sustainability challenges. We posted sales of $1.08 billion while ramping up our use of renewable energy, cutting waste, and unlocking the secrets to carpet recycling. Yet many of us also had a growing sense that the company I had founded back in 1973, and had reinvented in 1994, needed to be reinvented again to reach our Mission Zero goal.

That was another tall order, and the timing was far from perfect. As I write, 2008 is shaping up to be a very challenging year on many, many fronts. We've seen a historic storm in energy costs, the bursting of the housing market bubble, a credit crisis, a liquidity freeze, and the federal takeover of financial institutions. Bankruptcies and foreclosures are in every direction you look. And the year has a quarter to go! What will the next months, next year, bring?

Setting the stage for the Brasstown Valley meeting, our CEO since 2001, Dan Hendrix, observed, "Many are bracing for an economic slowdown."

Was that an understatement!

"But," Dan continued, "I feel the time is ripe to energize our associates around our most powerful, unifying element, which is also our most compelling strategic advantage—sustainability. We've got to be willing to explore the unknown, challenge our own assumptions, shake up our expectations, and find new ways forward."

But how? Surely not by having him or me stand up there in front of our people and tell them, *Just go for it!* As Paul Hawken said in his new book, *Blessed Unrest,* "The current state of the world reflects a problem-solving methodology never seen in nature: remedies from above imposed upon the excluded." Though I don't think anyone at Interface would say they feel "excluded," what Paul and Dan were both saying was that we needed a fresh approach.

For one thing, how do we know there are only seven faces to Mount Sustainability? Does this mountain have an eighth face? A ninth? How can we find and identify something we suspect but haven't yet seen?

Wouldn't a fresh approach to discovering the best route to the summit still be one that leveraged our past successes and harnessed our entrepreneurial way of doing business? Wouldn't we still hold to our companywide faith that the person closest to a problem has the best ideas of how to solve it? Or should we discard all preconceptions?

An outsider might have suggested right there that there were just too many questions, and that we ought to wait until Wall Street settled down, or energy costs stabilized (or even better, collapsed); or at least until the words "real estate" and "toxic loans" stopped showing up in the same sentence. I suppose a company with only a toe in the waters of sustainability might be excused if they decided against taking on any other big challenges until they figured out these more conventional ones.

But Interface has a deeper commitment than that. It isn't just some flavor of the month. It isn't greenwash to win over unsuspecting customers. It is in our DNA, pure and simple. And we have seen (and now, you have, too) that our Mission Zero quest has made excellent business sense, no matter how you might choose to define "sense." Why on earth would we abandon something so right, so smart?

Incorporating sustainability as a defining element has greatly improved our competitiveness—a good thing in hard times. It has enhanced our brand and our reputation, reduced our costs, and boosted our productivity. It has awarded us access to the very best talent, energized our entire company from the factory floor to the corner office, and spurred innovation.

If those things aren't useful in tough times, I don't know what might be.

And as this new set of values has become part of the cultural core of the company, we all have begun to look at the world differently. Sustainability at work has become sustainability at home, in school, at church, and in city hall. An evolutionary growth process had moved the entire company and its people in ways and to places I could never have guessed when I stood in front of that task force long ago.

Now, many of these same energized, motivated, evolved, and aware people wanted to know how we were going to make it to the top of Mount Sustainability in the time we had set for ourselves. They knew from their own hard work that truly amazing things were not only possible, but required. But they also knew that to get where we wanted to go meant climbing higher than ever on some familiar fronts, as well as thinking deeply and together in some important new areas, perhaps about that elusive eighth face.

The whole front of social sustainability comes immediately to mind here. Was this, by itself, the eighth face of Mount Sustainability? Our people were very good at measuring waste reduction, BTUs saved, and kilowatt-hours of renewable power generated and bought. But what about fairness? What about equal opportunity? What about making our senior management team look more like the communities where we have our plants? What about putting those plants closer to the markets they are supposed to serve? Or building and operating factories to the same high standards everywhere? What about developing greater sensitivity, and, for example, finding a better corporate definition of pregnancy than "a short-term disability"?

Some felt that the sixth face, sensitizing stakeholders, had adequately addressed social equity, but truly, we'd never thought deeply about some of these things before. And now, with fourteen years of experience behind us, we had an appreciation for just how hard the work of sustainability could be. There was more than a little impatience, too. I think Dave Gustashaw, our vice president for engineering and the man who pushed our landfill gas project through, voiced some of that early on. "We took four years to get our landfill gas plant in LaGrange up and running," he said. "We've got only twelve years to go until 2020—our Mission Zero goal. That's just three projects away. Can we do that?"

As you might expect, a lot of people have taken a hard look at Interface's climb toward sustainability. I've seen business school case studies and articles that wondered whether we were truly serious about Mission Zero. Zero impact? Was that something that Interface—or any company—could ever really achieve? Is it honestly possible to be 100 percent environmentally, financially, and socially sustainable and still be in business, still make things?

Or was our Mission Zero plan just a clever "stretch goal" concocted by management to bring out the best in our associates? Or was it a source of inspiration that would allow us to achieve things we might never have thought possible, but not something to take literally?

In a way, these questions reminded me of the ones I heard in 1994. Is Anderson serious? Does he really think that's going to work? When is he going to realize that he's trying to drive his company with the brakes on?

Well, as you've seen, our environmental and financial metrics have decisively answered all of those questions. Beyond any doubt. But it was time to get people together to find some new answers to some different questions. And so we found ourselves at the Brasstown Valley Resort for this challenging gathering to plan the Next Ascent.

The resort sits on the brow of a beautiful, forested mountain with long, green views in just about every direction. The setting might be what you'd see in your mind's eye if I asked you to close your eyes and picture that perfect place where you feel most calm, happy, and secure. Furthermore, Brasstown encourages green practices, and it is far enough away from Atlanta to allow local folks to get away from their day-to-day routines.

Designed by Jim Hartzfeld, the Next Ascent would have three main goals:

- celebrate and reflect on our progress to date;
- seek consensus on the direction necessary to achieve the next level of Mission Zero; and,
- help senior officers and other sustainability leaders develop detailed action plans and objectives to hit those Mission Zero goals.

In turn, each goal contained six areas of inquiry:

1. How do we attract, develop, and retain talent at all levels?
2. How can we engage and cultivate the commitment of people at all levels to implement a cohesive and bold vision of Mission Zero with its target date, 2020?

3. How do we foster an entrepreneurial and global organizational culture?
4. How should we invest in, and encourage innovation in, technology to advance environmental sustainability within the limits of financial sustainability?
5. How do we measure, invest in, and innovate around social sustainability within a context of financial sustainability?
6. How can we continue to build strong external connections to our customers, our suppliers, our communities, our investors, and our various governments?

The sixty participants from around the world represented our top global leadership, as well as those in the company responsible for taking the lead on sustainability. We wanted to hear all of their stories, good, bad, and indifferent. We took pains to make sure there was a very wide diversity in terms of job description, business unit, gender, and geography.

Jim paid special attention to making sure we had a good mix of those who had a long history of working at Interface and relatively new associates who'd come to Interface because of our sustainability mission. The first group knew firsthand that what some experts had said was impossible was anything but impossible. The second group had never once doubted the underlying wisdom of becoming a sustainable enterprise.

Working groups were formed to consider each of the six areas of inquiry, and every day at Brasstown was devoted to a specific task. They were:

- **Day One: Discovering the Best of What Is.** Our strengths, our accomplishments, what we've done (and how we've done it) when we were absolutely at our best. The appreciative inquiry approach developed by Dr. David Cooperrider of Case Western Reserve, in which Jim had become very proficient.
- **Day Two: Discovering What Can Be.** How we can use what has worked well in the past to push all six areas of inquiry forward in the direction of our Mission Zero goal?
- **Day Three: Imagine and Dream.** Building on what was discovered in days 1 and 2, people were encouraged to reach beyond the probable to the possible—to think big—and asked to prepare a

final five-minute, high-level summary of their best ideas. The presentation would include:

1. a provocative proposition;
2. key initiatives;
3. next steps; and
4. opportunities for additional dialogue.

I experienced a bit of déjà vu when Jim asked me to give the kickoff speech for the Next Ascent summit. Unlike that other one I had delivered so long ago, I knew I was on familiar ground. We'd all come so far and done so well, and had moved this company in directions not even I would have been bold enough to imagine back in 1994. You could say the speech wrote itself.

So that first night, with everyone gathered in a big pavilion with its sides wide open to the fresh, spring breeze, with everyone still focused on our first day's assignment—what we'd done right these many years—I got up in the spotlight and talked about my own proudest Interface moments:

- April 6, 1973, the day when I finally had the money in hand to start Interface—our company's birthday.
- December 1975, closing out our first profitable year.
- April 13, 1983, the date of our initial public offering, when Interface stock traded at twenty times the previous year's earnings then doubled in one year.
- The day we bought out our old UK equity partner, Carpets International Plc, in 1984.
- Surviving the 1991–1993 recession intact.
- August 1994, our *Mid-Course Correction*, which put Interface on the path to being the first name in industrial ecology, and completely sustainable by 2020.
- Surviving our self-inflicted wounds of 1997, when we bought and herded our installers into an exclusive network, ignored the resulting pain in our sales force, and found our largest supplier to be our biggest competitor.
- Being named by *Fortune* magazine as one of the "100 Best Companies to Work For" in 1998 and 1999.

- Realizing when the 2001 dot-com bubble burst and our market in office interiors contracted by more than 36 percent, that our sustainability strategy was instrumental in keeping the company profitable and viable.
- Reading the latest 2007 sustainability metrics, fresh off the press, demonstrating that we were 71 percent of the way to the top of that high, high mountain on the greenhouse gas emissions face, a peak we could not even see when we began this climb back in 1994.

Well, I thought that was a good place to end it, so I stopped and opened up the meeting to questions. One of our associates from Australia wondered when my new book would be finished, and I had to tell him that the world of publishing ran on its own schedule, that my own was pretty full, but to stand by. It was coming.

Then Joyce LaValle stood up at the back of the room. Joyce is our head of marketing for InterfaceFLOR-Commercial. She was also the one who'd sent me Hawken's book in 1994 when I was struggling with the question, *What is Interface doing for the environment?* And it was Joyce's daughter who'd sent her the same copy of *The Ecology of Commerce* after hearing Paul Hawken speak. Joyce is a constant source of inspiration, so I was eager to hear what she had to say.

"Ray," she began, "we've heard the good news about our environmental performance this year. But we've heard very little about how we are doing in the area of social sustainability. I'm not sure we would all agree about what social sustainability even means. Could you give us your own definition and tell us how you think we're doing?"

The room went dead quiet as everyone turned to me for some words of wisdom. Immediately thoughts began tumbling through my head, thoughts of all the training efforts we'd sponsored, the women who occupied leadership positions in the company, the diversity programs we participated in, the educational outreach of our tiny environmental foundation, the chair at Georgia Institute of Technology, our improving safety record in our plants, our marketing efforts through minority-owned dealers, the community legacy projects performed at every sales meeting. There was so much, yet I knew, not enough.

And the more I tried to put it into words (a skill that normally comes easily enough to me), the more diffuse and subjective it seemed, and the more difficult it became to offer a simple definition (like take nothing, do no harm). So I batted it back and said, "Joyce, if you don't know what social sustainability is, we're all in trouble." Joyce had no reply either. On my part, it was a glib answer, and one that didn't really satisfy me.

As we adjourned for dinner, I felt uneasy about the question, and my lack of a simple, clear response to Joyce. Why was it so difficult to talk about equity and social sustainability? We were doing a lot—all the things I shared in chapter 10. But there was no denying that I was a lot more comfortable talking about reducing our greenhouse gas emissions and boosting climate neutrality. I could instantly put my finger on a precise number on how far we'd come in those areas.

But what were the comparable metrics when it came to fairness? Diversity? Equality of opportunity? Community involvement? I knew how many tons of nylon we'd recycled. But how do you quantify what is so much the qualitative? How much social sustainability had we created, and how much was enough? My right brain seemed inadequate for the challenge.

Fortunately, our guest speaker that night, Majora Carter, a visionary voice in city planning who views urban renewal through an environmental lens, had a lot to say to us about some of these things.

Carter was awarded a 2005 MacArthur "genius" grant after founding Sustainable South Bronx, a community organization that pushes for eco-friendly practices (such as green and cool roofs). Equally important are job training and green-related economic development for her neighborhood. She currently runs a green economic consulting firm that bears her name.

Her talk to us that night, "Greening the Ghetto," put a spotlight on some of our toughest challenges. She also pointed out a path we could take to advance our social sustainability performance, to put it on par with our environmental and financial successes.

"I come from the South Bronx. When it comes to *un*sustainability," she began, "we are the canaries in the coal mine. Our city was redlined long before anyone had ever heard of the term. They ran elevated highways right through our neighborhoods, sometimes giving people only one month to clear out before the bulldozers showed up. Property values collapsed, and my parents were not able to sell their hard-won home at any price. It became more profitable to burn down apartment buildings and homes than to stick around to collect the rent. Crime was the only job in town. I grew up with a crack house across the street. My brother survived Vietnam only to be killed—gunned down—in our own neighborhood."

She told us that her community was always selected to host a new waste-treatment facility or garbage dump, though the South Bronx already handled 40 percent of all of New York City's commercial waste and all of the Bronx's municipal waste. That there were four power stations and a sewer sludge–pelletizing plant, but that the only new construction project intended for people was a prison.

She told us that being a woman of color made it twice as likely that she would suffer health problems from air pollution, and five times as likely that she could walk out her front door and see a chemical plant or a power station. She, like a great many other poor people, lived in zones of "environmental injustice," a term she had defined before uttering it.

I listened closely as Majora spoke, remembering the poor people who had been forced to endure the municipal landfill in LaGrange, and that perpetual cloud of buzzards that used to circle it before we got the gas project up and running. It had surely been another environmental injustice zone, but now it was not. There was an important lesson in that.

"*Economic* degradation," she said, "begets *environmental* degradation. And environmental degradation begets *social* degradation. The linkage is absolute. No exceptions. It's not a menu. You can't pick and choose which one of those three you'd like to address. You've got to address them all."

I thought back to the *Natural Step*'s fourth rule:

### 4. *Fairness and efficiency are linked.*

*The fourth rule is the social principle, which flows directly from the science-based principles. It mandates fair and efficient use of resources to meet humanity's basic needs. Because there are so many genuine needs, they must be met in the most resource-efficient manner possible.*

"While I know you guys at Interface are different," she said, "I don't expect most businesses to make the world a better place because it's right or moral. They just won't change their ways out of a sense of right and wrong. It's all about the bottom line. But what *kind* of bottom line?

"How long can a business continue to earn a good profit while, literally, trashing the environment or the people who are part of it? It's a good thing not to waste barrels of oil. A really good thing. I've heard Ray Anderson say we waste 90 percent of all the energy that goes into making things. But let's not add *wasting people* to that count.

"Profits, people, and the environment. That's the true triple bottom line we're aiming for. And the only way we're going to see some of those triple bottom line profits is through sustainable development. We need to bring everyone to the table and give them a reason to care. It doesn't matter if you're building a riverside park made from a brownfield industrial waste-land, attending job training in ecological restoration, working in a factory making carpet tiles, or holding down a green collar job installing photovol-taic panels. We are all responsible for the future we create.

"We all come from very different stations in life," she concluded, "but we all share one thing. We have nothing to lose by changing how business with a big 'B' is done. Nothing," she said, "but we've got everything to gain."

I thought about what Majora was getting at as she stayed onstage and fielded questions. Her message of inclusiveness—and hope—fit in with ev-erything I knew to be true. You cannot keep earning profits indefinitely at the environment's expense anymore than you can keep earning them at the expense of the people who work for you or live near you, or of your custom-ers or your installers. When it comes to sustainable enterprise, it really was all or nothing. And it really is true that we are all in it together.

Mentally, I took a step back and considered all of the challenges Inter-face had met, and those that were still to come. Energy prices were high, and that made our raw materials and transportation costs high, though re-cycled materials were becoming more competitive. Even recovering carpets for recycling was sensitive to the price of diesel fuel. While price fluctua-tions were certain, the overall general trends in pricing, generated by a static supply and a growing demand, seemed clear enough.

I knew that we'd wrung a lot of savings out of our operations—in energy, material, water, and waste. Then I thought about all those people in Majora's community. What could we do now to keep from wasting those most pre-cious resources—human ingenuity, resourcefulness, and determination?

I stepped back once more and realized that Majora Carter's hometown of the South Bronx was surrounded by some of the biggest, richest markets for Interface products. Where a lot of new carpets go in, a lot of old ones come out. A recycling facility located close to a resource like that ought to make pretty good business sense.

I wondered, *Could a community that had been on the short end of the stick for so long, people who'd lived in an "environmental injustice zone," play a part in closing the loop, returning precious organic molecules back to us to use again and again?* It would surely be meaningful work, and it would cut our virgin raw material use, our transport costs, and the embodied energy in our products—our whole carbon footprint. This could be the perfect integration of environmental responsibility, financial success, and social equity.

Win, win, and win. That's the way the system should work when people are the abundant resource and nature is scarce and diminishing.

I had to leave the Next Ascent summit that evening. But from the buzz I heard when it was all said and done, and from the final recommendations that Jim assembled, I knew that I had lots of company in thinking these thoughts. New thinking works in the social arena, too.

As our people gathered in working groups, and reached back for their strengths and forward to their dreams, some important things began to become clear. Yes, our Mission Zero goal was inspirational and very powerful. But it was also as real as we were willing to make it. We knew where we stood. We knew where we had to go. We had a compass now, and a map. The top of the mountain was right there, within sight. For the most part, the technologies existed. And nothing was going to stop us from standing together on that high summit. As for the eighth face, social sustainability, which some thought was incorporated adequately in that sixth face, this amorphous, unmeasurable quality that we knew was key to our ultimate success was becoming as clear as a mountain stream.

Just take a look at these six visions that emerged about who and what we will be when the year 2020 comes around. You'll see how inspiration, commitment, and determination, as well as Majora's people, profits, and the environment, come shining right through.

1. In 2020, *Interface is the number one place to work based on its undisputed leadership in environmental and social sustainability. Interface sets the standard for a diverse workforce in all aspects of diversity, reflecting Interface values while respecting cultural sensitivity. Interface develops every associate to her/his greatest potential, utilizing the principles of our strengths-based culture, which the Gallup organization has helped us develop.*

2. In 2020, *Interface is an organic, restorative corporation, meeting the needs of our employees, customers, and communities. We design,*

*create, and provide products and services in ways that support the conditions conducive to an enriched life. Energized by our strengths, we are passionate, connected, self-empowered, happy, highly engaged, transparent, diverse, and damn good!*

**3.** In 2020, *courage is the lifeblood of our company. We foster individual ownership through vision and accountability. We value passion, perseverance, curiosity, belief, and a sense of purpose. We embody the essence of our brand and our company. We embrace and capitalize on our uniqueness and diversity around the globe.*

**4.** In 2020, *Interface is an organization that demonstrates the end of the industrial revolution and the reality of the new—the sustainable economy. We are a company that grows or reclaims our own raw materials in a socially sustainable manner; manufactures our product utilizing only renewable energy and at locations near our markets and customers; and provides a beneficial use (which may be within our organization) for our legacy projects.*

**5.** In 2020, *Interface is the first name in social sustainability through our deliberate efforts to maximize human potential and the quality of life in the entire global community.*

**6.** In 2020, *through natural design, Interface is the first name in restorative commerce; a place where everything connects.*

Reading those results added another proudest moment to my list, and I think you can see why.

In his book *Collapse*, Jared Diamond makes the point that the forces that rose up and overwhelmed such diverse societies as the Greenland Norse and the Polynesians of Easter Island—environmental destruction, population overshoot, and resource depletion—need not be our fate. "Collapse isn't inevitable," he wrote, "but depends on a society's choices."

I've made mine, and I've never had a reason to turn back. Look at those six "2020 statements" and imagine your company, your university, your town's name instead of ours. We have made our choices.

Dare I ask, What about you?

# 16 | Every Reason for Hope

come from the private sector. My job has always been to find solutions and put them into practice, beginning with my own company. The fundamental transformation of Interface is, I believe—and I hope will continue to be—a phenomenon of the first order of magnitude, providing ultimate meaning to its original creation.

It is a business school case study brought to life, and one that other businesses would be smart to take a good look at. For what company, what economy, what civilization can exist without the services provided by nature; air; water purification and distribution (the hydrologic cycle); soil creation and maintenance, thus food; energy; raw materials; climate regulation; pollination; seed dispersal; nutrient cycling; an ultraviolet radiation shield; flood and insect control; and net primary production, the product of photosynthesis? Without any of them, provided by nature, there would be no economy in the first place.

Beginning at the headwaters of my personal journey, framed to some unknowable extent from my earliest days growing up in tiny West Point, Georgia, to that milestone moment of my epiphany in 1994, I have come at last to a remarkable and fulfilling place: a perch more than halfway to the summit of a mountain whose top I could scarcely imagine when my associates and I began this climb.

From this place, this perch, I can see clearly what we might accomplish as we shed the kind of thinking that had us nearly, but not quite, trapped. I can spot the dangers—and there are plenty of them—but I see even more opportunities. I have seen remarkable examples of the kind of new thinking the industrial systems absolutely must have.

I have seen a mechanical engineer design a new production line to manufacture the same product at the same rate as one he designed ten years earlier. Except this time he designs it to use 93 percent less horsepower (one fourteenth as much!) by using large straight pipes on one level rather than small, bendy ones that span several levels. Friction losses are cut dramatically, allowing for small pumps rather than large ones. Oh yes, the new production line cost less to build than the one built ten years earlier, and far less to operate. He has practiced whole system optimization, in which getting the job done well has replaced just getting the job done.

I have seen another factory engineer ask his counterpart at city hall how much methane gas was being produced at the local landfill. The city engineer checks, and he is amazed at how much there is, and at how offensive it is to the nearby African American neighborhood and the people who live there, in what Majora Carter calls an environmental injustice zone.

The two engineers collaborate, and a year later a public-private partnership is born. The city commits $3 million to capture and pipe the methane to a factory. The factory commits $50,000 to adapt its boilers. The two agree on a price for gas that is 30 percent less than natural gas. With a calculated life of the landfill gas project of forty years, that translates into a financial value for the city (at present value) of some $35 million for a $3 million investment!

As methane is drawn down, the capacity of the landfill is expanded, allowing the city to postpone opening a new one for an estimated fifteen years. The smell of methane that used to blanket the adjoining neighborhoods? It's gone. And the earth is spared enough greenhouse gas emissions (methane is especially potent) to render the engineer's factory entirely climate neutral.

And I've seen the marketing arm of that factory realize the appeal of a climate-neutral product and dub it Cool Carpet, and I have watched that product become a huge success, contributing incremental sales and lifting the company's image in ways no amount of advertising ever could.

I've also seen a factory manager in Southern California muse over the possibility of using solar photovoltaics to produce some of his plant's electricity. He uncovers state and federal assistance for such a system, but the accountants (who are only looking at costs) tell him it still won't "pencil out." That manager doesn't give up. His sales people are sure that a product made with the help of sunlight will generate new sales, and they are right. The result?

The solar system connects 127 kilowatts of peak voltage to the California grid, and generates enough energy to tuft a million square yards of Solar-made™ carpet, which generates incremental sales the accountant overlooked in his preoccupation with costs.

I have seen a product designer, frustrated with the lack of progress in implementing sustainable design, plead, "Let's do something, anything!" So his team redesigns a product to use 4 percent less of its most expensive and energy-intensive material component (in this case, DuPont nylon). The redesigned product performs well in all the usual tests, but an engineer is still curious. He wonders what the effect of that 4 percent savings means upstream (in other words, incorporating the embodied energy expended by the maker of that nylon). So he asks DuPont a question DuPont has never been asked before, and gets a *very* big number for an answer.

When that number is applied theoretically across the entire product line, it turns out that eliminating just 4 percent of the nylon used each year saves enough energy (not used by DuPont) to run the designer's entire factory for half a year. I have seen that savings grow over the years, until that theoretical 4 percent reduction now stands at a real 17 percent, and it even has a name all its own: dematerialization through conscious design, a concept with far-reaching implications for a voracious industrial system.

I've seen a multidisciplinary team of engineers, production people, and product designers collaborate to find a new way to produce patterned carpet.

The old way was to print the pattern on a plain-colored carpet base. But printing was very water intensive and required harsh dyes, steam (think energy) to fix the dyes, washing to remove the excess (where the dyes become chemically hazardous waste), energy-intensive drying to remove the wash water, and chemical treatment to the wash water and dyes before they could be released into a river.

But innovation results in a patented invention, a new process that uses a computerized tufting machine to place yarn of specific colors precisely to form intricate patterns. The old wet-printing machines are scrapped, the bridge burned, the investment written off, and the old technology abandoned. I have seen our people invent their way out of a water-, chemical-, and energy-intensive problem, and into a family of new products that give us a proprietary edge in our marketplace rather than a competitive handicap.

One of the first products to benefit from the new tufting machines has its origins in an outrageous assignment issued by our chief designer to his design team: Go out into a forest and see how nature designs a floor covering. Looking to nature as a mentor and inspiration, that team spends a day studying forest floors and streambeds. They find it to be chaotic—no two sticks, no two stones, no two leaves, no two square feet are the same. Yet there is a pleasant harmony in the disorder.

They return to their studios and design a carpet tile in which no two tile faces are alike. All are similar, but none are identical, contrary to the prevailing industrial paradigm that demands cookie-cutter perfection from every mass-produced item—Six Sigma uniformity. Nature, the inspiration, is anything but uniform. She doesn't know Six Sigma, but she is very effective. This new product is given a name, Entropy,® and in a year and a half it rises to the top of the bestseller list, faster than any other product ever has before.

I have seen another design team dream up and address a weird challenge: How does a gecko cling upside down to a ceiling? The question arises in a session intended to figure out how to completely eliminate glue from the installation of carpet tiles. Glue uses harsh, petro-derived chemicals and can be a devilish source of outgased volatile organic compounds long after a carpet is installed. Not a pleasant smell or healthy place to work!

Though the answer to a how a gecko manages to anchor himself in the most unlikely places—van der Waals forces—is not the answer to the glue question, it gets people thinking new thoughts about the problem, and a solution is found: a small, 2.5 inch square of releasable adhesive tape is applied to the underside of tiles where the corners meet, with the sticky side facing up. This way all the tiles are connected laterally, not to the floor but to one another, and their own combined weight keeps them anchored in place. And it accomplishes all of that using the special tape on less than 2 percent of each tile's undersurface to produce a glue-and-chemical-free installation. The bottom line? One more market differentiator for the company and its products, and no more glue fumes for its customers.

Upside down thinking? Maybe as conventional wisdom. But at Interface this has become normal. I have seen firsthand how all of these examples evolved naturally from our Mission Zero drive. And they all represent new thinking, important aspects of sustainability in action on the factory floor.

- Whole system optimization: big, short, straight, level pipes and small motors, not the other way around.
- Waste as "food": polluting methane gas converted to a revenue stream, an energy source, a greenhouse gas offset, Cool Carpet, a multimillion-dollar cost avoidance for a city, and an environmental injustice removed.
- In the round investment decisions: justified by more than cost; considering customers, market demand, the value of leadership, and incremental sales as factors in the go/no-go decision.
- Dematerialization through conscious design and upstream thinking (the real leverage may be up there).
- Burn the bridges: abandoning high-impact technologies for low-impact, sustainable technologies that also yield better, more innovative product designs.
- Biomimicry: using nature's time-tested engineering to create products that appeal to our deep appreciation of the natural world.
- Thinking upside down.

As I have heard Amory Lovins say countless times, "The best way to have good new ideas is just to stop having bad old ideas."

This is sustainability in action. Fourteen years of near total immersion in it has provided me with these and many other insights; and perhaps I have covered most of them already in this book and there will be nothing new in them for you, but for the sake of clarity and emphasis, allow me to repeat myself. These examples of new thinking are very definitely drawn from real life and represent the before and after views of reality that the people of Interface have experienced on our transformative journey.

As big as the challenge of sustainability is for one company like yours or mine—newer, better products and processes that help us in our climb toward sustainability rather than hold us back—a far bigger challenge remains for all of society. How in the world will we do it?

I am convinced that having a sustainable society for the indefinite future—whether that means seven generations or a thousand or more—depends totally and absolutely on the vast, ethically driven redesign of the industrial system about which I have written, triggered by an equally vast mind-shift. But—and this is the hard part—that shift must happen one mind at a time, one organization at a time, one technology at a time, one building, one company, one university curriculum, one community, one region, one industry at a time, one product at a time until we look around one day and see that there is a new norm at work, and that the entire system has been transformed.

I cling to an observation by Paul Paydos, an associate in the now-divested fabrics business. "I have never known an ex-environmentalist. Once you get it, you cannot un-get it." The movement is like a ratchet; it only moves in one direction. There's every reason for hope in that observation.

By picking up this book you have created the possibility that perhaps another mind will be added to the green side of the balance sheet and the ratchet will go "click." That would please me greatly.

And yet, it seems to me that our culture, with all of its taboos, assumptions, and mores is a reflection of something a lot bigger: a whole society's mind-set. So, what about the mind-set that underlies our culture? As you have read, I strongly suggest that we have been, and still are, in the grips of a flawed view of reality—a flawed paradigm, a flawed world view—and it pervades our culture, putting us on Jared Diamond's biological collision course with collapse. It is the paradigm that is reflected in our culture's infatuation with stuff and our willful ignorance of nature.

I unconsciously held the old flawed view of reality before I read Paul Hawken's book. The new view (the post-Hawken view) will undergird any sustainable society that I can imagine. Here are the pieces that must come together. Please pay attention to them, for they represent the way out of the trap we have so artfully built for ourselves.

The old, flawed view of reality that I refer to is the one that treats earth as if it were infinite in its ability to supply the stuff to feed the industrial system's metabolism, or treats earth as if it were an infinite sink into which to pour our poisonous waste, including greenhouse gases into the atmosphere.

*A sustainable society, into the indefinite future, will accept and honor the fragile finiteness of earth.*

That old, flawed view of reality is the one that adopts the life of a human being as its relevant time frame for caring about the consequences of our decisions—more likely, the working life—rather than recognizing the true long-term, evolutionary time. It holds onto the notion that earth was made for humankind to conquer and rule, to take whatever we want from nature without regard for the other species that depend on, and even comprise, nature—nature, of which we too are a part, not separate. What we do to the web of life we do to ourselves.

*A sustainable society will adopt the truly long view and put humans in their proper relationship with and within nature.*

The old, flawed view of reality holds that technology, coupled with left-brained human intelligence, will see us through without our having to address the extractive, abusive attributes of technology that are part of the problem, and without appreciating the right-brain attributes of intelligence that include the human spirit.

*A sustainable society will build on the ascendancy of women in business, the professions, government, and education.*

Technology must stop destroying the true wealth of nations by its extractive, linear, fossil fuel–driven, abusive, wasteful nature that is focused on labor productivity. It has proven itself all too capable of being a big part of the problem. It must become an even bigger part of the solution.

*In a sustainable society, technologies will share different general characteristics. They will be renewable, cyclical, solar-driven, waste-free, benign, and focused on resource-productivity.*

That old flawed view of reality holds that the invisible hand of the market is an honest broker. Yet the market is as blind as a bat if prices are dishonest.

> *A sustainable society will insist on ecologically honest prices that will enable a sighted market to work for sustainability rather than against sustainability.*

The old, flawed view of reality holds that increasing labor productivity is the route to abundance for all, when it is obvious in a world of diminishing nature and increasing human population that the route to abundance for all is through increasing resource-productivity. That's the logic behind all recycling efforts. Even inorganic materials have embodied energy that can be salvaged, and one very important result of increasing resource-productivity is that it puts people to work in the process. For clearly, at the heart of the challenge humanity faces is the imperative to lift the poorest among us out of grinding poverty while healing the already badly damaged earth in the process.

> *A sustainable society will respect nature's limits and draw inspiration from them for innovative ways to conserve resources and simultaneously address poverty.*

The old, flawed view of reality holds that happiness is to be found in abundance and material wealth (the trappings of affluence), when we know there is more to happiness than just piling up more stuff. We know that consumerism will not bring real happiness, despite the messages with which our children (and we) are bombarded through advertising saturation.

> *A sustainable society will seek higher levels of awareness and transcendent meaning in life—more true happiness with less stuff.*

Remember the modification we made to Paul Ehrlich's environmental impact equation to move technology (T) from the numerator to the denominator?

$$I = \frac{P \times A}{T_2}$$

Let's revisit it and ask ourselves how to make that equation reflect the new worldview I am describing. What about that capital A for affluence? To me it suggests that affluence is an end in itself. But what if we thought of it as a lowercase, a, suggesting that it's merely a means to a different end, and that that end is happiness?

We might then rewrite the equation again as . . .

$$I = \frac{P \times a}{T_2 \times H}$$

. . . in which H stands for happiness, the real end we seek. More happiness with less stuff! This describes a new, sustainable civilization, in which environmental impacts become vanishingly small, and generations into the indefinite future will be born into a livable world.

And what about the largest, most pervasive, wealthiest institution on earth, the one now doing the greatest damage? How does it become a leader in transforming society?

The old, flawed view of reality holds to the belief that business exists to make a profit, when we know in our hearts that business makes a profit to exist, and it must surely exist for some higher purpose. What CEO really expects to stand before her or his Maker someday and talk about shareholder value? Or market share? Or the clever manipulation of a gullible public?

*A sustainable society will realize that done right, the triple bottom line of corporate social responsibility—economy, environment, social equity—can come together under the banner of authenticity to create a truly superior, totally ethical, financial bottom line—a better way to bigger and more legitimate profits, a better business model.*

The old, flawed view of reality holds that the environment is a subset of the economy, the pollution part. In our new enlightenment we acknowledge that the economy is the wholly owned subsidiary of the environment, to quote the late U.S. senator Gaylord Nelson, who was quoting the archbishop of Canterbury. The environment is the parent; the economy is the child. It is not the other way around, as most of our economists still seem to believe.

> *A sustainable society will develop a system of economics that gets the prices right ecologically and economically by internalizing the externalities, and thus lovingly protects the parent, nature—the goose that lays all the golden eggs.*

So, will we shift paradigms in time and embrace this new view of reality? That is the question of our era. The hell of it is, it's up to you and me, and you now know where I stand.

I began this chapter by reminding you that I am an industrialist. I do not profess to be a politician, a think-tank guru, nor a B-school wonder. I come from the world of business and industry. I used to accept as fact the economist's view that there were no twenty-dollar bills lying in the street, that opportunities naturally attract entrepreneurs to jump on the next big thing.

But after all these years I have come to some very different conclusions. We found hundreds of millions of dollars in eliminating the concept of waste at Interface. We found new products, new processes, new markets, new sources of profit in a changed mind-set and new thinking. So I think it's quite conservative to say that, on a national scale, many billions of dollars are waiting to be found by someone.

Perhaps you are that someone; and unless you lead the charge to pick them up, perhaps no one will.

Yes, it has been a big challenge. But I also know it is far from impossible. Will we Homo sapiens (self-named wise man) shed our hubris, shift paradigms, and opt for survival in time to avoid a global version of Jared Diamond's *Collapse*? Will business and industry lead the way, and by doing so seize the biggest global market to come along in centuries? Or will business draw back and see nature withdraw her irreplaceable support?

Those are the questions of our era. And to answer them we have to ask ourselves another one: If someone's got to lead (and profit), why not us?

I can promise you that there's no greater challenge. There's no greater reward, and now there's a compass and a map. They are yours to use and follow.

After all, in 1994 I spun the wheel and turned one very oil-dependent company in a new and better direction. There was no map at all, yet today, we're well on the way to the top of that high, high mountain, one higher than Everest.

We've shown that there's a way to the summit that is good and green and profitable and right and smart. If we've been able to do all that, then, by definition, it must be possible. And, given the kind of company we are, if we can do it, anyone can. And if anyone can do it, there's truly every reason to believe that everyone can.

In March 1996, I gave a talk about our still new environmental mission to the sales force at our Bentley Mills operation in Southern California, the plant that would go on to design and install what was at the time the country's largest industrial solar electric system.

At first I could not say what kind of an impression I was making; it's sometimes hard for me to tell. People seemed to get what I was talking about and they made nice comments; but then, they were sitting in a room listening to Interface's founder and CEO, so naturally they would say nice things.

When I received an e-mail from one of them a few days later, it came totally out of the blue. It was a poem written by one of the Bentley folks. His name was Glenn Thomas, and it was one of the most encouraging moments of my life.

It told me that—for sure—at least one person sitting in that meeting room had really gotten it, right down to his soul. Here's the poem. Read it now and see for yourself.

### TOMORROW'S CHILD

*Without a name; an unseen face,*
*and knowing not your time or place,*
*Tomorrow's Child, though yet unborn,*
*I met you first last Tuesday morn.*

> *A wise friend introduced us two,*
> *and through his shining point of view*
> *I saw a day that you would see;*
> *a day for you, but not for me.*
> *Knowing you has changed my thinking,*
> *for I had never had an inkling*
> *that perhaps the things I do*
> *might someday, somehow, threaten you.*
> *Tomorrow's Child, my daughter-son,*
> *I'm afraid I've just begun*
> *to think of you and of your good,*
> *though always having known I should.*
> *Begin I will to weigh the cost*
> *of what I squander, what is lost.*
> *If ever I forget that you*
> *will someday come to live here, too.*

Every day of my life since then, "Tomorrow's Child" has spoken to me with one simple but profound message, which I am presuming to share with you: We are each part of the web of life—the continuum of humanity, sure, but in a large sense, the web of life itself. We have a choice to make during our brief visit to this beautiful blue and green living planet. We can hurt it or we can help it. For you, it is your choice.

# Epilogue

## *Off the Grid in Lost Valley, North Carolina*

In the early autumn of 2000, Pat said, "I would like to have a house in the mountains. A log cabin. Would you?"

My immediate answer was *Yes!* Especially if we could build it on a south-facing slope to take advantage of solar heating and electricity, and maybe even keep it totally off the utility grid. Was there such a place reasonably close by? We were determined to find out.

The mountains that are most easily accessible from our home in Atlanta are the Appalachian and Blue Ridge ranges of north Georgia, eastern Tennessee, and western North Carolina. We took weekend trips to comb them, hunting for just the right piece of land. Our hunt began to narrow in on the area around Highlands, North Carolina.

On a glorious weekend in late October, with the trees in full color, we found ourselves turning off the highway, driving through a pair of old stone columns and down three and a half miles of narrow, twisting, turning road to the bottom of a secluded valley. The map called it Lost Valley, and I could sure see why. There a bubbling stream ran gin clear and ice cold. We crossed the stream on a small bridge and began to drive up the opposite side of the valley.

The way grew steep, and I was about ready to turn back, but Pat wanted to keep exploring. We eventually climbed out of the trees and found ourselves on a cleared knoll. We stopped, got out, and stood there in awe.

The view went on for miles and miles, southward down the valley all the way to Georgia. The mountains were covered with an autumn carpet of red, yellow, gold, and orange foliage. The listing said the whole tract, some eighty-seven acres contiguous with National Forest Service land, was for sale.

It took our breath away. We'd found what we were looking for.

A year and a day after we bought the land (an interval dictated by the tax code), we signed an agreement with the Chattowah Open Land Trust to put seventy-nine of those acres into a "forever wild" conservation easement. Meanwhile, we had set about planning our off-the-grid log cabin in the mountains, and a division of labor had taken effect. Pat handled the aesthetics while I took on the construction and engineering. We both worked with our architect on the size and location of the rooms.

High on my list of must-haves was for our cabin to be truly off the grid, meaning no connection to any of the public utilities we take for granted in the city: no utility power, no water or sewerage pipes, no natural gas. For a while I did consider connecting our planned solar power plant to the local utility grid, selling our electricity back to them when our photovoltaic panels' output exceeded our modest demands. But the utility wanted forty thousand dollars (if they didn't hit rocks) to run a buried line to our house, and would buy solar electric power from us at one quarter of the price they charged.

We never called them back.

There were serious design challenges in trying to make a twenty-five-hundred-square-foot log cabin energy efficient. Air infiltration through cracks and crevices is the bane of any superinsulated home, as ours had to be. And what house has more cracks and crevices than a log cabin? But with the help of some great architects, engineers, carpenters, and contractors, we solved that problem—and all the others that presented themselves as planning, design, and then construction proceeded apace.

The construction phase, from beginning to end, took about a year and a half (though we moved in with furniture while work was still going on around us). What did we end up with?

A two-story cabin built of Engleman spruce, the logs harvested from a stand of dead trees (victim of an insect infestation forty years earlier) and assembled into thick, highly insulated walls. Gleaming yellow pine floors, five small bedrooms, a big living room with a roaring fireplace, a study, and a place for guests to retreat when they'd had enough visiting. Big windows for cross ventilation. A kitchen with all the usual appliances (though they are the most energy-efficient models available), four full baths, and two half-baths.

The cabin is heated by the sun in the winter and cooled by mountain breezes in the summer. The heavy, insulated log walls hold indoor temperatures nearly constant, no matter what the weather might be doing outside. Our water comes from our own deep well via a pump powered by the sun. Solar heat is gathered by five roof-mounted panels that circulate hot water to radiant coils embedded beneath the floor and to the domestic hot-water tank. The radiant heat never feels hot underfoot, but the floors never feel cold, either. No one has ever run out of hot water yet, and Pat makes sure that there are always plenty of clean sheets and towels for family and guests alike.

Electricity is provided by thirty-two photovoltaic panels that deliver five peak kilowatts, enough to supply all of our electrical needs when we're around, and to recharge the batteries that provide power when we're not. A propane tank delivers gas to boost the hot water system when necessary and to run our "backup" generator, which keeps the batteries topped off during long, cloudy spells. Propane provides gas-fired cooking and clothes drying, too. Our total utility bill is the cost of about nine hundred gallons of propane a year. I like to imagine that, because of the forever wild easement, the carbon sequestered by seventy-nine acres of southern hardwoods and pines makes us very nearly climate neutral. I really don't know for sure, but there are lots of trees left standing compared with what would be left if the property were fully developed.

We love our log house in the mountains—off the grid, in our forever wild slice of Lost Valley. Sitting on the porch, looking out across the forests, listening to the rush and tumble of Shoal Creek in the hollow far below, it is easy to imagine, as in the visualization game I sometimes ask my audiences to play, that I have found my own perfect place. Safe, serene, and far removed from all the cares of the world.

But it's not entirely so. While the outside world does not intrude here in Lost Valley, and while the regional power grid could fail entirely and we might never know about it until we read the local paper, the outside world is very much on my mind.

You see, four months have passed since I finished the prologue to this book. Four months that have not only *not* seen a solution to a truly global financial crisis, but rather have seen a deepening of it. Right now, Brugge and my laptop view of the financial meltdown seem like a century ago.

An economic hurricane has made landfall. Like Katrina, what began small and far away as a problem in the mortgage market has blown up into a category 5 monster that threatens to leave much of Wall Street (and Main Street, and my street, and yours) looking like the Ninth Ward of New Orleans.

Now you may think that if anywhere would be insulated from all of that it would be an off-the-grid cabin in the mountains of North Carolina. And in a superficial way that's true; but we are not insulated from the economic shocks that began reverberating through global financial markets in mid-2008. The credit freeze and financial meltdown I watched by laptop from Brugge have taken their toll around the world. At Interface, as at so many other companies, we have taken the painful action of rightsizing our company, releasing people, and closing facilities to better match capacities with demand. Still, our shareholders have experienced punishing loss in share price.

Yet I am confident that Interface is prepared for heavy weather. That is not to say we can prevent or hold this storm at bay, or swim against the tide (excuse the mixed metaphors). But just as we insulated our cabin in Lost Valley against the cold, selected the most efficient appliances, and powered them with the sun, Interface's drive toward the summit of Mount Sustainability has made it both green and lean, and prepared us to outperform our corporate peers—and competitors—whatever market conditions we encounter. We believe the competitive advantages we have realized in our Mission Zero quest will still be there throughout the hard times that are upon us. We are counting especially on the hard-won goodwill of our loyal customers.

I know that my credibility and the credibility of this book depend on the veracity of the preceding paragraph, and I expect to be fully vindicated. So, let us return to the larger issues of the times.

The chain reaction pileup that began when a bunch of predatory lenders convinced some gullible people that they could buy a house far beyond their means (because they could always sell it to some other gullible person) is now widespread, painful, and deeply troubling. Some economists pin the blame on deregulation, on laissez-faire free market shenanigans. Others cite a triumph of greed over common sense that allowed homeowners to believe they could have their house and spend it, too; or a market failure that allowed Wall Street whizzes to convince themselves that if they chopped up and bundled enough bad investments and spread them around they would magically become good ones. No less a financial expert than former Federal Reserve chairman Alan Greenspan professes to be shocked at how corporations were no longer "acting in their own best self-interests."

But I think this crisis has deeper roots than just a string of bad mortgages or a tidal wave of global money seeking risky returns. I think it stems from our dangerous faith in what is clearly a broken industrial model that is yoked to our infatuation with stuff—namely, consumerism.

I use the word *infatuation* deliberately, as in "a state of mind characterized by intrusive thinking, longing, uncertainty, hope, misperception, fantasies, and passion." Here's an example:

I read the other day about a woman who went to the mall for some "retail therapy" and used her credit card to buy a pair of shoes. They cost about forty dollars—a bargain. But at the end of the month, after paying her mortgage, her health insurance, her food, gasoline, and utilities, she didn't have enough to go around. A few months later, her credit card company notified her that those forty-dollar shoes, with all the late fees and penalties added in, were now going to cost her twelve hundred dollars. And by the way, her interest rate was now sky-high, too.

Whether it's buying cheap shoes or burning cheap coal, what seems like a bargain in the short term can get awfully pricey in a hurry. The bill will come due, and it must be paid.

Some might even call the way we insist on gauging our economic health by how much stuff we consume (and throw away) a kind of temporary insanity—"temporary" because, while reading this book, you have seen (as I have) that consumerism is absolutely unsustainable. Like that letter from the credit card company, a day of reckoning will come.

Looking at the smoking ruins of once mighty banks, the threatened devaluation of national currencies, the epidemic of foreclosures and bankruptcies, and the way those are spilling over into the rest of the real economy, can any of us say that our lives have not been materially harmed by an unhealthy infatuation with stuff? Now that America has become the biggest debtor on earth, can we say this has truly served us well? Or that flipping houses (or derivatives, or credit default swaps) is the same thing as earning money by actually making or improving something?

The United States maintained a healthy trade balance with the world right up through the mid-1960s. We built things that many other countries bought. Life was far from perfect back then, but has abandoning so much of our manufacturing sector been anything like an improvement (other than on Wall Street)?

I don't know how anyone can fail to see that drowning in a sea of red ink might put a damper on our ability to invest in a sustainable future, one that protects the environment and ourselves. But thumbing our nose at the environment and a sustainable future has contributed to the financial crisis, too. Let me take a shot at making that case once more.

At first blush the connection between ignoring sustainability and a global financial meltdown seems tenuous at best. Perhaps high energy costs, especially gasoline, stemming from dependence on foreign oil and exacerbated by hurricane activity, served to tip some home owners into default on their subprime mortgage loans. However, this is likely to have been a very minor factor, and is probably unquantifiable.

So, what are the deeper, less obvious connections? Well, as the banking crisis has unfolded, the magnitude of the subprime (read, high interest rate!) mortgage portfolios held by failing financial institutions around the world has begun to become apparent. Something on the order of $3 trillion (at present count) bad loans spawned losses in all kinds of high-risk derivative financial instruments—exposure perhaps on the order of $60 trillion!

What was at the heart of this debacle? I suggest—and I know this is heresy—that Milton Friedman was at the heart, along with a generation of economists and bankers who have blindly followed his mantra: "Business exists to make a profit."

Really? This credo is at the heart of the world view that I've already written about—the fundamentally flawed paradigm, the mind-set that underlies the industrial system—and I suggest that that same mind-set also underlies the global financial system. I further suggest that Gordon Gekko's fictional proclamation in the film *Wall Street*, "Greed is good," is as widely accepted as Friedman's credo, one hand-in-glove with the other, throughout the high-flying financial world. That's a real double whammy!

So, with trillions of dollars seeking instant gratification in short-term profits, with the financial industry coming up with ever-more esoteric and risky ways of satisfying that demand, with a ratings industry turning a blind eye to risk and stamping triple-A on too many pieces of paper (because if one agency didn't, another would), something had to give, and it did.

The system began to clog up (to use Secretary Paulson's term again), and the first casualty was trust, trust among banks, and trust by the general public in its banks. As trust evaporates, fear rushes in to fill the vacuum, and confidence quickly follows trust into oblivion. That pattern has been plain to see.

What does this scenario have to do with sustainability? Quite a lot.

Stephen Covey, author of *The 7 Habits of Highly Successful People*, tells us that trust is earned by trustworthiness, which in turn stems from competence and good character. And, furthermore, suppose that Milton Friedman was just dead wrong; and (dream a little) the newly enlightened economists would now accept a new view of reality: "Business makes a profit to exist, and must surely exist for some higher purpose."

Looking for evidence of good character? How about a higher purpose? How about concern for the common good?

How does the common good relate to sustainability? The answer is, in countless ways. A big, pseudo-profitable bank that spews toxic mortgages into the global financial community is pretty much the same as a big pseudo-profitable factory that spews toxic chemicals into the biosphere. Each of them can show a pseudo-healthy balance sheet for a while, but the bill always comes due in the end.

So the link between trust and confidence on the one hand and sustainability and character on the other, as reflected in good corporate citizenship and concern for the common good, becomes compelling. Conversely, the effect of the absence of character and the absence of trust is proving to be overwhelming.

Björn Stigson, president of the World Business Council for Sustainable Development, an association of some two hundred of the world's largest and most environmentally progressive companies, makes much the same point when he suggests that banks in general have been slow to take a real interest in sustainability, and it shows in lost reputation and lost trust. What's a reputation worth? What's trust worth? Seems pretty clear to me—a lot!

Maybe there is still another crippling flaw in banking systems around the world, one that condemns them to repeat boom-bust cycles over and over. The concentration of wealth and power, as big banks swallow small banks in their Pac-Man strategies, has been both obvious and admired, but may not be a good thing after all. The big banks get bigger but not smarter; the not quite so big banks—the ones who actually know something about their customers—disappear into the big.

One effect of a bank's getting bigger is an increase in the efficiency of the bank, which is measured by the ratio of revenue to fixed (largely personnel) costs. Layoffs invariably follow acquisitions, and even if the new bank's revenue turns out to be less than the preacquisition combined total (bankers call this loss "runoff"), more than enough cost is eliminated to make the resulting efficiency greater.

The problem this Pac-Man process produces, as Bernard Lietaer, a European economist who helped create the euro, has shown, is that efficiency and resilience in any system are inversely related. So there is a tradeoff between the two. Efficiency, pushed too far, produces a loss of resilience. When a big investment bank fails (read, Lehman Brothers), a big part of the system goes with it. That's lack of resilience.

Lietaer advocates looking to natural ecosystems for the model for redesigning and balancing, and thus optimizing, the tradeoff between resilience and efficiency in the financial system. Ecosystems specialize in self-organizing resilience, based on diversity. As Daniel Quinn, the author of *Ishmael*, who gave us the example of the flawed aerodynamic design for a civilization that won't "fly," says, "God's passion in nature is diversity."

How interesting! Nature! That's the same place Interface has looked for its guide in redesigning an industrial company. Diversity and resilience begin to look and sound a lot like sustainability to me.

But back to us humans. Our heedless worship of stuff has been, at best, a very mixed blessing. As a people, as a nation, as a species, we have piled up a mountain of debt that we are now hard-pressed to pay off. Our infatuation with stuff, whether it's cheap shirts from China, cheap oil from Saudi Arabia, or cheap mortgages for houses, has made us deeply dependent upon a world that is increasingly unwilling to foot our bills. It is a world that has been willing to underwrite this American way of life (read, overconsumption) for decades, but, I think, no longer. I fully expect one result on the other side of this recession (cum depression?) will be that a lot of excesses is squeezed out of the system.

I've written quite a bit about how excesses and consumerism have put us crosswise with the earth. How the take-make-waste industrial paradigm was leading us all, lemming-like, to a high cliff. But it now has put us at odds with our own financial health, too. It has not made us free, and as I sit here looking out across my own perfect place in Lost Valley, I know that the thoughtless pursuit and accumulation of ever cheaper goods have not made us happy, either.

Now, a good many of our fellow citizens are more than not happy; they are miserable. Trillions of dollars of family savings have "vanished." Huge companies teeter on the edge of insolvency. Jobs are vanishing. How are we to get them back? How should we rebuild? What is to be done?

Well, in business, when something isn't working out, a wise CEO tries something new. This whole book has been about that something new, new thinking, and that better way. Sustainability in all its forms, from the personal to the corporate to the national to the world at large, is and must surely be our better way. But in times as unsettling as these, can we afford to pay attention to something as esoteric sounding as sustainability?

I think we cannot afford not to. When a hurricane strikes, when storm surges swamp barrier islands and winds level whole towns, the old mind-set would have us return to the scene of devastation and rebuild everything just as it was.

Wouldn't it be smarter to build with a new mind-set? With channelized rivers freed to meander again, to deliver sand and silt to rebuild those barrier islands? With marshes revitalized, and with homes and towns built on higher ground and to a higher standard of construction?

Hurricanes, nature's trail, revitalized marshes, rebuilt homes, higher ground—all these are metaphors that remind us that common sense still has a role to play, and the search for a better way makes the most sense of all. And there is an enormous opportunity waiting for us.

Remember what Bill Clinton said: "Creating a low carbon economy will lead to the greatest economic boom in the United States since we mobilized for World War II." Bill Clinton may not have gotten everything right. Not by a long shot. But in this, he is definitely on target. He could have added, with sufficient prescience, that we are going to need that boom to get us out of the 2008–2009 (and maybe 10, 11, and 12) mess.

What should we do now to begin to move away from the old, unsustainable business model and to generate new jobs and new wealth? Here's a beginning:

We have homes to insulate.

We have energy-efficient appliances and industrial machinery to invent and sell.

We have benign chemistry to develop to eliminate toxics from our waste streams and products.

We have recycling technology to invent, build, install, and operate to get rid of the waste streams and give precious energy-intensive molecules life after life.

We have unlimited, renewable power from that marvelous fusion reactor eight minutes away at the speed of light to tap into and distribute from one end of our country to the other.

We have an electrical "interstate highway system" for direct current (low line loss) electricity to build.

We have a world waiting to buy our renewable technologies.

We have hybrid and all-electric vehicles to pioneer, to breathe life into our auto industry and to bring back skilled jobs that pay good wages.

We have a financial system to rethink and redesign.

We have a leadership vacuum to fill.

Sitting here on the deck of my mountain cabin, watching the sun drop below the far hills that mark the western edge of Lost Valley, listening to the birds get quiet and the crickets crank up, I sometimes think that all these things are just too much for us to handle; that they are all just "blue sky" dreams, and I'm just a dreamer who has poured a lot of his time, energy, and stockholder money into lofty ideas about ecology and sustainability instead of the bottom line.

But you have seen that I'm as profit-minded, and as competitive, as anyone you're likely to meet. You have read how I took the entrepreneurial plunge and founded Interface with nothing more than a good idea, my life's savings, and the faith of a few brave investors. You have seen how that company became the world leader in carpet tiles, with annual sales of more than a billion dollars.

I have told you the story of how, at age sixty in 1994, I steered my company on a new course—one designed to reduce our environmental footprint while increasing our profits, and to be the first corporation in history to become truly sustainable, to shut down its smokestacks, close off its effluent pipes, do no harm to the environment, and take nothing from the earth not easily renewed by the earth. We have turned on its head the myth that you could do well in business or do good, but not both. We have shown the world, by example, that you can run a big business both profitably and in an environmentally responsible way, even in the face of economic downturn.

An impossible dream, said some. But if it exists, it must be possible, as Amory Lovins says. And today this new paradigm faces an enormous test in a shrinking marketplace. But we press on and we are well on the way up that high, high mountain. Will the way ahead to the summit be difficult? Certainly. But is it impossible? Not a chance. Will the new business model—investing in a truly sustainable future, a future characterized by new thinking, new products, and new profits—see us through the economic downturn? I say, yes, and my money—my personal investment—is where my mouth is. And if we can do it, anybody can. If anybody can, everybody can.

This is the challenge. This is humankind's opportunity. This is the better way. That way is sustainability: the survival option.

# Appendix A

## LCA Comparison of Two Carpet Tile Backing Types

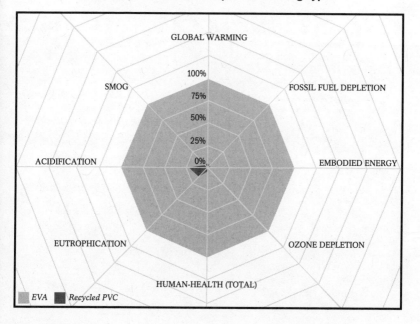

The spidergraph (so named because it resembles a spider web) is a visual comparison of environmental impacts. It can be used to compare one material versus another, or one product versus another, or one process versus another; even one company versus another.

In the example above, one carpet tile backing compound, based on recycled polyvinylchloride (PVC) polymer, is compared with a commonly used alternative backing compound, based on ethylene vinyl acetate (EVA) polymer. Each spoke (axis) in the diagram represents a dimension of sustainability; in the example there are eight dimensions. These were chosen because the scientific databases for these eight are considered by Interface scientists to be the most scientifically rigorous of some twenty possible dimensions.

The impacts for EVA are plotted as 100% along each spoke, forming the outer "footprint." The impacts for recycled PVC are plotted as percentages of the comparable EVA value. Manufacturers' recommended installation methods are included in determining impacts for each. Connecting the points specific to each compound produces the relative "footprint" of each.

In the example, recycled PVC has much the smaller footprint, and EVA has the larger (worse) footprint along all of the spokes of the spider graph, making recycled PVC compound a clear choice, environmentally.

# Appendix B

## MASTER EVERGREEN LEASE AND SERVICES AGREEMENT

THIS MASTER EVERGREEN LEASE AND
SERVICES AGREEMENT ("Agreement")
is made and entered into effective this——day of————,————,
by and between INTERFACE EVERGREEN, INC.,
a Georgia corporation                    ("Interface"),
and_____("Customer").

**Background.** Customer desires to implement a program to lease carpet from Interface and, in connection therewith, have Interface and its associated dealers deliver and install the carpet, and provide certain maintenance and selective carpet replacement services during the lease term. Interface desires to lease such carpet and provide such services to Customer on the terms and conditions contained herein. Therefore, for and in consideration of the premises and the mutual covenants and agreements contained herein, and other good and valuable consideration, the receipt and sufficiency of which are herby acknowledged, Customer and Interface agree as follows:

**1. Lease of Carpet; Term.** Interface will install and lease carpet ("Carpet") to Customer as requested by Customer pursuant to the terms and conditions of the Agreement. Customer shall enjoy the full right to keep and use the Carpet installed for a period of seven (7) years from the date of installation plus any renewal term. The lease term at a particular Customer Location shall be referred to as the "Location Term."

**2. Carpet Services.** Interface will professionally maintain the Carpet in accordance with mutually agreed-upon procedures and schedules. In addition, Interface will replace up to 2% of the installed Carpet with new carpet each year during the applicable Location Term as necessary due to unusual wear, spills, spotting or other similar occurrences, regardless of cause (such replacement carpet shall, upon installation, be considered leased "Carpet" hereunder). Interface shall provide such maintenance and selective replacement services (collectively, the "Carpet Services") through the Location Term.

**3. Addenda.** At the time Customer requests that Carpet be leased at a particular Customer Location, the parties shall meet and agree upon styles and colors, rent and

Carpet Services payments, and installation and maintenance requirements and schedules for Carpet at such Customer Location. Such terms shall be incorporated into this Agreement by a written Addendum executed by both parties in the form attached hereto as Exhibit "A."

**4. Payments.** Rent payments and Carpet Service payments for Customer Location shall be paid to Interface monthly in accordance with the applicable Addendum. The amount of the monthly rent shall remain fixed during the Location Term. The price of monthly Carpet Services shall be adjusted as of January 1$^{st}$ each year to account for inflation (or deflation) and other changes in costs incurred by Interface in providing ongoing services, including changes in labor cost. The amount of such adjustment shall be calculated pursuant to the formula and terms set forth at Exhibit B hereto. All amounts due to Interface under this Agreement shall be payable in full at Interface's office at 1503 Orchard Hill Road, LaGrange, Georgia 30241 (or such other place as Interface may direct).

**6. Ownership of Carpet.** During the lease term, nothing contained herein shall give to Customer any right, title or interest in or to the Carpet except as a lessee. At all times, legal title to the Carpet shall remain with Interface, and the Carpet shall not be considered a fixture for any purpose regardless of the degree of its installation in or affixation to real property.

**7. General Terms and Conditions.** This Agreement includes the General Terms and Conditions set forth as Exhibit "C," which are incorporated herein by reference.

**8. Notices.** Except as otherwise expressly provided herein, any notice required or permitted to be given pursuant to this Agreement shall be in writing and shall be deemed to have been duly made and given upon delivery in person or upon the expiration of five business days after the date of posting if mailed by registered or certified mail, postage prepaid, to the following addresses: **If to Interface:** Interface Evergreen, Inc., 1503 Orchard Hill Road, LaGrange, Georgia 30241, Attention: VP Finance; **If to Customer:**————————————. Either party may change the address to which notices to such party are to be sent by giving notice to the other party at the address and in the manner provided herein.

**9. Entire Agreement.** This Agreement includes Exhibits A, B and C and each subsequently executed Addendum, all of which are incorporated herein by reference. This Agreement supersedes all prior discussions and agreements between the parties with respect to the subject matter hereof, and contains the sole and entire agreement between the parties with respect to the matters covered hereby.

**10. Modification.** This agreement shall not be modified or amended except by an Addendum or other instrument in writing signed by the parties hereto.

**IN WITNESS WHEREOF,** the undersigned have caused this Agreement to be executed by their respective duly authorized officers or representatives, as of the day and year first above written.

**INTERFACE EVERGREEN, INC.**

By:

Name:

Title:

**Lessee:**

By:

Name:

Title:

# Appendix C

THE INTERFACE MODEL

## Typical Unsustainable Company of the 20th Century

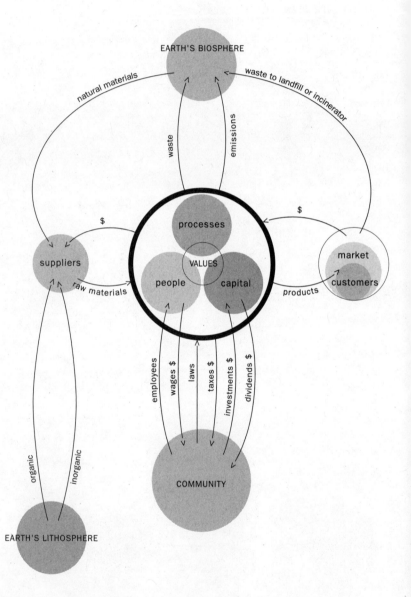

FIG. 1
(For further explanation, please visit www.rayanderson.com.)

# THE INTERFACE MODEL

## Prototypical Company of the 21st Century, One That Has Climbed the Seven Faces of Mount Sustainability

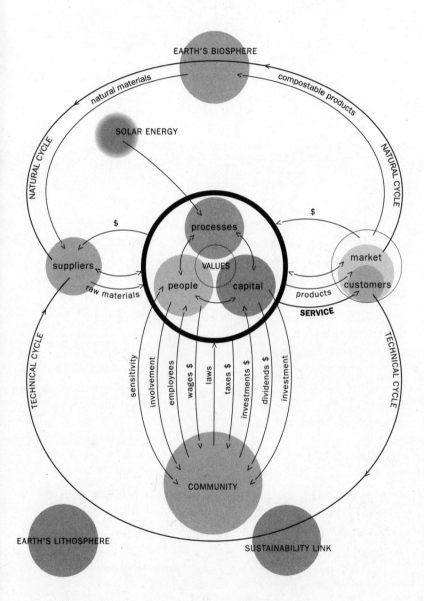

FIG. 2

# Index

St. Martin's Press has aimed for sustainability in all aspects of this book's production:

—The paper is 100 percent recycled made from 100 percent post-consumer waste, certified by the Forest Stewardship Council, and ancient-forest friendly.

—We used soy-based inks, which are more biodegradable than standard petroleum-based inks.

—Instead of using petroleum-based plastic laminate on the cover, we've opted for a varnish, which is recyclable.

—The book is held together with two kinds of glue, both of which are recyclable under certain processes.

—We are using printers that are close to our warehouse to minimize emissions from transport. Both the text and cover printers are FSC-certified.